The Future of Inter-American Relations

The Future of Inter-American Relations

EDITED BY JORGE I. DOMÍNGUEZ

An Inter-American Dialogue Book

Routledge
New York and London

Published in 2000 by
Routledge
29 West 35th Street
New York, NY 10001

Published in Great Britain by
Routledge
11 New Fetter Lane
London EC4P 4EE

Copyright © 2000 by Routledge

Printed in the United States of America on acid-free paper.

Library of Congress Cataloging-in-Publication Data

The future of inter-American relations / edited by Jorge I. Domínguez.
        p.   cm. — (An Inter-American Dialogue book)
    Includes bibliographical references.
    ISBN 0–415–92215–1 (hb.). — ISBN 0–415–92216–X (pb.)
        1. Latin America—Foreign relations—United States. 2. United States—
Foreign relations—Latin America. I. Domínguez, Jorge I., 1945–   . II. Series.
    F1418.F92   1999
    327'.097—dc21   99–35000
                                                                                 CIP

Contents

PART III
International Civil Society

List of Illustrations

Preface

The idea for this volume emerged from an exchange among Inter-American Dialogue staff in 1997 as part of a larger effort to set and shape the Dialogue's programmatic agenda in a systematic way. We thought it was important not only to react to breaking events and take advantage of opportunities as they arise in Washington and throughout the hemisphere but also to probe deeper and anticipate questions that may not be readily evident. In addition to commissioning a half a dozen brief papers on a variety of key hemispheric themes, we decided to undertake a forward-looking examination of the inter-American agenda. Two leading analysts—one from Latin America and the Caribbean, the other from the United States—were called on to consider one of six salient issues in inter-American relations: trade; the role of international financial institutions; migration; international support of democracy; transnational crime; and security.

From the outset, Jorge Domínguez, founding Dialogue member and associated fellow and director of the Weatherhead Center for International Affairs at Harvard University, has made an invaluable contribution to this exercise. He played an instrumental role in every phase of the entire effort, including identifying topics, selecting authors, and providing critical feedback and intellectual guidance on succeeding drafts. He directed with characteristic skill and efficiency the focus on the inter-American agenda, the product of which is this volume.

Initial drafts of the papers on hemispheric challenges and inter-American relations topics were discussed at a March 1998 meeting at the Brookings Institution in Washington, D.C. The sessions benefited from the input of Washington-based analysts, U.S. policy officials, a number of Latin American and Caribbean ambassadors, and representatives of multilateral institutions. The discussions substantially informed and enriched the Dialogue's Linowitz Forum plenary meeting, held the following May. In September 1998, at a meeting held at Harvard University and hosted by the Weatherhead Center, more advanced draft chapters for the current volume were thoroughly discussed.

The Dialogue expresses its deep thanks to the Weatherhead Center for a productive collaboration—for funding, organizing, and sponsoring the September meeting. We are grateful to the David Rockefeller Center for Latin American Studies for providing some support to prepare the index. Warm thanks are in order for Rosaline deButts and Theresa Spinale for their work in staffing the Harvard conference, and to Amanda Pearson for her superb effort in the production stage of the book. Jennifer Burrell has ably managed the final part of the project from the Dialogue.

The Inter-American Dialogue's research and publications are designed to improve the quality of public debate on key issues in Western Hemisphere affairs. The Dialogue is both a forum for sustained exchange among leaders and an independent, nonpartisan center for policy analysis on U.S.-Latin American economic and political relations. The Dialogue's one hundred members—from the United States, Canada, Latin America, and the Caribbean—include prominent political, business, labor, academic, media, military, and religious leaders. At periodic plenary sessions, members analyze key hemispheric issues and formulate recommendations for policy and action. The Dialogue presents its findings in comprehensive reports circulated throughout the Americas. Its research agenda focuses on four broad themes: democratic governance; inter-American cooperation; economic integration; and social equity.

The Inter-American Dialogue wishes to express its gratitude to the Swedish Agency for International Development for their support for Latin American participation in the project. We are also pleased to acknowledge the broader support that the Dialogue has obtained from the Ford, A. W. Mellon, and William and Flora Hewlett foundations and from the Carnegie Corporation of New York.

Michael Shifter
Senior Fellow and Program Director
Inter-American Dialogue

PART ONE

Risks of Violence, Hopes for Peace

1

The Future of Inter-American Relations: States, Challenges, and Likely Responses

JORGE I. DOMÍNGUEZ

In 1821, U.S. Secretary of State John Quincy Adams expressed the view that Latin Americans "are not likely to promote the spirit either of freedom or order by their example. They have not the first elements of good or free government. Arbitrary power, military and ecclesiastical, is stamped upon their education, upon their habits, and upon all their institutions. . . . I have little expectation of any beneficial result to their country from any future connection with them, political or commercial." Adams's views were quoted approvingly in a 1950 secret memorandum by George F. Kennan, who was the premier U.S. government diplomatic thinker at the birth of the cold war. Kennan was at the height of his intellectual influence shortly after penning for *Foreign Affairs* magazine his justly famous "X" article on U.S. policy toward the Soviet Union. Following John Quincy Adams, Kennan argued that the United States should not depart "in any way from the principle of formal disinterestedness in the domestic affairs of these countries." Kennan was also deeply skeptical of multilateralism as an instrument in U.S.-Latin American relations, "which represents at bottom a form of agreeable and easy escapism from the real problems of foreign policy." Instead, he thought it "important to keep before ourselves and the Latin American peoples at all times the reality of the thesis that we are a great power; that we are by and large much less in need of them than they are in need of us; that we are entirely prepared to leave to themselves those who evince no particular desire for the forms of collaboration that we have to offer; that the danger of a failure to exhaust the possibilities of our mutual relationship is always greater to them than to us; that we can afford to wait, patiently and good naturedly; and that we are more concerned to be respected than to be liked or understood."[1] The foregoing sentence is as pertinent in 2000 as it was in 1950. Kennan's views were informed not only by the onset of the cold war or competition with the Soviet Union but also by a deep and renewed skepticism about the efficacy of the League of Nations, the

United Nations, and the Organization of American States. He was impressed by the capacity of the United States to deploy its power during World War II. And he had just toured Latin America, noting the rebirth of dictatorships which marked the region from the late 1940s through much of the 1950s.

These passages summarize key intellectual themes in U.S. policy toward Latin America until the end of the cold war in Europe at the end of the 1980s. They are at the heart of a "realist" perspective in international affairs: conscious of the centrality of asymmetrical power in inter-American affairs, unconvinced about the utility of multilateralism, and doubtful that the United States should seek to promote democracy or any other domestic arrangements in the Americas.[2] Elements in Kennan's realist diagnosis and policy recommendations linger. At the birth of the new millennium (just as a half century ago), the United States is "much less in need of [Latin Americans] than they are in need of us." In the late 1990s, the U.S. Congress repeatedly rejected fast-track authorization for negotiations over a Free Trade Area of the Americas, "entirely prepared to leave to themselves those who evince no particular desire for the forms of collaboration that we have to offer"—a policy view that extends to U.S. policies toward Latin America over drug trafficking and migration. Alas, the United States "can afford to wait," whereas Latin Americans in the early twenty-first century felt urgency for action in international and domestic arenas. Asymmetry remains at the heart of U.S.-Latin American relations, yesterday, today, and tomorrow, as Boris Yopo's chapter in this book reminds us.

The U.S. foreign policy establishment's relative disinterest in Latin America has been highlighted in various ways. Richard Nixon was the only U.S. president to appoint a presidential commission to make comprehensive recommendations on the totality of U.S. policies toward Latin America. Chaired by Nelson Rockefeller, then governor of the State of New York, this report's tone differed from Kennan's lugubriousness: "We went to visit neighbors and found brothers."[3] The Rockefeller report emphasized Latin America's high and enduring significance for the United States. The Nixon administration ignored the findings.[4]

In the fall of 1997, the magazine *Foreign Affairs,* an occasional voice for the aging[5] U.S. foreign policy establishment, published a special edition in honor of its own seventy-fifth anniversary. Arguments focused on every part of the world except Latin America and Africa. Latin America made a cameo appearance only as part of a worry whether ethnicity and immigration would undermine a conception of an American national interest in foreign policy.[6]

U.S. attention toward Latin America has oscillated between moments of forgetfulness and panic. Deliberately ignored during much of the cold war in the routine conduct of foreign policy except when it "inexplicably" became a crisis, Latin America's low salience for leading U.S. foreign policy elites in the post-cold-war years still echoes George Kennan's thoughts.

In the 1990s, an array of changes made possible a different relationship between the United States and Latin America. The collapse of the Soviet Union and the end of the cold war in Europe freed U.S. foreign policy, at long last, from its obsession with communism. The collapse of Latin America's economies in the 1980s gradually opened the way to a double transformation in the region: the discrediting and replacement of authoritarian regimes and the discrediting and replacement of statist interventionist economic models. Latin America in the 1990s was characterized by freer politics and markets. This triple transformation permitted Latin America and the Caribbean to find common cause with the United States in the defense of democracy, the promotion of free trade, and the maintenance of interstate peace in the Americas to an extent unprecedented in two centuries of independent existence.

In this chapter,[7] I argue that Latin America, the Caribbean, and the United States matter to each other.[8] Latin America and the Caribbean affect significant aspects of the quality of life in the United States, including the composition of the nation's people, the maintenance of public order, and the prospects for prosperity; there is no question, of course, about the high impact of the United States on the rest of the hemisphere. I forecast that both financial instability and significant levels of interstate and intrastate violence are likely to recur throughout the first decade of the twenty-first century for reasons already evident in the 1990s. Financial crises in Latin America are akin to earthquakes in seismic zones: their timing is difficult to forecast, but the likelihood of their occurrence is high.

Asymmetrical power remains central for inter-American relations, but multilateral institutions and procedures at the hemispheric and subregional levels have begun to address it more effectively and are the predominant trend for the early twenty-first century. Multilateralization has become the "equilibrium solution" to shared inter-American problems in finance, trade, international security, the defense and promotion of democracy, crime control, and even migration. U.S. unilateralism is also likely to endure into the twenty-first century, especially with regard to issues that the United States considers within its domestic domain (crime and migration). I explain why multilateralist and unilateralist trends are likely to persist and why there are theoretical and practical reasons for the visible shift in favor of regionalist multilateralism.

The chapter concludes by a consideration of the construction and strengthening of an inter-American civil society in the expectation that it will grow further during the opening years of the next millennium. I sketch the wide-ranging and urgent debate about the quality of democratic institutions and the relationship between democracy and other worthwhile goals, such as peace and prosperity, evident throughout the hemisphere and even within the pages of this book. Finally, at the interstate level, I argue that in the early 1990s the United States—across presidential administrations of different political parties—committed itself in actual practice to join Latin American and Caribbean countries to defend democratic institutions throughout the Americas. This is a major change from the policy predisposition so well articulated by George Kennan. These themes with regard to democracy, too, are likely to prevail at the opening of the new millennium.

And Yet They Matter to One Another

The importance of the United States for Latin America requires little demonstration, yet in light of the foregoing the importance of Latin America for the United States should not be overlooked. The following examples illustrate this general point while the chapters that follow provide greater depth.

Economic Issues

In the 1990s U.S. exports to Latin America and the Caribbean increased at an average annual rate 50 percent above that of U.S. exports to the world as a whole, as Roberto Bouzas indicates in his chapter. Much of this export growth occurred between the United States and Mexico within the terms of the North American Free Trade Agreement (NAFTA), which since 1994 joined the United States, Canada, and Mexico. In the 1990s, Canada was the most important trading partner of the United States, and Mexico—not Japan, not Germany—was second. By the end of the 1990s, intra-NAFTA exports accounted for more than half the exports of the NAFTA partners, itself an historic record.[9] In addition, however, the rate of U.S. export growth to the southern South American countries was two-and-a-half times faster than the rate of growth of U.S. worldwide exports; while some of these baselines were low, Latin America was nonetheless significant because in the 1990s U.S. exports did not perform as well in other regions of the world.

The United States, Canada, and Latin American and Caribbean countries have locked themselves into a process to create a Free Trade Area of the Americas (FTAA), as Robert Devlin, Antoni Estevadeordal, and Luis Garay explain. This ongoing work is likely to foster trade in the Americas and to provide for newer and deeper means of engagement between the countries of the hemisphere.

Latin America in the 1990s became once again a player in the international financial system, as Pamela Starr's chapter indicates. Although international bank loans were of only modest significance in the 1990s, the flow of direct foreign investment and portfolio investment surpassed prior benchmarks. Latin America became interesting again for international investors, both at moments of euphoria and at those of concern.

Security Issues

Latin American countries have foresworn weapons of mass destruction even though Argentina and Brazil had for some years embarked in programs that could have led to the development of nuclear weapons. In the 1990s, the Argentine and Brazilian governments, and other governments within the region including Cuba, banished these and chemical and biological weapons from Latin America and the Caribbean.[10] Thanks to their statesmanship, Latin American countries do not pose high security threats to the United States.

The United States has also repeatedly deployed massive military force in various near-neighboring countries, as David Mares's chapter notes. Thousands of U.S. troops were deployed to the Dominican Republic in 1965, to Grenada in 1983, to Panama in 1989, and to Haiti in 1994. U.S. military forces readied for nuclear war in the environs of Cuba in 1962. Since the mid-1980s smaller deployments of U.S. troops have participated in military antidrug operations in several Latin American countries. U.S. military assistance missions have been significant in various wars in Latin American countries, most recently in several Central American countries in the 1980s. Note that the U.S. invasions of Panama and Haiti occurred after the cold war had ended in Europe and the Berlin Wall had fallen. Latin America, and especially the Caribbean, should expect future U.S. military interventions because the United States believes that its own security reasons justify them.

Societal Issues

In 1998, the most common name recorded in birth registries in the State of California was Jose. Many years earlier salsa (the condiment) had begun to outsell ketchup in U.S. supermarkets, while salsa (the dance) began to make an impact on dance floors beyond the U.S. Latino community. The impact of Latin American-origin peoples in the United States, already large, is likely to grow.

As Christopher Mitchell notes in his chapter, more than twelve million people born in Latin America and the Caribbean lived in the United States in the mid-1990s; two-thirds of these entered the United States after 1980. The United States is one of the largest Spanish-speaking countries in the world. As such, it is a source of Spanish-language literature, music, journalism, and social science. Early in the twenty-first century, U.S. Latinos will become a larger minority than African-Americans in the United States. As Mitchell also notes, the mobile transnational character of Latin American and Caribbean migration connects the source countries to the United States in an ongoing network of continuing population movement in both directions. Emigration is but one of many movements between home and host country; indeed, the meaning of "host" and "home" begin to blur.

South, Central, and North America are also connected by the scourge of transnational crime, as Ivelaw Griffith and Mónica Serrano make evident. Bolivia, Peru, and Colombia are the leading producers of coca and cocaine for the U.S. market. In the late 1990s, the U.S. Office of National Drug Control Policy estimated that the available cocaine supply in the United States was approximately 240 metric tons. The optimistic U.S. government national strategic goal was to reduce that amount to 120 metric tons during the following decade.[11] There is a tragic though decisive future for cocaine as an issue in inter-American relations, and as the chapters by Griffith and Serrano make clear, also for other crime-related issues.

Democracy and Inter-American Actions

The United States was founded with the ringing words of the Declaration of Independence, affirming its belief that "all men are created equal," that their "inalienable rights" include "life, liberty, and the pursuit of happiness," and that governments are established to secure these rights deriving their "just powers from the consent of the governed." And yet, as the opening passages of this chapter recall, U.S. policy toward Latin America was mostly not based on these principles. In the twentieth century, actively pro-democratic policies were adopted by President Woodrow Wilson with disastrous results: U.S. troops intervened in Mexico, allegedly for the sake of democracy, only to fuel the fires of the Mexican revolution.[12]

At the conclusion of World War II, more open politics spread through various Latin American countries. At that moment, the Organization of American States (OAS) was founded. A shared creation of the United States and Latin America, the Charter bristles with democratic affirmation. The Preamble states that the signatories are "convinced that the historic mission of America is to offer to man a land of liberty." They are "confident" that the organization's mission is "the consolidation on this continent, within the framework of democratic institutions, of a system of individual liberty and social justice based on respect for the essential rights of man."[13]

The OAS did not succeed at protecting democratic governance in the 1940s or in the decades that followed, in part because the U.S. government behaved as Kennan and others had recommended, but mainly because dictatorship, not democracy, remained the norm in Latin America. President John F. Kennedy's administration supported democratic politics, but by 1964 the United States backed a military coup that overthrew Brazil's constitutional government on suspicions of being soft on communism, among other sins.[14] President Jimmy Carter's administration followed a human rights policy and favored democratic openings, but it met with resistance at the high point of dictatorial power in Latin America's contemporary history.[15]

By the 1990s, however, as the chapters by Anita Isaacs and Heraldo Muñoz make clear, there developed a shared inter-American interest in the defense and promotion of democracy in the Americas. John Quincy Adams was at last proven wrong. Latin Americans struggled successfully to overcome the barriers that had prevented them from achieving freedom and order. The spread of constitutional government throughout Latin America, along with an evolving political consensus in the United States, crystallized the joint support for democracy among the countries of the hemisphere to an unprecedented extent.[16] Meeting in Santiago, Chile, in 1991, the member governments of the Organization of American States (led among others by Chile and the United States) approved Resolution 1080, agreeing to defend democratic governments if they were to face a threat of overthrow. In the United States, both the administrations of Presidents George Bush and Bill Clinton took significant steps to defend and promote constitutional government in the Americas.

The United States has always mattered for Latin America and the Caribbean, and in the 1990s Latin America and the Caribbean certainly mattered to the United States. Drug trafficking, migration, and the commitment to democracy affect the character of private and public life in the United States, moving beyond the "realist" diagnosis that George Kennan and others had formulated in mid-twentieth century. The hemisphere matters to the United States because it affects the quality of life in the United States, not because it threatens the prospects for U.S. survival in an anarchic international system. The Americas have come to share their histories in ways unsuspected a half century ago. This joint history is likely to endure into the new millennium.

Likely Challenges

The two most important likely challenges for inter-American relations in the first decade of the twenty-first century are likely to be financial instability in Latin America and the Caribbean, on the one hand, and persistently high levels of transnational violence, on the other. These two problems share a key characteristic: there are strong reasons to forecast that they will occur, but it is impossible to make specific or "point" predictions about the timing of the worst events.

Financial Instability

In the last quarter of the twentieth century, Latin America triggered (or contributed to) a major-to-moderate international financial crisis every few years. In 1982–1983, the region's financial crisis posed a grave threat to the solvency of major U.S. money center banks. During the 1980s, the major international banks survived and prospered in the end, but one cost was Latin America's second great economic depression of the twentieth century.[17]

In late 1994, Mexico's financial debacle—marked by a sharp and sudden devaluation of the peso, the collapse of its stock market, and a severe economic recession—led the U.S. government to arrange a large and complex financial rescue that protected international investors and enabled Mexico to recover much faster than its experience in the 1980s.[18]

Latin American countries weathered well the initial fallout from the East Asian financial crisis that began in mid-1997. In the aftermath of the Russian financial collapse of August 1998, however, Brazil's international financial exposure seemed especially vulnerable. The International Monetary Fund (IMF) organized a large financial rescue effort to defend the Brazilian exchange rate. In early 1999, however, Brazil first devalued the currency and then let it float, whereupon the devaluation deepened dramatically. Even before the Brazilian crisis, most Latin American economies were headed for a growth slowdown, or outright recession, as the century lurched to an end, and the Brazilian collapse guaranteed it. There was no regionwide growth in per capita gross domestic product in the 1998–2000 period.

In the 1990s, economic reform advanced in all Latin American countries far more than might have been believed possible a decade earlier. Yet there are three broad reasons why financial crises should be expected in various Latin American countries early in the twenty-first century: (1) the economic and political legacies of the previous economic development model; (2) the transformation of international capital markets; and (3) the evident unpreparedness of political institutions to cope with these problems.

Until the mid-1970s in Chile, and until the second half of the 1980s in most of Latin America, import-substitution industrialization was the dominant economic development model. This economic model favored autarkic economic policies. One of its consequences was the very low profile of their exports other than primary commodities. Another consequence was a general lack of experience by firms, government officials, and ordinary citizens with the workings of markets untrammeled by highly intrusive government intervention. Rates of inflation were significantly higher than those prevailing in world markets. Consequently there were periodic exchange rate crises, savings rates were low by some comparative standards, and capital markets were underdeveloped.[19] Politicians believed that they knew best how to design effective economic policies.

Several legacies of that model persist in the early twenty-first century. To be sure, there is considerable variation among Latin American countries, but the following observations still apply throughout much of the region. Latin America's export profile retains a large concentration in primary commodities, highly vulnerable to international trade shocks that contribute to financial crises. Even in Mexico, which has a more diversified export profile, the national government depends disproportionately on petroleum for its fiscal revenues. Most Latin American countries still suffer inflation rates above those prevailing in North America and Western Europe. A great many Latin American business firms remain inexperienced in world markets. Savings rates have risen in some countries, but generally they remain insufficient to finance domestic economic growth. Most Latin American financial markets are weakly regulated. Latin American governments and firms often rely on volatile short-term external capital to finance short-term needs. Meanwhile, many politicians still believe that their intervention in the economy is both providential and salutary. As the twentieth century closed, the latter beliefs were especially widespread in Brazil, Venezuela, and Ecuador. The 1999 Brazilian devaluation crisis was sparked, for example, by the decision of former president Itamar Franco, a conservative but also a populist, then governor of the State of Minas Gerais (Brazil's third largest state in economic importance), to default on his state's obligations to the federal government. These various political and economic factors are likely to contribute to economic turbulence from time to time. (Specific crises require more specific explanations, of course.) Latin America's economic volatility has been and is likely to remain for some time worse than in the North Atlantic world.[20]

As Latin America made its economic transition in the 1980s and 1990s, the international financial system was transformed. Starr's chapter in this book sketches the vast dimensions of international capital markets as the millennium closed. Large sums of money slushed around the world, moving instantly from one market to another thanks to a technological revolution in electronic communications and transfers, and thanks also to new financial liquidity in the 1990s born from rapidly rising stock markets, especially in the United States.

Latin America's circumstances on the capital account changed substantially. From 1982 until 1990, Latin America suffered consistently negative net transfers of resources (net capital inflows minus net payments of profits and interest). Since 1991, net transfers have been consistently positive, but they have also been highly volatile. For example, net transfers amounted to $31 billion in 1993, dropped to below $8 billion in 1994, more than doubled to over $16 billion in 1995, and nearly doubled again by the end of 1997.[21]

Latin America's own capital markets remained thin and relatively illiquid. Historically, the region's stock markets had been overregulated into inactivity; in the 1990s, many lacked basic financial rules to ensure minimally acceptable levels of transparency and accountability. These vast sums of international capital flowed into—and then pulled out of—these markets. The constraint on capital inflows from 1993 to 1994 is one part of the explanation for the Mexican financial panic of late 1994 and for the recession that followed in Mexico and, to a lesser degree, in Argentina. Latin American governments believe that they must keep their capital accounts liberal enough to attract international funds. Some governments (Chile and Colombia especially) have attempted policies to cushion the impact of capital flow volatility, with moderate success, but all countries remain vulnerable to sudden shifts of favor with emerging markets.

In this context, the political institutions of most Latin American countries are strikingly unprepared to cope with these problems. Consider some simple examples from the two most important countries. Mexican institutions were implicitly designed to operate for a de facto one-party system. When the long-governing Institutional Revolutionary Party (PRI) lost its majority in the Chamber of Deputies in the nationwide 1997 elections, the new opposition heads of congressional committees found no professional civil service staff and no records to help them act responsibly. The Congress had usually received the draft budget proposal from the executive late in the year and approved it in a few weeks; there were no procedures for a congressional "continuing resolution" on the budget in the event that president and Congress were to differ.

Brazil's Constitution of 1988 exemplifies the "Christmas tree" approach to constitution making. It includes every realizable and every unrealizable dream of Brazilians of quite diverse political opinions. As one of Brazil's leading social scientists, Bolívar Lamounier, characterized it, the 1988 constituent assembly "entrenched a bewildering variety of old-fashioned statist economic concepts as well as corporate interests into the extremely detailed and rigid 1988 Constitution."[22] The Brazilian Congress has spent much of the 1990s amending the economic and social provisions of this constitution. Brazil's central and federal institutions are still hobbled by unworkable constitutional requirements that help to expose the country and render it vulnerable to exogenous economic shocks.[23]

Brazil's financial difficulties in 1997–1999 help to pinpoint the nature of the problem more sharply, however. Brazil responded effectively to the mid-1997 East Asian financial crisis. As the crisis seemed about to engulf Brazil, President Fernando Henrique Cardoso took economic measures to demonstrate Brazilian macroeconomic responsibility. Presidential decisions alone did not suffice. The president took his proposals to the Congress, which enacted them into law. The crisis subsided. Brazil avoided the East Asian financial panic because its democratic institutions credibly demonstrated a broadly supported commitment to sound policies. In the wake of the August 1998 Russian financial panic, the IMF orchestrated an anticipatory financial rescue package for Brazil contingent on its undertaking important austerity measures and economic reforms. Brazilian members of Congress balked, however, because they thought that the IMF would be raining dollars and euros upon Brazil. Congress as such was not the problem; the effective flow of information to members of Congress and the internal procedures of the Congress were the problem. Institutional reform is required but within the framework of democratic constitutionalism.

In the 1990s Latin American countries made admirable progress toward reforming their economies, making them more internationally open and efficient. Among the most impressive changes has been the liberalization of trade. But much remains to be done, especially with regard to international financial issues. Most Latin American countries continue to need international financing, yet they still lack the institutional and market conditions to make stable, effective use of those international resources. Financial crises should be expected, therefore. These crises may involve only a few countries at a time, as was the case in 1994–1995 when the Mexican crisis had a severe impact only on Argentina and Uruguay. But their recurrence will bring suffering to the countries affected, most probably increase the cost of capital to the region as a whole, and injure a fair number of international firms operating in Latin American markets. The path to prosperity in the early twenty-first century may likely be punctured by occasional financial crises.

Domestic and International Violence

There are three likely sources of violence in the early twenty-first century: (1) Militarized interstate disputes, especially in the circum-Caribbean region; (2) transnational crime; and (3) U.S. military interventions.

From the late 1970s to the late 1990s, most Latin American countries made major strides toward achieving interstate peace and a domestic democratic order. International and civil wars swirling about Nicaragua, El Salvador, and Guatemala ended. One unintended positive effect of the great depression of the 1980s, as Mares notes in his chapter, was to stop and reverse the arms races that had threatened to spiral out of control in the 1970s. By the early 1990s, for Latin America as a whole (including Cuba), military expenditures represented only about 1.5 percent of gross national product—the smallest proportion for any region of the world. The number of soldiers per thousand people fell from about 4.5 during the first half of the 1980s to about 3.5 during the first half of the 1990s.[24] A genuine diplomatic transformation occurred in the southern cone of South America, markedly improving the quality of bilateral relations especially between Argentina and Chile (see also Yopo's chapter), between Argentina and Brazil, and even between Argentina and the United Kingdom.[25]

And yet, as evident in Table 2.2 in Mares's chapter, the frequency and intensity of displays and use of military force to address bilateral disputes between Latin American countries remain high. There has been at least one militarized interstate dispute per year in Latin America and the Caribbean since 1991; the frequency of such militarized disputes actually increased in the second half of the 1990s. The worst incident was the full-scale war between Ecuador and Peru in

1995 that led to hundreds of casualties and other costs, but interstate disputes are also common in Central America and between Venezuela and Colombia.

The experience of reaching a far-reaching agreement in 1998 that could settle the Ecuador-Peru dispute definitively points to a choice for the inter-American community. Left to themselves, Ecuador and Peru would probably have been unable to reach such an agreement. A major effort had to be made by Argentina, Brazil, Chile, and the United States to broker a settlement. So too it goes in Central America, and between Venezuela and Colombia, in the early twenty-first century: left to themselves, militarized interstate disputes are likely to recur. But there is a good chance of definitive settlements, most of all in Central America, if the inter-American community is willing to invest its resources to bring them about. In some instances, as in the joint effort by Honduras and El Salvador to honor the 1992 judgment of the International Court at The Hague to demarcate their boundary definitively, one problem is the lack of funds to carry out the demarcation on the ground, relocate people, pay appropriate compensation, and launch joint border area development projects.

Within countries, the trends concerning civil-military relations and civil wars have been positive. In the early 1990s, there were violent military mutinies or overt coup attempts in Argentina, Guatemala, Haiti, Panama, Peru, Trinidad-Tobago, and twice in Venezuela. The good news is that all attempts failed except in Haiti and Peru. The Peruvian case is more ambiguous because it was led by Alberto Fujimori, the constitutionally elected civilian president, against the Congress, the courts, and the political parties. Since 1994, there has been only one such coup attempt (in Paraguay), which also failed. Also in the 1990s, terrorism and guerrilla actions subsided in Peru compared to the extremely high levels reached in the late 1980s and early 1990s. Civil war ended in Suriname, and Central America's civil wars also ended.

Severe problems persist, however. The threats to constitutional government seem strongest in Haiti, Paraguay, and possibly Venezuela. The quality of constitutional government in helping citizens achieve reasonable goals has been particularly poor along the Andean mountain chain from Bolivia to Venezuela, but to some degree democratic political systems are being seriously challenged everywhere in the region. The level of civil violence in Colombia remains extraordinarily high. It involves communist guerrillas that are legacies from the 1960s, powerful right-wing paramilitary forces, and the quasi-military forces of drug cartels. As the chapters by Serrano and Griffith make clear, moreover, the level of criminal violence remains stunningly high throughout the Americas. Griffith notes that there have been dramatic and recurrent terrorist acts in the 1990s in Argentina, Colombia, Peru, and the United States. There have been lesser terrorist acts in most other Latin American and Caribbean countries during this decade, all well past the end of the cold war in Europe.

Transnational violence took a turn for the worse in the 1990s. New technology made it easier to transport weapons and people associated with transnational crime, to transfer funds electronically for money laundering, and to communicate effectively in order to coordinate transnational criminal activities across countries. International weapons markets flourished, supplying weapons for terrorists, criminals, and kidnappers. (To be sure, new technology at airports and border crossings has also helped in the attempt to prevent and deter the commission of some crimes.) Both Serrano and Griffith note the problem posed by large volumes of private arms transfers from the United States to Latin America and the Caribbean. By the second half of the 1990s, the United States was receiving approximately a hundred requests per day from other countries in the hemisphere to trace weapons used in crime. In the mid-1990s, about ten thousand weapons per year were being confiscated in Mexico, nine-tenths of which came from the United States.

Serrano's chapter suggests a new "security dilemma" for neighboring countries. The successful efforts of some states to improve their security with regard to drug trafficking undermines the security of other states because of the shift in trafficking routes and the development of new markets. The success of some states may force some drug cartels to transnationalize their operations even more in order to spread risks and ensure that some deliveries will get through to finance their full operations. Thus one state's "victory" in the drug war may come at the expense of worsening security for other states. This has been, in part, the story of shifting security threats from drug trafficking throughout the Caribbean and Central America, generally, and between Colombia and Mexico, more specifically.

U.S. antidrug policies increase the price of illegal drugs, making the business enormously lucrative. U.S. policies that emphasize reduction of supply at the source have forced Latin American countries to militarize their police forces and increase their expenditures on these operations while generally contributing to very high levels of violence in Latin American and Caribbean countries. Latin American countries are forced to do more, at greater cost, to yield less security—the security dilemma, indeed.

U.S. invasions of its neighbors have been one source of past international conflict. After the end of the cold war in Europe, the United States demonstrated that its willingness to invade its near neighbors was not just a response to fears about Soviet meddling. U.S. military occupations of Panama in 1989 and Haiti in 1994 responded to concerns over drug trafficking, migration, and democracy, among others.

What are, therefore, the most likely scenarios for U.S. military intervention in one of its neighboring countries early in the twenty-first century? The first scenario could develop from heightened U.S. concern over drug traffic operations. If the government of a Caribbean island country were cooperating with traffickers more than with the United States, then U.S. forces might invade to replace this government, as was one of the justifications for the U.S. invasion of Panama in 1989. Caribbean countries, as Griffith's chapter makes clear, are highly vulnerable to the operations of drug traffickers. Since the late 1970s, several have come under attack or penetration from transnational criminal forces.[26] And U.S. forces can occupy Caribbean countries easily and at relatively low cost.

The second scenario could be a U.S. military intervention in Cuba. By the late 1990s, Fidel Castro's health was not good (he was born in 1926). Important features of Cuba's domestic economic and political systems were changing under severe strain. A wider transition is likely to occur in Cuba in the first decade of the twenty-first century. The circumstances of that transition remain elusive.[27] Some possible patterns of change may involve violence, perhaps including U.S. citizens who, as Cuban Americans, claim the right to participate in the politics of their home country and the equal right to demand the military and political support of their adopted country. In the 1990s, moreover, U.S. policy toward Cuba became quite inflexible, as Yopo notes in his chapter, making it more difficult for the United States to respond to a Cuban crisis through nonmilitary means. The range of feasible U.S. options was radically simplified through an act of Congress (the Helms-Burton Act). Thus, in the face of civil violence in Cuba, the likelihood that the United States might use military force has increased.

Finally, as Mares notes, the United States has militarized the U.S.-Mexican border. At times, literally, some U.S. troops have been deployed to the border; in these cases, the U.S. military operate under specific constraints. Forces associated with the Border Patrol or the Drug Enforcement Administration employ weapons along the border to enforce U.S. policies. A general disposition developed making it appropriate for U.S. authorities to use force at the U.S.-Mexican border in certain cases.

Latin America and the Caribbean have made important progress toward constructing a democratic order. Argentina, Brazil, and Chile are exceptional because they seem to have ended the threat of war between themselves. But militarized interstate disputes remain a problem in much of Latin America. The spread and growth of transnational crime poses severe threats to the security of states and persons. Possibly the United States would yet again intervene militarily in the affairs of a neighboring country. Peace is not likely to be at hand in the first decade of the twenty-first century.

Likely Responses

There are three likely responses to many of the challenges that will face the hemisphere. First, to a degree greater than many would have thought possible, multilateral[28] responses became common and more effective during the 1990s and are likely to become predominant in the new century. Second, U.S. unilateralism is a long-standing practice. It will persist, but the United States, too, has discovered the utility of inter-American multilateralism. Third, an inter-American civil society has emerged and will probably strengthen. Nongovernmental associations are likely to become means for coping with inter-American problems.

Multilateralism, Multilateralism Everywhere

The construction of inter-American relations in the 1990s and the likely trajectory for the twenty-first century highlights the importance of multilateral institutions in widely different fields of international endeavor, perhaps to George Kennan's dismay. The salience, methods, and impact of these international institutions vary from one issue area to another, but multilateralization of inter-American relations seems likely to endure.

The oldest of the significant institutions in inter-American relations are the international financial institutions—the International Monetary Fund (IMF), the World Bank, and the Inter-American Development Bank (IDB)—which are discussed in the chapters by Wendy Hunter and Pamela Starr. Latin American governments were cofounders of all three. The two banks played a significant role in the development of infrastructure in Latin America in the 1950s and 1960s.[29] Especially since the 1980s, all three international financial institutions play informational, not just financial, roles. They have been incubators and transmitters of ideas about economic development, the management of macroeconomic projects, and the design of projects, as Hunter in particular shows in her chapter. They helped to train and nurture generations of economists and other professionals who, upon returning to their home countries, spread the faith that markets foster more efficient growth. Their willingness to finance or cofinance projects, even if their cash allocations are modest, signal to international private institutions that the countries are credit-worthy. They help to marshall and manage syndication efforts for the largest financial packages (as they did with regard to Brazil in 1998–1999), and they provide explicit and implicit insurance for large international efforts involving many creditors. They are implicit bill collectors for creditor governments and private banks, threatening noncompliance with penalties. They form and foster international and domestic coalitions to thwart policies they oppose and to promote policies they support. And since the 1990s they seek to reshape the domestic institutions of governance, especially property rights and the professional behavior of courts. By comparison, especially with regard to the larger Latin American countries, in the 1990s their financial contributions were not so significant because their share of international financing had dropped markedly.

These international financial institutions remain a routine part of the landscape of the international political economy of Latin America and the

Caribbean. Governments still need them, even if they have come to depend on international private capital for most sources of financing. The multilateralization of the international financial relations of Latin America and the Caribbean is firmly established.

The region's countries had a troubled relationship with the international trade regime. Many Latin American and Caribbean countries were reluctant to join the General Agreement on Tariffs and Trade (GATT), and some did so quite late (Mexico publicly debated whether to join the GATT and decided against it in 1980, only to do so in 1986). For many years, Latin American members of the GATT invoked loopholes to retain levels of trade protection above GATT standards.

In the 1990s, Latin American and Caribbean countries were full members of the World Trade Organization (WTO), the GATT's successor, and went on to rely on trade multilateralism to reshape their commerce. (Bouzas, and Devlin, Estevadeordal, and Garay discuss many of these issues in their respective chapters.) NAFTA went into effect in January 1994; by 1998, the value of intra-NAFTA exports exceeded $500 billion, more than twice their worth in 1990. The second most important regional trade integration agreement is MERCOSUR, or southern common market, which groups Argentina, Brazil, Paraguay, and Uruguay. It went into effect in January 1995, though partial and preparatory agreements had been under way for some years. By 1998, the value of intra-MERCOSUR exports was more than $21 billion, in nominal U.S. dollar terms more than five times their worth in 1990.

Three other small regional trade integration agreements dating from the 1960s were revitalized in the 1990s. The Andean Community grouped Bolivia, Peru, Ecuador, Colombia, and Venezuela; it was reactivated and reshaped through decisions taken in 1988 and 1996. The value of intra-Andean exports in 1998 exceeded $5 billion, again in nominal U.S. dollar terms more than four times their worth in 1990. The Central American Common Market (CACM) was reactivated in 1990; it included Costa Rica, Nicaragua, Honduras, El Salvador, and Guatemala. In 1998, the value of intra-Central American exports was more than $2 billion, exceeding three times their worth in 1990. Finally, the Caribbean Community (CARICOM) was constituted of the Anglophone Caribbean island and mainland countries; it underwent significant reforms beginning in 1989–1990. The value of intra-CARICOM exports surpassed $800 million in 1995, about 50 percent over their worth in 1990.[30]

The growth rate of intraregional exports has been much faster than the growth rate of extraregional exports for each of these regions. This comparison of growth rates has contributed to persuade the Latin American countries, and to a lesser degree the United States, that multilateral regional trade agreements work for them better than simple reliance on the WTO processes. The following countries send more than a quarter of their exports to their respective regions: Argentina and Uruguay to MERCOSUR, and Guatemala and El Salvador to CACM. And two others, Paraguay to MERCOSUR and Mexico to NAFTA, export more than two-thirds of their exports to their respective regions.

Supplementing and crisscrossing these major multilateral trade agreements are many other trade agreements that create various narrower free trade areas. For example, Chile is not a formal member of any of the regional trade blocs just mentioned, but it has trade agreements to foster trade with MERCOSUR and also separately and individually (signed between 1991 and 1998) with Mexico, Venezuela, Bolivia, Colombia, Ecuador, Canada, and Peru. Mexico is a member of NAFTA, but it also has a free trade agreement with the Central American Common Market as well as separate subsequent individual ones with Costa Rica and Nicaragua, and further individualized free trade agreements with Chile and Bolivia and with the Colombia-Venezuela twosome. The Central Americans have persistently sought, to no avail, special treatment under NAFTA, but their success has been limited to separate trade agreements between their CACM, on the one hand, and Mexico, Colombia, Venezuela, and the Dominican Republic, on the other.[31]

The march of multilateralism in the international political economy of the Americas has responded both to Latin American and to U.S. and Canadian preferences. The administration of President Ronald Reagan signed the U.S.-Canadian free-trade agreement with Prime Minister Brian Mulroney's government. The Bush administration signed NAFTA, while the Clinton administration steered its approval through Congress. All three administrations relied on the international financial institutions to help to orchestrate financial rescues in the region at moments of distress, and with the decline in U.S. official foreign assistance, all three came to rely on these institutions as an instrument to finance economic development. Multilateral institutions "solve" the matching of continental preferences concerning international economic relations in the hemisphere.

Multilateral approaches seem likely to retain a significant role in the opening decade of the twenty-first century. The inter-American summits have launched a process of trade negotiation seeking to reach a Free Trade Area of the Americas (FTAA) within this first decade of the century. This is the subject of the chapter by Devlin, Estevadeordal, and Garay. A series of trade ministerial meetings and associated specialized working groups have been keeping all governments closely engaged for several years. The summit process begun at Miami in 1994 and continued in Santiago, Chile, in 1998 has already succeeded in multilateralizing the continent's international trade relations. In the 1990s, freer trade in the Americas consolidated economic reforms, created new international markets for trade, prepared Latin America and the Caribbean for globalization, and fostered cooperation among the governments of the region.

There are several analytic and practical reasons to proceed with the FTAA, as Devlin and his associates make clear. The FTAA signals to the wider international community a sustained commitment to trade liberalization and helps to lock in domestic market-oriented reforms. It takes place under the umbrella of the WTO to ensure that it develops consistently with global free-trade rules. It is likely to have positive externalities beyond the trade area, as is already evident in the MERCOSUR's commitment to the defense of democratic institutions (see below). The FTAA is likely to foster transparency and lower the transaction costs that have emerged unintentionally from the mushrooming of crisscrossing bilateral free-trade agreements. And, on the practical side, the FTAA is the most likely instrument to liberalize trade in agriculture and textile and apparel sectors, to restrain U.S. use of antidumping procedures, and to generate reliable trade dispute settlement mechanisms. The FTAA process was slowed down by the repeated refusal of the U.S. Congress in the late 1990s to approve "fast-track" legislation to facilitate the trade negotiations, but the governments of the Americas proceeded with preparatory work in anticipation that the United States will, in the end, be prepared to implement what has long been its policy preference: freer trade.

The multilateralist zeal, as Mares and Yopo indicate, has spread as well to political and security areas especially in the 1990s. The United Nations played a leading role in bringing to an end the international and civil wars that plagued Nicaragua, El Salvador, and Guatemala in the late 1980s and 1990s, while the OAS played a supportive role in these cases and a leading role in ending civil war in Suriname. The Rio Protocol Guarantors (Argentina, Brazil, Chile, and the United States) played a decisive role in stopping the 1995 war between Ecuador and Peru and patiently constructed the framework for a broadly supported peace agreement reached late in 1998.

Muñoz and Isaacs detail the extensive array of multilateral actions designed to support democratic institutions and practices in the Americas. As Muñoz puts it in his chapter, a new international political regime in the Americas seeks to promote democracy, prevent its breakdown, and react to a collapse of democratic government in order to restore it. As noted earlier, a turning point was the OAS decision in 1991 to adopt Resolution 1080, committing the member states to react to a threat to constitutional government. The OAS did react to such threats in the 1990s in Haiti, Peru, Guatemala, and Paraguay, with particular success in the latter two. Through its "Unit for Democracy," the OAS has also provided other services in support for democracy, in particular international election observation—one of the key practices in the international support for democracy of the closing decade of the twentieth century.

"Democracy defense" clauses have spread to other regional institutions. CARICOM has a long, honorable trajectory of democratic defense. Its members have always assisted democratic governments facing threats from criminal forces, adventurers, or coup attempts. In 1997, the Rio Group—founded in the 1980s around the Central American crisis but refocused on opportunities for multilateral cooperation—adopted procedures similar to OAS Resolution 1080 to help defend constitutional government. MERCOSUR, too, evolved from a mere trade association to become a successful instrument to defend constitutional government in one of its member countries, Paraguay. In 1996, as General Lino Oviedo was on the verge of overthrowing the constitutional government, MERCOSUR countries, with support from the OAS Secretary-General César Gaviria and the U.S. government, helped to prevent the coup from succeeding. In 1998, as Muñoz notes, the MERCOSUR countries also held Paraguayan politicians to the fixed date to transfer presidential power.

Multilateral approaches have also become important in attempts to combat international crime, as Griffith's chapter reports. By the late 1980s and through the 1990s, as Table 4.2 shows, on average one major international treaty was negotiated and signed every year to improve the collective capacity to combat transnational crime and its associated effects. A panoply of intergovernmental organizations sought to carry out these agreements. Some were global, like the International Criminal Police Organization (Interpol) and the Financial Action Task Force, designed by the leading industrial states to combat money laundering. Others were regional, like the Regional Security System (which provides for police and military collaboration in the eastern Caribbean) or the Caribbean Financial Action Task Force (the regional counterpart of the global entity).

There is even a hint of multilateralism in the evolution of international migration relations. As Mitchell notes, at Mexico's initiative, a Regional Conference on Migration was established in 1996 and has met various times at the vice-ministerial level, with staff follow-through on various noncontroversial albeit important questions pertaining to migration relations in the Americas. Rafael Fernández de Castro and Carlos Rosales point out in their chapter that there has also been a significant bilateralization of policies at the U.S.-Mexican border through the creation of institutions for intergovernmental liaison, for coordination of illegal alien deportation procedures, and for the protection of the legal rights of Mexicans in the United States.

Inter-American institutions were built during the twentieth century on the bedrock of a grand bargain: Latin American and Caribbean governments acceded to the policy wishes of the United States; in exchange, the United States agreed to restrain its behavior and acceded to significant influence over its own policies. The United States sought compliance; Latin American and Caribbean countries sought voice.[32] Yet, as Yopo observes, in the 1990s significant international institutions developed also among Latin American and

Caribbean countries apart from the United States. The architecture of Anglophone Caribbean political, economic, and military cooperation has long been impressive. And, among the Latin Americans, MERCOSUR prospered and the Rio Group evolved successfully in the 1990s.

In the 1990s, the visible general shift in favor of regionalist multilateralism results from the interaction of four factors. (1) The end of the cold war in Europe freed the United States to participate in fashioning the end of the cold war in Latin America outside of Cuba and it enabled Latin American and Caribbean governments to think of the United States as an ally over issues other than the cold war. Ever suspicious of unilateral U.S. military intervention, Latin American and Caribbean countries sought to contain U.S. power while simultaneously seeking U.S. support through multilateral institutions in order to address security problems such as terminating Central America's wars and the war between Peru and Ecuador as well as combating transnational crime. Long involved in the Central American wars and deeply affected by continuing transnational crime, the United States found these new multilateral processes cost effective. It could not end Central America's wars on its own because it had been a participant. And it could combat transnational crime more effectively if it had willing partners.

(2) One consequence of the U.S. federal budget battles during the last fifth of the twentieth century was the U.S. withdrawal, in practice, from providing international economic assistance. The United States came to rely increasingly on international financial institutions to manage economic crises outside the advanced market economies; these institutions were funded by many countries, not just by the U.S. taxpayer. These crises mattered to the United States because they repeatedly shook the pillars of the world economy in the 1990s. Latin American countries turned to these institutions to cope with their financial instability and promote their development prospects.

(3) The collapse of the long-standing import-substitution industrialization model turned all the countries of Latin America and the Caribbean to search for international markets. To open the markets of other countries, they had to open their own. For its part, the United States, fearful of continental protectionism in the European Union and perhaps East Asia, looked for free-trade partners within the Americas. Freer trade became the shared elite mantra for the end of the millennium. Multilateral institutions constructed the rules and dispute settlement instruments to free the power of trade.

(4) The collapse of communist regimes in Europe and of most authoritarian regimes in Latin America enabled political leaders across the Americas to embrace democracy, for the first time ever, as a normative value that was shared in practice. The defense and promotion of democratic institutions seemed to work more effectively when it was promoted multilaterally rather than simply as

the "cover" to hide less noble interests of some governments. Democratic values were cherished on their own term but they also provided an ideological justification for military, financial, trade, and political cooperation.

More generally, in the 1990s inter-American institutions and procedures developed in the belief that they would facilitate cooperation, not just ward off trouble.[33] These international institutions help to organize interstate relations in mutually beneficial ways. Actors conform to practices, as Robert Keohane has written, not because they are uniquely best but because others conform to them as well. Such international institutions establish mutual expectations about the patterns of behavior of others and they develop working relations that allow the parties to adapt their practices to new situations.

International institutions also alter the relative costs of transactions. They prohibit discriminatory policies except under clearly specific conditions (such as the imposition of sanctions on a rule breaker). The main insurance against violation is not some centralized authority, but rather the growing linkage among issues and the interpenetration of economies, most advanced for the NAFTA and MERCOSUR countries. The transaction costs of misbehavior rise at the same time that transaction costs of lawful behavior lower. It is cheaper for governments and firms to reach agreements and make deals once a stable international regime has been instituted; firms can take advantage of economies of scale. Governments, too, find it easier to reach agreements beyond the one that founded a specific international regime. For example, MERCOSUR was established as a trade regime, with few supranational organizations to implement its rules. Nonetheless, by the second half of the 1990s it had evolved into a defense-of-democracy regime.

International institutions reduce uncertainty and facilitate the transfer of information. NAFTA helped the United States and Mexico contain the financial panic in early 1995. As Hunter's chapter shows, the transfer of information (analyses, evidence, and so forth) is at the heart of the activities of the international financial institutions. Multilateralism, therefore, is not a fad. It is a practical solution to the enduring problem of international asymmetry in the Americas.[34]

Multilateralism is not a panacea, however. Multilateral institutions are slow to act because they operate best only when consensus has been established. Multilateral institutions may often choose suboptimal solutions because only these can secure consensus. Multilateral institutions are vulnerable to unilateral decisions to withhold dues payments and other financial obligations of member countries, as the United States too often did in the closing years of the twentieth century. And yet, the very process of deliberation, frustrating as it often is, tends to create the foundations and commitments for sustained agreement and implementation. This capacity of multilateralism to generate credible commitments has finally recommended the approach to many governments. Therefore, multilateralism is likely to remain and to grow in the twenty-first century as a means for inter-American collaboration.

Unilateralism, Unilateralism Everywhere?

A central problem in inter-American relations has been the propensity of the United States to act unilaterally, as Yopo's chapter makes clear and as George Kennan had preferred, and in so doing to presume that its own vision of the hemisphere is widely shared by other governments and peoples of the Americas.

As the twentieth century ended, nowhere was this unilateralist predisposition stronger than with regard to migration and drug trafficking. As Mitchell and Fernández de Castro and Rosales explain, the U.S. Congress in the mid-1990s provided fertile soil for sprouting unilateral initiatives affecting migration. Led by the new Republican majority in the House and Senate, the U.S. government increased deportations of illegal aliens, including many who were in the process of regularizing their status. The U.S. government accelerated deportations of illegal aliens who had committed crimes and denied a number of welfare benefits to legal residents of the United States. In so acting, the United States consulted none of its neighbors.

Several of these acts of Congress had unintended consequences, as Mitchell also notes. The policy against legal residents generated a huge jump in their applications for U.S. citizenship. It may also have galvanized many naturalized citizens in California—the state where these issues were most acute—to defeat the Republican party in the 1998 elections for governor, the state house, and Congress.

For inter-American relations, this bundle of policies had diverse effects on security, political, and economic issues, as Fernández de Castro and Rosales and Mitchell explain. Deportations of criminal aliens had important effects on security issues, as these authors and also Griffith make evident. The number of criminal deportees jumped suddenly from 36,967 in Fiscal Year 1996 to 50,165 in Fiscal Year 1997. In the latter year, about 5 criminals per day landed in the airports of the Dominican Republic while more than 100 criminals per day were deported to Mexico.[35]

A petty thief might have entered the United States illegally from the Dominican Republic. In the streets of New York, this thief may learn English, how to use assault weapons and cell telephones, and perhaps join a far-flung criminal organization. Upon deportation to the Dominican Republic, this high-tech tooled-up criminal may be no match for underpaid, occasionally corrupt, often unprofessional Dominican police officers—and a transnational criminal network could thereby be strengthened.

The policy of tightening up on the U.S. handling of political asylum cases mobilized the Central American governments into joint action. These governments feared that the United States would deport large numbers of Central Americans, who had fled the region's civil wars in the 1980s, back to their countries of birth. The Central American governments joined to lobby the U.S. government to return to the status quo to the extent possible. (This is a key theme in the case studies in the Fernández de Castro and Rosales chapter.) Nicaragua and El Salvador, in particular, focused on reversing this U.S. decision, committing significant resources of their governments to this effort. The economies of Central America and the Caribbean depended significantly on migrant remittances; in the view of these Central American governments, the U.S. Congress was threatening the goose that lays the golden eggs.[36] Along with domestic lobbying (in part stimulated by the Central American governments) and some belated leadership by the White House, these efforts brought about new congressional legislation.

The unilateralist vocation of U.S. policy toward Latin America is also evident regarding drug trafficking issues. As Serrano's chapter indicates, since 1986 U.S. law has required the executive to certify or decertify countries according to their degree of cooperation with unilaterally determined U.S. policies toward the drug trade. Such U.S. policies made relations between the United States, Mexico, and the Andean countries rancorous and cooperation more difficult. U.S. decertification and associated policies toward Colombia in the 1990s, moreover, threatened the stability of its constitutional government.

During the Bush and Clinton presidencies, the United States developed some bilateral policies to promote elements of cooperation short of a multilateral regime. The most elaborate scheme was constructed between the United States and Mexico. In March 1996, the United States and Mexico created the United States-Mexico High Level Contact Group for drug control, which has met on a regular basis ever since.[37] Tragically, in February 1997, General Jesús Gutiérrez Rebollo, Mexico's drug czar, was arrested on allegations of drug corruption, provoking a serious political crisis within Mexico and in U.S.-Mexican relations.

Yet U.S. actions against drug trafficking retained a markedly unilateral character even after such a formal agreement with Mexico. In May 1998, the U.S. government reaped the fruits of a three-year-long covert operation against Mexican banks and bankers implicated in money laundering. The substantive results were modest. However, the U.S. government had systematically misinformed the Mexican government about this operation both before and after the establishment of the High Level Contact Group; the actions of various U.S. agents may have violated Mexican law.[38] Unilateralism triumphed by sheer force of habit.

U.S. unilateralist propensities also threaten inter-American trade cooperation, as Bouzas argues in his chapter. U.S. trade policies imposing antidumping and countervailing duty penalties and generally pursuing an aggressive unilateralism to advance U.S. objectives no doubt contributed to the cause of negotiating the NAFTA and WTO agreements, but they also left a residue of anxiety: Would the United States live up to its multilateral trade commitments? The refusal of the U.S. Congress to authorize fast-track legislation to negotiate a Free Trade Area of the Americas—or even just to negotiate free trade with Chile—raised concerns among Latin Americans about the depth of the U.S. commitment to implement the trade agreements reached at the Miami and Santiago inter-American summits of the mid-1990s.

The reasons for U.S. unilateralism were summarized by George Kennan's views quoted at the outset of this chapter. The United States has the power and the tradition to act swiftly and decisively; the costs of noncollaboration in this asymmetrical international relationship fall disproportionately on other countries. The United States is more likely to act unilaterally with regard to those issues ordinarily considered matters of domestic jurisdiction, such as immigration and law enforcement.

Despite the persistence of unilateralism through the twentieth century, despite its likely continuation into the twenty-first century, the relative balance between multilateral and unilateral U.S. actions in the Americas shifted in favor of the former during the Bush and Clinton presidencies. President Bush negotiated the NAFTA and proposed an initiative for free trade in the Americas. President Clinton obtained NAFTA's ratification and opened the negotiations toward the FTAA. Both administrations made greater use of the IMF, the World Bank, and the Inter-American Development Bank to ward off financial crises in Latin America, promote economic stabilization and structural adjustment policies, and contribute to economic development. Both administrations obtained significant capital replenishments for these international financial institutions from the U.S. Congress.

The Bush administration welcomed the United Nations to make peace in the Nicaraguan war in 1989–1990, and again soon thereafter in the war in El Salvador. The Clinton administration behaved similarly, welcoming the United Nations as the lead peacemaker in Guatemala's war. The OAS helped implement the peace agreements in these three cases. Under OAS Resolution 1080 in support of democracy, the Bush administration acted multilaterally in response to coups in Haiti in 1991 and Peru in 1992. The Clinton administration continued these actions. And the latter sought formal U.N. Security Council approval prior to the U.S. military occupation of Haiti in 1994—the first time ever that the United States had sought United Nations approval prior to undertaking a military action in the Americas.

The reasons for the U.S. shift toward hemispheric multilateralism are not difficult to discern: in the 1990s, multilateralism was more cost-effective. It was cheaper for the United States to promote the IMF to take a lead role to contain the consequences of Brazil's financial crisis in 1999 than for the United

States to play a solo role, as it did during the Mexican financial crisis in 1995 at considerable political cost to President Clinton in his relations with Congress. Free-trade practices can only be implemented by the consent of the governments of the Americas; it is impossible for the United States to impose them. The United States can cut its programs of economic assistance knowing that international financial institutions may take up some of the slack. It is more effective to promote and defend democratic institutions in Latin America and the Caribbean with the consent and participation of the states of the region than by U.S. imposition. The United States alone could not pacify Nicaragua or El Salvador, because it was a party to each conflict. When the United States exhorted Mexico to liberalize its economy, little happened; however, when the United States cooperated with Mexico toward that same end, major transformations occurred. And the successful mediation of the territorial dispute between Peru and Ecuador, reached in late 1998, would have been more difficult had the United States alone sought to forward its views.

This cumulative shift toward multilateralism across two presidential administrations of different political parties suggests the possibility that the trend will persist into the twenty-first century. The shift toward multilateralism has been grounded in the self-interest of the United States, Latin America, and the Caribbean. The United States will no doubt act alone in many instances, but it became less likely to do so as the millennium closed. This was not the peculiar preference of one president or one secretary of state, rather the considered judgment of the government of the United States.

An Inter-American Civil Society

Nongovernment organizations—international firms, missionary churches and societies, the Lion's and Rotary Clubs, professional associations, sports clubs, and the like—have long mattered in inter-American relations. Caribbean music from various island traditions became a part of popular music in the United States, just as jazz, rock, and other forms of popular entertainment became part of mass culture in many countries. Exiles have played a significant role in creating an inter-American civil society. Political exiles sought to mount from one country the overthrow of governments they opposed in other countries. Literary exiles created for the first time the worldwide literature of the Spanish-speaking peoples, written in one country, published in another, read everywhere. The heart and soul of the Spanish language migrated from Castile to Buenos Aires, Lima, and Mexico city, but also to New York, San Antonio, Los Angeles, Chicago, and Miami.

These inter-American trends became stronger in the second half of the twentieth century thanks in part to the much greater ease of transportation and communications. As the millennium closed, more passengers from U.S.

airports flew south toward Latin America and the Caribbean than east to
Europe or west to Asia. As Mitchell notes, many of these were transnational
migrants shuttling back and forth between homes in two countries, but in so
doing, they tightened inter-American societal bonds.

The liberalization of trade and investment throughout Latin America and
the Caribbean, and the establishment of free-trade agreements in a patchwork
across the continent, led to the heightened international involvement of business firms. Free trade lowered the transaction costs of internationalization for
many medium-sized and smaller firms, greatly diversifying the pool of firms
constructing an inter-American business environment.

Religious evangelizing intensified as well in the closing decades of the
twentieth century. Pentecostals, Mormons, Jehovah's Witnesses, and many
other communities of faith made significant inroads in various Latin
American countries. From Puerto Rico to Brazil, from Guatemala to Chile, the
newly plural voices of Christianity constructed wider and tighter inter-
American communities of faith. The Roman Catholic Church, led by Pope
John Paul II, modernized its organization and deepened transnational links
among Roman Catholics. Many U.S. Roman Catholic bishops came to realize
that the source of growth in their congregations was Spanish-speaking Roman
Catholics. Migration from Latin America helped to change Roman
Catholicism in the United States as the century ended and led the U.S. Roman
Catholic bishops to focus afresh on Latin America.

These and many other nongovernmental organizations provide the fabric
of an expanding inter-American civil society. Its members are frequent-flying
Dallas business executives who feel at home in Buenos Aires; Dominican
grandmothers visiting their extended families in New York city and Lawrence,
Massachusetts; the Cardinal Archbishop of Boston celebrating mass with
noteworthy regularity in Havana's Roman Catholic cathedral; members of
transnational and inter-American Central American peasant movements;[39]
Latin American authors whose book sales are greater in the United States than
in their home countries; and letterwriting members of Amnesty International
who care about political prisoners in Latin American jails.

The actions of many within this inter-American civil society promote and
help to consolidate constitutional government and democratic practices, as
Isaacs and Muñoz make clear. Muñoz points out the contributions of civil
society entities from Latin American countries, Chile especially, to the promotion of democracy elsewhere in the continent. Isaacs calls attention to the fed-
erations of political parties, and particularly of foundations associated with
the main German political parties, that contributed to democratic transitions
and that assist in aspects of democratic consolidation. She notes, too, that several large foundations in the United States, notably the Ford and MacArthur

Foundations, have helped to sustain inter-American civic life. Election observation in many Latin American and Caribbean countries has developed into a specialized and effective task mainly by nongovernmental organizations, especially by former President Jimmy Carter's center. Bilateral official assistance from Canada, Scandinavian countries, Spain, and the United States has supported many civil society organizations. Isaacs discusses as well problems associated with this form of international assistance, but on balance, the aid has been positive. More generally, nongovernmental organizations have contributed to a rise in environmental standards in the hemisphere, strengthened networks of human rights monitors and defenders, and generated exchanges among legislators seeking to design codes to help prevent violence against women.[40] The construction of an inter-American civil society has advanced democratic and other "good government" practices in the Americas.

An Inter-American Democratic Debate

In the 1980s and 1990s, a vigorous debate opened in Latin America about the relationship between democracy, on the one hand, and other "good things," on the other. Was democracy just a "consumption item," a good for its own sake, or was it likely to retard or promote the achievement of other "good things"? This debate will shape the choice of responses in crises. The debate occurs within countries but also across the Western Hemisphere; this continental dimension is a genuine late-twentieth-century novelty.

Some of the news is good. No constitutionally elected president has been overthrown in an Iberoamerican country since 1976. Transitions toward more open politics, and in most cases toward democratic political systems, have occurred throughout Latin America and the Caribbean. A political transition toward more open politics is slow moving only in Cuba. Yet the quality of democratic life remains poor in many countries of the region, as Isaacs notes in her chapter. Large parts of Colombia and Peru are under military state-of-siege provisions. The levels of professionalism of the police and the courts remain low throughout Latin America. Significant violations of human rights, property rights, and judicial due process remain the norm as well. Journalists are often intimidated, and from Argentina to Mexico, they have been victims of political assassination. There is a rising, vigorous debate about the quality of democratic politics in both Latin America and the Caribbean. Concern exists about widespread corruption and about declining rates of electoral turnout in countries of long-standing democratic credentials, such as Venezuela and the Anglophone Caribbean.[41]

But there is another democratic debate concerning the utility of democracy to achieve other worthwhile social goals. Can democracy—a worthwhile goal in itself—also provide effective governance to perform the central tasks of a capable state? Can it generate peace, domestic order, and prosperity? This debate echoes through the chapters in this book, too. Mares observes that democracy has failed to prevent the outbreak of various militarized interstate disputes in Latin America in the 1990s.[42] Indeed, both Ecuador and Peru had constitutional governments when they went to war in 1995. Mitchell accounted for the enactment of anti-immigrant provisions in the United States in the mid-1990s as an outcome of democratic politics: anti-immigrant feelings in public opinion converted into policy through the nationwide Republican congressional victory in 1994. Bouzas worries about the dangers of protectionism in North and South America, in part because protectionist business lobbies exert pressure through democratic constitutional procedures—a point first developed elegantly by C. E. Lindblom who called it "the privileged position of business" in democratic politics.[43]

Serrano argues that democratic regimes seem particularly vulnerable to blackmail and penetration by drug traffickers, on the one hand, while the more successful antinarcotics operations have taken place in nondemocracies. International organized crime, she notes, imperils the constitutional order of democratic states because the latter—unlike authoritarian regimes—are constrained by the rule of law in combating this new international menace. In contrast, effective operations against drug traffickers have been carried out in Pinochet's Chile and Castro's Cuba. While some authoritarian regimes have been deeply involved with drug trafficking—General García Meza's in Bolivia, General Noriega's in Panama—no democratic regime yet has successfully overcome a major drug-trafficking threat.

Starr and Isaacs, in turn, worry that market-oriented economic reforms may undermine democratic practices and that the latter may impede the consolidation of the former. Starr argues that democratic regimes may find it difficult to enact unpopular reforms, given electoral constraints, while the volatility of international financial capital may undermine economic adjustment and structural reform programs and imperil constitutional government. Isaacs argues forcefully that the neoliberal economic model may obstruct democratic deepening. Budget cuts shred weak social safety nets and contribute to poverty and inequality levels incompatible with democratic objectives. Government accountability to the electorate is impaired if governments must be responsive, above all, to the international financial community. Without the tools to build social democracy in Latin America, she concludes, procedural democracy stands on shaky ground.

On the other hand, Fernández de Castro and Rosales indicate that Nicaragua and El Salvador succeeded in changing aspects of U.S. immigration policies through the effective use of democratic procedures in the United

States. Devlin notes that free trade in the Americas was probably facilitated by Latin America's democratic transition and that trade growth propelled Latin American economies in the 1990s helping to consolidate constitutional government. Muñoz and Yopo detail various ways in which concerted political action was facilitated by the shared democratic commitments of key southern South American governments and how these governments have acted internationally to defend democratic institutions in neighboring countries.

I share many of these concerns and these hopes. My own research suggests a somewhat hopeful conclusion. With regard to the prospects for international peace, constitutional government and democracy in Latin America provide no guarantee of avoidance of war or of militarized interstate disputes. Nonetheless, these democracies are not war-prone. They exhibit a status-quo bias: they find it difficult to make peace, though they can at times, but they also find it difficult to break the peace, though they can also do that. They characteristically persevere along inherited pathways.[44]

With regard to the relationship between democracy and markets, I have argued that democracies can help to consolidate market economies. Statist economic arrangements often foster close connections between economic and political elites, fostering corruption and reducing the likelihood that profits would derive from efficiency or quality. Statist economics privileges the powerful, even if they are inept, inefficient, and crooked. A long history of authoritarian power—not the recent democratic experiments—constructed the legacy of poverty and inequality. Market reforms can cut the ties that facilitate corrupt and rent-seeking behavior and may reduce the scope of arbitrary action when compared to authoritarian regimes under statist economics (though they do not always deliver on this potential). Democracy can lower certain transaction costs: revolutions and other acts of violence need not be mounted to overthrow dictators. Elections provide a more effective means to sweep away the failed policies and politicians of the past to start afresh. And democratic procedures, particularly when congress and political parties are involved directly in making economic policy, may better meet the rational expectations of economic actors because they are more likely to ensure that market rules are adopted by the consent of the governed. Under those circumstances, democracies are more credible than dictatorships in asserting that today's market rules will also be tomorrow's. The empirical record of most Latin American and Caribbean governments in the 1990s demonstrates that democracies can and have enacted important market reforms and that the success of the reforms required adherence to constitutional practice.[45]

For the reader, the question should remain open, as it remains throughout most of the Americas. The purpose in sketching the disagreements among scholars, even within the pages of this book, is to provide insight into the wider, deeper, and important debate about the prospects for democracy, peace, order, and prosperity in the hemisphere. This is an inter-American debate, for the obstacles, the answers, and the complexities combine the international and the domestic. Rulers and citizens learn from the collective experience of their neighbors and this shared inter-American disputation is part of the history of the future about to begin.

Notes

1. "Memorandum by the Counselor of the Department (Kennan) to the Secretary of State," *Foreign Relations of the United States, 1950,* vol. 2 (Washington, D.C.: U.S. Government Printing Office), 598–624. Specific quotations, respectively, come from pp. 615, 620, 622.
2. For an account of varieties of realist arguments, see Stephen G. Brooks, "Dueling Realisms," *International Organization* 51, no. 3 (summer 1997): 445–77.
3. *The Rockefeller Report on the Americas* (Chicago: Quadrangle Books, 1969), 17.
4. A more influential report, taken seriously by the Carter administration, was that issued in 1975 by the Commission on United States-Latin American Relations, chaired by Sol M. Linowitz. See its text in *The Americas in a Changing World* (New York: Quadrangle Books, 1975).
5. The median age for the authors in this issue was about seventy.
6. *Foreign Affairs* 76, no. 5 (September/October 1997).
7. This is not a free-standing chapter. Instead, it calls attention to and, to some degree, summarizes themes that emerge from the chapters in this book. This chapter relies on textual references to other chapters, but my debt to the authors of this book is much greater than these citations suggest. I am also grateful to Roberto Bouzas, Peter Hakim, Michael Shifter, and Viron P. Vaky for excellent comments on an earlier draft. The views expressed here are mine alone, however. The authors are at liberty to claim that all the errors in this chapter are mine and all the insights are theirs. All mistakes are certainly mine alone.
8. For a thoughtful discussion of prospective European-Latin American relations in the early twenty-first century, see Instituto de Relaciones Europeo-Latinoamericanas, "América Latina y Europa: Más allá del año 2000," *Dossier,* no. 65 (Madrid: IRELA, 1998).
9. Inter-American Development Bank, *Integration and Trade in the Americas: A Preliminary Estimate of 1998 Trade* (Washington, D.C.: 1998), Annex A.
10. Carlos Escudé and Andrés Fontana, "Argentina's Security Policies"; and Mônica Hirst, "Security Policies, Democratization, and Regional Integration in the Southern Cone," both in *International Security and Democracy: Latin America and the Caribbean in the Post-Cold War Era,* ed. Jorge I. Domínguez (Pittsburgh: University of Pittsburgh Press, 1998).
11. U.S. Executive Office of the President, Office of National Drug Control Policy, *Blueprint for a Drug Free America: Assessing the Performance of the National Drug Control Strategy* (Washington, D.C.: 1997), 14.
12. Robert E. Quirk, *An Affair of Honor: Woodrow Wilson and the Occupation of Vera Cruz* (New York: McGraw-Hill, 1962).
13. The Charter was signed in 1948 at the Ninth International Conference of American States in Bogotá, Colombia.
14. For a thoughtful discussion of these issues, with specific attention to the Kennedy administration, see Robert Packenham, *Liberal America and the Third World* (Princeton: Princeton University Press, 1973).
15. Lars Schoultz, *Human Rights and United States Policy toward Latin America* (Princeton: Princeton University Press, 1981).
16. For the evolving policy consensus, see Thomas Carothers, *In the Name of Democracy: U.S. Policy toward Latin America in the Reagan Years* (Berkeley and Los Angeles: University of California Press, 1991).

17. For analysis, see Jeffrey Sachs, ed., *Developing Country Debt and Economic Performance* (Chicago: University of Chicago Press, 1989); Pedro Pablo Kuczynski, *Latin American Debt* (Baltimore: Johns Hopkins University Press, 1988).

18. For general discussion in a wider context, see Barry Eichengreen and Albert Fishlow, *Contending with Capital Flows: What is Different About the 1990s?* (New York: Council on Foreign Relations, 1996).

19. Sebastian Edwards, *Crisis and Reform in Latin America: From Despair to Hope* (New York: Oxford University Press, 1995), chap. 7.

20. Inter-American Development Bank, "Overcoming Volatility," *Economic and Social Progress in Latin America: 1995 Report* (Washington, D.C.: Johns Hopkins University Press, 1995), 207–18.

21. United Nations, Economic Commission for Latin America and the Caribbean, *Preliminary Overview of the Economy of Latin America and the Caribbean, 1992* LC/G.1751 (New York: United Nations, 1992), 55; ibid., *1997* (Santiago, Chile: United Nations, 1997), 57.

22. Bolívar Lamounier, "Brazil: The Hyperactive Paralysis Syndrome," in *Constructing Democratic Governance: South America*, ed. Jorge I. Domínguez and Abraham F. Lowenthal (Baltimore: Johns Hopkins University Press, 1996), 171.

23. For discussion, see the special issue of the *Journal of Interamerican Studies and World Affairs* 40, no. 4 (winter 1998). In particular, see David Fleischer, "The Cardoso Government's Reform Agenda: A View from the National Congress, 1995–1998"; and Timothy Power, "Brazilian Politicians and Neoliberalism: Mapping Support for the Cardoso Reforms, 1994–1997."

24. U.S. Arms Control and Disarmament Agency, *World Military Expenditures and Arms Transfers, 1991–92* (Washington, D.C.: U.S. Government Printing Office, 1994); Francisco Rojas Aravena, "El proceso de asignación del gasto militar en América Latina," in *Gasto militar en América Latina*, ed. Francisco Rojas Aravena (Santiago: CINDE-FLACSO, 1994); and Daniel P. Hewitt, "Military Expenditures 1972–1990: The Reasons Behind the Post–1985 Fall in World Military Spending," *IMF Working Paper*, no. WP/93/18 (Washington, D.C.: International Monetary Fund, 1993).

25. Jorge I. Domínguez, "Security, Peace, and Democracy in Latin America and the Caribbean: Challenges for the Post–Cold War Era," in *International Security and Democracy*, ed. Domínguez.

26. See also Anthony P. Maingot, "The Illicit Drug Trade in the Caribbean: Use, Transshipment, and Violent Crime," in *International Security and Democracy*, ed. Domínguez.

27. For discussion of scenarios, see Jorge I. Domínguez, *Democratic Politics in Latin America and the Caribbean* (Baltimore: Johns Hopkins University Press, 1998), chap. 6.

28. "Multilateral" in this chapter refers to the intergovernmental institutions at the inter-American and subregional level within the Americas. When global multilateral institutions are discussed, the context makes it clear. In only one chapter is the usage different. Devlin, Estevadeordal, and Garay typically use the word "multilateral" when they are referring to global institutions, such as the World Trade Organization, and reserve the word "regional" when discussing the FTAA and similar arrangements.

29. Three other smaller regional public banks deserve mention. The Caribbean Development Bank and the Central American Bank for Economic Integration function in ways similar to the IDB: they are subregional banks with special commitments to their respective member countries but with much less money. The Eastern Caribbean Central Bank and the Eastern Caribbean dollar predate the European Central Bank and the Euro by decades; most Eastern Caribbean Anglophone countries have long been governed by a uniform monetary and fixed exchange rate regime under a regional central bank that operates as a multilateral currency board.

30. *Integration and Trade in the Americas, 1998*, Annex A.

31. For a partial list of agreements, see Edwards, *Crisis and Reform in Latin America*, 143–47.

32. For a parallel argument about the evolution of the European Union in the 1990s, see Joseph Grieco, "The Maastricht Treaty, Economic and Monetary Union, and the Neo-realist Research Programme," *Review of International Studies* 21, no. 1 (January 1995): 34.

33. This and the next paragraphs draw from Robert O. Keohane, *After Hegemony: Cooperation and Discord in the World Political Economy* (Princeton: Princeton University Press, 1984), 85–95.

34. For a trenchant general critique of institutionalist arguments similar to mine, however, see John J. Mearsheimer, "The False Promise of International Institutions," *International Security* 19, no. 3 (winter 1994–95): 5–49.

35. Computed from Margaret Taylor and T. Alexander Aleinikoff, *Deportation of Criminal Aliens: A Geopolitical Perspective* (Washington, D.C.: Inter-American Dialogue, 1998), 4.

36. Rodolfo de la Garza, Manuel Orozco, and Miguel Baraona, "Binational Impact of Latino Remittances," *Policy Brief* (The Tomás Rivera Institute) (March 1997): 1–12; Deborah Waller Meyers, "Migrant Remittances to Latin America: Reviewing the Literature," *Working Paper* (Inter-American Dialogue and Tomás Rivera Institute) (May 1998): 1–22.

37. See, among others, *US/Mexico Bi-National Drug Strategy* (Washington, D.C.: U.S. Office of National Drug Control Policy Information Clearing House, 1998).

38. "Statement made by the Attorney General of Mexico, Jorge Madrazo Cuéllar, regarding Operation Casablanca," May 22, 1998, courtesy of the Office for Political and Congressional Affairs of the Embassy of Mexico to the United States.

39. Marc Edelman, "Transnational Peasant Politics in Central America," *Latin American Research Review* 33, no. 3 (1998): 49–86.

40. For case studies on these three issue areas, see Margaret Keck and Kathryn Sikkink, *Activists Beyond Borders: Advocacy Networks in International Politics* (Ithaca: Cornell University Press, 1998), chap. 3–5.

41. See, for example, thoughtful discussions by Michael Coppedge, "Venezuela: The Rise and Fall of Partyarchy"; and Trevor Munroe, "Caribbean Democracy: Decay or Renewal?" both in *Constructing Democratic Governance,* ed. Domínguez and Lowenthal.

42. For an assessment of the broader international issue, consistent with Mares's argument about Latin America, see Joanne Gowa, "Democratic States and International Disputes," *International Organization* 49, no. 3 (summer 1995): 511–22.

43. C. E. Lindblom, *Politics and Markets* (New York: Basic Books, 1977), chap. 13.

44. Domínguez, "Security, Peace, and Democracy in Latin America and the Caribbean," 21–25.

45. Jorge I. Domínguez, "Free Politics and Free Markets in Latin America," *Journal of Democracy* 9, no. 4 (October 1998): 70–84.

2

Securing Peace in the Americas
in the Next Decade

DAVID R. MARES

The Security Agenda in the Americas: Nagged by the Old, Challenged by the New

The security agenda in the Americas has experienced some positive and dramatic changes in the 1990s.[1] Redemocratization lowered the level of tension in some interstate rivalries (Peru-Chile and Argentina-Chile[2]) and mitigated the fear of transnational revolutionary alliances.[3] The end of the cold war reduced the severity of ideological competition, thereby helping to end the Central American civil wars. Even the economic collapse associated with the debt crisis had its positive impact on hemispheric security by effectively ending the arms races, which had been gathering speed since the mid-1970s. The Americas can look back on this decade, therefore, with a good measure of satisfaction.

Nevertheless, the traditional issues of border disputes, competition for natural resources, and migration pressures still animate security relations among many states in the hemisphere. Borders, both land and sea, remain contentious between Guatemala and Belize, Nicaragua and Colombia, Colombia and Venezuela, Ecuador and Peru, Bolivia and Chile, and among Honduras, El Salvador, and Nicaragua. Competition for resources affects relations between Venezuela and Trinidad and Tobago (petroleum) and states in the Gulf of Fonseca (fisheries). Migrations can also heighten interstate tensions when one side uses its military to "regain control over its borders." Of late illegal migrations are affecting relations between the United States and Mexico, Nicaragua and its neighbors Honduras and Costa Rica, Haiti and the Dominican Republic, as well as Colombia and Venezuela. Cross-border guerrilla activity also causes security problems for three of Colombia's neighbors: Ecuador, Venezuela, and Panama (see Table 2.1).

In addition, issues that had been with us for a long time, but had never become identified as threats to national security, have now been elevated to such standing, thereby increasing tensions among some hemispheric states. In

Table 2.1

Interstate Disputes in Contemporary Latin America

Countries	Issue
	Major Disputes
Guatemala-Belize	Demarcation of border
Honduras-El Salvador	Implementation of Interamerican Court of Justice decision on border demarcation; migration
Honduras-El Salvador-Nicaragua	Demarcation of maritime borders in Gulf of Fonseca; depletion of fisheries
Honduras-Nicaragua	Demarcation of maritime border in Atlantic; migration
Nicaragua-Costa Rica	Border demarcation; migration
Nicaragua-Colombia	Territorial dispute over San Andres and Providencia Islands
Colombia-Venezuela	Thirty-four points on border in dispute; migration; guerrillas; contraband, including but not limited to drugs
Venezuela-Trinidad & Tobago	Maritime boundaries; resources
Haiti-Dominican Republic	Migration; border demarcation
Bolivia-Chile	Territorial dispute: outlet to the Pacific
	Minor but Active Disputes
Argentina-Chile	Ratification of Campos de Hielo agreement
Chile-Peru	Final implementation of 1929 treaty covering Peruvian access to Chilean port at Arica
	Latent Disputes
Venezuela-Guayana	Territorial dispute: Venezuela claims 40 percent of Guyanese claimed territory
Antartica	Issue of national claims
Argentina-Great Britain	Malvinas/Falklands, Georgias and Sandwich Sur
United States-Cuba	Guantanamo

Sources: Adapted from Francisco Rojas Aravena, "Latin America: Alternatives and Mechanisms of Prevention in Situations Related to Territorial Sovereignty," *Peace and Security in the Americas* no. 13 (Oct. 1997): 2–7; Noti-Sur.

the name of one of these new issues—drug trafficking—large-scale military force was used against the government of another country (U.S. invasion of Panama in 1989). The overthrow of democracy is now considered a threat to hemispheric security.[4] The region averted another use of military force on this issue only at the last minute in Haiti. In addition, industrialized nations' concerns over the potential environmental threat emanating from the destruction of the Amazonian ecosystem animate Brazilian security analysts.

Perhaps most depressing of all, the return of democracy to the region has not yet led to peaceful relations among democracies (see Table 2.2). Since a number of these democracies have passed through the ten-year transition period the literature on the democratic peace identifies as necessary for salutary effects to occur,[5] the experience of the Western Hemisphere suggests that it is not democracy per se which matters for interstate violence. Rather it may be something about the type of information a democratic public receives, the values its society holds beyond that of "ballots over bullets," and the degree of economic interdependence among potential adversaries that matter.[6]

In summary, the security situation in the hemisphere has certainly improved during the last decade. Yet the likelihood of further movement in the direction toward peaceful interstate relations in the forthcoming decade is decreased by the emergence of these new factors and the persistence of historical disputes. The hemisphere would benefit immensely if it were possible to move into a new phase of interstate relations characterized by mutual accommodation in the security realm.

What Is Currently Being Done?

Political and military actors in the hemisphere have been active in addressing some of these security issues. These efforts fall into three categories: diplomatic negotiations to resolve outstanding disputes; confidence-building measures to mitigate the possibility of misunderstandings developing into armed confrontations; and modernizing defense establishments to ensure the credibility of deterrence.

Diplomatic Negotiations

Most interstate conflict resolution efforts are oriented toward *border disputes.* Despite a flurry of international, regional, and bilateral activity, only one set of countries appears to have virtually resolved their disputes. When Chile and Argentina began their current efforts, twenty-four points of contention were outstanding; today, solutions have been negotiated and implemented on twenty-three of these. The last agreement (concerning the Campos de Hielo) awaits full legislative approval in both countries, but delay in implementation has not produced tension on the border.

Table 2.2

Militarized Disputes Involving Latin American Countries
1990–1998

Year	Dyad	Hostility Level[a]	Democracy
1990	NONE		
1991	Honduras/Nicaragua	4	yes/yes
	Peru/Ecuador	3	yes/yes
1992	U.S./Haiti	4	yes/no
1993	U.S./Haiti	4	yes/no
1994	U.S./Haiti	4	yes/no
1995	Ecuador/Peru	5	yes/yes
	Ecuador/Peru	4	yes/yes
	Colombia/Venezuela	4	yes/yes
	Nicaragua/Honduras	4	yes/yes
	Nicaragua/Colombia	2	yes/yes
1996	Nicaragua/Honduras	4	yes/yes
	Nicaragua/El Salvador	4	yes/yes
	Honduras/El Salvador	4	yes/yes
1997	Honduras/Nicaragua	4	yes/yes
	Nicaragua/Costa Rica	3	yes/yes
	El Salvador/Honduras	3	yes/yes
	Venezuela/Trinidad and Tobago	4	yes/yes
	Venezuela/Colombia	4	yes/yes
	Belize/Guatemala	4	yes/yes
1998	Ecuador-Peru	4	yes/yes
	Ecuador-Peru	3	yes/yes
	Costa Rica-Nicaragua	3	yes/yes

Source: MID data base to 1992, Keesing's International Archives, ChipNews, Noti-Sur, *Hoy*
(Quito, Ecuador) and *La Nación* (San José, Costa Rica).

a. Hostility levels are: 1=no threat to use force; 2=threat; 3=display of force; 4=use of force;
   5=outbreak of war. Charles S. Gochman and Zeev Maoz, "Militarized Interstate Disputes,
   1816–1976," *Journal of Conflict Resolution* 28, no. 4 (Dec. 1984): 605–12.

Ecuador and Peru seem finally to have resolved the territorial issues that
produced a number of wars between the two countries since independence
170 years ago. Bilateral negotiations were problematic for three years after
their last war in 1995. But after a number of Peruvian soldiers had been
maimed by land mines, important arms purchases by both sides, and mobi-
lizations of both militaries in August 1998, the two sides agreed to arbitrate
their dispute. Hopefully, the decision by the four arbiters (United States, Chile,
Argentina, and Brazil) will prove lasting despite initial negative reactions by
many people in both countries.[7]

Resolution of the Salvadoran-Honduran land border has foundered on the details of sorting out citizenship and property rights of people caught on the "wrong" side of the border settlement determined by the International Court of Justice in 1992. Unfortunately, the inability of a binational commission of experts working since 1992 to settle the problem has produced unilateral action by local government and citizens, which turned violent in 1997.[8]

Negotiations among Honduras, El Salvador, and Nicaragua over constructing a system of border markers in the Gulf of Fonseca are stymied. In 1997 the dispute heated up and Nicaraguan patrol boats fired on Honduran fishing vessels. Honduras's defense minister responded by proclaiming that the country's military forces would know how to defend the country.[9]

Guatemala and Belize also seem stuck after the courageous unilateral decision by Guatemala's then-President Jorge Serrano to recognize the existence of Belize in 1992. In February 1997 talks began on delimiting the border, but in that summer Belizean troops expelled Guatemalans from the Peten. Guatemala responded by increasing its patrolling of the disputed area.[10]

Interstate conflicts in the Western Hemisphere are not limited to border disputes. Migration is a contentious regional issue, which at times escalates into the verbal and physical use of military force by one of the countries to influence the other nation's policy on uncontrolled migratory movements. The perception that military force is unable to produce security in this complex relationship is increasingly challenged. Faced with an inward flow of people (as well as drugs), the United States has been steadily militarizing its border with Mexico in an attempt to control these new "threats." The U.S. public and its leaders may not believe war is thinkable with Mexico, but they are coming to believe that using military force against Mexico is a legitimate way to address particularly pressing problems. Costa Rica and Nicaragua have held talks to deal with the problem of illegal Nicaraguan migrants, and Venezuela has expressed its concerns over Colombian migrants; these migration issues have contributed to Nicaragua's aggressive stance over the access by Costa Rica's police forces (the country has no military establishment) to the San Juan River, and Venezuela's militarized response to Colombian guerrilla incursions.[11]

Unfortunately, other disputes that have heated up in the past are not even being negotiated. Venezuela continues to reject Colombia's call for negotiations on the thirty-two points in dispute on their border, and Colombia rejects outright Nicaragua's claims on the San Andres Islands. In 1996 Bolivia raised the issue of an outlet to the sea (previous talks were broken off during the war scare of the late 1970s). Upon winning the 1997 presidential elections, Hugo Banzer (who had been dictator during the previous negotiations), demanded Chilean concessions on this issue and denounced Chilean mines on the border. Chile, however, refuses to negotiate under pressure. The absence of full diplomatic relations between the two countries limits negotiations on such a sensitive issue.

Confidence-Building Measures

U.S. defense establishments are active in initiating confidence-building measures, often getting out in front of their civilian counterparts. The U.S. Department of Defense has always perceived training programs that bring together officers from multiple Latin American countries as providing the indirect benefit of building personal relationships, which in turn provide mutual confidence among Latin American defense establishments so that tense moments can be resolved peacefully. The United States continues to carry out such training programs, but they are under increasing attack because of the past behavior of the Latin American military as well as the current reticence of some Latin American militaries to submit to effective civilian control at home.

Latin American militaries too have been actively engaged in confidence-building measures. After Honduran and Nicaraguan ships exchanged fire in the summer of 1997 naval authorities negotiated a buffer zone and agreed to initiate joint patrols. But in the absence of border delimitation and joint management of the progressive depletion of maritime resources in the area such measures may be difficult to sustain.[12] Since 1995 Ecuadorian and Peruvian military leaders have engaged in bilateral and multilateral efforts designed to make border defense activities transparent so as to demonstrate their nonoffensive character. In 1992 both sides agreed that they would not use threats or force against each other, yet they were at war three years later. Consequently, the recent peace agreement contemplates continued efforts at military confidence building. Meanwhile Chile and Argentina performed joint military exercises in 1998.[13]

Latin American civilians have also been active in confidence-building efforts, at times encouraging their defense establishments to engage in joint activities (e.g., Argentina). With the exception of Chile and Ecuador (and perhaps Brazil), civilian efforts are oriented more toward increasing confidence in peaceful management of conflict by decreasing the destructive power of military establishments. Panama and Haiti have traveled farthest, abolishing their armed forces in 1992 and 1994, respectively.

Unilateral force reductions, however, may increase the likelihood of violence in the short-term. Panama's weakened ability to defend its border has made it easier for Colombian rebels to cross into Panama. The resulting border tensions suggest that if a country chooses to abolish its military it should have an alternative available. Costa Rica, which eliminated its military in 1948, has been able to count on both a professionally trained and equipped police and third-party intervention when the former proved insufficient.[14]

Diplomatic efforts have focused on the control and limitation of conventional weapons because the relevant players have all foresworn weapons of mass destruction.[15] Discussions surrounding the Treaty for Democratic Security in Central America address the issue of conventional weapons via efforts to limit military budgets. At the moment, talks are stalled, partly over the definition of adequate military spending levels. Once again Oscar Arias has staked out a bold position, this time by proposing (in conjunction with eleven other Nobel Peace Prize Laureates), a code of conduct concerning the arms trade. It requires increased control and vigilance of arms trading, including registries of arms produced and sold, plus international collaboration to exchange the intelligence that allows one to increase the transparency in the trade.[16]

A successful code will require international and not just Latin American cooperation because the international arms market is extremely lucrative. The good intentions of presidents is not enough, as evidenced by the current scandal in Argentina. Despite the Menem government's dispatch of peacekeeping troops to the former Yugoslavia and Argentina's role as a guarantor of the 1942 peace treaty between Ecuador and Peru, cabinet and high-ranking military officials have been implicated in the sale of arms to Croatia and Ecuador during periods of armed conflict (1991 and 1995, respectively).[17]

There is also an increasingly vocal demand in Latin America that the United States cooperate on regulating the flow of small arms to the region. In an interesting twist to what we commonly hear in the United States, on this matter Latin America wants the United States to control its borders!

Deterrence and Force Modernization

Many countries in the hemisphere, including the United States, are reluctant to pin the entire defense of their interests on diplomacy and confidence-building measures. Saddled with outdated and even inoperable equipment, force modernization is increasingly the order of the day. In addition, Ecuador's performance in the 1995 war demonstrated that smaller armies equipped with modern weapons could hold out against larger, but less-well-equipped and -trained armies. Peru may not have learned this lesson well as it subsequently purchased MIG-29 aircraft from former Soviet states, without the service contracts that will keep them flying. Chile, on the other hand, is taking a more prudent course, buying planes from Belgium's NATO forces and pursuing the U.S.-made F-16. Argentina recently pursued the special status of a U.S. non-NATO ally, partly in hopes of gaining special access to U.S. weapons.[18]

The U.S. decision in the fall of 1997 to sell sophisticated weapons to Latin America will facilitate force modernization. But such modernization will not depend on U.S. policies. The international arms market and the internal Latin American political demands for keeping the military out of domestic politics produce the dynamics that make such a process inevitable.

The security conditions in the hemisphere at this time are not acute enough to escalate force modernization into arms racing. The Western Hemisphere, however, is a region in which states continue to use military force to signal and negotiate.[19] If the traditional and new issues on the hemispheric security agenda remain contentious into the future, then the groundwork will have been laid for hard negotiating tactics to escalate into violent military confrontations.

The Role of International Institutions

International institutions have had a weak record in previous conflict-management schemes, largely because of the unilateral behavior of the United States in the OAS and its insistence on marginalizing the UN in the hemisphere. But in the 1980s the UN became a joint actor in conflict management with the OAS in Central America, and Latin American states have subsequently played an active role in UN peacekeeping operations elsewhere in the world.[20] Thus the UN is now a legitimate player in hemispheric security affairs.

The OAS is attempting to construct an effective inter-American security system. Defense ministerial meetings could be a major step in this direction, particularly as the number of civilian defense ministers increases. The Special Commission on Hemispheric Security focuses on trying to prevent conflict and not just manage it. It has discussed confidence- and security-building measures, the creation of a Conflict Prevention Center, and linking the regional system to the United Nations efforts in the area of preventive diplomacy, peacemaking, and peacekeeping. Most Latin American nations, however, are still reluctant to provide the OAS with any effective security functions.

Subregional efforts to institutionalize security management are also under way. The Permanent Mechanism for Joint Political Action, known as the Rio Group, was developed in the midst of the Central American civil wars and continues to seek peaceful and negotiated mechanisms to deal with conflict in the region.[21] In the summer of 1997 Argentina proposed that MERCOSUR (Southern Common Market) create a multilateral security force that could respond to domestic disturbances, drug trafficking, or terrorist acts.[22] A "Framework Treaty on Democratic Security in Central America" was signed in 1995,[23] but there has been little progress on its implementation.

Assessment of Progress and Policy Recommendations

New Issues of "National Security"

As redefinitions of security proliferate both internationally and bilaterally, it is useful to evaluate the advantages and disadvantages of a broad or narrow definition of "security." Security as a political concept in international relations is an empowering device. To attach this label to an issue affects its relative standing in a country's agenda, the resources upon which policymakers may call, and the degree of risks, as well as costs, one is willing to entertain in formulating appropriate related policies. Perhaps most importantly for students of international politics, the concept legitimizes state actions that would otherwise face condemnation. One must remember its use by the far right and left to justify internal wars against "enemies."

The concept's utility in providing resources and a broad range of actions to address problems leads even analysts who disdain the traditional militarized definitions of security to frame the new issues in terms of "security," rather than adopt a less-politicized notion. We should ask, however, in the context of inter-American relations, whether categorizing a new range of issues that affect interstate relations as "security" issues helps or hinders their mutually beneficial resolution.

Granting the short-term advantage of attracting increased resources to resolve a problem, broadening the definition of security carries significant risk. Security issues may legitimately be addressed in a unilateral fashion if cooperative efforts fail. Yet most of the "new" issues on the bilateral agenda cannot be resolved by unilateral action. For example, if drug trafficking were to be truly perceived as a security threat, as Nazism or communism were, then the U.S. public would demand that its leaders unilaterally "solve" the threat since cooperation with the Colombian government (to take but one example) has clearly "failed." Since the problem of drug consumption in the United States is at least as much a problem of demand as of supply, forcing any Latin American government to increase dramatically the effectiveness of its antidrug policies would cause severe internal turmoil and bring the United States only marginal benefits.

Preventive Diplomacy

Preventive diplomacy requires an important first step: recognizing the existence of an interstate disagreement and its potential for escalation. Diplomatic efforts are consequently oriented toward resolving the dispute before it escalates to military threats or action. The efficacy of preventive diplomacy is the sign of a mature security community.

The traditional approach to conflict management in the Americas ignored bilateral disputes so long as active fighting did not occur. Despite the diplomatic rhetoric concerning early-warning and preventive diplomacy, the traditional approach remains the de facto mode of conflict management in the hemisphere. The OAS, the Rio Group, and others all remain unwilling to insist that countries resolve their traditional disputes and cooperate effectively in addressing the new security issues. The inter-American community is willing to sanction a country for the overthrow of democracy and violations of human rights (previously seen as the inviolable domain of sovereign states), but it remains toothless concerning the issues that have traditionally led to the use of military force in the hemisphere.

The Americas might take a lesson from Europe's insistence on resolving central European borders before accepting former Soviet allies as full partners. Although former U.S. National Security Advisor Richard Feinberg proposes such a link for accession to the Free Trade of the Americas Agreement (FTAA) by the date of its implementation in 2005,[24] no one seems to have seconded the call. Since the FTAA itself is in serious trouble as a result of the U.S. Congress's rejection of fast-track negotiating authority for the president, this may no longer be a particularly attractive carrot.

Activation of Civil Society on These Issues

For too long these issues have been left to the elites. Just as now we are learning that the stability of democracy requires a strong and active civil society, we should also recognize that international cooperation cannot be left to elites. Individual voters are more likely to benefit from resolving these disputes than from spending their taxes, and at times lives, for maximalist positions.

Nongovernmental organizations must take the lead on activating civil society in these matters. Because of the sensitivity of national identities and histories, local NGOs should be in the forefront.[25] The task is to provide a peaceful and cooperative framework within which to conceptualize both the importance of the issues and the possible solutions. In the absence of an alternative framework the contending issues will continue to be conceptualized and debated in the context of competitive nationalisms. In this vein, Chilean, Argentine, and Brazilian NGOs might be particularly useful since their societies have moved beyond the disputes that had them on the brink of war in the past.

Public opinion polling is one way to break the elite's hold on these issues. In Ecuador a private consulting firm began including questions about the border dispute with Peru in its monthly surveys. Some very interesting material is now available, but the press in Ecuador remains *oficialista*, largely reporting official commentary and ignoring alternative sources of information and opinion. The communications revolution, expressed in satellite TV and news on-line presents some interesting possibilities for breaking the silence on these issues. The international news media such as CNN or the *International Miami*

Herald could play a role here in publicizing this type of news, perhaps thereby pushing national sources into addressing them as well.

Private foundations, such as the Fundacíon Arias para la Paz y el Progreso Humano in Costa Rica, are organizing public events as well as private meetings with public policy and opinion leaders to focus attention on these problematic issues. They are often helped by developed country NGOs such as the German Friedrich Ebert Foundation and the Dutch Clingendael Institute.

Ratification and Implementation of Agreements

A number of settlements stall in national legislatures that refuse to ratify or implement the agreements. The hemispheric community should address this problem. Examples include the aforementioned Campos de Hielos dispute between Argentina and Chile and the Salvadoran-Honduran implementation of the terms of their peace agreement. Ecuador and Peru suffered as a result of not implementing all of the provisions of the 1942 treaty that ended their previous war. Hopefully, the new agreement reached by arbitration meets a better fate. Confidence in the diplomatic path to conflict resolution is at stake.

Legitimate Defense Requirements

Arms control and CBMs are not simple issues, dependent solely upon political will and an unmitigated good. Rather they are complex, with potential spillovers often not considered. OAS resolutions frequently refer to "legitimate defense requirements" when discussing curbing arms proliferation, but what does the phrase mean in practice? Arms registries in principle contribute to confidence building, but they are less meaningful in the absence of agreement on what constitutes stable force levels. It will be difficult to make meaningful progress on minimizing force levels in the region without addressing this issue. The continued underlying distrust of Chile by its neighbors is a direct result of fundamental disagreements over what is necessary to address legitimate defense requirements. The publication of its Defense White Paper this year may help assuage neighbors, but it still reflects a Chilean deterrent emphasis. In Central America, the dramatically different approaches to the topic by Costa Rica and its neighbors constitutes a roadblock to further substantial progress on regional security cooperation.

The identification of legitimate defense requirements plays a particularly important role in a context in which military force is used to influence diplomatic bargaining. In Latin America fear of a costly war has kept militarized bargaining from escalating into full-scale war.[26] If the ability of states to inflict costly damage were decreased (e.g., via proposals to reduce drastically equipment and munitions) without resolving their disputes, the likelihood increases that a militarized dispute will escalate under the pressure of crisis bargaining.

Avoid Creating a Hemispheric Defense Force

Proposals for managing interstate conflict in the Americas by creating a hemispheric defense force, whether under the auspices of the OAS or a subregional group like MERCOSUR, should continue to be rejected. In a context of militarized bargaining, a weak challenger to the status quo will certainly find it useful to provoke an incident in the expectation that the Inter-American Peacekeeping Force would intervene and force the stronger defender of the status quo to make concessions in the name of peace. Ironically, peacekeeping forces in the hemisphere would probably increase interstate instability.

Conclusion

Interstate peace in the Americas is fragile. Expectations of an easy peace after the cold war were misplaced because the global bipolar conflict appeared before the traditional disputes in the Western Hemisphere had been resolved.[27] If the end of the cold war has a major impact on inter-American relations it may be to remove some prudent constraints on the use of force to affect many of the laudable goals previously subordinated to U.S. containment policies: defense of democracy and human rights as well as combating international crime (especially drug-related operations).

Democracy and economic interdependence may contribute to the peaceful resolution of some disputes. But the process by which these political and economic interests recast national interests is neither automatic nor fast in the hemisphere. Empowering the people before chauvinistic national histories are reinterpreted may push leaders facing electoral accountability into playing up either external threats or unrealistic offers to resolve a dispute in the nation's favor. Opening markets and the inflow of capital and technology are making previously inaccessible areas more valuable. Unfortunately, sharing the resources is neither natural nor easy, especially in those maritime zones in which global demand is producing overfishing.

Our conclusion should not be to limit democracy and economic interdependence. Rather we need to recognize the interstate context within which such processes are occurring and devise strategies to promote cooperation. Careful examination of the benefits and liabilities of particular conflict resolution policies will serve the inter-American community better than a headlong rush into idealistic formulas.

Some aspects of the recent peace agreement between Ecuador and Peru may provide a model for securing peace in the Americas in the next decade. The international community pledged $3 billion in financial aid for joint development projects. The two presidents acted courageously in requesting international arbitration and defending the decision at home in the face of opposition not only from some sectors in the military but also from large segments of civil society. And not least, intellectuals and public opinion leaders have committed themselves to revising the history texts with which the next generation of citizens will be educated.[28]

Notes

1. I would like to thank Jorge I. Domínguez and Richard Feinberg for providing helpful comments. All responsibility for this paper rests with me alone.
2. From 1973 to 1978 the leftist Peruvian military government and rightist Chilean military government rekindled tensions that had laid dormant since 1929, while the two military governments in Chile and Argentina were on the verge of war between 1977 and 1982. Redemocratization in Peru and Argentina corresponded with a changed attitude in those two countries vis-à-vis Chile.
3. The opening of political space for the democratic center-left in Central America during the 1980s weakened the social bases of radical insurgents who looked to the Sandinistas in Nicaragua or to Cuba for aid at home. Democratization of Nicaragua subsequently and effectively sidelined Sandinista efforts to promote revolution in the region, while the collapse of the USSR greatly weakened Cuban capabilities in most respects.
4. See Ana Julia Faya, "Los Cambios en el Sistema Interamericano de los Años 90," *Paz y Seguridad en las Americas* 11 (July 1997): 13–20.
5. Edward D. Mansfield and Jack Snyder, "Democratization and the Danger of War," *International Security* 20, no. 1 (summer 1995): 5–38.
6. See Samuel P. Huntington, "The Clash of Civilizations?" *Foreign Affairs* (summer 1993); and Paul A. Papayoanou, "Interdependence, Institutions, and the Balance of Power: Britain, Germany, and World War I," *International Security* 20, no. 4 (spring 1996): 42–76.
7. On the general conflict, see David R. Mares "Deterrence in the Ecuador-Peru Enduring Rivalry: Designing Around Weakness," *Security Studies* 6, no. 2 (winter 1996/97). For the 1998 events, see *Hoy* (Quito), Aug.–Oct. 1998.
8. "Constant Border Disputes Represent Latent Danger for Central American Integration Initiatives," Latin American Data Base, Noti-Sur, ISSN 1089–1560, 1, no. 18 (Oct. 17, 1996).
9. Ibid.
10. "Border Tensions with Belize Flare Again," Noti-Sur, ISSN 1060–4189, 7, no. 28 (Aug. 8, 1997).
11. Mauricio Herrera Ulloa, "Asamblea nica anularía acuerdo," *La Nación* (San Jose, Costa Rica), Aug. 12, 1998, 16A; and *El Diario de Caracas*, Mar. 15, 1995, 22.
12. "Honduran, Salvadoran and Nicaraguan Naval Forces Agree to Reduce Tensions in Gulf of Fonseca," *EcoCentral* 2, no. 32 (Sept. 4, 1977).
13. Argentine-Chilean security relations are discussed in Francisco Rojas Aravena, "El diálogo argentino-chileno en temas de seguridad y defensa," *Fuerzas Armadas y Sociedad* 1, no. 2 (Apr.–June 1997): 3–12.
14. In 1955 the United States sent its air force to Costa Rica when the Nicaraguan dictator Somoza was encouraging dissidents to overthrow the Costa Rican government. In the 1980s Venezuelan F-16s flew into Costa Rican airspace when the Sandinistas in Nicaragua were threatening Costa Rica over its support for the Contras. J. Lloyd Mecham, *The United States and Inter-American Security, 1889–1960* (Austin: University of Texas Press, 1962), 402–6; and Andrés Serbin, "Percepciones de Amenazas y Equipamiento Militar en Venezuela," in *Percepciones de Amenaza y Políticas de Defensa en América Latina*, ed. V. A. Rigoberto Cruz Johnson and Augusto Varas Fernández (Santiago: FLACSO, 1993), 310; and the special issue "Países Desmilitarizados en América: Defensa y Seguridad" of *Paz y Seguridad en Las Américas* no. 12 (July 1997).
15. The Andean Group presidents renounced weapons of mass destruction in December 1991 (Declaration of Cartagena). In 1991 Argentina, Brazil, and Chile signed accords to proscribe chemical and biological weapons and subsequently signed the Cartagena Agreement, foreswearing all weapons of mass destruction.

16. Oscar Arias Sánchez, "El Mundo Después de la Guerra Fría: Los Principales Retos," *Paz y Seguridad en Las Américas* no. 9 (Dec. 1996): 8–9.
17. "ARGENTINA: President Menem Accused of Interfering With Arms-Scandal Investigation," Noti-Sur, ISSN 1060–4189, 8, no. 41 (Nov. 6, 1998).
18. "Old Latin American Rivalries Re-emerge, Generating Concerns About U.S. Diplomacy in the Region," Noti-Sur, ISSN 1060–4189, 7, no. 31 (Aug. 29, 1997).
19. David R. Mares, *Violent Peace: Militarized Bargaining in Latin America's Interstate Relations* (New York: Columbia University Press, forthcoming).
20. Fernando Zeledón Torres, "Security, Agenda, and Military Balance in Central America: Limits to Democratic Consolidation in the 1990s," and Antonio L. Palá, "Peacekeeping and Its Effects on Civil-Military Relations" both in *International Security and Democracy: Latin America and the Caribbean in the Post-Cold War Era*, ed. Jorge I. Domínguez (Pittsburgh, Pa.: University of Pittsburgh Press, 1998), 239–41, 130–36.
21. Francisco Rojas Aravena, "Security Regimes in the Western Hemisphere: A View from Latin America" in *Security, Democracy, and Development in U.S.-Latin American Relations*, ed. Lars Schoultz, William C. Smith, and Augusto Varas (New Brunswick, N.J.: Transaction Books for the North-South Center, University of Miami, 1994), 183–89.
22. "Argentina Proposes Military Integration for MERCOSUR," Noti-Sur–Latin American Affairs, ISSN 1060–4189, 7, no. 27 (Aug. 1, 1997).
23. Caesar D. Sereseres, "Central American Regional Security: Postwar Prospects for Peace and Democracy," in *International Security and Democracy,* ed. Domínguez, 218–19.
24. Richard Feinberg, personal communication with author, July 9, 1998.
25. For a similar argument concerning NGOs in the human rights arena, see Sergio Aguayo, "Del Anonimato al Protagonismo: los organismos no gubernamentales y el éxodo centroamericano," *Foro Internacional* XXXII, no. 3 (Jan.–Mar. 1992): 323–41.
26. Mares, *Violent Peace.*
27. David R. Mares, "La Guerra Fría en los Conflictos Latinoamericanos: Mitos y Realidades," *Fuerzas Armadas y Sociedad,* 10, no. 2 (Apr.–June 1995).
28. See the papers presented at the conference "Ecuador y Peru: Vecinos Amigos," organized by FLACSO-Ecuador and DESCO-Peru and sponsored by the W. K. Kellogg Foundation, Quito, Ecuador, Oct. 19–20, 1998.

3

Hemispheric Security: Toward the Twenty-First Century

BORIS H. YOPO

At the start of the 1990s, as the cold war ended, the spread of democracy throughout Latin America and the convergence of free-market economic policies provoked great optimism about the potential consequences of these trends for hemispheric security.[1] In particular, many actors believed that this new scenario provided an historic opportunity for fruitful cooperation between the United States and Latin America. Such cooperation had not been realized in the past for three distinct reasons: first, contrary to what had often been affirmed, there was neither a convergence of interests nor a shared perception of "threats" in the region; second, there was widening divergence about the most appropriate means to address crisis situations in the hemisphere; and third, the formal U.S. commitment to "nonintervention" and multilateralism had always been subordinate to U.S. policies of intervention and unilateral action within a context of marked asymmetry between U.S. power and that of its southern neighbors.

These differences have not been fully resolved, nor are they likely to be so given the domestic bases of U.S. foreign policy and global interests. Nonetheless, the end of bipolar confrontation, the growing costs of unilateralism, the emergence of new shared security problems that require joint action, and the convergence among political systems in the Americas are among the factors that have created room for cooperative policies concerning hemispheric security to an extent unthinkable just a few years ago. The Santiago Declaration of 1991, the collective actions in defense of democracy, and the meetings among defense ministers are examples of these new patterns in the areas of politics and security.

Two worldviews stand, nevertheless, in the way of defining a flexible and realistic policy to promote security cooperation. On the one hand, some affirm that nothing has changed in hemispheric relations and propose to adhere to the most classical definitions of nonintervention. On the other hand, others ignore the complexities and diversity of interests that prevail in the hemisphere and rush to create new hemispheric security structures. This second view fails to consider the difficulties of such a process, the lack of consensus over security issues, and the lack of interest of several significant countries in the region in strengthening and using inter-American institutions to settle regional security problems.

U.S. Security Interests in the Hemisphere

The more productive approach to address hemispheric security within the new global context is, on the one hand, to make progress in those areas where there is a fundamental convergence of interests and assessments between the United States and Latin American countries. On the other hand, fora for permanent consultation should be developed or strengthened to address issues where the United States and the major Latin American countries still differ. This twin approach became particularly important in the 1990s because the greater opening of most economies and the greater permeability of borders made the United States itself more vulnerable to problems that once existed just within other countries.

It is worrisome, therefore, that various problems affecting daily life in the United States, such as illegal migration, drug trafficking, transnational crime, or environmental degradation, are perceived as negative consequences of a relationship with Latin America. These undesirable consequences from the process of globalization generate a "negative interdependency" and require a continuing hemispheric dialogue and cooperation. These problems cannot be addressed effectively through unilateral policies. Yet there is the risk that domestic politics in the United States could inject tension over these issues in hemispheric relations, as has occurred at various times in the 1990s. Fortunately, there is a hemispheric convergence at the level of principles: it is worthwhile to address these problems jointly.

The United States is less flexible and less likely to accommodate Latin American proposals when U.S. "vital interests" are at stake. Nor is it possible to solve complex hemispheric security problems if the United States is openly opposed to strategies worked out in Latin America. On the other hand, there are instances of U.S. "nonpolicies," marked by few U.S. initiatives with regard to hemispheric relations; these provide an opportunity to propose policies that the United States might eventually adopt, given its lack of alternatives to address certain regional problems.

Therefore, it is essential to identify which are the U.S. priority interests in the hemisphere, because they shape decisively both the regional security agenda and the likelihood of cooperation over it. There are three interrelated and fundamental U.S. hemispheric security concerns:

1. The major key permanent U.S. geo-strategic concern, unchanged by the end of the cold war, is for the hemisphere to remain relatively stable and secure at low cost in order to avoid diverting and calling upon U.S. defense assets assigned to other more unstable areas of the world that are truly vital for U.S. strategic interests, such as the Middle East and the Asia-Pacific region. The U.S. view of Latin America as its "strategic rear" is not limited, therefore, just to preventing the presence of a hostile rival power in the hemisphere; it includes avoiding instabilities and tensions that might make the region yet another object of concern for a major power that is already "overextended" in attempting to fulfill its global commitments.

2. Contemporary objectives of some relevance for U.S. hemispheric defense planning include secure access to vital energy resources such as petroleum, the normalization of relations with military institutions including the sale of sophisticated weapons after a two-decade-long pro-hibition of such commerce and collaboration with countries in the region over international peacekeeping operations.

3. U.S. Defense and State Department documents and official statements concerning old and new "threats" to hemispheric security have identified the following principal problems: the instability of democratic political systems; drug trafficking; terrorism; persisting border disputes; the pro-liferation of light weapons and of weapons of mass destruction; and humanitarian emergencies that spiral out of control and generate star-vation, violence, and massive migrations, among other events. The United States also seeks to ensure an orderly transfer of the Panama Canal to Panama and to reduce the likelihood that political conflicts with Cuba would lead to a U.S.-Cuban military confrontation.

The Hemispheric Security Agenda: Convergence over Broad Principles, Divergence in Strategies for Action

Various U.S. officials reiterate that the convergence of perspectives concerning key issues is the distinctive feature of contemporary inter-American relations. Examples are the consolidation of democracy, the strengthening of market-oriented economic policies, and the development of cooperative approaches toward security issues. Differences remain, however, between the United States and Latin American countries, as among the latter, concerning the better ways to approach security problems, the rank order of priorities on the security agenda, and the choice of appropriate fora and means to address hemispheric security crises. For example, some countries support reexamining the pertinence of the concept of sovereignty in times of emergency, while others uphold the classical doctrine that no doubt should be cast upon the nonintervention principle even if many states have been compelled to accept international intervention "voluntarily" either to receive international assistance or to resolve domestic conflicts with active international participation.

These reflections bear on the debate about the possible future use of force as part of a collective security strategy of multilateral deterrence. There is still, to be sure, a general rejection of this idea among Latin American countries because of the long and still-current history of U.S. intervention in the hemisphere. Yet the case of Haiti in 1994 could open a new chapter with regard to emergencies. A joint action between the Organization of American States (OAS) and the United Nations could legitimate a policy of "coercive diplomacy" in instances where a government violates international and humanitarian law systematically.

Moreover, the insertion of the so-called "new transnational issues" in the international security agenda has triggered a debate, yet to be resolved, concerning their scope. Should the concept of security be restricted to its military dimension, or should it be expanded within the new context of hemispheric issues? The new issues certainly threaten security when they have a significant impact on domestic political stability, the international regional order, or relations between states. In such circumstances, they can provoke conflict and greater military activity in the area. In general, it is inadvisable to set an agenda closed to the consideration of the new issues, but it is equally ill-advised to accord to every issue the rank of "security threat." In the latter instance, an open agenda would become unmanageable; it would also distort the handling of problems that require policies different from those bearing on military and security issues.

There have been differences between the United States and various Latin American governments over the best policies to address problems, such as drug trafficking, that affect many countries in the region. Various countries resist the policies of "militarizing and regionalizing" the management of the drug-trafficking issue and of imposing unilateral sanctions focused on production and trafficking, rather than on consumption. These countries disagree with the approach, methods, or priority allocated to these matters, particularly where drugs are not a vital security issue. In addition, some see the attempt to involve the military in playing a leading role in the war on drugs as a new form of military "politicization" at the very moment when the goal is to consolidate a framework for the armed forces focused on their traditional defense tasks.

Drug trafficking and production is, nevertheless, a national security problem for various countries in the region whenever it affects the capacity of states to guarantee order and ensure the physical integrity of their national territory. U.S. authorities, moreover, have come to include in their formulation of a comprehensive strategy to combat drug trafficking a greater attention to the complex social problems involved in coca and other drug production as well as a greater willingness to assume responsibility for effectively reducing consumption. Both of these observations explain a greater convergence of interests that could facilitate the development of joint strategies to confront this problem, which is so difficult to solve definitively.

Similarly, countries with large temperate or tropical forests are reluctant to consider the environment as a problem of regional security. They oppose increased foreign monitoring of an issue that they hope to preserve as their exclusive domestic prerogative. The discussions of this topic are still preliminary, but it is plain that environmental degradation increasingly crosses national borders and can affect the well-being of other societies. Large-scale natural disasters could also require international military cooperation when emergencies spiral out of control. For example, Brazil has offered the services of its Amazonian monitoring system (SIVAM) to the other countries of the Amazon basin in order to strengthen environmental protection and combat drug trafficking.

Access to and conservation of natural and mineral resources, especially nonrenewable resources, pose a similar concern for international security in the twenty-first century. Latin America is well endowed with raw materials that could be embroiled in controversies if scarcities develop that adversely affect the interests and needs of various countries. This issue is particularly serious if the resources are found in disputed territories. Disputes over fisheries in some maritime zones provide one example. Therefore, the resolution of the border disputes that persist in the region should be a significant priority, as is the utility of exploring the prospects for subregional cooperation to facilitate the joint exploitation of nonrenewable resources.

Another persisting security concern in the post–cold war is Cuba's situation. There is a general rejection in Latin America of the U.S. policy that promotes the worsening of Cuba's social and economic conditions, even if there is also greater Latin American ideological disagreement with the Cuban government. Countries geographically close to Cuba are especially opposed to such U.S. policies because they fear the direct effects of a Cuban crisis; for these countries, the Cuban question affects their security.

There is no disagreement between the United States and the countries of the region with regard to the goal of seeking a democratic opening in Cuba, however. During the cold war, a Latin American version of "détente" policies was the doctrine of "ideological pluralism," which gave the Cuban government some margin for maneuver at the regional level; however, this margin no longer exists. The bases for that doctrine disappeared once the global confrontation ended and pluralist democracies spread throughout the region. Thus Cuba remains outside of various important means for regional cooperation and joint action because being a representative democracy has become an essential prerequisite to belong to, and be a full member of, such entities as the OAS, the Rio Group, or subregional associations such as the MERCOSUR (the common market that joins Argentina, Brazil, Paraguay, and Uruguay). The Caribbean countries, however, have brought Cuba into several of their schemes for cooperation and integration, as might be expected given the political and commercial impact that the largest of the Caribbean countries has on its immediate geographic neighbors.

Beyond the subtle differences that may exist within various subregions in the respective policies toward Cuba, no one supports a policy of isolating Havana. On the contrary, there is a growing view that the most important security objective is to help to avert any crisis situation or a traumatic change in Cuba that could have deep effects on regional stability. This concern with avoiding instability is at the root of policies seeking to maintain open dialogue with the Cuban authorities and to involve the Cuban government in those fora where the nature of its political regime is not an obstacle. Thus, for example, in the late 1990s Cuba joined the Latin American Integration Association (ALADI).

This approach toward Cuba is based on a shared diagnosis among many political leaders in the region. They observe that all the strategies so far employed to bring about change in Cuba have failed; thus they conclude that international pressure has only a limited impact on Cuba's leaders. These failed strategies include embargoes, diplomatic isolation, and subversive activities as well as rapprochement policies that provide incentives for economic cooperation. But, from a security perspective, this approach also rests on the assessment that the Cuban government's cooperation is required to address some of the so-called "new transnational issues." Cuba is strategically located astride the air and maritime corridor that connects the southern hemisphere to the United States, and it could have a positive influence in persuading guerrilla movements to join processes of reconciliation. Thus security concerns require the maintenance of a dialogue with the Cuban government and the promotion of confidence-building measures to avoid conflicts such as the shooting down of small aircraft that occurred over the Straits of Florida in 1996.

The activities of insurgent groups have declined across the region, but guerrillas remain important domestic and international problems in some cases. They threaten the stability of some international subregions when they operate in border regions, provoking conflicts between neighboring countries. One example is the border between Venezuela and Colombia; the growing presence of Colombian guerrillas who frequently cross the border has resulted in a growing deployment of the Venezuelan Army in this area.

In the past, the U.S.-supported counterinsurgency policies made it virtually impossible to formulate flexible strategies for negotiation, which were often required in those instances where insurgencies had social support. The United States was, therefore, incapable of serving as mediator in the resolution of some of these conflicts, although its policies began to change with the end of the cold war. (In Central America, for example, the Contadora Group and the European Union played the initial roles of international mediation.) U.S. policies had also been interpreted by some armies as a "green light" to apply unlawful procedures, thereby undermining yet another objective of U.S. regional policy: respect for human rights.

A new hemispheric security policy to promote and fortify the stability and strength of democratic institutions requires a different approach toward these conflicts. The strategies employed to combat insurgents should not result in weakening the rule of law in whose name the actions are being taken. Relations between U.S. officials and Latin American armies must be governed by the policies and procedures set by civilian authorities; they must avoid the "parallel channels" that at times in the past had contributed to subvert the democratic institutions of some of the countries in the region.

In the 1990s, the sale of weapons became also an issue of high concern in the hemisphere because of its possible repercussions for regional security. In fact, the growth of military expenditures as such does not generate conflicts; there must be other factors such as unstable situations, power vacuums, the rise of powers with hegemonic ambitions, disputes over land or maritime areas rich in natural resources, unresolved border disputes, or instances where countries address their domestic conflicts by means of aggressive policies toward their neighbors. Nevertheless, large purchases of weapons may at times be made in order to improve a country's bargaining capacity within a context of subregional tension. This could have a trigger effect. Dormant conflicts could come to pose a risk of war when a substantial upgrading of weapons inventories, along with the other factors just mentioned, permits some actors that may harbor territorial ambitions to realize them along with their other strategic objectives.

There is also the risk of an arms race in the region because two trends coincide: there is a surplus of weapons in international markets and the economic wherewithal in Latin America to acquire new military technologies. Latin America's economic growth during the 1990s, the deterioration of other markets where weapons had been sold in large quantities in the past (Africa and the Middle East), and the sense of crisis and fierce competition evident in the military industries of developed countries have rendered the hemisphere an increasingly attractive market for military sales, given an otherwise weak global demand.

Therefore, the development of policies of transparency and of advance notification of plans to purchase new weapons must proceed. The adoption of a regional code of conduct should also accompany the acquisition of new military technologies. The code should commit governments to keep a lid on military expenditures and to formulate symmetrical policies while developing their military capabilities, seeking agreements with their neighbors about what constitutes a "reasonable" level of military expenditure. Thus standard procedures must be developed to measure defense expenditures; an international organization could develop a methodology to compare the cost and quality of defense expenditures in the region's countries.

Beyond the technical means to build confidence between the countries of the hemisphere, the historical record makes it evident that political will at the highest levels is indispensable in order to sustain these peace processes in the long term. The South American regional conditions that prevailed in the 1990s could strengthen the peace; the European experience shows that the consolidation of democracy and the processes of economic integration can render obsolete the old strategies and war hypotheses about relations between neighboring countries. But such an achievement will require much time and responsible military policies to reach the goal.

Since the Santiago Declaration in 1991, there has been significant hemispheric coordination to defend democracy under stress in Guatemala, Peru, Haiti, and Paraguay. In addition to the role of the OAS in these pro-democracy efforts, some subregional instruments like MERCOSUR have also adopted the so-called "democratic clause," which commits member countries to act whenever there is an attempt to interrupt the democratic process, as occurred in Paraguay. As the twentieth century closed, the defense of democracy became part of an expanded conception of hemispheric security for two reasons: first, the defense of democratic systems was an end in itself; and second, democracy was the best guarantee to ensure regional stability and to deepen economic integration processes.

These joint actions to protect democratic order no longer respond to U.S. imposition. They stem from a convergence of interests between the countries of the hemisphere, seeking to prevent reversals of the democratic process that the continent enjoys. There are, nevertheless, some problems that still require resolution. "Early-warning" instruments should be strengthened, as should preventive actions applied early on in a crisis. On the other hand, the "restoration of the democratic system" has at times been incomplete. An exaggerated presidentialism, or the continued "tutelary" role of the armed forces in some countries, weakens other institutions that serve as counterweights in consolidated democratic systems. Finally, as shown by the case of Haiti, instability and institutional weakness may require a prolonged international role. It may thus be necessary to discuss "second-generation" policies to strengthen the steps already undertaken with regard to defense and democratic consolidation.

Chile and Hemispheric Security

The return to democracy in Chile coincided chronologically with the end of the cold war. Chile's participation in hemispheric affairs thus underwent important changes soon after the transition to a democratic government in 1990. Perhaps the most visible example of this change was the new government's decision to reinsert Chile fully in its obvious geographic environs, Latin America. Until 1990, the military government's relative political isolation and the priority accorded to extrahemispheric relations over relations within the region had constrained Chile's participation and significance in the region.

The new democratic government accorded a high priority in its foreign policy to relations with Latin America and, in particular, with countries in South America's southern cone. This rapprochement responded to the decision to restore what had been a Chilean foreign policy of long-standing as well as to more specific considerations related to democratic consolidation and the economic model that Chile has implemented with success for more than a decade.

The new government sought to make progress as quickly as possible to resolve the border disputes still pending with Argentina in order to ensure that these would not become obstacles to the growing relations of economic integration that would develop during the 1990s. Thus twenty-three of the twenty-four border disputes were resolved soon. The settlement agreement over the southern glaciers was amended by both governments in 1998 and subsequently ratified by the congresses of both countries.

Chile supports steps to strengthen all multilateral institutions that could contribute to political and military stability and to democratic consolidation in the hemisphere. Thus in 1991, Chile, Argentina, and Brazil signed the Mendoza Commitment, which bans chemical and biological weapons in the southern cone. In 1992, Chile joined the Rio Group. As an associate member of MERCO-SUR, it also participates in the dialogues over security that take place in that forum; at the last MERCOSUR presidential summit held in Ushuaia, Argentina, in July 1998, there was an agreement to establish a "zone of peace" in the southern cone. Moreover, as one of the guarantor countries to the Rio Protocol of 1942 Chile joined other countries to contribute to the search for a definitive solution to the dispute that led Ecuador and Peru to war in 1995.

Chile's basic hypothesis in its policies within the southern cone subregion is that the growing economic and commercial interdependence requires as well a greater cooperation over defense and security to ensure that the latter concerns would not adversely affect the deepening of the political and economic links built during the 1990s. The greater permeability of borders also facilitates the diffusion of problems that had been settled hitherto within national domains; these problems could generate conflicts unless there is a collective approach to addressing them.

At the hemispheric level, the Chilean government supports strengthening the OAS procedures that bear on security issues. Chile had a leading role in the establishment of means to defend democracy in the region (the 1991 Santiago Declaration), as it did in the organization of conferences to promote hemispheric confidence-building measures (one of these conferences was held in Santiago in 1995, the other in San Salvador in 1998). The confidence-building conference processes and the work of the OAS Commission on Hemispheric Security have fostered the formulation of joint assessments of actual regional security risks, which is a necessary step prior to the effective design of new shared strategies concerning security.

Despite the limitations of the inter-American system, the OAS is the only forum with sufficient institutionalization to gather together all the countries of the region, facilitate meetings, and provide a source of legitimacy for the approval of measures to protect regional order and stability. The meetings of foreign ministers called to address the interruption of democratic governments in various instances provide one example; another is the possibility of joint action with the United Nations in Haiti, under the rule of law, duly authorized by prior OAS decisions.

Chile has also pursued a pragmatic approach to the management of hemispheric security problems, understanding that security challenges frequently vary from one subregion to the next and that for the sake of their own national interests some countries give precedence to some instruments over others. There must be flexibility, therefore, in the choice of appropriate instruments to face up to a specific crisis. For example, the OAS had the leading role in addressing the constitutional crises in Guatemala and Haiti; in the Peruvian constitutional crisis, both the OAS and the Rio Group were important, while the MERCOSUR was the most important international actor in working toward the positive outcome in the Paraguayan constitutional crisis.

The key in the final analysis is the existence of the capacity to act collectively to face up to the principal regional security challenges. Only through gradual and practical steps that prove successful can a new institutionality be built over time to address hemispheric security issues. The new scheme will probably feature, unlike in the past, a plurality of subregional instruments and hemispheric fora that will coexist with the role held by the inter-American security system during the past several decades.

Reforming Hemispheric Security Institutions

Because of the significant changes in Latin America during the 1990s, the reform of the institutions of inter-American security that had lost their efficacy and legitimacy during the cold war is on the hemispheric agenda. These institutions proved incapable of addressing conflicts between states in the Americas (e.g., Nicaragua versus the United States) or the actions of an extra-hemispheric power in the hemisphere (e.g., the Malvinas War). The lack of consensus concerning the objectives and the very definition of what was encompassed under regional "collective security" helps to explain the inefficacy of treaties and institutions such as the Inter-American Treaty for Reciprocal Assistance (the Rio Treaty) and the Inter-American Defense Board (IADB). As a result, Latin American governments created other fora and alternative instruments to face up to crises: the Contadora Group in the 1980s was one example. The United States, in turn, came to rely more on unilateral responses to address problems that touched on its hemispheric interests.

The OAS Charter features the juridical bases to reform or to abolish the inter-American security institutions created during the cold war. At the OAS Bogotá Conference in 1948, the Latin American governments opposed the U.S. proposal to transform the IADB (created in 1942 during World War II) into the OAS defense institution. Instead, the IADB was accorded consultative status relative to the OAS; the hemispheric governments also agreed that the IADB could be abolished if two-thirds of the members of the inter-American system came to believe that the IADB had outlived its usefulness.

The problem of institutional reform is not legal but political. There is no convergence of interests to authorize radical institutional reforms because some important countries in the Americas oppose structural reforms in the schemes for inter-American security, while others prefer to manage their priority concerns outside the OAS framework. A realistic approach, therefore, suggests the value of a flexible and pragmatic approach to solve specific problems within the framework of the instruments available within the system. In this fashion, for example, in the 1990s the IADB played a permanent advisory role concerning certain issues of interest for the hemispheric community. It worked on demining (especially in Central America), promoting confidence-building measures, monitoring disarmament and cease fire processes, and convening seminars on current issues of international security, among others.

The current inter-American security institutions are characterized by a "flexible geometry." Countries participate simultaneously in various entities that contribute to the management of regional security problems. At the inter-American level, for example, the OAS Commission on Hemispheric Security now exists alongside the IADB. The commission makes recommendations to the member states on various security issues; it also sponsors specialized conferences to foster common views for action. In addition, in 1989–1990 the OAS had created ad hoc security instruments such as the commissions to provide support and verification services (OAS–CIAV) to oversee the disarmament and social reintegration of insurgent groups in Nicaragua and Honduras. It adopted a similar procedure in 1992 in Suriname, helping thereby to foster national reconciliation in that country.

The summits of defense ministers seek to strengthen the role of civilian authorities responsible for defense and to promote cooperation among them. These meetings supplement those focused on economic and social questions, especially the summits of the Americas that were also held outside the OAS structure. This further shows that some countries prefer the creation of parallel instruments when they propose initiatives of particular interest to them and when they hope for concrete results in a short time.

Within the existing security institutions, other regional institutions address specific topics, such as the OPANAL which prohibits nuclear weapons and the already cited Mendoza Commitment which bans chemical weapons in the southern cone. Caribbean countries have also developed ad hoc instruments to cope with crises. Central American countries did the same in order to reach a joint agreement to reduce the level of armaments. So too occurred in South America among the 1942 Rio Protocol guarantors to oversee and mediate a settlement to the 1995 Ecuador-Peru War; the guarantor states (including the United States) played an essential role to prevent a new military escalation in the disputed area.

The coordination among interior ministers of the MERCOSUR countries to prevent terrorist activities across the boundaries of Argentina, Brazil, and Paraguay, or the proximate use of the Amazon vigilance system (SIVAM) by the Amazon basin countries to combat drug trafficking and environmental degradation are among other examples of initiatives undertaken in the 1990s to address nonconventional security challenges in the post–cold war. Moreover, by the late 1990s bilateral arrangements for security cooperation were developed between Chile and Argentina and between Argentina and Brazil; these processes are likely to be strengthened early in the twenty-first century as a result of the growing integration in the southern cone.

Future Prospects and Recommendations

As the twentieth century ends, there is convergence in policies and assessments with regard to security, but there remain no less significant differences with regard to the shape of the hemispheric security agenda, the best institutions to work on security issues, and the diagnosis and handling of specific issues. These differences are likely to become more important as a result of the impact of some regional problems on the domestic affairs of the United States and other countries. Differences may also grow because most of the contemporary security risks have a more diffuse character than in the past, which makes it more difficult to reach a shared assessment of their significance and to identify common strategies to address them.

Certain traditional problems persist, such as boundary and territorial disputes. In some instances these can lead to war, as occurred in 1995 between Peru and Ecuador, or as happens less severely and occasionally between the states that border on the Fonseca Gulf in Central America. These disputes in border regions become more difficult to cope with because of illegal migrant flows, guerrilla operations in such areas, and other illegal commercial flows that violate land and maritime boundaries.

There is, however, no consensus either to reform the structures of the hemispheric security system or to abolish the institutions that constitute it. During the 1990s, the principal trend was toward the coexistence and plurality of security organizations and fora in the absence of a single or unifying regional security structure. Thus the decision to appeal to one institution or to another depends on the conflict at issue, the political and legal options that each institution offers to settle specific conflicts, and, of course, the priority that the United States and the major Latin American countries accord to some fora over others.

Therefore, the preferred strategy toward the next decade should give priority to substantive progress, not to the institutional redesign for inter-American security. A more comprehensive and up-to-date hemispheric security system is more likely to emerge, in any event, from diverse incremental steps and cumulative actions. Thus attempts to launch ambitious reforms that lack support from the principal regional actors will not prosper, may provoke regression rather than advance, and may reinforce either unilateralist temptations or those that seek to create parallel institutions that would weaken the role of the OAS in security issues. A more viable strategy, instead, would make use of the effective and legitimate fora and institutions already available to make substantive progress in topics of interest for hemispheric security. This includes strengthening democracy, reducing the risks of interstate conflict, preventing arms races, and, above all, promoting joint multilateral approaches to address the instabilities that plague the region.

Progress is also needed early in the twenty-first century to formalize the division of labor and the coordination among the institutions and instruments that participate in handling security problems, given that there will be no single system for hemispheric security. The purpose of such coordination will be to avoid jurisdictional conflicts and contradictions and to foster all efforts toward settling security issues.

The OAS will retain a significant role because it is the only entity at the hemispheric level that can confer legitimacy to decisions in matters of security. Besides, it commits the United States and other large countries through multilateral obligations and, therefore, it is more likely to search for responses that are proportional to the threats to be deterred. It is, therefore, advisable whenever possible to strengthen its capacity for action. This is not incompatible, of course, with the role that subregional organizations may play to the extent that these fashion their actions following the same principles that have guided the OAS in the post-cold-war years.

The key point is that, increasingly, the security problems that are most likely to affect the region are the unwanted legacy of the growing interdependence evident in our continent. The free flows of goods, investments, services, and people also generate a greater vulnerability to transborder problems that require joint action in order to manage them. This includes drug trafficking, money laundering, illegal weapons transfers, guerrilla operations in border regions, and the external consequences of domestic crises. These problems cannot be solved without the cooperation of the governments and other concerned key actors.

Thus it is especially encouraging that official U.S. statements from the second half of the 1990s began from these very premises to analyze U.S. security relations with Latin America.[2] Nevertheless, in order to make progress in inter-American cooperation, the United States and Latin America will have to agree on a joint definition of security risks and threats incorporating both the permanent interests of the United States as well as the perspectives and concerns of the other countries in the region. It is thus worrisome that some U.S. policies respond to short-term interests, generating inconsistent and counterproductive actions even in matters that the United States considers its vital interests.

Starting from a "shared vision and responsibility," a new political institutionalization may emerge. Over the long term, it may foster horizontal cooperation to address issues that do not respond to unilateral solutions. The management of common problems that affect regional security will require a sustained commitment from governments. From that basis, a new hemispheric "security architecture" may eventually be constructed. The region's economic development in the 1990s and its future sustainability depend as well on ensuring stable conditions in the continent in order to be able to face up successfully to the challenges from globalization as the twenty-first century begins.

Notes

1. This chapter expresses my individual views exclusively. The government of Chile and other institutions with which I am associated bear no responsibility for these comments. Jorge Domínguez was the translator from the Spanish original.
2. U.S. Department of Defense, *United States Security Strategy for the Americas* (Washington, D.C.: U.S. Department of Defense, 1995).

4

Transnational Crime in the Americas: A Reality Check

IVELAW GRIFFITH

Diplomatic history is replete with blunders that dramatize the veracity of a statement made six decades ago by British statesman Anthony Eden: "There is nothing more dangerous than a foreign policy based on unreality." Needless to say, the statement applies to security and other policy areas as well. Scholars and statesmen, therefore, need periodically to undertake reality checks, especially during periods of change.

Like most periods of change, the twenty-first century is approached by many citizens, statesmen, and scholars in the Americas with a combined sense of expectancy and apprehension. The expectancy stems partly from hope that the new age will see more discernable benefits of the end of the cold-war era that colored and constrained policies and practices in this hemisphere and elsewhere for almost half of the twentieth century. It is also driven by a somewhat metaphysical notion that having (virtually) hit bottom in many areas, improvement is inevitable, no matter how small the increment. The apprehension, on the other hand, is driven by the many unknowns that the changing dynamics of inter-American (and broader international) relations hold for the future. Apprehension, however, is not a function only of the unknown; it feeds also on what is known, especially when some of what is known portends danger. Yet it is important to guard against having expectancy lead to false expectations and apprehension develop into fatalism.

People concerned with transnational crime (TNC) in the Americas are not exempt from feelings of expectancy and apprehension. One way to deal with this—and to avoid false expectations and fatalism—is to understand some of the "What," "Why," and "How" of TNC by adopting a matrix approach. The matrix can be viewed as having three sets of elements: *content* ("what" questions); *consequences* ("what" and "how" questions); and *countermeasures* (questions of "what" and "how"). These elements are linked in that content affects consequences, and countermeasures are a function of the dynamics of the two others. A multidisciplinary approach to the issue is necessary because it has aspects of political science, international political economy, criminal justice, and foreign policy, among other areas. Moreover, there are two central realities: TNC content, consequences, and countermeasures in the Americas, as elsewhere, involve both state and nonstate actors; and TNC in the Americas has connections beyond the Americas.

Transnational Crime in the Americas

A few preliminary observations are warranted before examining some specifics of TNC in the Americas. First, in broad conceptual terms transnational criminal activities constitute what one noted scholar calls "interdependence issues"—issues "distinguished from conventional issues by the fact that they span national boundaries and thus cannot be addressed much less resolved through actions undertaken at the national or local level."[1] Second, TNC is transnational, multidimensional, and organized. On the last feature, two writers correctly assert: "Organization is key. Yet, there is no standardized organizational chart for a developed criminal organization. There are varying types of criminal patterns."[2] Third, transnational crimes generally fall within the parameters of "gray areas," where "gray area phenomena can be defined as threats to the stability of nation-states by non-state actors and non-governmental processes and organizations."[3] Transnationality apart, these features of TNC distinguish it generally from domestic crime: high-threat capacity to undermine governance; vertical and horizontal criminal alliances; scope and multidimensionality; and necessity for extrastate responses.

The criminal justice literature offers several crime typologies. One sees two basic types of crime: enforcement crimes, and business crimes. Another posits three kinds of crimes: consensual crimes; expressive crimes; and instrumental crimes. A third speaks to the following kinds of crime: multinational; white collar; political; organized; professional; and conventional.[4] However, the kinds of TNC confronting societies in our region—related to drugs, arms trafficking, migrant smuggling, prostitution, terrorism, car theft, the smuggling of cigarettes, art, gold, and other products, among other things—defy strict typological construction; they extend across categories and types.

These activities involve state and nonstate actors in varying ways. Some have similar contexts and consequences; others have markedly different ones. And they all are met with a multiplicity of countermeasures. However, while all of these TNC areas deserve assessment, space and scope limitations here preclude analysis of all of them. Thus, it seems reasonable to discuss those with hemispheric salience, reflected in: (1) their impact on a meaningful number of nations—at least twelve; about one-third of the membership of the

Organization of American States (OAS), the largest hemispheric body; (2) significance in scope and intensity of threats and apprehensions, both within and among states, with threat definition coming essentially from local political and security elites but also from regional or hemispheric actors; (3) the amount of interstate and intrastate conflict precipitated, with armed conflict, violent crime, seizures, kidnappings, diplomatic protests and warnings, and economic sanctions being manifestations of conflict interactions. Based on these parameters, narcotics, terrorism, and arms trafficking clearly warrant discussion.

The Narcotics Phenomenon

The issue of drugs as a TNC matter entails more than illegal-drug production and trafficking. The narcotics phenomenon is multidimensional in content as well as in consequences. While all the content and consequence elements do not have equally weighted TNC dimensions, it is useful to appreciate the complete package. My approach to doing this is reflected in the concept of geonarcotics. As Figure 4.1 indicates, it posits, first, that the narcotics phenomenon is multidimensional, with four main problem areas (drug production, consumption-abuse, trafficking, and money laundering); second, that these give rise to actual and potential threats to the security of states, including crime, arms trafficking, and narco-terrorism; and third, that the drug operations and the activities they spawn precipitate both cooperation and conflict among various state and nonstate actors.

The narcotics phenomenon has developed out of—and is still developing—relationships among three factors besides drugs: geography; power; and politics. Geography is a factor because of the global spatial dispersion of drug operations, and because certain physical and social geographic features of numerous countries facilitate drug operations. Power involves the ability of individuals and groups to secure compliant action. This power is both state and nonstate in origin, and in some cases nonstate sources exercise more power than state entities. Politics revolves around resource allocation in the sense of the ability of power brokers to determine who gets what, how, and when. Since power in this milieu is not only state power, resource allocation is, correspondingly, not exclusive to state power holders. Moreover, politics becomes perverted, and all the more so where it already was perverted.

The geonarcotics milieu involves a variety of state and nonstate actors, which vary in how they affect and are affected by the various problem areas as well as in their countermeasures. Drug operations generate two basic kinds of interactions: cooperation, and conflict. These are bilateral and multilateral and do not all involve force. Some involve nonmilitary pressures, such as economic and political sanctions by the United States against countries, which, in

Figure 4.1

Geonarcotics: A Framework

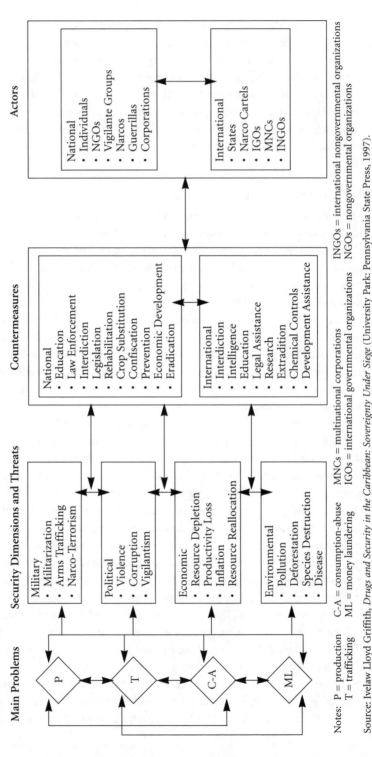

Notes: P = production   C-A = consumption-abuse   MNCs = multinational corporations   INGOs = international nongovernmental organizations

T = trafficking   ML = money laundering   IGOs = international governmental organizations   NGOs = nongovernmental organizations

Source: Ivelaw Lloyd Griffith, *Drugs and Security in the Caribbean: Sovereignty Under Siege* (University Park: Pennsylvania State Press, 1997).

Washington's estimation, are not proactive enough in fighting drugs. Some actors engage simultaneously in both cooperation and conflict; examples are the United States and Mexico, and the United States and Colombia, especially between the 1994 inauguration of Colombian President Ernesto Semper and the ensuing June 1998 election of President Andrés Pastrana. The geonarcotics approach does not view the "war on drugs" as purely a military matter. The application of military countermeasures alone is, therefore, considered impractical. International countermeasures are necessary, especially since all states face resource constraints. However, collaboration among states may result in conflict not only over sovereignty concerns but also because of disputes over the nature and severity of threats and, therefore, the appropriate measures to deal with them.[5]

There is no uniformity in how narcotics problems or their consequences are manifested in the Americas. Although Tables 4.1 and 4.2 offer merely a glimpse of production and trafficking levels, they suggest variability in production and other areas. In the production area, for instance, Bolivia, Colombia, and Peru are the largest cocaine producers. Bolivia by itself produced some 25 percent of the world's coca leaf in 1997, while Colombia produced some 70 percent of the world's cocaine that year. However, even though there was an 18 percent increase in coca leaf production in Colombia in 1997, most of the cocaine paste comes from other countries. As far as heroin is concerned, Colombia and Mexico rank first and second, respectively, in production in the Americas.[6] No cocaine is produced in the Caribbean, but, along with the United States, Mexico, and Colombia, Caribbean countries are among the world's largest marijuana producers. In relation to the United States, the 1998 *National Drug Control Strategy* indicates three million marijuana plants were eradicated in 1996; their potential yield was 1,389 metric tons of marijuana. In 1997 more than 300,000 plants were eradicated in 4,400 sites *in national parks alone.*[7]

In the consumption-abuse area, the United States has the dubious distinction of being the world's single largest consumer of narcotics, although addiction levels in some areas have declined since 1979. One U.S. official estimated that 300 metric tons of the approximately 575 metric tons of cocaine available worldwide in 1994 was consumed in the United States.[8] Between 287 and 376 metric tons of cocaine alone were estimated to have been smuggled into the United States in 1995. Yet the United States, with its 13 million drug users (in 1996)—6.1 percent of the population above twelve years of age—is not the only country in the Americas facing serious consumption-abuse problems; many in South and Central America and the Caribbean face them also. As two Mexican scholars rightly indicate, "Despite the fact that most of the drugs are destined for export, mostly to the United States, a considerable (and probably increasing) proportion stays within the region."[9]

Table 4.1

Estimated Narcotics Crop Cultivation (Hectares)

Crop/Country	1990	1991	1992	1993	1994	1995	1996	1997
Opium poppy								
Colombia	NA	1,160	20,000	20,000	20,000	6,540	6,300	6,600
Guatemala	845	1,145	730	438	50	39	0	0
Mexico	3,310	3,765	3,310	3,960	5,795	5,050	5,100	4,000
Coca leaf								
Bolivia	50,300	47,900	45,500	47,200	48,100	48,600	48,100	45,800
Colombia	40,100	37,500	37,100	39,700	45,000	50,900	67,200	79,500
Peru	121,300	120,800	129,100	108,800	108,600	115,300	94,400	68,800
Cannabis								
Colombia	1,500	2,000	2,000	5,000	4,986	5,000	8,000	5,000
Jamaica	1,120	950	389	744	308	305	527	317
Mexico	35,050	17,915	16,420	11,220	10,550	6,900	6,500	4,800

Source: U.S. Dept. of State, *International Narcotics Control Strategy Report,* 1991–1998.

Table 4.2

Cocaine Seizures in the Americas (Metric Tons)

Country	1990	1991	1992	1993	1994	1995	1996	1997
Bahamas	3.53	5.26	4.80	1.80	0.49	0.39	0.12	2.58
Belize	0.60	0.13	0.85	0.01	0.14	0.84	0.09	2.70
Bolivia	12.46	3.44	8.40	5.61	7.46	8.19	9.95	10.39
Brazil	2.20	3.70	2.81	7.70	11.80	5.70	3.10	4.00
Colombia	53.07	86.35	37.73	32.16	62.00	41.00	41.00	44.00
Costa Rica	1.14	0.46	1.80	0.61	1.38	0.05	1.99	7.74
Dominican Rep.	2.59	1.81	2.36	1.07	2.80	3.60	2.14	1.35
Guatemala	15.50	15.40	9.50	7.60	2.00	1.00	4.00	5.60
Haiti	NA	0.19	0.06	0.16	0.72	0.55	NA	2.1
Jamaica	0.76	0.06	0.49	0.16	0.18	0.57	0.24	0.41
Mexico	48.50	50.30	38.80	46.20	22.10	22.20	23.60	34.90
Panama	4.00	9.30	9.80	5.68	8.60	5.89	7.80	7.85
Peru	8.50	5.17	6.93	5.77	10.70	22.65	19.69	11.10
Venezuela	NA	9.80	5.80	3.30	6.70	7.77	7.20	17.19

Source: U.S. Dept. of State, *International Narcotics Control Strategy Report,* 1991–1998.

This is true not only for South and Central American producer countries but also for many Caribbean countries that are deeply implicated in trafficking, such as the Dominican Republic, Jamaica, Puerto Rico, Guyana, and Haiti. Drugs are increasingly available by design and default in these countries, even when they themselves are not the intended destinations (although in many cases they are). In the former case they are used in lieu of cash for the payment of services, and in the latter instance failed trafficking operations often result in the availability of drugs intended for elsewhere. Even Cuba is facing this, as indicated by their national prosecutor in a November 1995 interview with *Granma*: "Years ago, since this merchandise had no commercial value, everyone who found a packet of this type handed it over to the authorities. Now people have discovered how much that's worth and they don't always hand it over."[10]

Terrorism

Following Laqueur, terrorism is viewed here as "the sub-state organization of violence or threatened violence intended to sow panic in society, to weaken or even overthrow the incumbents, and to bring about political change."[11] Brian Jenkins is also correct in deeming terrorism "violence for effect…not only, and sometimes not at all, for the effect on the actual victims of the terrorists. In fact, the victims may be totally unrelated to the terrorists' cause."[12] As with the narcotics phenomenon, terrorism involves both state and nonstate actors, and it can be sponsored by both kinds of actors. But unlike two decades ago when both state- and non-state-sponsored terrorism were part of this hemisphere's landscape of political violence, terrorism now is solely a function of the pursuits of nonstate actors. However, the contemporary salience of the issue has less to do with this transformation and more with the proximity and scale of terrorist actions recently.

For many people in the United States, for example, terrorism ceased to be a foreign phenomenon with the World Trade Center bombing on February 26, 1993, which killed six people and injured more than one thousand, and the Oklahoma Federal Building bombing on April 19, 1995, which killed 168 and injured hundreds. Elsewhere in the hemisphere, the issue gained prominence because of the dramatic terrorist actions in Argentina, Peru, Colombia, Venezuela, among other places. In one 1994 incident in Argentina, eighty-six people were killed and some three hundred were injured in the bombing of the Argentine Jewish Mutual Association in Buenos Aires. One Peruvian case involved fewer fatalities, but was more dramatic, partly because it was played out over five months. In December 1996 more than five hundred people— government ministers, military and police officials, businessmen, diplomats, and foreign officials—were taken hostage by the Tupac Amaru Revolutionary

Movement (MRTA) at the Japanese embassy. The matter was brought to closure in April 1997 when Peruvian military forces stormed the embassy and rescued the hostages. Although there was regret over the loss of life of one hostage, two Peruvian soldiers, and all fourteen of the MRTA operatives, most observers seem to have agreed that the action by the Peruvian authorities was necessary to resolve the issue.[13]

Most of the "significant" terrorist incidents during the past few years have occurred in South and Central America. But the contemporary history of the Caribbean shows that the region has not been immunized against terrorism; neither by state actors—in Cuba, Haiti, Grenada, and Guyana, for example—nor by nonstate actors. As a matter of fact, the Caribbean was the scene of one of the most dramatic nonstate terrorist acts in the hemisphere during the mid-1970s: on October 6, 1976, shortly after departing Barbados, a Cubana Air airplane en route from Guyana to Cuba exploded. All seventy-three people on the flight—fifty-seven Cubans, eleven Guyanese, and five North Koreans—were killed. Anti-Castro exiles based in Venezuela later claimed responsibility for the action. (On August 1, 1998, while on a visit to Barbados President Fidel Castro dedicated a monument to the victims of the incident.)[14] Cuba suffered numerous other bombings at tourist locations during 1997, perpetrated allegedly by anti-Castro Cuban exiles in Miami and Central America.[15]

Terrorism, whether in the United States, Peru, Cuba, Colombia, or elsewhere, reflects some of the key elements of TNC mentioned earlier: it is transnational, multidimensional, and organized. Of course, the extent of these features depends on variables such as the history of the actor(s), motive, size, funding, ideology, organization, and the political-institutional environment involved. Nevertheless, it is fairly easy to appreciate that the frequency and scope of action by groups such as the Revolutionary Armed Forces (FARC) and the National Liberation Army (ENL) of Colombia, Sendero Luminoso and MRTA of Peru, and the Popular Revolutionary Army (EPR) of Mexico, and by individuals such as Timothy McVeigh (Oklahoma bombing) and Ramzi Ahmed Yousef (World Trade Center bombing) could not be accomplished without transnational linkages—even beyond the Americas—and often skillful organization. Paul Wilkinson's decade-old assertion about terrorism certainly is true in the Americas today: "Terrorism is inherently international in character, so that, paradoxically, the more individual states improve their national measures, the more it becomes attractive for the terrorists to cross national frontiers."[16]

Beyond all this, terrorism is salient partly because of the high premium placed on the (re)construction and maintenance of democracy, and because terrorism serves to undermine democracy by threatening the exercise of various civil and political rights that are fundamental to it. Indeed, as the OAS secretary-general told the OAS special conference on terrorism in Peru in April

1996, the first Summit of the Americas Declaration states, "National and inter-national terrorism constitute a systematic and deliberate violation of the rights of individuals and an assault on democracy." David Apter captures the essence of why hemispheric leaders would view terrorism as antithetical to democra-cy: "In democratic societies, political violence suggests institutional weakness and blockages, or normative insufficiencies, injustices, or inequities, i.e. wrongs to be righted."[17] Countries in Latin American and the Caribbean where the (re)construction or consolidation of democracy is a major political project are, therefore, more sensitive to the actual and potential impact of ter-rorism on democracy.

Arms Trafficking

One critical concern about arms trafficking pertains to its linkages to the two other TNC issues examined in this study. In his foreword to a 1996 book on arms trafficking Oscar Arias notes, "The arms trade and drug trafficking con-tribute a sinister quid pro quo in a market of death and suffering for millions of human beings. On our continent, the heart of this market lies in the unin-terrupted displacement of thousands of kilos of cocaine to the north and thousands of weapons to the south."[18] Findings about the drugs-arms connec-tion in the Caribbean have even greater relevance to elsewhere in the hemi-sphere. They suggest that the ownership of guns and ammunition are considered vital to the successful conduct of some drug operations, especially production and trafficking. Weapons are used for both symbolic and substan-tive purposes, notably for protection of drugs and drug operatives, the com-mission of murders, robberies, and acts of narco-terrorism, and for intimidation of clients as well as other drug operators.[19]

Understandably, though, the salience of arms trafficking goes beyond the connections to drugs and terrorism; it exists also because of connections to crim-inal gangs, murders in general, robberies, political instability, and the climate of violence to which it contributes. The murder of prostitutes and street children, extrajudicial killings, and politically motivated killings that are not necessarily terrorist-related are alarming manifestations of the climate of violence. For instance, in relation to Brazil, there was the 1993 killing of street children who were sleeping outside a church in Rio De Janeiro, and the 1995 incident in Rondonia where paramilitary police opened fire on a group of five hundred fam-ilies that had been squatting on the Santa Elina farm. Nine of the squatters were killed, mostly shot in the back, and one hundred thirty were wounded.[20]

Moreover, the issue is germane because, in many societies, arms circulate within several levels outside the military and the police. Drug operators, guer-rilla and terrorist groups, private militias, gangs, private security companies, and ordinary citizens own them. One Colombian analyst, Daniel García-Pena Jaramillo, for example, estimates that there are about one million legally obtained firearms in the hands of private Colombian citizens. The government had issued 823,245 permits to individual citizens before 1994; and in 1994, from January to June, 191,120 people applied for permits for guns already in their possession, but not previously registered, bringing the total number of legally owned weapons to a little more than one million. However, the number of guns illegally obtained is said to be greater—about two to five million.[21]

Arms trafficking has clear multidimensional and transnational dynamics. Some of the arms circulating in countries are from licit arms purchases, with some coming from intraregional arms trading. In the area of small arms, for example, Argentina, Brazil, and Chile produce pistols, rifles, submachine guns, hand grenades, land mines, and mortars; Colombia, the Dominican Republic, and Guatemala produce rifles; Mexico produces rifles and submachine guns; and Venezuela produces pistols and rifles.[22] Light weapons, of course, are not the only category of weapons produced in South America. Some of the arms are acquired through illegal transactions, both within Latin America and through smuggling from the United States and Europe. According to Andrés Oppenheimer, for instance, during 1997 in Mexico alone authorities seized 9,750 firearms, most of them smuggled from the United States.[23]

Mexico is not the only country that secures illegal weapons from the United States. Examination of the Justice Department's "Significant Export Control Cases, January 1, 1981 to May 31, 1995" revealed numerous other countries and cases, including: a 1983 conspiracy to export M-16 rifles, grenades, and other weapons to overthrow the government of Guyana; the 1985 scheme to export automatic weapons to Belize in exchange for marijuana; a 1988 effort to smuggle hand grenades, automatic rifles, and bullet-proof vests to Colombia; a 1989 attempt to smuggle grenades, rockets, and other weapons to El Salvador; a 1990 case where the aim was to export twelve Stinger antiaircraft missiles to Colombian drug lords; the exportation of more than one hundred assault rifles, shotguns, and ammunition used in the 1990 coup attempt in Trinidad and Tobago; a conspiracy in 1990 to export a large quantity of weapons, including M-16 rifles, grenades, and antitank rockets to Mexican drug traffickers; and the 1994 scheme to purchase Stinger missiles, antiarmor weapons, and C-4 explosives for an attack on Cuba.[24]

The United States is, however, not the only source of illegal weapons for nonstate actors in Latin America. For example, according to the U.S. Drug Enforcement Administration (DEA), between June and September 1997 several Russian vessels made port calls at Turbo, Colombia, and are believed to have unloaded shipments of AK-47 assault rifles and rocket-propelled grenades, exchanging some for drugs.[25] Moreover, the United States itself has been the intended destination of illegal trafficking initiatives. For instance, in April 1998, two Lithuanians, Alexander Darichev and Aleksandr Pogrebezskij, were convicted in Florida, on charges of conspiring to smuggle forty Russian-made missiles from Bulgaria to the United States. The arrest followed a two-and-a-half-year sting operation during which U.S. Custom's officials posed as drug brokers.[26]

Within the last two decades, the arms trafficking also has been driven by theft of weapons from arms warehouses, covert gunrunning by the United States, the USSR, Cuba, and other countries, the sale of weapons by soldiers and policemen, and the sale of end-user certificates—the documents used for legal arms purchases. In an October 1993 Bolivian case ten civilians and three high-ranking generals, including the general manager and a former general manager of the Armed Forces Development Corporation (Cofadena), were charged with selling fraudulent end-user certificates to European and Middle Eastern arms dealers for $300 each. The certificates listed Bolivia as the intended destination of thousands of rifles, pistols, grenades, and other weapons.[27]

Some Consequences of Transnational Crime

As with the content, TNC consequences are also multidimensional. They are direct and collateral and affect governance in a variety of ways. Obviously, this chapter is unable to examine all of them, but some are too important to overlook.

Corruption

Some consequences, such as corruption, help to "cause" or facilitate TNC. In many cases the economic context provides a powerful driving force, and often the financial lure is irresistible. In relation to drug-related corruption, for example, Ethan Nadelmann remarks, "The bribes paid by drug traffickers are much greater, both in an absolute sense, and in proportion to government salaries, than those paid by any other type of criminal. Moreover, unlike the sizeable bribes paid by foreign corporations, which are available only to a select group of high-level officials, drug traffickers' bribes are available to all who can place themselves in the right place at the right time."[28]

It must be stated at the outset that the February 1997 arrest of General José de Jesus Gutiérrez Robello in Mexico[29] and other high-profile South and Central American cases notwithstanding, corruption is not peculiar to Latin America; it is found throughout the hemisphere because the TNC which it facilitates and spawns is pan-hemispheric; indeed, it is global. Peruvian lawyer Ricardo Soberón is right: "The existing relationship between corruption and illegal drug trafficking does not occur exclusively in institutionally weak, drug-producing countries."[30] One media investigation reveals, for instance, that 10 to 15 percent of the drugs smuggled into the United States from Mexico each year cross the border with help from corrupt U.S. officials.[31] Moreover, the U.S. drug czar told the Senate in March 1997 that "34 percent of the FBI's conviction of U.S. state and local public officials and law enforcement officers on corruption charges between 1991 and 1995 were drug related," and "indictments of U.S. officials for offenses involving the abuse of public office averaged 625 a year between 1973 and 1983, and 1,262 a year between 1984 and 1994."[32]

Quite important also is that the cases of corruption uncovered by criminal investigations, governmental probes, media investigations, and academic research clearly indicate that the corruption associated with drugs, arms trafficking, and terrorism is not simply sporadic; it is often systemic and institutionalized.[33] Moreover, it often is facilitated by what Jean Cartier-Bresson calls "corruption networks," which are "structured in a clandestine manner by mobilizing multiple 'resources,' such as financial interests, obedience to hierarchy, solidarity, family, friends."[34]

Although most corruption cases fall within the executive branch of governments, there is also corruption in legislatures and judiciaries. Outrage is often significant when the corruption is government-related, and justifiably so, especially when military or police officials are involved. This kind of corruption compromises these institutions, with the result that (1) their capacity for effective action is undermined, and (2) individuals and groups become inclined to resort to vigilante justice because of that diminished capacity, or a perception of it. But, there is also corruption in the private sector, which is not to be underestimated, either in scope or importance, especially considering the neoliberal economic emphasis on the private sector as "the engine of growth." But, whether in the public or private sector, corruption involves acts of commission and omission that violate both laws and norms and have deleterious effects on governance. The Inter-American Convention against Corruption summarizes the impact cogently: "Corruption undermines the legitimacy of public institutions and strikes at society, moral order, and justice, as well as the comprehensive development of peoples."[35]

Criminal Justice

Crime is also a critical consequence of TNC in the Americas, although all crime is not TNC-related. As noted earlier, it cuts across categories. It also correlates differently with variables such as income, education, gender, age, race, and political affiliation among countries. It affects the state, corporate entities, and individual citizens, rural and urban areas, and is both violent and nonviolent.

Understandably, there is variation in the nature and volume of crime among countries. In 1992 Medellín, Colombia, had 6,625 *recorded* homicides—about 18 murders a day.[36] Since then the statistics often have been even more dramatic. Statistics from Mexico City's Attorney General's Office indicate the committal of an average of 700 crimes daily in 1997, including an average of three murders and four rapes per day. Robberies numbered 391 per day—about 33 every hour.[37] Indeed, crime increased 25 percent in November 1998 after Mexico City's government declared a "war on crime."[38] Kidnappings are also on the rise; Mexico is now second to Colombia, and ahead of Brazil, in kidnappings, with close to 3,000 kidnappings for ransom between 1993 and 1997.[39] The situation in Brazil is even more alarming:

> According to the UN survey, Brazil has by far the largest number of firearm homicides—41,000 per year—and places a close second to South Africa in the rate of killings per population. The murder rate in Sao Paulo has reached one per hour, and 90 percent are committed with firearms. There are an estimated 18.5 million firearms in the country, only one-third of which are registered. In Brazil, as elsewhere, as the general level of violence goes up, so does the number of citizens that carry personal guns, and confidence in the police's ability to provide public safety declines.[40]

In the United States, the Unified Crime Reports for 1996 provide a very revealing crime portrait: one property crime every three seconds; one violent crime every nineteen seconds; one aggravated assault every thirty-one seconds; one robbery every fifty-nine seconds; one forcible rape every six seconds; one murder every twenty-seven minutes; one motor vehicle theft every twenty-three seconds. In the Caribbean, Puerto Rico had the highest per capita murder rate in the United States in 1995, and 64 percent of the 850 murders were drug-related. Murders increased dramatically in 1996—to 868—and 80 percent of them were drug-related. In Jamaica, the number of murders went from 690 in 1994 to 780 in 1995, and in 1996 it was 921, 17 percent more than in 1995. The situation has deteriorated to the point where one territorial governor—Governor Roy L. Schneider of the U.S. Virgin Islands—felt compelled to carry a Glock semiautomatic pistol when he did not have his official security detail, a fact he disclosed to the *Washington Post* and the *Virgin Island Daily News* in January 1997.[41]

The backward and forward criminal linkages within the hemisphere have several dimensions. A reporter gives a glimpse of one dimension: "Mexican drug mafias reach into Hispanic neighborhoods of U.S. border cities with ease, enlisting street gangs to support their criminal enterprise."[42] The deportation of criminals is another dimension. During its 1997 fiscal year (October 1996 to September 1997), the United States deported more than 100,000 aliens, almost half of them convicts. The large deportations to Latin America and the Caribbean were: Mexico, 84,899—45 percent of them being criminal deportees; Dominican Republic, 2,603—74 percent criminal deportees; El Salvador,

3,743—40 percent criminal deportees; Jamaica, 1,730—68 percent criminal deportees; Honduras, 3,732—29 percent criminal deportees; Guatemala, 3,392—23 percent criminals. During 1993–1997, Latin America and the Caribbean received an enormous number of criminal deportees: 112,000 to Mexico; 5,524 to the Dominican Republic; 4,428 to El Salvador; and 3, 918 to Jamaica.[43] However, the United States is not the only country that returns criminals to their homelands. For example, of the people returned to Jamaica in 1997, 257 were from Canada, and 121 were from the United Kingdom.[44] Suriname and French Guiana frequently return people to Guyana, while the Cayman Islands is constantly deporting Jamaicans.

Although criminal deportation has many benefits in terms of counter-drug and anticrime strategies and economic and criminal justice measures for sending countries, it presents several headaches to receiving countries, especially in relation to crime. Governments throughout Central American and the Caribbean have complained that deportees tend to become involved locally in criminal networks, using the "skills" garnered in the North. According to one Caribbean police official, "They leave our islands as high school criminals and are returned to us as post-graduate criminals." In one May 1997 case in Guyana, a bungled burglary and shooting incident at the home of the former chairman of the Elections Commission, Rudy Collins, involved the use of laser-guided weapons by the would-be robbers, all five of whom were killed in a shoot-out with police; several of the bandits had been deportees.[45]

Because of increased crime, prisons have become overcrowded, which serves to further aggravate the criminal justice situation. The situation is further complicated because of the deportees. Moreover, in many cases the prisoners are incarcerated for TNC-related offenses and allegations. In Trinidad and Tobago, most of the seven penal institutions house three and four times the number of people for which they were intended. The Port of Spain prison, for instance, built in 1812 to house 250 inmates, had a 1993 daily average inmate population of 978, up from the 1992 figure of 916. It housed an average of 1,100 people daily during 1994 and a little less in 1995. The deplorable conditions of prisons in Trinidad were highlighted in July 1998 when Justice Peter Jamadar blocked the execution of a death row inmate—Darrin Thomas—on grounds that he had already been subjected to cruel and inhuman punishment by virtue of his imprisonment over the years his trial worked its way back and forth in the criminal justice system.[46]

One 1996 report on prison conditions in Latin American revealed, among other things, that: La Victoria prison in the Dominican Republic held about 5,000 prisoners, some five times its official capacity; Caracas's Reten de Catia prison, built to hold 700 inmates, housed 1,758 people during November 1997; in April 1996, a prison riot at Argentina's Sierra Chica prison spread to eighteen other jails, leaving twenty-one people dead and thirty-five wounded; a macabre "death lottery" to execute four inmates was announced by prisoners in July 1996 at the Santa Ana jail in El Salvador, where inmates were so tightly packed that they were forced to sleep in shifts; in Venezuela, only 27 percent of the nation's 24,840 inmates had been convicted of a crime; and in Brazil some 400,000 arrest warrants remained unexecuted due to limited prison space.[47]

The dramatic increase in crime and the limitations of criminal justice systems have contributed to a dramatic increase in the number of private security outfits in some countries. In Jamaica, 231 private security companies, with some 15,000 guards were registered in 1994 under the Private Security Regulation Act, adopted in 1992 to regulate the growing private security business. By mid-1996 the number of guards had exceeded 20,000. Mexico's Federal District alone had some twelve hundred private security companies in 1997, but only about forty of them were considered "quality operations."[48] The increase in private security has several implications—for the capacity of the state to provide law and order, economic and cost factors, the regulation and management of such outfits, and the false sense of security that some of them provide because of inadequate training and poor and unreliable equipment used. Cost creates a certain security class differentiation. Still, high cost does not guarantee security; expensive private security can deter some potential criminals, but it also can simply divert them toward other potential victims.

Yet, for all the ills they bear for the criminal justice system, crime and corruption, whether ad hoc or organized, but more so if organized, have a fundamental impact on the kind of democratic governance maintained in the Americas. As two scholars presciently observe, "The threat of organized crime to democracy is basic. While it rests upon many supports, democracy depends upon the faith of people in the institutions and practices that sustain and operationalize it. Integrity and a sense of fair play are critical components of that faith. It is precisely these that criminal organizations challenge."[49] Moreover, Oscar Arias highlights the issue of resource allocation, which features in the geonarcotics framework: "Weapons feed violence in all forms: military, political, and economic. Even worse, weapons cause many governments to neglect the most basic needs of their populations: arms budgets divert a great deal of resources that otherwise would be dedicated to improving health, education, and housing, to mention only a few needs."[50]

TNC Countermeasures

Although understanding TNC content and consequences is important, even more critical for the avoidance of false expectations and fatalism is an appreciation of some of the countermeasures.

Policy Options

TNC countermeasures need to be multidimensional and multilevel (national, regional, and international) because TNC is both transnational and multifaceted. They also should be multiactor because (1) states are not the only actors with vested interests that are affected, and (2) many states have such capability limitations that their individual actions are inconsequential. International governmental organizations (IGOs), therefore, become important. Cooperation is necessary, not simply desirable. More than this, though, bilateral and multilateral cooperation should not be viewed in zero-sum terms. As a matter of fact, bilateral measures are sometimes more desirable from the standpoint of political expediency, given that generally they can be designed and implemented more quickly, which means that policymakers can showcase their efforts to "solve" problems and "get results." Moreover, from a bureaucratic standpoint, there may be budgetary imperatives to act quickly.

This makes it incumbent on policymakers to:

- determine what combination of bilateral and multilateral measures best suits their national interest, bearing in mind the nature and salience of issues, their capabilities, the efficacy of proceeding individually or collectively, and time considerations;

- pursue bilateral measures that do not contradict or undermine multilateral efforts initiated earlier; (of course, there is the right to revisit multilateral game plans);

- be cognizant of the institutional resource implications of initiating numerous bilateral mechanisms or several combinations of bilateral and multilateral ones, considering that they also are pursuing bilateral and multilateral initiatives outside the Americas.

But, multilateralism has its limitations, one of which is incrementalism. This is a function of several factors: bureaucratic power politics, within both domestic agencies and international organizations; the realities of power asymmetries in the Americas; the fact that both state and nonstate actors are involved; the need for the larger state and nonstate actors in the partnership to be mindful that "leadership" does not become "dictation." All of this also means that (1) the process of policy decision making and project design will be time consuming, and (2) the delivery of the multilateral product(s) might be delayed, sometimes to the point where little or nothing appears to be happening.

Whether viewed from the bilateral or multilateral standpoint, the necessity for cooperation should not mask the reality that conflict may ensue, in relation to capabilities and sovereignty, among other things. As noted elsewhere, the capability challenge does not arise merely because of the actual money, equipment, and other constraints on the part of partnership actors. It does also because inherent in the capability disparities of cooperating partners, especially in a multilateral context, is the expectation that those with less limitations will give relatively more to the cooperative effort. This is not always achievable for a variety of reasons, including political leadership changes, public opinion, and the fact that policymakers in the relatively better-off states are sometimes unsure that there will be commensurate national interest returns on their national investments.[51]

Michael Dziedzic assets that sovereignty is "the fundamental constraint on the evolution of an effective Inter-American drug control regime."[52] This statement is true for countermeasures in relation to arms trafficking and terrorism as well, and it holds true even for some bilateral efforts. For understandable reasons sovereignty tends to be more closely guarded by the smallest and least powerful states in the hemisphere. Sometimes protestations over sovereignty violations are justified, although at times they are nothing more than an excuse for the absence of political will, or a reflection of the vicissitudes of domestic politics. Nevertheless, it behooves the larger states in the hemisphere to be mindful of sovereignty sensibilities, in relation to both the design and execution of multilateral (and bilateral) initiatives.[53] Policymakers should bear this in mind and create formal and informal mechanisms to resolve conflicts that arise and not have the success of initiatives jeopardized by conflicts.

Although sovereignty conflicts have surfaced over arms trafficking and terrorism, most of them have dealt with narcotics issues. In geonarcotics terms, there may be convergence of perception on the nature and gravity of threats, but there is divergence on the nature of the strategies and tactics needed to deal with them. This is precisely the case in the 1996–1997 "shiprider" dispute involving the United States and Barbados and Jamaica. The Caribbean countries acknowledged that it was in their interest and the interest of the United States that trafficking be combated through maritime interdiction. But they refused to sign agreements with terms that they felt stood to undermine their sovereignty. The matter was resolved at the May 10, 1997, United States-Caribbean Summit in Barbados, with the signature of agreements with slightly different provisions.

Conflict over sovereignty, strategy, and tactics also have driven the disputes on the issue of drug certification. The issue has both symbolic and substantive aspects. It has been seen as a powerful demonstration of United States unilateralism over a phenomenon—an interdependence issue—that is best approached multilaterally. Moreover, sometimes it highlights the contradictions in United States foreign policy in relation to which countries are certified and which are not. The concern also stems from the fact that tangible political and economic sanctions are attached to decertification. These could include loss of bilateral aid, opposition to loan requests in multilateral financial institutions, visa denials, and suspension of air services, among other things.

Still, the United States certification policy has had positive-sum value for countries in Latin America and the Caribbean. For one, it allowed political leaders there to use the threat of decertification to build domestic consensus, to get legislation and policies adopted, and to secure agency cooperation. In other words, it often has been a positive instrument of local politics outside the United States, where it clearly has been a tool of domestic politics. On balance, though, certification has been viewed as having more negative aspects than positive ones, which has served to temper the willingness of states to engage in genuine bilateral as well as multilateral collaboration. Thus, at the second Summit of the Americas, leaders agreed to "establish an objective procedure for the multilateral evaluation of actions and cooperation to prevent and combat all aspects of the drug problem and related crimes, based on the principles of sovereignty, territorial integrity, and with a comprehensive and bilateral approach." Canada and Chile were later identified as coleaders of efforts to develop a multilateral evaluation mechanism.

Regimes

A survey of the hemisphere reveals the existence of all the elements mentioned above: multinational, multilevel, and multiactor initiatives; unilateralism, bilateralism, and multilateralism; and conflicts over capabilities and sovereignty, some of which were noted. Moreover, some of the bilateral and multilateral initiatives involve states and IGOs outside the Americas. As a case in point, Britain, France, and the Netherlands, play invaluable roles in the counternarcotics area, especially in relation to money laundering and trafficking in the Caribbean. There is a certain understandable self-interest in their actions, of course, as these countries have dependencies (and Départments d'Outre Mer in the case of France) in the Americas. But two other factors also motivate their actions: one, they are affected by drugs, arms trafficking, and terrorism; and two, they recognize that the multidimensionality and transnationality of these matters make it imperative that they lend their support to the manifestations of them in the Americas. However, it is not just individual states outside the Americas that are involved; nonstate actors outside the area are also. Two examples are the European Union and the Financial Action Task Force (FATF), which was formed in 1989 with Britain, Canada, Germany, France, Italy, Japan, and the United States as members. The FATF has been a prime actor in the creation and operation of the Caribbean Financial Action Task Force (CFATF), which is the multilateral leader in anti-money-laundering efforts in the Caribbean Basin.[54]

Because the narcotics phenomenon, arms trafficking, and terrorism are interdependence issues, it has been necessary for states to go beyond bilateralism to multilateralism and form a variety of anti-TNC regimes, in conjunction with IGOs such as the OAS, the UN, the Regional Security System, and the International Criminal Police Organization (Interpol). Table 4.3 shows some of these regimes. But it also suggests that states in the Americas understand the regional-global nexus of these interdependence issues and, therefore, have joined not only hemispheric regimes but also global ones. In that regard, a state in the Americas—the Bahamas—had the distinction of being the first to ratify the 1988 UN Convention against Illicit Trafficking in Narcotic Drugs and Psychotropic Substances, on January 30, 1989.

The most recent regime instrument in the Americas is the Inter-American Convention against the Illicit Manufacturing of and Trafficking in Firearms, the first of its kind in the international system. It was signed on November 14, 1997, by twenty-nine OAS member states; the other three members have since signed it, the last being St. Lucia, on June 3, 1998. Yet, up to the end of September 1998, only three had ratified it: Belize (January 12, 1998); Mexico (June 8, 1998); and the Bahamas (June 30, 1998).[55] However, since Article XXV of the convention provides for it to come into force with the second ratification, it came into force in June 1998. To help ensure that arms are transferred to legitimate users, parties to the convention are required to establish or maintain an effective licensing or authorization system for the export, import, and transit of firearms, ammunition, explosives, and other related materials. To improve the ability to track down the sources of illegal firearms, they are required to seek, at the time of manufacture and for importation, the markings of firearms, with the name, place of manufacture, and serial number.

As testimony to the importance their countries attach to the convention, both President Bill Clinton and Mexican President Ernesto Zedillo went to the OAS Secretariat for its signing. They both offered a sense of the scope and gravity of arms trafficking. President Clinton indicated, "Last year, the U.S. Bureau of Alcohol, Tobacco, and Firearms received approximately 30,000 requests just from OAS member states to trace weapons used in crimes. Gun trafficking is an issue of national security for all of us, and a matter of neighborhood security for the Americas." The Mexican president identified some of the TNC linkages involved: "This commerce in violence fuels serious offences, such as drug trafficking that wreaks destruction and aspires to impose a code of death and corruption; organized crime that abducts, commits violent assaults, and undermines public security; and terrorism that seeks to block the path to democracy and enshrine dogmatism and intolerance."[56]

Meaningful multilateral countermeasures, however, require going beyond platitudes and signings; they obligate states to follow through, to implement the

Table 4.3

Transnational Crime Regime Countermeasures in the Americas

Regime	Year Adopted
Convention on Offenses and Certain other Acts Committed on Board Aircraft	1963
Convention for the Suppression of Unlawful Seizure of Aircraft	1970
Convention for the Suppression of Unlawful Acts against the Safety of Civil Aviation	1971
Convention to Prevent and Punish the Acts of Terrorism Taking the Forms of Crimes against Persons and Related Extortion that Are of International Significance	1971
Convention on the Prevention and Punishment of Crimes against Internationally Protected Persons	1973
Inter-American Convention on Conflict of Laws concerning Bills of Exchange, Promissory Notes, and Invoices	1975
Convention on the Physical Protection of Nuclear Material	1979
International Convention against the Taking of Hostages	1979
Inter-American Convention on Extradition	1981
Protocol for the Suppression of Unlawful Acts of Violence at Airports Serving International Civil Aviation	1988
Protocol for the Suppression of Unlawful Acts against the Safety of Maritime Navigation, with Related Protocol	1988
UN Convention against Illicit Trafficking in Narcotic Drugs and Psychotropic Substances	1988
Convention on the Marking of Plastic Explosives for the Purpose of Identification	1991
Inter-American Convention on Mutual Assistance in Criminal Matters	1992
Inter-American Convention on International Traffic in Minors	1995
Plan of Action in Hemispheric Cooperation to Prevent, Combat, and Eliminate Terrorism	1996
Inter-American Convention against Corruption	1996
Action Plan for the Implementation of the Anti-Drug Strategy of the Hemisphere	1997
Inter-American Convention against the Illicit Manufacturing of and Trafficking in Firearms	1997

Source: Organization of American States, 1998.

terms and pursue the mandates to which they signaled commitment. Many states in the hemisphere are delinquent in this area for differing reasons, including technical and financial capability limitations, administrative lethargy, the lack of political will, and bureaucratic disputes among executing agencies. The point was made elsewhere that while the implementation of many provisions of multilateral plans and instruments demonstrate the need for confidence building among states, it also often reflects the importance of confidence building within states. Moreover, states have to be constantly mindful of needing to overcome several challenges, in relation to the setting of priorities, the design of policies, and battles for turf and resources among executing agencies.[57]

Conclusion

The connectivity among content, consequences, and countermeasures warrants stressing. Not only do content elements affect consequences but also countermeasures are a function of both content and consequences. Hence, we should be mindful, for instance, that a multilateral evaluation mechanism that fails adequately to address the symbolic and substantive shortcomings of the U.S. certification measure is likely, at best, to lead to lukewarm production suppression efforts by states, resulting in sustained or increased production. Governments that improve the effectiveness of terrorism countermeasures but also focus only on their domestic jurisdiction increase the likelihood that terrorists will (1) explore international linkages generally, with no net improvement in global counterterrorism, (2) test the pressure points of neighboring countries, which could lead to sour relations with proximate states, and (3) form alliances with criminals whose area of enterprise is narcotics or weapons smuggling.

Thus, desired outcomes should not only be defined in terms of reducing the scope and impact of, say, drugs or weapons trafficking, or crime. They should also be defined in terms of mitigating the potential deleterious impact of action in one area on another area. In other words, a desirable outcome should be to avoid successful anti-drug-trafficking efforts leading to increased arms trafficking, for example. An even more important desired outcome is that policymakers and managers not lose their humanity in combating TNC, and that the rule of law be preserved in dealing with it. Having laws and applying them is, therefore, crucial. Yet, although legislation is necessary, the mere passage of legislation is not sufficient. Indeed, legislation by itself could undermine desired outcomes. For example, tough laws could help worsen prison overcrowding and lead judges to use fines instead of imprisonment, thereby (1) putting criminals back in the society, and into other societies given cross-national operations, and (2) undermining the willingness of police and prosecutors to vigorously enforce laws. Policymakers, therefore, should not only give "teeth" to domestic legislation by allocating adequate resources for policy execution but also pay increased attention to international criminal justice measures, such as extradition and witness protection, as an extension of domestic rule of law.

This reality check suggests that inter-American relations in the twenty-first century will continue to witness dynamic interplay among state and non-state actors in gray areas that are complicated by the vicissitudes of power, some of which are beyond the control of individual states. We are likely to witness an accentuation of multilateral countermeasures, as the limitations of unilateralism become more apparent. The TNC issues examined here will not be "solved" at the dawn of the new decade, perhaps not even during it. Hence, avoiding false expectations is just as important as preventing fatalism. In order to do this TNC policymakers and practitioners might find it useful to

- rise above platitudes, implementing and executing conventions and policies;

- set practical missions and achievable goals (don't let countermeasures be driven by political dictates for quick fixes, as none of the issues is amenable to such);

- avoid seeing countermeasures in zero-sum terms, but reduce duplication and working at cross-purposes, both within and among countries; and

- accept that there will be conflicts over sovereignty and capabilities, but create and strengthen mechanisms to resolve them quickly, as TNC actors will exploit any discord that arises.

Notes

1. James N. Rosenau, *Turbulence in World Politics* (Princeton: Princeton University Press, 1990), 106.
2. Roy Godson and Wm. J. Olson, *International Organized Crime: Emerging Threat to U.S. Security* (Washington, D.C.: National Strategy Information Center, 1993), 5.
3. J. F. Holden-Rhodes and Peter A. Lupsha, "Horsemen of the Apocalypse," in *Global Dimensions of High Intensity Crime and Low Intensity Conflict*, ed. Graham H. Turbville, Jr. (Chicago: University of Illinois Office of International Criminal Justice, 1995), 10.
4. See, for example, Mark A. Kleiman, *Marijuana: Costs of Abuse, Costs of Control* (Westport, Conn.: Greenwood Press, 1989), 109–17; M. Douglas Anglin and George Speckart, "Narcotics Use and Crime: A Multisample, Multimethod Analysis," *Criminology* 26, no. 2 (1988): 197–231; and John M. Martin and Anne T. Roman, *Multinational Crime: Terrorism, Espionage, Drugs, and Arms Trafficking* (London: Sage Publications, 1992).
5. For more on geonarcotics, see Ivelaw L. Griffith, "From Cold War Geopolitics to Post-Cold War Geonarcotics," *International Journal* 48 (1993–1994): 1–36.
6. U.S. Department of State, *International Narcotics Control Strategy Report* [hereafter *INCSR*], March 1998, 65, 81.
7. United States, Office of National Drug Control Policy, *National Drug Control Strategy, 1998* available at http://www.whitehouse.gov/policy/98ndcs/iic/html.
8. Gen. Barry R. McCaffrey, "Lessons of 1994: Prognosis for 1995 and Beyond" (presentation at the U.S. Southern Command-National Defense University Annual Strategy Symposium, Miami, Apr. 25, 1995).

9. María Elena Medina-Mora and María del Carmen Mariño, "Drug Abuse in Latin America," in *Drug Policy in the Americas*, ed. Peter A. Smith (Boulder: Westview, 1992), 46. For more on drug abuse (and the trafficking of drugs and precursors, and money laundering) in Latin America and the Caribbean, see United Nations International Drug Control Program, *World Drug Report* (New York: Oxford University Press, 1997); the 1998 *INCSR*; and visit http://www.oas.org./EN/PROG/w3/Boletin97.

10. This interview is reported in Rensselaer W. Lee, III, "Drugs: The Cuba Connection," *Current History* (1996): 57.

11. Walter Laqueur, "Postmodern Terrorism," *Foreign Affairs* 75 (1996): 24–25.

12. Brian Jenkins, *International Terrorism: A New Mode of Conflict* (Los Angeles: Crescent Publications, 1975), 1.

13. For a discussion of the incident and its outcome, see George Gedda, "U.S. Urges Hard Line in Lima," *Washington Post*, Dec. 18, 1996; Peter Grier and Alex Emery, "Strong Tactics Win Big," *Christian Science Monitor*, Apr. 24, 1997; and "The Peru Crisis: A Chronology," *Christian Science Monitor*, Apr. 24, 1997.

14. For examination of the incident, see Dion E. Phillips, "Terrorism and Security in the Caribbean: The 1976 Cubana Disaster off Barbados," *Terrorism* 14, no. 4 (1991): 209–19. On the dedication, see "Castro to Dedicate Monument to Cubana Crash Victims," *Barbados Nation*, Aug. 1, 1998, available at http://www.nationnews.com.

15. See Larry Rohter, "Cuba Arrests Salvadorean in Hotel Blasts," *New York Times*, Sept. 12, 1997; and Ann Louise Bardach and Larry Rohter, "Bombers Tale; A Cuban Exile Details a 'Horrendous Matter' of a Bombing Campaign," *New York Times*, July 12, 1998.

16. Paul Wilkinson, "Trends in International Terrorism and the American Response," in *Terrorism and International Order*, ed. Lawrence Freeman et al. (London: Routledge and Kegan Paul, 1986), 49.

17. David E. Apter, "Political Violence in Analytic Perspective," in *The Legitimization of Violence*, ed. David E. Apter (New York: New York University Press, 1997), 7.

18. In Michael Klare and David Andersen, *A Scourge of Guns: The Diffusion of Small Arms and Light Weapons in Latin America* (Washington, D.C.: Federation of American Scientists, 1996), i.

19. Ivelaw Lloyd Griffith, *Drugs and Security in the Caribbean: Sovereignty Under Siege* (University Park: Pennsylvania State University Press, 1997), 154.

20. Klare and Andersen, *Scourge*, 8.

21. Cited in Klare and Andersen, *Scourge*, 5–6, 52.

22. For more on the kinds and amounts of weapons produced in these and other Latin American countries, see Klare and Andersen, *Scourge*, 16–25, and the Appendix.

23. Andrés Oppenheimer, "U.S. Aid Sought in War on Guns," *Miami Herald*, Apr. 6, 1998, 8A.

24. See Klare and Andersen, *Scourge*, 67–71.

25. Ivelaw L. Griffith, "Caribbean Geopolitics and Geonarcotics: New Dynamics, Same Old Dilemma," *Naval War College Review* 51 (1998): 60.

26. Frank Davies, "Tales of $3.2 Million Missile Deal Unfold Like a Good Spy Novel," *Miami Herald*, Apr. 19, 1998, 1B, 13b; and Frank Davies, "Arms Brokers Convicted in Weapons Smuggling," *Miami Herald*, Apr. 24, 1998, 1B, 2B.

27. Klare and Andersen, *Scourge*, 66.

28. Ethan A. Nadelmann, *Cops Across Borders: The Internationalization of U.S. Criminal Law Enforcement* (University Park: Pennsylvania State University Press, 1993), 258.

29. For a discussion of the Gutiérrez case, see Carlos Fazio, "Mexico: The Narco General Case," in *Crime in Uniform: Corruption and Impunity in Latin America*, ed. Theo Roncken (Amsterdam: Transnational Institute, 1997).

30. Ricardo Soberón Garrido, "Corruption, Drug Trafficking, and the Armed Forces: An Approximation for Latin America," in Roncken, ed., *Crime in Uniform*, 1.

31. William Branigan and John Ward Anderson, "Drug Corruption Heads North," *Washington Post*, Nov. 3, 1997, 1.

32. See "March 12, 1997 Statement by Barry R. McCaffrey, Director, ONDCP, on U.S.-Mexico Counterdrug Cooperation," Senate Foreign Relations Committee, Subcommittee on Western Hemisphere and Peace Corps, available at http://www.ncjrs.org/mxshort.htm.

33. For more on sporadic, systemic, and institutionalized corruption, see Nadelmann, *Cops*

Across Borders, 251–312; Peter Andreas, "Profits, Poverty, and Illegality: The Logic of Drug Corruption," *NACLA Report on the Americas* 27 (1993): 22ff; and Anthony P. Maingot, "Confronting Corruption in the Hemisphere: A Sociological Perspective," *Journal of Interamerican Studies and World Affairs* 36 (1994): 49–74.

34. See Jean Cartier-Bresson, "Corruption Networks, Transaction Security, and Illegal Social Exchange," *Political Studies* 44 (1997): 469, 470.

35. "Inter-American Convention Against Corruption," OEA/Ser.K/XXXIV.1.CICOR/doc14/96rev.2, March 29, 1996, 1.

36. Godson and Olson, *International Organized Crime,* 23.

37. Kelly Librera, "On Guard," *Business Mexico* 8–3 (1998): 9.

38. Julia Preston, "Reported Violence Soars as Mexico Cracks Down on Crime in Capital," *Miami Herald,* Nov. 18, 1998, 10A.

39. Ibid.

40. Michael Renner, *Small Arms, Big Impact: The Next Challenge of Disarmament,* World Watch Paper No. 137, Oct. 1997, 22. The United Nations study to which Renner refers is the July 1997 "Report of the Panel of Governmental Experts on Small Arms."

41. Visit http://www.fbi.gov/UCR/CIUS/96Crime/96CRIME2.PDF; and see Griffith, *Drugs and Security in the Caribbean,* 119–23.

42. Molly Moore, "Tijuana Cartel Escalates Violence," *Washington Post,* Nov. 4, 1997, 1.

43. See Margaret H. Taylor and J. Alexander Aleinikoff, *Deportation of Criminal Aliens: A Geopolitical Perspective,* Inter-American Dialogue Paper, June 1998, available at http://www.iaddialog.org/taylor.html.

44. Telephone interview with Commander Chris Annamunthodo, Chief of Military Intelligence, Jamaica Defense Force, by author, Apr. 14, 1998.

45. Albert Alstrom and Andrew Richards, "Cops Kill Five Men—Robbery Foiled," *Stabroek News Online,* May 5, 1997, available at http://www.trinidad.net/stabroek.htm.

46. For more on prison conditions in the Caribbean, see Griffith, *Drugs and Security in the Caribbean,* 143–47. The actions of Justice Jamadar are reported in *Miami Herald,* "Trinidad and Tobago Judge Blocks Execution of Convicted Murderer," July 23, 1998, 10A.

47. See Tim Johnson, "It's a Vile, Violent World Behind Bars," *Miami Herald,* Dec. 22, 1996, available at http://www.herald.com/americas/archive/prisons/docs/prison22.htm.

48. Griffith, *Drugs and Security in the Caribbean,* 118; and Librera, "On Guard," 10.

49. Godson and Olson, *International Organized Crime,* 22.

50. Klare and Andersen, *Scourge,* i.

51. Some of the observations in the preceding paragraphs come from Ivelaw L. Griffith, "The Caribbean Security Landscape: A Reality Check," *Caribbean Affairs* 7 (1997): 35–44.

52. Michael J. Dziedzic, "The Organization of American States and Drug Control in the Americas," in *International Handbook on Drug Control,* ed. Scott B. MacDonald and Bruce Zagaris (Westport, Conn.: Greenwood Press, 1992), 411.

53. In this respect, it is pleasing the note a statement on page 32 of the 1997 U.S. *National Drug Control Strategy:* "While seeking to reduce drug availability, we must respect the rule of law and sovereignty of our partners."

54. For more on the role of the European Union and FATF, see European Union, *The Caribbean and the Drugs Problem: Report of the EU Experts Group,* Brussels, Apr. 1996; Institute For European-Latin American Relations, *Base Document for the Third European Union-Rio Group Dialogue on Security Issues,* Madrid, Dec. 1997; and INCSR 1988, 555–65.

55. Communication to author from Dr. Ricardo Mario Rodríguez, Minister at the Venezuelan Embassy to the OAS on Aug. 4, 1998 and Oct. 8, 1998.

56. "Remarks by Presidents Clinton and Zedillo at Signing of Hemispheric Arms Trafficking Convention," Nov. 14, 1997, available at http://www2.whitehouse.gov/WH/new/19971114-3126.html.

57. See Ivelaw L. Griffith, "Security Collaboration and Confidence Building in the Americas," in *International Security and Democracy: Latin American and the Caribbean in the Post-Cold War Era,* ed. Jorge I. Domínguez (Pittsburgh, Pa.: University of Pittsburgh Press, 1998), 183–86.

5

Transnational Crime in the Western Hemisphere

MÓNICA SERRANO

International organized crime affects different states and regimes in different ways. Its impact is conditioned not only by the domestic and international dimensions of the state's strength but also by the nature of the regime at risk. The most basic notion of a state's strength refers to its capacity to "preserve itself and the territory and people over which it claims control," as well as to guarantee security from external and internal challenges to its monopoly of organized force. In its ideal form, a strong state should be capable of performing a variety of "functional responsibilities" ranging from economic policy and security to welfare. Toward the other end of the spectrum are the weak states, which are unable to impose the rule of law or to provide its people with basic services. Falling off the end of the spectrum are collapsed states, in which the structure, authority, law, and political order have fallen apart.[1] To the extent that state strength is a relational quality, it may not be possible to establish a categorical division between strong and weak states. Yet the phenomenon of transnational crime enables one to propose a working definition of the division, as follows: the weak state is one which will tend to be favored by international criminals for their operations.

When facing international organized crime, weak states will tend to resort to approaches that could best be defined as "making policy by default." The deeper question about these states, however, concerns the dynamic between the domestic and international dimensions of their weaknesses. The interplay between a state's location in the international system, the structural characteristics of its state apparatus, the relative autonomy of the state vis-à-vis the dominant classes, and the overall balance of power in civil society are all pertinent factors. Not least, they determine the state's vulnerability to transnational criminal organizations (TCO).[2]

My discussion opens by considering the background to the transformation of organized crime from an old contender of the authority of weak states

into a significant transnational rival. In assessing the major trends in transboundary criminal activities that have flourished in the Western Hemisphere,
I examine the effects of transnational organized crime on government institutions, economic performance, and more broadly the rule of law in those countries facing this predicament in the Americas. I reserve a final question
concerning the nature of the political regimes at risk for the conclusion. While
it is a major premise of my argument that weak states are less able than strong
ones to contain transboundary criminal activities, what conclusions are to be
drawn about the normative relations between strong and weak states, on the
one hand, and democratic and authoritarian regimes, on the other? In the
context of economic globalization, this question is further complicated. The
decision of a state to deregulate its economy also has a bearing on any answer
to the question about its weakening.

Crime Globalization

The drift toward the internationalization of crime is closely related to two parallel processes in operation: the emergence of a global market economy, and
changes enforced upon the traditional functions and responsibilities of states.
Clearly, rapid technological and financial transformation and the integration of
national economies into a global market economy have weakened the authority
of all governments. More deeply, some of the state's fundamental responsibilities have been abdicated, with a consequent erosion of governance.[3]

A preliminary explanation of this would stress both the changes in the
boundaries of the state's authority (its contraction in both society and the
economy) and their impact upon the dynamics associated with the emergence
of other "loci or sources of authority." A subsequent interpretation would highlight the changes in the traditional "purposes of states" themselves. Although
the rise of the "competition state" over the welfare state is among the most visible of these changes, the performance of many other tasks linked to both economic and military security have also been significantly transformed.[4] In the
past decades, as the state's authority has declined and become diffused among
other collective forms of nonstate authority (including organized crime), even
the integrity of territorial borders of the state have gradually dwindled. But central to the debate about this decline and diffusion of state authority is the distinction between those nonstate sources of authority that may reinforce the
state and those that challenge and threaten its legitimacy and power. While
many of these actors operate in gray areas and are ambiguously perceived, it is
widely assumed that organized crime represents a rival, a "counterauthority" to
the state. Indeed, criminal organizations have emerged as the net beneficiaries
of the decline of state control over their territories.[5]

Organized crime is an old contender of state authority, yet its character-istics have changed over time. Fast growth and global reach have given it an unprecedented capacity to challenge states. There is little doubt that the transnational scope achieved by organized crime during the past decades has to be seen within the context of the changes taking place in the global econo-my. Transnational criminal organizations are now closely connected in intense forms of interaction that have led to an exponential expansion of illegal mar-kets. The local and regional base of organized crime that first reached transat-lantic proportions is now "clearly global."[6]

Available evidence suggests the criminal organizations that have gained international ascendancy are the Latin American, more specifically the Colombian and Mexican, drug cartels. According to some criminologists, the new conditions created by NAFTA's trade liberalization between Mexico and the United States led Colombian cartels to buy and acquire businesses in Mexico. Similarly, the advantages offered by free trade in Chile seem to have influenced the decision of Mexican baron Amado Carrillo to relocate to Chile.[7] According to the Chilean Justice Minister María Soledad Alvear, Carrillo was attracted to Chile by both the degree of openness of the Chilean economy and the entry prerogatives granted by Chilean authorities to foreign investors.[8]

A more disputed case has been that pointing to links between the Latin American cartels and the Russian Mafia. Thus, the details of an allegedly joint report by the Drug Administration Agency (DEA) and the Colombian National Police connecting Colombian and Mexican cartels with the Russian Mafia were contested by the Mexican embassy in Colombia, but its funda-mental hypothesis (about a possible deal of cocaine for arms) was acknowl-edged by Colombian authorities in Mexico City. Moreover, the international reach of the Mexican cartels had been confirmed in 1997 by the former head of the Instituto Nacional de Combate a las Drogas (INCD), Francisco Molina, who affirmed that members of the Tijuana cartel had received special military training by Israeli private security services. Possible links between the Russian Mafia and Mexican cartels have also been traced in a number of alleged visits made by the former drug lord Amado Carrillo to Russia before his death in 1997. Similarly, the Chilean ambassador in Mexico, Luis Maira, referred to the possibility of a distribution network being negotiated between Carrillo and Italian gangs. In that same year the head of Interpol in Mexico, Juan Miguel Ponce, corroborated that a group of Russians who had been deported in July were carrying arms and a substantial amount of cash.[9]

The power acquired by Russian Mafias in the past years has relied on a manpower base of more than 80,000 "agents" that have spread their operations around forty countries.[10] Similarly, recent reports on international organized crime in Canada, a NAFTA member, have not only made clear the presence of Mexican organizations but also their strength. Mexican cartels have evolved from providing services subcontracted by Colombian cartels to establishing direct links with local mafias including the Italian, Colombian, Russian, and Asian organizations. These studies estimate that growing demand of cocaine in the United States could encourage Mexican cartels to establish processing laboratories in Canadian territory, which has emerged as one of the main centers of operation of international mafias.[11]

Changes in the international political economy are central to understanding this evolution. There is little doubt that the integration of national economies into a global market economy, the revolution in communication and transportation, and the consequent porosity of national borders have opened "unprecedented opportunities for international criminal activity."[12] The rapid expansion of transnational economic activity in the past decades has eroded the regulating capacity of states. The increase in transnational flows of merchandise and people have not been accompanied by a parallel increase in the capacity of states to survey and regulate such flows. This has encouraged the movement across borders of illicit commodities and unlawful transactions. In August 1997 the U.S. drug czar Barry MacCaffrey publicly acknowledged the incapacity of U.S. authorities to inspect the nine million containers arriving each year into U.S. ports. In Mexico, the customs general administrator, Luis Carlos Moreno, conceded that it was almost impossible to detect and stop the illicit flow of arms and other commodities to that country. U.S. Customs now estimate that only 3 percent of the nine million containers are inspected; and of the five thousand trucks entering daily only two hundred are searched. On the Mexican side of the border only 15 percent of the vehicles crossing the border in Tijuana are inspected by Mexican customs authorities, where more than 27 million crossings were registered by the U.S. Immigration and Naturalization Service in 1996.[13] Even without these human and material restrictions, there is an argument that stricter customs regulations would lead to significant trade disruption and may even stimulate corruption. Similarly, by limiting the states' capacity to control financial flows the internationalization of financial markets has also facilitated international financial crime.

So, the operation of criminal organizations has become transnational, and their behavior has increasingly come to parallel that of transnational firms. The new generation of criminal organizations and transnational drug cartels share many of the geo-economic characteristics of their legitimate counterparts: the powers to operate across borders; to expediently mobilize resources at different stages of the "industrial" process; to swiftly respond to changes or constraints in demand; to establish strategic alliances to improve and open new markets and/or reduce operations risk; and even to subcontract private security forces. Another common analogy is that they both, in their very different forms, have the power to hold the liberal state hostage to their interests.

In an important sense, multinational corporations (MNCs) tend to exercise a disproportionate influence on public policy through their discretionary economic powers over investment, resources, and employment. In their dealings with governments, corporations often condition their cooperation upon policy making and fully exploit their discretionary power.[14] But while there is an argument that legal transnationals revalidate a state's authority by negotiating their access to territory and markets with it, no such argument can be made for international criminal organizations. Unlike transnational corporations, criminal organizations achieve access to states through "circumvention," through bypassing their control.

Yet there is a further relevance to the comparison between MNCs and TCOs. Undoubtedly, the rise of MNCs as one of the main agents of integration of the world system has altered relationships among these companies and states, forcing them down new bargaining avenues. If states cannot any longer direct international production, then firms continue to seek countries and governments that provide a stable, "temperate environment" and favorable regulatory regimes. Corporation planning systems increasingly demand from governments stability in the regulation of business environments, so that long-term and large-scale resource investments can be guaranteed.

In clear contrast, favorable conditions for transboundary criminal organizations are more often found in countries troubled by instability and weak or illegitimate state institutions. Moreover, while governments may look for firms that will be "good citizens, productive expanding and loyal," it is difficult to imagine socializing cartels into having more soulful public objectives, popular mythology about Pablo Escobar notwithstanding.[15]

The new forms of operation observed among TCOs (international networks, subcontracting agreements, "strategic alliances") have made clear their similarities with MNCs, in particular their increased transnational mobility and adaptability. This in turn underlines the magnitude of their challenge to state authority and to traditional conceptions of national and international security.

Major Trends in Transboundary Criminal Activities in the Western Hemisphere

In the past decade the variety in the forms of transboundary illicit activities, including illicit flows of money, arms, stolen cars, and people as well as drugs, has intensified. Other industries such as kidnapping and security blackmailing have also proliferated. Many of these enterprises are often interconnected, turning organized crime into an assortment of different illicit activities. This is particularly the case with drug trafficking, which not only represents by far the biggest illegal market but also entails important ramifications in other areas. Drug trafficking is indeed often referred to as a complex of associated crimes including, among others, arms trafficking, money laundering, and the illicit trade of chemical precursors.

In the Americas, as in many other parts of the world, the impact of globalization has varied among different states depending on the interplay of the countries' domestic and international choices and constraints. What is already clear is that the shift from import substitution industrialization (ISI) toward outwardly oriented economic development entailed important implications for the internal and external security of regional states. Apart from the security effects associated with economic integration arrangements and globalization more generally, what is evident is that ISI policies were closely linked to state-building processes in Latin America. This trend came to an end in the 1980s.

The rollback of the state in the region would appear to have negatively affected previous sources of order. Furthermore, while the contraction of the state has not necessarily resulted in greater efficiency or re-regulation, overall state power appears to have declined. The process of "reinventing" government and institutions has not taken hold, either as a result of the ascendancy of "apolitical and technocratic views of what this 'reinvention' entails," or simply because the resources needed to guarantee the transition to an "effective state" capable of maintaining a significant degree of political power and authority are lacking.[16]

The developments in areas like drug trafficking, money laundering, extortion, illicit arms transfers, and illegal migration suggest a serious erosion of the capacity of states to guarantee the security of its citizens and to maintain law and order. The continued indebtedness and the fiscal crisis of the state have severely reduced the capacity of regional governments to fulfill many of their basic public responsibilities, including the preservation of law and order. Corrupt and inefficient police forces have long been evident throughout the region, but the magnitude of the crisis of public order in countries like Brazil, Colombia, Mexico, and Peru have brought to light the precarious conditions under which these institutions operate. The fragility of these institutions has been further complicated by the emergence or exacerbation of new problems, most specifically transnational organized crime.[17]

Drug Trafficking

The exacerbation of drug trafficking since the mid-1980s has spawned new and menacing threats to both the internal and external security of regional states. This situation is the result of the combination of at least three factors: first, the boom in consumption, particularly in the United States; second, the intensification of antidrug policies focused on the supply of narcotics; and third, the emergence of a new generation of drug organizations that turned drug trafficking into a major global enterprise. Clearly, the explosion of drug trafficking in Latin America could not be explained simply in terms of the lack of interest or unwillingness of regional states to enforce the prohibition norm, that is, to address the problem. Instead, increased efforts to combat drug trafficking have tended to produce more violence, to deplete states' institutions, to threaten internal peace in a number of important ways, and, finally, to poison relations between neighboring states.

Explanations for the exacerbation of the drug problem in the Western Hemisphere in the 1980s should be sought in the interaction between the explosive global growth in drug production and trafficking, on the one hand, and the implementation of flawed and excessively onerous policies of prohibition, on the other. These policies have not only failed in their ultimate objective of checking the expansion of the drug market but also have brought disastrous consequences. Unquestionably, such policies that have sought to reduce the ingress and consumption of drugs by sealing the U.S. borders (thus seeking to increase the price of narcotics) have been accompanied by ever-more undesirable consequences in both the domestic and international spheres. Such disastrous consequences call to mind Hirschman's well-known "perversity thesis," by which a given policy remains in place even though it continues to backfire. At the least, such consequences should entail comprehensive estimations of the costs of antinarcotic policies. These costs are institutional and international as well as financial.

The tendency of profitability to increase when a trade in goods or services has been declared illegal has received considerable attention.[18] What is now abundantly clear is that the changes observed in the global market economy together with the increased emphasis on repressive policies in the Western Hemisphere have significantly contributed to the growth and strengthening of criminal drug organizations, in many cases at the expense of the solidity of the state.

The institutional costs of drug trafficking for regional states like Colombia and Mexico have been high. Drug organizations can penetrate not only the state apparatus but also political parties and important areas of the private sector. The extraordinary financial capacity in the hands of drug traffickers enables them, at least, to challenge the institutional capacity of the state and, at worst, to generate a climate of ungovernability by depleting the state's authority.[19] Clearly, the penetration of government institutions significantly erodes the capacity of states to enforce law and order. This is a situation further aggravated by the opportunity cost associated with the diversion of institutional efforts toward fighting the drug war. Institutions like the judiciary, the police, and the armed forces are cut off from the activities that provide their raison d'être, to become instead involved in missions not entirely connected with their original purposes.

Although the estimation of economic profits linked to drug trafficking remains a cause for controversy, most observers now tend to agree that direct and indirect economic costs simply outweigh potential benefits such as employment or temporary stabilization of exchange rates. Indeed, in addition to mounting economic resources invested in the war against drugs, drug profits introduce serious economic distortions and undermine the economic integrity of markets. In Colombia, for example, inflows of drug money are estimated at around 2–8 percent of GDP. Although this figure is relatively small, it is far from negligible. In macroeconomic terms, drug earnings undoubtedly contributed to cushion an exchange crisis and to make the debt crisis more manageable. Yet the direct economic costs of the war on drugs are dramatic. Colombia's former president, Cesar Gaviria, estimated that the country spent $1 billion annually fighting the drug trade and lost a similar amount in foreign investment, foreign exchange, and taxes.[20]

There is a cost to the political legitimacy of the state as well. Drug traffickers have often manipulated the judiciary and taken advantage of the loopholes present in complex and inadequate legal systems. They have thus often been able to recover not only their freedom but also confiscated properties. Some efforts have been made to improve the administration of criminal justice by including in antiorganized crime legislation a variety of legal forms—conspiracy, attempt, and aiding and abetting—as juridically defined crimes. These attempts notwithstanding, judicial systems have so far failed to act as credible deterrents to drug traffickers' operations.[21] To these drawbacks one also has to add insufficient regulatory capabilities in customs procedures, air and transport norms, as well as import and export regulations.

In Colombia as in Mexico, drug barons, when finally brought to trial have often been acquitted either by corrupt or intimidated judges or by judicial authorities devoted to "judicial formalities that ultimately benefit traffickers."[22] Furthermore, in these countries the majority of the resources allocated to the administration of justice has been diverted to the war against drugs.

This war has also been excessively onerous to the health of the coercive apparatus of many Latin American republics. In Colombia, killings of policemen and judges active in drug-control policies became more frequent from the mid-1970s on. This was particularly the case in the city of Medellín, where car bombings of police posts and assassinations of policemen took place "almost weekly." By the mid-1980s the estimated armed power of Pablo

Escobar in Medellín (around 1,500 people organized in gangs) rivaled the 2,500 men in the city's police force. The legacy of drug-control policies for Colombian police forces in the period between 1982 and 1992 was a total of nearly 3,000 policemen killed on duty.[23]

In the case of Mexico, U.S. authorities have made public their concern about the spillover of violence across the border and the high rate of policemen killed on duty in areas dominated by drug trafficking.[24] This vulnerability of police forces partly accounts for the rise of an alarming trend toward the enrollment of the armed forces in antinarcotic policies. Although the vulnerability of already corrupt and fragile police corps to drug bribery and violence helps to explain this trend, equally important was the decision to militarize the war against drugs, which resulted from the decision of the U.S. government to proclaim drug trafficking a national security threat.

In Colombia, as in Mexico or Peru, the military's increased role in antinarcotics operations has rendered the armed forces in turn more vulnerable to corruption, threatening their institutional cohesion. The penetration and infiltration of police forces and the military has further weakened the credibility of already deeply defective institutions by fomenting internal distrust, deepening conflicts among different corps, and undermining their unity and discipline. Equally important is the fact that increased involvement in antinarcotics operations has also entailed the risk of "armed fragmentation," with significant implications for both the armed institution itself and civil-military balances.[25]

In the three countries here studied the institutional damage has been evident in the increasing numbers of national police officers, soldiers, and generals who have been dismissed and prosecuted on corruption charges. In Colombia in the last four years more than 14,000 national police officers have been dismissed for corruption. In Peru at the end of 1994 more than one hundred soldiers, most of them officers, including two former regional commanders for the Upper Huallaga Valley, had been indicted or convicted for complicity in the drug trade. Whereas in Mexico, although scandals are by no means new, the arrest in February 1997 of the antinarcotics czar, General Jesús Gutiérrez Rebollo, on drug-corruption charges forced the armed institution to accept publicly the charges and to prosecute thirty-four army officers for drug-related offenses during the first half of that year. Similarly, successive police reforms have involved the dismissal of increasing numbers of officers. In 1996 alone more than 1,300 policemen were removed on corruption or incompetence charges. In some regional states meanwhile, organized crime has produced serious hemorrhages of police corps. In Morelos, during the first half of 1998, the 2,000-strong police force lost at least 25 percent of its members on charges of participation in kidnappings, drug trafficking, and car theft.[26]

In addition to such institutional damage, it is also important to recall the direct cost of diverting efforts and resources to assignments clearly detached from the original missions for which these institutions were created. Throughout these years the cost of the war on drugs has been evident in rising budgets for the police and military forces. By contrast to current trends observable in the rest of the region, in both Mexico and Colombia the apparent internal decay, and the ever-more complex problems of order generated by drug trafficking and insurgent movements, have pushed security spending upward. Since 1992–1993 the share of Colombian security spending has risen from approximately 1.4 percent to 3.5 percent of GDP, while in Mexico similar trends account for the rapid expansion of the armed forces and an increase in defense expenditure from $1, 206 billion in 1990 to $2,310 in 1993 and $2.9 billion by 1997. Its share in total government expenditures increased from 1.96 percent in 1990 to 5.20 percent in 1995.[27]

Gray Areas: Violence and Crime

At the heart of current discussions on the crisis of public order in the region lies the key question of political competition in the absence of a sovereign or under the shadow of an impotent sovereign. Under such conditions a continuity between organized violence and other violent criminal activities might be found, and the political aim of violence may not even always be what one might consider the foremost target: the state.[28]

The Colombian experience illustrates only too clearly this situation. In this country where violence now permeates almost all spheres of public and private life, the overlapping of different criminal activities has produced vicious circulatory patterns of violence with cross-fertilization among different actors. As Gonzalo Sánchez notes, one can observe a constant circulation among actors, with insurgents becoming paramilitaries, and drug lords and criminal organizations offering their services to revolutionaries.[29] This violent, Hobbesian landscape, where the frontiers between social protest, political violence, and criminal activities have been blurred, is the result of both confrontations and alliances between state agencies, drug traffickers, paramilitaries, self-defense groups, and guerrilla movements. The legacy of more than a decade of internecine wars among these various actors in Colombia has pushed the homicide rate and the overall numbers of disappearances to tragic levels.[30] These are not just crime statistics; behind them political considerations are at stake. Although drug traffickers do not seek the destruction of either the state or the market, their actions often aspire to sway both state and market decisions. The assassination of political candidates, judges, and members of the armed branch of the state is just one consequence.

Such an onslaught on government authorities, especially at the local level, has resulted in the impotence of the state in two key areas: the control over organized violence, and the provision of basic security to citizens. Colombia has accordingly been depicted as a "new country without a state."[31] A particularly distressing manifestation of the internal vulnerability of such states is the erosion of central authority and the consequent risk of the balkanization and feudalization. The salient cases here concern the power accumulated by drug lords, guerrillas, and criminal organizations over portions of the territory of Peru and Colombia as well as over some remote regions in Mexico. Such states' monopoly over organized violence and their capacity to enforce the rule of law are being questioned in practical terms.

ALLIANCES BETWEEN DRUG TRAFFICKERS AND GUERRILLAS Illegal crops tend to be cultivated in remote areas where the presence of the state is weak or plainly absent. The challenge to central authority has become ever-more serious where alliances with guerrillas have been established, helping these actors to secure control of sometimes strategic portions of the territory.[32] To take the least obvious case, in Mexico until recently specialists agreed that, despite the intermittent outburst of violence in various parts of the territory, the authority of the state remained in place. Yet, the power accumulated by drug traffickers in the states of Sinaloa, Durango, Chihuahua, Guerrero, Veracruz, and Oaxaca has now clearly disturbed civil-military balances in many of these states.[33] As a consequence, sanctuaries dominated by drug cartels and guerrilla movements have become a major problem challenging central state authority, even weakening the state's ability to control its borders. Clearly, in many of these regions an alternative system of "profit and power," a surrogate social and economic order has emerged, in which organized violence plays a role and openly defies the state's supremacy.[34]

Although the link between drug trafficking and insurgency has not received sufficient attention from analysts, events in Colombia, Mexico, and Peru have evidenced how the interests of these two actors may at least temporarily converge. While it is true that the term *narco-guerrilla* was popularized in the mid-1980s when the U.S. government declared the drug problem a national security threat, evidence of potential links clearly preceded this decision. U.S. perceptions of the guerrilla movements of that time notwithstanding, the drug trade can indeed be manipulated by political forces either seeking additional resources or the weakening of adversaries.[35] In Latin America the term *narco-guerrilla* was first used in Colombia in 1984 when the authorities discovered that the cocaine-processing laboratories in Tranquilandia were being protected by the Fuerzas Armadas Revolucionarias (FARC).[36]

There is little doubt that the growth of drug trafficking in Colombia since the late 1970s contributed to the reactivation of insurgent movements. In Mexico, on the other hand, some observers see in the deployment of a vigorous antinarcotic campaign in the 1970s a preemptive measure: the Echeverría government may have intensified drug-control policies in an effort to reassert central authority and to avoid the risk of violent rural responses against police forces and the army.[37]

The increasing resources associated with illegal activities, including drug trafficking, have benefited guerrilla movements. Even more clearly though, by weakening state institutions, such resources also facilitated the expansion of these movements. Although the combination of social and political violence can act as incubator of international organized crime, some rebel movements may present higher fertility rates than others. Not only has political violence varied in its objects, intentionality, methods, and organization but also it is clear that certain guerrilla movements are more prone to exploit rent-seeking opportunities and to enter into relations of "cooperative conflict." Variations between movements in connection to the "proper" as opposed to the "improper uses of violence" may depend on the significance of the movement's symbolic capital—complex connections between violence and ethical beliefs—and the value granted to interest and negotiated settlements. Those movements that see political violence as a "form of exchange" might be more prone to consider "money and power" as their object.[38]

In Colombia, the expansion of coca plantations produced a peculiar, pragmatic relationship between drug traffickers and guerrilla movements against state control, which produced in turn mutual economic and military benefits. This alliance both opened new sources of arms supplies for the guerrillas and increased the number of opportunities for political control. Insurgent movements offered protection to plantations in exchange for regulatory powers to limit their number, as well as to extract a levy on coca leaf and paste transactions. By 1993–1994 the Colombian government estimated that the FARC's income from the coca trade could reach $20–30 million annually.[39]

Drawing on the tendency of the new generation of Colombian insurgencies to flourish in the same areas troubled by the "Violencia" of the 1950s, some authors have thus explained their increased reliance on criminal practices such as kidnapping and extortion. In Colombia, this trend has allowed guerrilla movements to become significantly stronger both in economic and military terms, but in a significant way it has also blurred the frontiers between unlawful and criminal activities, fomenting circular forms of mobility among the various actors of violence.[40] This vicious cycle may, in the long term, weaken the guerrillas; however, in the short term, financial resources obtained through ransoms and taxes have not only strengthened the ELN (Ejército de

Liberación Nacional) and the FARC but also have enabled these movements to perform "para-state" functions in the several regions under their control. Moreover, underlying the apparent impasse reached between the guerrillas and the Colombian Armed Forces may lie not a stalemate of forces, but rather a common interest in maintaining a situation that confers legitimacy to "actions that in peacetime would be punishable as crimes." Indeed, rent-seeking opportunities can help explain both the protracted nature of some conflicts and the presence of various forms of "cooperative conflict."[41]

Similarly, in Mexico, the emergence of the EPR (Ejército Popular Revolucionario) in the state of Guerrero has been linked to the combination of drug trafficking and high rates of robberies and kidnappings. Evidence of the presence of armed groups in the southern state had been mounting before the EPR came to the surface in 1996. Local authorities had already acknowledged the emergence and proliferation of rural self-defense groups as well as considerable arms flows. Guerrero is also one of the most important producers of opium poppies in the country. Between April 1993 and May 1994, fifty-five kidnappings were reported in the state and the total ransom collected by organized crime reached more than $4 million. Although kidnappings have increased throughout the region, Mexico now holds the second place after Colombia.

It is true that long-term collaboration between drug traffickers and guerrilla movements is limited by their respective and conflicting political objectives.[42] Whereas insurgent movements aspire to subvert the existing political order, drug trafficking only seeks the debilitation of the state. Although some guerrilla movements still believe in the possibility of fundamentally altering the capitalist order, the profits obtained from drug trafficking are intimately dependent on the maintenance of free-market economies.

The alliance between drug traffickers and guerrilla movements is temporary as well as violent, yet it has aggravated the crisis of the state: it has provided the womb within which other forms of nonorganized, criminal, and indiscriminate violence have been incubated. The "dynamism" observed in industries linked to arms flows, kidnapping, security blackmailing, and illegal migration provide ample evidence about the conflict-economies produced by violence.[43]

ARMS FLOWS As has been widely documented, stability in various states in Central America, and more recently in southern Mexico, was significantly affected by the availability of arms in neighboring states, leading to transnational flows. The decision of the United Nations to monitor arms transfers in Central America was, to an important extent, motivated by an appreciation of the dangers of arms flows for regional stability.

The booming of the illicit arms market in the region has also been linked to the internationalization of drug cartels. The illegal market of arms across the U.S.-Mexican border has emerged as an important issue in the bilateral agenda between these two countries. In Mexico, in early 1998, the undersecretary of foreign affairs, Juan Rebolledo, identified the U.S.-Mexican understanding to strengthen efforts in the control of arms trafficking as a triumph of Mexican diplomacy, particularly since the flow of arms along the border originates almost entirely in the U.S. (In 1996 the *Los Angeles Times* reported that at least 90 percent of confiscated arms in Mexico originated in the United States.) During 1994 and 1995 more than 20,000 firearms were confiscated in Mexico, of which 39 percent were linked to drug-related crimes. Three years later, the seizure by the San Diego police of arms contraband en route to Mexico seemed to confirm the views of Mexican officials that the United States had become a critical market for the cartels' arms procurement.[44] Similarly, the alleged arms for cocaine deal between the Russian Mafia and the Colombian cartels may have enabled the latter to supply insurgents in Colombia and possibly too in Peru.[45]

KIDNAPPINGS The "industry" of kidnappings in Colombia, Brazil, and Mexico has also expanded. The total numbers reported in 1994 were 4,000 in Colombia; 800 in Mexico; 800 in Brazil; and 3 in Argentina.[46] In Mexico, the number of kidnappings officially registered by offices of justice procurement at the state level reached 1,460 a year, but according to both officials of the prosecutor's office and private security firms, this figure could be doubled if nonreported abductions were to be included. The states accounting for the majority of cases (which are increasingly including middle-income victims) are Michoacán, Guerrero, Jalisco, Morelos, Chiapas, Sinaloa, and the Federal District.[47]

A surplus of qualified security-trained personnel readily available for private hire, either resulting from police reforms, state-contraction and redundancy policies, or deportation of "violence-wielding criminals," may in the short run trigger higher crime, and in the medium- and long term stimulate the booming private security sector. The privatization of security is often associated with escalating crime and public frustration at the inadequate performance of poorly paid police forces.[48] What is clear is that rising levels of violence and the mushrooming of various forms of extortion tend to boost the demand for protection.

In Colombia as in Mexico, efforts to combat kidnapping and, more generally, organized crime have been hindered by the police protection offered to criminals. Scandals have spread in Mexico revealing protection granted by police officers to criminal activities. This has, of course, been particularly evident in cases pointing to drug-related corruption.[49] However, in places like Morelos, where police reforms produced a surplus of available security personnel, soaring crime could be explained by badly managed police reforms.[50]

The External Dimension

There are also external threats associated with transnational criminal activities and, more specifically, drug trafficking. International surveys have made clear the vulnerability of states to clandestine penetration by those criminal organizations seeking new routes or networks of production and distribution. The power of these organizations, in some cases rivaling that of governments, has undermined the ability of states to exercise their sovereign prerogatives and to effectively control their borders. Border incidents associated with drug-related violence and international organized crime (IOC) have been present along the U.S.-Mexican border, and the frontier between Colombia and Venezuela where the Colombian ELN (National Liberation Army) has clashed with the Venezuelan Armed Forces. The inability of the Colombian Armed Forces to contain rebel activity has had negative effects in all neighboring countries, but particularly in Venezuela where the army has been compelled to increase its border presence by some 10 000 troops.[51]

The vulnerability of states to drug power is also closely related to the underlying interdependent dynamics produced by drug-control policies. Past experience has shown how drug activities, when faced with stronger drug-control efforts, simply migrate to areas where the ability of governments to enforce law and order appears to be weaker, or to countries where their activities will, at least temporarily, be tolerated. These are among the most harmful counterproductive effects of antinarcotic measures at the international level.

The Security Dilemma of Drug Trafficking

Relatively successful drug-control policies, then, can push the international relations of certain states into a potential negative interdependence whose dynamic parallels that which characterizes the "security dilemma." The successful efforts of states to improve their security vis-à-vis drug trafficking can undermine the security of other countries by shifting routes or fostering the development of new markets. This has been particularly clear in the interaction between Colombia and Mexico since the 1970s.

In the 1970s the successful twin assault on Mexican and Jamaican marijuana production opened the door for Colombia's ascendancy to the "big leagues of drug trafficking." A few years later, the combination of the frontal war on drugs declared in Colombia by the governments of Belisario Betancur and Virgilio Barco and increased U.S. efforts in "sealing" Florida turned

Mexico into the main transit route for Colombian cocaine. Subsequently, mounting external pressures, the revival of the threat of extradition and the intensification of drug-control policies in Colombia all opened a window of opportunity to the rise of more powerful and violent cartels in Mexico.[52] Drug-control policies lead states into external vicious circles even as the effective combat of drug trafficking increasingly comes to depend on international cooperation.

The Certification Process

Drug-driven countries are vulnerable to a range of external menaces that range from economic sanctions to direct military or police intervention by external powers. The annual certification process inaugurated by the U.S. government increased the vulnerability of these states to U.S. sanctions. These include: the cancellation of 50 percent of bilateral aid (with the exception of some humanitarian aid); a negative U.S. vote for loan concessions in international financial institutions; and the denial of access to Export-Import Bank credits for U.S. exporters selling to decertified countries. The certification process has been strongly criticized as discriminatory and ineffectual since its inception in 1986 when the U.S. Congress amended the Foreign Assistance Act to require the president to certify whether or not drug-producing countries and transit countries were fully cooperating with antinarcotic efforts. Since then the certification mechanism has developed into a thorny issue in inter-American relations. This has been particularly so after 1995, when Colombia, Bolivia, and Peru were "conditionally certified" on the basis of strategic considerations, only for Colombia to be totally decertified one year later. By 1997 fear of decertification prompted the congresses of both Mexico and Colombia to pass resolutions condemning this practice.[53]

While it could be argued that mounting pressures forced Colombian authorities to take drug issues seriously, the results of Colombia's three-year decertification appear disputable. Despite rising U.S. pressure (unleashed to punish the funding of Ernesto Samper's 1994 campaign with drug-money from the Cali cartel), the Colombian president remained in power for the whole of his term. Although the Samper administration showed greater willingness to cooperate throughout these years,[54] decertification was sustained with counterproductive results on various fronts, including coca cultivation.[55] The same applied to the pressures exerted on the Zedillo administration after the Casablanca anti-money-laundering operation leading to the arrest in 1998 in the United States of a dozen white-collar criminals from Mexico through deceptive tactics. To the extent that this operation brought to light fissures in U.S.-Mexico antinarcotic cooperation, Mexican officials claimed that it mostly benefited criminals.

Double standards have also been present in the U.S. certification policies toward the region. Despite clear evidence that Mexico had become the main corridor for more than 70 percent of the cocaine aimed for the U.S. market, this country was systematically certified. Strategic considerations, that is, have tainted the certification process. It increasingly became clear that the effectiveness of a country's antinarcotic efforts were not the only criteria upon which certification decisions depended. Countries of major importance for U.S. interests, such as China, Taiwan, Panama, Brazil, and, indeed, Mexico have usually been certified. According to one view, in 1996 full decertification of Colombia was in fact advocated upon the belief that this would make possible Mexico's full certification by the U.S. Congress. Exceptions have also been contemplated on the basis of political considerations; both Paraguay and Peru received special treatment in 1996 due to the fragility of the transition to democracy in the first case, and to avoid disrupting the peace process with Ecuador in the latter.[56]

Ever since certification gained salience in U.S.-Latin American relations, the scope for disagreement has grown. In March 1997, in the context of the second meeting of experts of the Rio Group, President Zedillo, backed by a solid domestic consensus shared by the main political parties, made public his opposition to the U.S. certification policy. Similarly, during the regional meeting of foreign ministers held in Paraguay in May of that year, Latin American representatives discussed possible alternatives to the certification process, by then regarded as an unilaterally illegitimate mechanism.

The lack of standard criteria to assess the efforts deployed by different countries and the distortion of certifications by the dynamics of U.S. domestic politics became the main targets of the mounting criticism. However, in spite of its deficiencies and the presence of more impartial alternatives (such as the annual report of the UN International Narcotics Control Board), the balance has not yet swung against the certification process. Although Barry MacCaffrey, the U.S. drug czar, acknowledged many of the flaws present in the certification process, it is likely to remain in place, largely because U.S. politicians, including the president, have much to lose by appearing weak on the drug issue. A change in policy has only been contemplated by U.S. authorities, including MacCaffrey, in the context of an unthinkable "success of international antinarcotic cooperation" in the future.

In the meantime certification continued to proceed on the assumption that it could compel governments to devote much-needed attention to drug trafficking, violence, and corruption that also threaten economic and political stability in their countries. However, the key question may not concern the potential for success or otherwise of this process, but the extent to which the same antinarcotic policies are responsible for such chronic instability as described above.[57]

Clearly, since the mid-1980s the definition by the U.S. government of the drug problem as a "security" issue paved the way to costly military responses to particularly complex problems, and foreshadowed new grounds for foreign intervention. The vulnerability of states to intervention has indeed increased, as first became clear with the U.S. military actions leading to the invasion of Panama in 1989.

The militarization of the war against drugs could not only endanger democratic rule and sovereign state institutions (in countries other than Panama) but also entails important regional security implications.[58] These range from violent resistance against antinarcotic policies, to shifts in regional military balances consequent upon arms transfers originally aimed at strengthening the capabilities of states besieged by drug traffickers.[59]

Democratic Vulnerability and State Strength

Dominant views about drug trafficking, transnational organized crime, and available policy options proceed on the assumption of the "formal equality of states." As should now be evident, the view presented here is that the actual weight of inequalities among states matters. So too does the nature of the regime, although in a more complex manner. Three preliminary observations are in order: first, that democratic regimes seem particularly vulnerable to various forms of blackmail and penetration by drug traffickers; second, many of the successful antinarcotic experiences reviewed in the literature have taken place within nondemocratic frameworks; and third, that the effects of transnational crime on government, economic performance, and the rule of law are nowhere equal. The comparison between the behavior of a democratic government and an authoritarian regime when faced with the threat of drug trafficking may shed some light on their relative capacities to contain the threat posed by international organized crime.

Like economic crises, IOC is a phenomenon that can strike these regimes equally. Unlike economic crises however, IOC unleashes a set of questions that go to the heart of the very constitutional basis of the state it attacks. If a democratic government finds itself threatened by these forms of crime, then its margin of maneuver will be seriously constrained by the rule of law, by the principle that government must be conducted according to law. If, on the other hand, we are dealing with an authoritarian regime, then that principle will not hold. To the degree that this regime is not subject to the control of law, the degrees to which it can disregard, manipulate, or overtly violate the rule of law, its margin of maneuver will consequently be widened.[60]

This contrast can be deepened if we look at the situation through the eyes of the criminal organizations themselves. Transnational organized crime, in particular drug trafficking, is of course an economic activity, but it is also characterized by political tendencies, the most pronounced of which is the infiltration of the political systems of the states within which it operates. A political system in which law making and judicial procedure are guided by the principles of impartiality and transparency might be more inviting to the criminal organizations than one which is closed. To mention the particularly dramatic example of Colombia, the legislature spent considerable time agonizing over the status of both the citizenship rights of its criminals, and—in attempting to draw a line between drug trafficking and narco-terrorism—the sui generis nature of their crime. Meanwhile in Chile, the dictator General Pinochet was able to pack the country's cartel leaders on a plane. The execution of General Ochoa on drug charges in Castro's Cuba provides another more ambiguous, but perhaps relevant, example of the capacity of authoritarian governments to control and regulate IOC. It is true that authoritarian governments such as General Noriega's in Panama could rely on the state apparatus to "administer" illicit markets. But this may also make these regimes more vulnerable to external intervention on both democratic and antinarcotic grounds.

Whereas democratic governments, when hit by organized crime appear to face an uncomfortable dilemma. They can opt for paralysis, by allowing criminals to take advantage of the loopholes within the law which represent their margin of political maneuver, they can set in motion antinarcotic policies which may well breach the rule of law by impinging on individual rights. As they combat one form of unregulated violence with another form of organized force, democratic governments may put us in mind of their contender, the authoritarian regime. Experiences like that of the case of Colombia teach us that it is possible for a democracy to sit on both horns of the dilemma at the same time.

It thus seems reasonable to conclude that democratic governments can get into troubles with drug trafficking and other forms of organized crime. But when they do, is this a sign that we are dealing with a weak democratic government, or with a particularly vulnerable juncture? Would it be possible to argue that the levels of uncertainty that often accompany democratic change can easily complicate the efforts of governments to maintain law and order? In Colombia (and more recently in Mexico) ambitious political reforms aimed at the liberalization and democratization of the political regime in fact coexisted with a period of rapid decay of public authority. The depth of the coincidence between the spread of democracy in Latin America and the spread of drug trafficking is at the least noteworthy.

Whatever one makes of that coincidence, periods of rapid change in the rules and institutions that govern political behavior and keep political systems in place can easily be exploited by powerful criminals seeking to advance their interests. Thus the infiltration by drug traffickers of the legislative or executive branches of government in order to gain additional immunity and to influence economic and political decisions has led some observers to refer to these states as "narcodemocracies" or "crime-challenged neo-democracies."[61]

Although states in these conditions can adopt safeguards to try to protect democratic institutions, what is incontrovertible is that the drug trade represents a major threat to democratic stability. The financial and armed power in the hands of drug traffickers has enabled these actors to fund political organizations and candidates, to intimidate aspirants, and to disrupt the electoral calendar. As the Colombian experience has amply demonstrated, these objectives are either pursued by corrupting and buying political actors, or through naked terrorist actions.[62]

Undoubtedly more shocking has been the determination of drug barons to engage in politics through directly violent means. It was indeed the systematic use of violence to confront the authorities and impede the state's actions which led to the coining of the term *narco-terrorism*. In Colombia the threat of extradition became the engine of a frontal attack by drug traffickers against the state. The subsequent "extradition war" produced the assassination in 1987 of the Attorney General Carlos Mauró Hoyos; the murder in 1989 of the presidential candidate Luis Carlos Galán and two other presidential candidates one year later; the blowing up of a civilian aircraft; and the destruction of the Departamento Administrativo de la Seguridad (DAS).[63]

In Mexico, although the capacity of drug traffickers to buy protection from government institutions came out into the open at the start of the 1990s, by the end of the decade it reached unanticipated levels. Similarly, the escalation of violence became dramatically visible as the decade came to its close. While evidence pointing to open political aspirations on the part of the drug traffickers has not been clear, the government's regulations regarding party finance sought to provide safeguards against this very possibility, while a rash of political assassinations raised concern about potential links within the body politic with drug trafficking.[64] In the context of increased violence along the U.S.-Mexican border, the U.S. drug czar MacCaffrey acknowledged that Mexico had become the target of a violent campaign carried out by powerful international criminal organizations representing an important threat for the viability of democratic institutions.

Concluding Remarks

The vulnerability of states became more acute as a new generation of more sophisticated and better-adapting drug-trafficking and criminal organizations emerged in the late 1970s. The drug organizations that proliferated throughout the 1980s have been characterized by their immediate access to exorbitant financial resources, their capacity to integrate and subcontract logistical services, to build their own private armies, to administer large-scale processing laboratories, as well as by their access to cutting-edge transport, smuggling, and money-laundering technologies.

Indeed, not only do trafficking organizations adapt and survive in Darwinian manner, making subsequent control efforts ever-more challenging, but also the latter are often accompanied by counterproductive and perverse effects. If one pursues the Darwinian analogy further, then one can conclude both that criminal transnational bodies show every sign of succeeding in making more complex adaptations in the future and that the cost of this success may increasingly be borne by the democratic states in the region, already struggling as they are to survive in the new global world economy.

Notes

1. Susan Strange, *The Retreat of the State: The Diffusion of Power in the World Economy* (Cambridge: Cambridge University Press, 1996), 73–82; David Keen, *The Economic Functions of Violence in Civil Wars,* Adelphi Paper Series No. 320 (Oxford: Oxford University Press for IISS, 1998); and William Zartman, "Introduction: Posing the Problem of State Collapse," in *Collapsed States: The Disintegration and Restoration of Legitimate Authority,* ed. W. Zartman (Boulder and London: Lynne Rienner Publishers, 1998), 1.

2. Andrew Hurrell and Ngaire Woods, "Globalization and Inequality," *Millennium* 24, no. 3 (1995): 458–60; Evelyn Huber, "Assessments of State Strength," in *Latin America in Comparative Perspective,* ed. Peter Smith (Boulder: Westview Press, 1995), 185.

3. Susan Strange, *Rival States, Rival Firms: Competition for World Market Shares* (Cambridge: Cambridge University Press, 1991), 19–20; and Strange, *The Retreat of the State,* 13–14.

4. Strange, *The Retreat of the State,* 73–82.

5. Strange, *The Retreat of the State,* 92–93; and Paul B. Stares, *Global Habit: The Drug Problem in a Borderless World* (Washington, D.C.: The Brookings Institution, 1996), 52.

6. This has been particularly clear in the activities deployed by drug cartels. See, among others, Strange, *The Retreat of the State,* 113–114; and Stares, *Global Habit.*

7. The connection between trade liberalization and international organized crime is neither necessary nor direct. This might be particularly the case within regional integration schemes, where trade liberalization has often increased intraregional trade. However, under certain circumstances, the reduction of trade barriers can facilitate the smuggling of illicit merchandise. This could be the case in the weakest flank of an economic area, or with items like illicit drugs, which can be concealed easily by smugglers and dealers.

8. Such decisions are also influenced by the magnitude of the pressures exerted by the implementation of antinarcotic policies. Consequently greater police pressure in Colombia could also account for the migration of Colombian drug traffickers toward Mexico and Brazil. Similarly, the intensification of the antinarcotics campaign in Mexico could have led Amado Carrillo to consider relocating his cartel's operations in Chile. *Reforma* (Mexico) Mar. 18 and May 28, 1998.

9. *Reforma,* Feb. 4 and 14, 1998.

10. See the declarations of Vladimir Vasiliev, deputy minister for the interior, reported in *El País* (Spain), Nov. 26, 1997; and *Reforma,* Feb. 4, 1998.

11. *Annual Report on Organized Crime in Canada 1997* reported in *Reforma,* Mar. 9, 1998.

12. Phil Williams, "Transnational Criminal Organizations and International Security," *Survival* 36, no. 1 (spring 1994): 97.

13. Stares, *Global Habit,* 69; *La Jornada* (Mexico), May 17 and Aug. 30, 1997.

14. Patrick Dunleavy and Brendan O'Leary, *Theories of the State: The Politics of Liberal Democracy* (London: MacMillan, 1987), 293–94.

15. Strange, *Rival States, Rival Firms*, 3; and Dunleavy and O'Leary, *Theories of the State*, 295.

16. Hurrell and Woods, "Globalization and Inequality," 453–56.

17. Mónica Serrano, "Latin America," in *The New Security Agenda: A Global Survey*, ed. Paul Stares (Tokyo: Japan Center for International Exchange, 1998).

18. As Nadelmann has pointed out, in the absence of substitutability, prohibition laws tend to affect the nature of the activity and the market, but they hardly influence the decisions of those determined to participate in the activity. Ethan A. Nadelman, "Global Prohibition Regimes: The evolution of Norms in International Society," *International Organization* 44, no.4 (autumn 1990): 512.

19. Laurence Whitehead, "Mexico's 'Near Ungovernability' Revisited," in *Governing Mexico: Political Parties and Elections*, ed. M. Serrano (London: Institute of Latin American Studies, 1998).

20. Stares, *Global Habit*, 95–96; and Jorge Orlando Melo, "The Drug-Trade, Politics and the Economy: The Colombian Experience," in *Latin America and the Multinational Drug-Trade*, ed. Elizabeth Joyce and Carlos Malamud (London: MacMillan in association with the Institute of Latin American Studies, 1998).

21. Fernando Cepeda Ulloa, "Introduction," in Joyce and Malamud, eds., *Latin America and the Multilateral Drug-Trade;* and Procuraduría General de la República, *XVI International Drug Enforcement Conference* (IDEC XIV Proceedings) México D.F., Procuraduría General de la República, Apr. 1996.

22. Orlando Melo, "The Drug-Trade, Politics and the Economy," 73.

23. Orlando Melo, "The Drug-Trade, Politics and the Economy," 82; Stares, *Global Habit*, 64; Washington Office on Latin America, "The Colombian National Police, Human Rights and US Drug Policy," Washington, D.C., May 1993.

24. *Reforma*, Aug. 23, 1997; and *La Jornada*, Aug. 30, 1997.

25. *Armed fragmentation* refers to the process by which the cohesion of the armed forces could be threatened by an officer holding control over a significant number of soldiers. This was the potential challenge posed by the former drug czar General Gutiérrez Rebollo who maintained control both of the military zone and of police corps in the state of Jalisco. Mónica Serrano, "Drug-Trafficking and Militarization: The Case of Mexico" (paper prepared for the conference "States of Violence: The Limits to National Sovereignty in Mexico," London, Institute of Latin American Studies, Nov. 1997).

26. Orlando Melo, "The Drug-Trade, Politics and the Economy," 83; Serrano, "Drug-Trafficking and Militarization"; A. Valenzuela, "Yes to Certification," *Washington Post*, Mar. 9, 1997; and *Reforma* June 2, 1998.

27. Edgar Reveiz, Javier Torres, and Mónica Hurtado, "Reforma política y proceso de decisión sobre el gasto en seguridad en Colombia: una economía para la paz," in *Gasto militar en América Latina: Procesos de decisiones y actores claves*, ed. Francisco Rojas Aravena (Santiago de Chile, and San Francisco, Calif.: CNDE and FLACSO, 1994), 217–20; Orlando Melo, "The Drug-Trade, Politics and the Economy," 89; Serrano, "Mexico: El pacto cívico-militar en los noventa," *L' Ordinaire Latinoamericain* no. 169 (Jui.–Sept. 1997): 93–106.

28. Malcom Deas, "Canjes violentos: reflexiones sobre la violencia política en Colombia," in *Dos ensayos especulativos sobre la violencia en Colombia*, ed. M. Deas and Fernando Gaitán Daza (Bogotá: FONADE/DNP, 1995), 23–24.

29. Gonzalo Sánchez, "Colombia: Violencias sin futuro," *Foro Internacional* 38, no. 1 (1998).

30. Between 1989 and 1992 the rate of intentional deaths was of 77.5 per 100,000 inhabitants. The homicide rate in Colombia is three times that of Brazil, the second most violent country in Latin America, and seventeen times that of Uruguay, the most "peaceful" country in the region. Sánchez, "Colombia: Violencias sin futuro."

31. Sánchez, "Colombia: Violencias sin futuro."

32. Cepeda Ulloa "Introduction," 10; and Orlando Melo "The Drug-Trade, Politics and the Economy," 80.

33. Richard B. Craig, "Mexican Narcotics Traffic: Binational Security Implications," in *The Latin American Narcotics Trade and US National Security*, ed. D. J. Mabry (New York,

Greenwood Press, 1989), 31; and Roderic A. Camp, *Generals in the Palacio: The Military in Modern Mexico* (New York: Oxford University Press, 1992).

34. David Keen, "When War Itself Is Privatized," *The Times Literary Supplement*, Dec. 29, 1995; Daniel Pecaut, "Presente, pasado y futuro de la violencia," *Análisis Político*, no. 30 (Jan.–Apr. 1997); Keen, *Economic Functions of Violence.*

35. In Southeast Asia, first France and subsequently the U.S. government relied on this trade to underwrite covert operations. Similarly, in Afghanistan, Pakistan, Burma, Peru, and Colombia, drug profits have helped support local insurgencies and separatist movements, while drug-related income has contributed to finance arms purchases for local conflicts in places like Somalia, Chiapas, Liberia, Kashmir, and the former Yugoslavia. Stares, *Global Habit*, 22, 54.

36. Orlando Melo, "The Drug-Trade, Politics and the Economy," 81.

37. María Celia Toro, "Mexico y Estados Unidos: el narcotráfico como amenaza a la seguridad nacional," in *En busca de la seguridad perdida: Aproximaciones a la seguridad nacional mexicana*, ed. Sergio Aguayo and Bruce Bagley (México D.F.: Siglo XXI Editores, 1990), 374; Jorge Chabat, "El narcotráfico en la relación México-Estados Unidos: lo que se ve es lo que hay," *Estados Unidos: Informe Trimestral* III, no. 3 (autumn): 5–14.

38. See David E. Apter, "Political Violence in Analytical Perspective," in *The Legitimization of Violence*, ed. D. E. Apter (New York: New York University Press, 1997), 12–15.

39. Orlando Melo, "The Drug-Trade, Politics and the Economy," 80–81; Eduardo Pizarro Leongómez, *Las FARC (1949–1966); De la Autodefensa a la combinación de todas las formas de lucha* (Bogotá: Instituto de Estudios Políticos y Relaciones Internacionales/Tercer Mundo Editores, 1991), 110.

40. Sánchez, "Colombia: Violencias sin futuro."

41. Keen, *Economic Functions of Violence*, 12, 17.

42. Jorge Chabat, "Seguridad Nacional y Narcotráfico: vínculos reales e imaginarios," *Política y Gobierno* 1, no. 1 (Jan.–June 1994): 112.

43. Keen, *Economic Functions of Violence*, 11.

44. Reacting to Mexican demands the U.S. government has more recently agreed to reduce from four- to one-year export arms permits. While in Mexico President Zedillo submitted to Congress a number of amendments increasing the penalties for illegal possession or transport of arms. *Reforma*, Dec. 10, 1996; Apr. 21, 1997; Feb. 8 and 14, 1998; and Apr. 29, 1998.

45. In Colombia, the armed forces have traced the replacement of the Israeli Gali guns for AK-47. *Reforma*, Feb. 5, 1998.

46. Sánchez, "Colombia, Violencias sin Futuro."

47. In an effort to combat rising kidnappings, in February of this year the Mexican Office of the General Attorney, jointly with the governments of nine states, decided to set up a new elite force. The Yaqui Group brings together ninety members of different state-judicial police forces that have received special training provided by retired Israeli military officers and French antikidnapping police units. Other measures include the creation of a data base, a register to be operated by the Specialized Unit of Kidnapping Research at the Office of the General Attorney as well as tentative plans to set up a security tax. *La Jornada*, May 5, 1998; *Reforma*, May 29, 1998; *Reforma*, May 31 and June 3, 1998.

48. Keen, *Economic Functions of Violence*, 33.

49. Investigations about police and military protection offered to drug lords spread in Mexico in the late 1990s. One of the most alarming cases was the arrest of the drug czar General Gutiérrez Rebollo in 1997.

50. As mentioned earlier, in Morelos more than 25 percent of the members of police corps resigned or were dismissed. The former head of the Morelos antikidnapping group, Armando Martínez Salgado, now under arrest, is among those suspected of granting police protection to criminals and responsible for turning the state into a haven of criminals and drug traffickers. *El País*, May 14, 1998; *Reforma*, May 30, 1998.

51. See Serrano, "Latin America"; and International Institute for Strategic Studies, *The Military Balance* (London: Oxford University Press for the IISS, 1997), 199.

52. M. C. Toro, "México y Estados Unidos," 367; Stares, *Global Habit*, 28–29; Guadalupe

González, "Régimen internacional y políticas nacionales de control de drogas: un análisis comparado de México y Colombia," in *Regionalismo y poder en América: los límites del neo-realismo*, ed. Arturo Borja et al. (México D.F.: Miguel Angel Porrúa/CIDE, 1996).

53. *Oxford Analytica*, Latin America Daily Brief, Mar. 4, 1997; The Latin American Program, "Drug Certification and US Policy in Latin America," Woodrow Wilson Center for Scholars, Apr. 1998; and Elizabeth Joyce, "Conclusion," in Joyce and Malamud, eds., *Latin America and the Multinational Drug-Trade*.

54. Orlando Melo emphasizes President Samper's success in imprisoning the leading "barons" of the Cali cartel and the significant increase registered in the volumes of drugs seized and crops destroyed during this administration. See Orlando Melo, "The Drug-Trade, Politics and the Economy," 96, n. 18.

55. Colombia had become the country with the largest number of hectares of coca cultivation. In 1996 a report by the inspector general of the State Department maintained that "the certification process has had limited success in improving counternarcotics performance overseas." According to some views, one year later, anticipating decertification, the Colombian authorities considered abandoning the eradication campaign altogether. See *La Jornada*, Mar. 7, 1997; and The Latin American Program, "Drug Certification and US Policy in Latin America," Apr. 1998.

56. Joyce, "Conclusion," 201–2.

57. *Oxford Analytica*, Latin America Daily Brief, Mar. 4, 1997; *La Jornada*, Mar. 7, 1997; *Reforma*, May 17, 1997; and *Reforma*, Feb. 7, 1998.

58. In Colombia, more vigorous eradication campaigns prompted angry farmers to occupy oil stations in 1994, a move that had international implications as it blocked the flow of Ecuadorian oil to the Pacific coast. In 1996 farmers occupied local airports to prevent the takeoff of eradicating planes. Most dramatically, as antinarcotic police measures stepped up in Colombia, police forces became the target of attacks by drug traffickers. Stares, *Global Habit*, 64; and Washington Office for Latin America, "The Colombian National Police, Human Rights and US Drug Policy" (Washington, D.C., 1993), 12, 14.

59. Under the Bush administration Colombia received more U.S. narcotics-related assistance than any other country. Total economic, military, and law enforcement assistance increased from $14 million to $143 million between 1988 and 1992. Military aid jumped from $4 million in 1988 to $92.3 million in 1990. Although the deterioration of relations with the United States leading to the 1996 decertification underlay the decline in U.S. assistance, the resumption of narcotics-related aid and new transfers of military equipment were announced in mid-August 1997. See WOLA, "The Colombian National Police," 3–5; and *Reforma*, Aug. 16, 1997; and *La Jornada*, Aug. 18, 1997.

60. As Nadelmann has pointed out criminal activities such as the trade of illicit narcotics are more likely to be effectively suppressed in those states "able and willing to employ totalitarian measures" or "states whose laws are bolstered by strong social sanctions." We could thus infer that drug trafficking is not only assisted by the relative ease with which drugs are produced, smuggled, and traded but also, above all, by the lack of all-embracing consensus needed to sustain the prohibition. See Ethan Nadelmann, "Global Prohibition Regimes," *International Organization* 44 (autumn 1990): 479–526, 486, n. 14.

61. Stares, *Global Habit*, 97; and Whitehead, "Mexico's 'Near Ungovernability' Revisited."

62. Cepeda Ulloa, "Introduction," 7.

63. Orlando Melo, "The Drug-Trade, Politics and the Economy," 71–72.

64. The assassination of more than seven delegates of the Office of the Attorney General in Baja California, most of whom collaborated in the northern office between 1994 and 1996 awoke speculation and rumors about a possible link with the murder of the Luis Donaldo Colosio in 1994. *Reforma*, July 18, Sept.15 and 23, 1996; and *Reforma*, Feb. 14, 1998.

PART TWO

Finance and Trade: Threats from International Shocks and the Search for Growth

6

International Financial Institutions: Changing Perspectives and Policy Prescriptions

WENDY HUNTER

Since their founding, the World Bank, Inter-American Development Bank (IDB), and International Monetary Fund have undergone a series of important changes with respect to the intensity of their intervention in the economies of Latin America, as well as the extensiveness of their reach into extraeconomic policy areas such as administrative reform and governance (e.g., the control of corruption and crime). Throughout their existence they have sought to be organizations with a distinctive development mission (especially the World Bank and IDB) as well as lending institutions in the conventional sense. But at times, emphasis has been placed on one role over the other. In their ideal self-conception, the influence they yield on borrowers stems not only from the money they disburse but also the knowledge and ideas they disseminate. Attempting to maintain the dual status of development organization/bank has not been an easy road to follow. It has generated internal tensions as well as external criticism. Acting in accordance with the strict economic calculations of banks has subjected international financial institutions (IFIs) to charges of insensitivity by developing countries and exhortations to broaden their concerns by First World nongovernment organizations (NGOs). But playing an expanded role in development carries risks of its own. For one, it often entails entry into sensitive political and social terrain, generating further criticism among Third World borrowers. How IFIs have responded to increasing public scrutiny has had important implications for issues ranging from the kinds of projects and programs they have pursued to the kinds of personnel they have hired to design and implement them.

    This chapter traces the evolution of IFI influence toward Latin America from the 1960s onward: the *intensity* of their influence over the economies of the region and the *extensiveness* of their reach (i.e., beyond the economy and into society and politics). It focuses on economic conditions and ideas about development as factors that have affected these variables. It ponders the following questions and arrives at some tentative answers. Where do the ideas that IFIs promote come from, from academic economists, experts within international organizations, or from states themselves? What is the role of economic and other events in shaping such ideas? Which ideas gain attention and become adopted, and why? What difference does leadership make in the policy orientation and effectiveness of IFIs?

This chapter emphasizes developments that have occurred in the last decade, asking what caused the shift in emphasis from market reform, narrowly construed, to the reform of social and political institutions, broadly conceived, in the 1990s? In other words, why did IFIs adopt a broader and more flexible approach after having prescribed strict recipes for stabilization and adjustment in the depth of economic crisis. I describe and explain the recent expansion of organizational goals—especially of the World Bank—as a response to the successful stabilization of many Latin American economies, the recognition that economic growth has been limited despite stabilization, and public criticism that the Bank address new issues, including governance, environmental, and human-resource related concerns. I conclude by pondering the consequences of recently expanded organizational goals for the public profile and internal composition of IFIs, the quality and effectiveness of their development projects (especially in an era of declining funds) and their ability to remain politically neutral vis-à-vis their clients.

Before proceeding, it should be noted explicitly that the evolution of IFI thinking that the chapter lays out—presented in the form of a decade-by-decade chronology—raises to prominence the changes that have occurred over time. These changes include real shifts as well as the "spin" put on programs by IFI leaders as they tack and weave through the forces of time. I focus less on continuity but draw attention to important elements of constancy where relevant. Two additional caveats are in order. First, there exist important differences among IFIs with respect to some of the general claims made about them in this chapter. Second, the considerable internal political complexity of IFIs should be borne in mind when understanding claims made even about specific IFIs. With respect to the first note of caution, the evolution of the ideas and the policy responses to them described below apply more to the World Bank and Inter-American Development Bank than to the IMF. For the most part, the World Bank and IDB have defined their mandates as agents of development in broader terms (with policies intended to apply over a longer-time horizon) than the IMF, whose organizational mission since its founding in 1944 has remained more narrowly confined to issues of short- and medium-term economic stabilization and fiscal adjustment. In exchange for providing loans, it has stipulated conditions—like austerity and high interest rates to bolster national currencies—that can trigger unemployment, recession, and political backlash.

In recent years, however, even the IMF has become somewhat more flexible and begun to adopt a slightly wider agenda (e.g., in the Mexican crisis of 1995 and more recently in Indonesia). It has become more aware of questions of political sustainability and the distributive consequences of its policies, as reflected in allowing greater spending to sustain subsidies in places like Indonesia, South Korea, and elsewhere, becoming more flexible on full repayment, and backing away from one of its standard austerity demands: a budget surplus.[1] Also, IMF conditionality has evolved in ways that concede some of the arguments of its critics. For example, the organization is increasingly sensitive to the criticism that it props up dictators and allows corruption or crony capitalism to persist. In Indonesia, for instance, the IMF forced the breakup of monopolies and an end to government aid to business ventures run by President Suharto's family and friends. Change of this kind has been limited, however, and criticism persists. Among the organization's most vocal critics of late has been its sister institution, the World Bank. With poverty alleviation remaining its main charge, the Bank has gone to great lengths to differentiate itself from the IMF.[2] In a speech to finance ministers and central bank governors from 182 nations meeting in Washington, D.C. in October 1998, Bank president James D. Wolfensohn argued that too little attention was being paid to poverty and to political stability in the rush to stabilize currencies and bring about economic reform.[3]

Important differences also exist between the World Bank and IDB. As discussed at greater length below, the IDB has a longer tradition than the World Bank in emphasizing antipoverty programs. It also initiated structural adjustment lending much later. The IDB, in which Latin American countries constitute the majority of shareholders and U.S. influence is less predominant (albeit still considerable), is arguably more popular among borrowing member nations than the World Bank. The comparative closeness of its relationship to borrowers is often said to provide the IDB with a greater ability to identify, design, and implement worthwhile projects. At the same time, inside observers acknowledge that patterns and practices deleterious to development often go unchecked given that the IDB leadership overlaps with the governments and officials associated with these compromising practices.[4]

With respect to the internal complexity of IFIs, a host of other factors condition the operation of any given program and the establishment, continuation, and markedness of any given trend. These factors include the specific project-type, sector, and country-team. The internal diversity of the international lending organizations at hand even extends to a matter as basic as field offices, which are present in some countries and not in others. The existence of a field office is significant insofar as it enhances the potential for closer communication between a bank and a borrowing member country and greater responsiveness on the part of the bank to local conditions. It also improves a bank's capacity to monitor programs. In short, a complete understanding of any specific IFI must include an appreciation for its internal diversity, something acknowledged but not treated at length in this chapter.

IFI Approaches over Time

Since the 1960s, the World Bank, Inter-American Development Bank, and to a lesser extent the International Monetary Fund have expanded their conception of what it means for a country to be developed, and their appreciation of how complex and difficult the development process is. Accordingly, they have taken on new roles and ventured into previously uncharted areas of borrowing member countries. Social and environmental considerations, in addition to technical criteria, have gained in importance over time. This shift has even influenced the kinds of personnel that fill their ranks. While economists still predominate in all three of these IFIs, progress has been made to harness the expertise of other kinds of social scientists as well.

Academic economists, development experts, and even IFI leaders (albeit to a lesser extent) have been the main sources of the changing views traced below. Events such as economic crises have often had a huge impact on shaping their ideas and, consequently, on development trends. In the complex interplay between the realm of ideas and real-life events, IFIs have been consumers as well as producers and exporters of development thinking. The political aptitude and commitment of IFI leaders to a given school of thought seems to make a difference in how thoroughly related policies get adopted.[5]

1960s

The central tenets of modernization theory informed IFI conduct in the 1960s. According to the modernization paradigm, economic growth would lead naturally to greater social equity as well as to political democracy.[6] This belief was politically convenient insofar as it kept multilateral lending agencies from having to confront social and political issues more directly. The subjects covered by the World Bank, however, were wider ranging than those of the IMF, a tradition that existed since the two multilaterals were established in the wake of WWII.[7] Nevertheless, under the premise that economic growth would engender economic distribution and political participation, coupled with a fair degree of optimism about Latin America's economic future, IFIs confined their policy initiatives largely to the economic realm: while the IMF concentrated on short-term economic stabilization, the World Bank and IDB emphasized the building of economic infrastructure.[8] In the years between 1950 and 1969, the World Bank committed 62.5 percent of lending to infrastructure (telecommunications, transportation, electric power, and other energy) and only 2 percent to the social sector (education, environment, population, urban development, water supply, and sanitation).[9] Similarly, after 1965, the IDB made a clear shift into lending policies that favored the productive sector and economic infrastructure projects. By 1965, the level of support for housing, water and sewer programs, and education (15 percent, 19 percent, and 2 percent, respectively) had dropped significantly from what it had been in 1962 (27.8 percent, 26.6 percent, and 3.7 percent). At the same time, funds dedicated to industry and mining more than doubled in these years (from 11.7 to 26 percent). By 1968, economic infrastructure had become dominant, taking up 48.5 percent of total lending allocations.[10]

In addition to the prevailing idea that "all things good" would ensue from economic growth, there were political reasons for focusing on narrow economic matters. In the context of the cold war, having an apolitical profile lent itself to working with as many kinds of governments as possible. This mattered less for regional organizations like the IDB than for ones thoroughly dominated by Western powers such as the IMF and World Bank, which since the 1950s had made a point of casting themselves as technocracies. The Articles of Agreement of the World Bank contain formal rules governing the World Bank's commitment to political neutrality—more specifically, the prohibition of political criteria in lending decisions. Yet they constitute a flexible document that the Bank itself reserves the right to interpret.[11]

The relatively favorable economic situation that existed throughout the 1960s inhibited deeper IFI involvement in the economies of the region as well. Under these conditions, the imposition of strict conditionality was not as necessary or as possible as in the 1980s and 1990s, when widespread economic crisis led the World Bank to divert its attention away from poverty initiatives and to focus more on macroeconomic problems and solutions (including structural adjustment and sectoral adjustment loans with policy conditioning of the type commonly associated with the IMF) and constrained countries to adhere to such adjustment programs. Whereas Brazilian President Juscelino Kubitschek (1956–1961) denounced IMF conditions in 1959 and proceeded with his own economic program just one year after agreeing to a tough stabilization program,[12] most presidents of major Latin American countries in the 1990s (e.g., Carlos Menem of Argentina, Alberto Fujimori of Peru, and Fernando Henrique Cardoso of Brazil) signed onto the "Washington Consensus," implementing tough stabilization plans and taking steps to restructure their economies.[13]

1970s

In the late 1960s and early 1970s, development economists shifted the focus of their attention away from the creation of aggregate wealth to the issue of distribution.[14] Latin American social scientists spearheaded the dependency approach to development. The idea that growth and distribution might be more contradictory than compatible gained sway.[15] The growing recognition that economic growth fell far short in alleviating poverty and enhancing equity in the developing world led the World Bank, under the energetic leadership of Robert McNamara from 1968 to 1979, to include and push "basic needs" in its agenda.[16] Education and welfare for the population, and not just the infrastructural trappings of modernity (e.g., tall buildings, pharaonic bridges, and dams) came to be understood as integral to "development." Although concerns about global poverty had been expressed prior to McNamara's appearance at the Bank, according to Martha Finnemore, "What McNamara and the Bank did was to institutionalize this concern, to make it an inextricable part of what development was all about."[17]

Robert McNamara was vital in the Bank's adoption of the basic needs perspective. For him, it was a moral imperative of wealthy nations to help the poor. Moreover, it was in their security interest insofar as poverty and gross disparities in welfare were frequently a cause of violence. Conflict stemming from poverty was often of a kind that military power faced limits in eliminating. McNamara articulated such views while still secretary of defense. And he put the full power of his position at the Bank behind an effort to revise development norms in the direction of poverty alleviation and to promulgate such views in the international system. The initial years of McNamara's tenure gave rise to studies sponsored by the Bank that showed the failure of most Third World growth strategies to achieve significant "trickle-down" effects. McNamara then commissioned more studies and brought into the Bank's orbit leading development economists like Hollis Chenery and experts in areas like education and population to propose new ideas about poverty alleviation. Many of these experts came from academic circles. Without the impetus, coordinating effort, and resources provided by the Bank, however, it is unlikely that their ideas would have coalesced and received such mainstream acceptance.

Also in the 1970s, Latin American governments began to play the dependency card, emphasizing the unequal distribution of wealth *between* the First and Third World and calling for a New International Economic Order to enhance the power of the latter. But LDCs as a whole were not pushing multilateral development banks to redirect their loans and projects toward poverty alleviation. The impetus came from IOs and development experts in the developed world.[18] Partly in response to the challenge posed by dependency theory, analysts in First World development circles underscored the inequitable distribution of wealth and privilege *within* most LDCs, thereby questioning the legitimacy of elites in these societies. Focusing its research, aid, and development projects increasingly on the poor (to compensate for the failure of LDC governments to do so themselves) the World Bank began to tread on social and political ground, generating greater controversy than the prior focus on economic development narrowly defined.

World Bank projects came to reflect a heightened concern with alleviating poverty and enhancing "human capital," launched with the hope that specific projects of this kind would bring about more equitable behavior in general by borrowers. Allocations directed to the social sector increased slightly over three times in the 1970s from where they stood in the prior decade (from 4 to 13 percent). This trend continued in the next two decades, as social expenditures climbed to 15 and 26 percent of total funds, respectively. At the same time, loans for economic infrastructure fell from 64 percent in the period 1960–1969 to 36 percent in the period 1970–1979, continuing to fall to 29 percent (1980–1989) and then to 24 percent (1990–1995).[19] The trend toward "basic needs" activism did not yet apply to the IDB in the 1970s, however. In fact, the IDB shifted more clearly into infrastructure in that decade, and lending to social sectors suffered, decreasing to 15 percent, down from nearly 25 percent of total lending in the 1960s. It took until the 1980s for the IDB to move in the same direction as the Bank. Social sectors transfers increased threefold in the 1979–1981 period alone.[20]

While the social sector at the World Bank grew in significance, aggressive measures of redistribution like land reform were not among the projects the World Bank pursued. Doubtless such measures would have generated greater political resistance among unwilling borrowers, which Bank officials were not willing to stand up to. If only to enhance the political viability of implementing such measures, the Bank would also have been obligated to hire a host of personnel other than economists and financial specialists, by far the predominant profession found within the institution. The shift two decades later to issues involving sectoral reform and governance, even more so, would require the Bank to venture into tricky political zones.

While the World Bank expanded the scope of its projects over Latin America and the rest of the developing world (with the IDB retaining the range of its projects), the level of IFI intervention in the economies of Latin America did not change significantly in the 1970s. Despite the hardships imposed by the oil shocks of 1973 and 1979, most Latin American countries prolonged the facade of prosperity and postponed adjusting to new constraints by incurring huge debts. Not only did most governments in the region not restrain their spending but countries like Mexico and Brazil went as far as laying out larger sums of money to build up their infrastructure. Only later when the debt crisis erupted (after 1982), did the IMF and other IFIs gain much greater leverage over the region's economies.

1980s

The 1980s witnessed an intensification of IFI intervention in the economies of Latin America and a retrenchment of IFI engagement in extraeconomic affairs. In this decade, neoliberal ideas gained clear predominance within the

IFI community. Moving away from development models predicated on a high degree of state interventionism, World Bank and even IDB officials followed the IMF and embraced many of the central aspects of neoliberal economic reform.[21] With this embrace of market forces, the gap narrowed between the World Bank and the IDB, whose thinking had previously been closer to that of ECLA (Economic Commission for Latin America), a source of intellectual inspiration in the 1950s and 1960s for ideas about economic dependency and state-led development.

While the early to mid-1980s witnessed the implementation of heterodox programs in many crisis-ridden countries (e.g., Argentina under President Alfonsín [1983–1989], Brazil under Sarney [1985–1990], and Peru under García [1985–1990]), Latin America moved decisively into neoliberalism after IFI adherents to the "Washington Consensus" promoted the shift via the economic research and sector analyses they conducted, the lending practices and dialogue they engaged in, and the conditions they imposed on their borrowers. This is not to say that IFI influence was the sole factor behind the widespread adoption of neoliberal reforms. Barbara Stallings, among others, emphasizes the strong pressure that international financial institutions— whose power grew with the debt crisis—imposed on Latin American countries.[22] But certainly, the obvious failure of a number of heterodox programs and the model of success provided by Chile also helped motivate the shift.[23]

In any event, because most Latin American economies had entered dire straits after 1982, the region became much more subject to conditions stipulated by the IMF and World Bank. Thus, while the World Bank paused in trying to expand its influence on other fronts (namely, the social and political), it became more intensely engaged in macroeconomic reform.[24] Pushing for the control of hyperinflation and promoting profound adjustment became the order of the day. Yet the World Bank differed somewhat from the IMF in the specific policies it emphasized. While the IMF continued to emphasize short-term stabilization and the restoration of economic equilibrium (policies like budget balancing and correcting trade deficits), the Bank pushed more for measures that would promote long-term structural adjustment (privatization, trade reform, deregulation, and so on), which (as discussed below) have proven to be equally if not more difficult to enact.

The strong and unequivocal push by IFIs for stabilization and adjustment beginning in the late 1980s led developing country governments and citizens to criticize them for being insensitive to the social impact of their policies. At the same time, NGOs, international and domestic, stepped up the campaign against the banks for failing to consider adequately the concerns of women, indigenous peoples, and the environment in their policies.[25] World Bank officials seemed to respond more to criticism of this kind than did the IMF or the IDB. The IMF was more used to and seemingly more accepting of public condemnation. The IDB, which was less involved with adjustment measures in the first place,[26] was also more insulated from criticism over social insensitivities by virtue of its regionally based leadership. The degree to which NGO critics pressured Congress contributed to the Reagan administration's choice of a former congressman—Barber Conable to head the Bank in 1986.[27] Donor funding was at stake for the Bank in having a president who could cultivate good relations with NGOs, as well as shareholders. While Conable continued the markets and private sector shift begun under his predecessor, A. W. Clausen, he also paved the way for the Bank to respond to public concerns about the social impact of adjustment policy and about the special problems of women, indigenous people, and the environment.

1990s

If the 1980s were for the most part an era of IFI pressure for hard-core neoliberal adjustment, the late 1980s and the decade of the 1990s witnessed a recognition by IFIs (the World Bank and IDB and to a lesser extent the IMF) that the promotion of development rests on more than unleashing market forces. They have therefore further extended their efforts to influence extraeconomic pursuits. Under the ambitious and effective leadership of Enrique Iglesias since 1988, the IDB has embarked on a vigorous program of social sector investment, while continuing to support economic and political liberalization. The Eighth Replenishment, for which negotiations were completed in 1994, resulted in the IDB becoming the multilateral lender with the largest capacity to lend to the Latin American and Caribbean region.[28]

What extraeconomic policies have IFIs pursued in the 1990s? One set of such policies emphasizes measures designed to enhance the palatability and popularity of IFIs and their programs. In this category are social investment funds intended to improve the welfare of people affected by market reforms, and projects oriented toward NGOs and the constituencies they represent. Another set of these pursuits, of greater eventual consequence in my view, has to do with laying the institutional groundwork for improved economic and social policy outcomes. In this category are "second-wave" reforms (e.g., improving the efficiency of the public sector in areas like health and education) as well as reforms intended to enhance "governance" (e.g., controlling corruption and crime). Each of these new programs and goals are treated below.

With most Latin American economies now stabilized, IFIs (including the IMF) have grown increasingly concerned with keeping adjustment politically viable by alleviating its social costs and attending to political demands.[29] They recognize that losers must be compensated and winners created in order for structural adjustment to advance further. Their strong support for social emergency funds and targeted social programs (or "safety nets") like the Social

Development and Compensation Fund (FONCODES) in Peru, as well as their growing tendency to consult with nongovernmental groups (for example, labor unions) about the acceptability of harsh economic measures they are intent on implementing, attests to this concern.[30] Social investment funds vary in some respects from country to country, but they all share a number of key characteristics. They try to target their benefits at the poor. Most projects under their supervision are demand-driven and involve the participation of local community groups. And, more of the money they allocate goes to improve education, health, nutrition, water supply, and sanitation. The first social investment fund was established in Bolivia in 1986.[31]

Deciding to work more with NGOs and to address the concerns by them constituted an additional response (especially by the World Bank) to the need to build support for adjustment in developing socieities and to abate the criticisms launched by liberal constituencies who control swing votes in donor countries and hence are positioned to reduce available funds.[32] The World Bank has worked to engage NGOs as partners in project implementation. NGOs typically provide technical, organizational, and political services to underrepresented groups. They are thought to improve upon the implementation of projects and the delivery of services due to their closer contacts with civil society (relative to those of large multilateral banks) and greater ability to involve the beneficiaries of projects in their operation.[33] A less common but growing kind of collaboration is where NGOs exercise influence over the design and evaluation of World Bank projects. A formal channel for policy dialogue and cooperation with NGOs is the NGO-World Bank committee.[34] The Bank's linkage to NGOs has many positive ramifications. Nevertheless, some analysts have expressed a concern that the World Bank's efforts to enhance its popularity with relevant publics might be detracting from the technical quality of its projects and the soundness of its policies more broadly.[35]

An additional activity pursued by IFIs in the 1990s involves their efforts to promote institutional reforms (for example, privatization in sectors where nationalist symbolism is high, greater flexibility in labor markets, the redesigning of education, health, and social security systems, etc.). Coming after stabilization, these are often referred to as "second-wave" reforms.[36] What caused the shift in emphasis from market reform, narrowly conceived, to the broader reform of social and political institutions? Beyond the common tendency of ideas (especially in their extreme form) to experience a swing of the pendulum, the fact that economic growth after structural adjustment has not been as robust as IFI officials and neoliberal experts had expected suggests the necessity of implementing policies beyond simple stabilization and adjustment. In particular, social sector lending—with specifications about the design and operation of sectoral institutions—has been a convenient way for IFIs to combine the dual goals of growth (through efficiency) and equity. Improving upon the financing, allocation, and delivery of services makes more sense for development than issuing blanket spending cuts. It might even be expected to generate less public criticism than slashing expenditures but, as discussed below, many factors complicate the realization of such improvements.

Efforts to promote second-wave reforms have arguably proven more difficult and elusive than the adoption (albeit not easy) of IMF-style stabilization and liberalization measures. The less strictly technical *content* of "stage-two" reforms and the more complex decision-making *process* entailed in their approval and implementation have rendered difficult their unfolding. With respect to content: after the failure of heterodox reforms, a technical consensus formed around specific issues like cutting down inflation. In this connection, the influence of official experts (in this case, IFI officials) can be assumed to be at a maximum when it comes to highly technical fields like macroeconomic policy making.[37] Issues like how social security and education systems are to be reformed allow for greater latitude or choice (i.e., they are not strictly technical issues). Consequently, they invite greater debate and fuel greater contestation among social and political forces. Moreover, because external intervention in these less technical and more political areas seems less legitimate, IFIs are less able to influence them. With respect to the issue of process: while the earlier ("stage-one") reforms are launched by a small circle of high-level officials in an atmosphere of secrecy and crisis, when many citizens accept dramatic government action (at least temporarily) in order to stem further economic deterioration,[38] most institutional reforms are put in place over a longer time frame and in a more open political context. Such a context increases the likelihood that politicians and interest groups will intervene (against contending domestic forces as well as IFI directives) and block reform efforts that work against their interests.[39] Because efforts to implement most "stage-two" reforms have taken place in a noncrisis context (compared with stage-one reforms), forces opposed to them are less likely to swallow them and self-interested politicians less likely to try to push them through.

The heightened difficulty experienced by IFIs in overseeing the successful completion of stage-two institutional reforms—reforms that entail challenging specific vested groups, that call upon the bureaucratic will and authority to promote collective over particularistic interests, and that require broader long-term political support in a noncrisis context—provides a preview of the tremendous challenge that IFIs face ahead in the twenty-first century as they strive to go even further and promote reforms broadly conceived under the rubric of "governance."

"Governance"—which includes securing the rule of law, respecting property rights, controlling corruption and crime, and promoting accountability and participation (for example, through decentralization)—has become an important aspect of IFI discourse and policy innovation in the 1990s.[40] Some governance issues are mere extensions of what used to be called "administrative reform" and "capacity building." Others that involve explicitly political issues, such as the call for a free press, go beyond what IFIs have aspired to influence in the past. Analysts view Latin America—afflicted by a "triple curse" on markets: corruption, crime, and an unpredictable judiciary—as particularly prone to problems of governance.[41]

Governance-type reforms are rooted in the notion that the market needs to be embedded in appropriate political, social, and cultural institutions for development to occur and remain robust over the long run. One specific motivation to address such issues was the sorry state of sub-Saharan Africa's economic performance despite massive aid and compliance with IFI programs, raising into sharp relief the political/social roots of economic decay (ethnic-based politics, clientelism, and so forth). More generally, the broadening of the reform agenda from the economic realm to the political and social realms can be seen as a natural consequence of structural adjustment, which requires that IFI officials examine the details of government policy and its implementation.[42]

In this vein, the World Bank and IDB have begun to take much more seriously the idea that entrepreneurs are less likely to invest in a country if problems ranging from ordinary crime to arbitrary government action put their physical safety as well as capital investments at risk. Crime, they note, hinders economic growth not only because the resources spent combating it could otherwise be used for development but because it erodes the state's legitimacy overall.[43] Corruption, which also undermines the image of state effectiveness, imposes extra costs on business and increases fiscal costs by impeding the delivery of basic state services. Broad societal participation is valuable insofar as it indicates what demands exist, reduces information problems, and increases the legitimacy of governments.[44] Moreover, the existence of a strong and independent news media is vital to expose the negative consequences of phenomena like "crony capitalism." In his opening speech at the meeting of the World Bank and the International Monetary Fund in October 1998, Bank president James D. Wolfensohn underscored how essential a free press is to "good governance" on which, he argued, sustainable economic progress depends.[45]

As part of the recent attention given to governance issues, the World Bank and IDB have even begun to embrace the idea of social capital[46] as a vital precondition for development.[47] The importance attributed to social capital, a communitarian concept, departs from an approach based on strict neoliberalism, which emphasizes individualism and competition. In this connection, the broad premise underlying the World Bank's efforts in the 1990s to bring about social, political, and administrative change among its borrowers is that good government is essential to development, and that this rests on an effective (not a minimalist) state. Essential functions of the state include addressing market failure and improving equity.

What are the real and potential consequences of the growing interest by IFIs in issues of administrative reform and governance? At the very least, this interest has reinforced a trend begun with "second-wave" institutional reforms in the hiring of noneconomists (e.g., anthropologists, sociologists, political scientists) with in-depth knowledge of the societies in which the projects of multilateral lending institutions are found.[48] Also, by drawing IFIs into overtly political and social issues, it has put them at risk of violating their own claims and rules about maintaining political neutrality. Moreover, it increases the likelihood that IFIs will enter into controversy with governments (and often nongovernmental groups) in borrowing countries, which will regard their efforts to influence a broader array of policies as an undue affront to national sovereignty. Finally, the overt recognition by IFIs that economic recovery and growth rest on political, social, and cultural preconditions (whether it be the rule of law for future investment or a domestic political consensus for tough stabilization) could enhance the leverage of Latin American borrowers. In short, by making it more legitimate to say that the broader preconditions for economic restructuring are weak or absent, Latin American governments may gain in their capacity to postpone the implementation of the toughest reform measures.

While the consequences of a serious promotion by IFIs of governance issues are many and significant, it is important to ask how much weight IFIs will really give to governance concerns. Miller-Adams notes of the World Bank that governance-related activities involve small amounts of money, occupy few staff members (approximately twenty-five), and are marginalized in terms of bureaucratic location. In short, they remain outside the mainstream of Bank lending. In her view, seeking to distance itself from political fallouts that could occur from promoting governance-related issues, the Bank has sought refuge in the apolitical mandate of its founding charter more than been constrained by it.[49] Clearly, the values and beliefs held by Bank leaders are most compatible with initiatives that steer clear of reforms that call for the enactment of explicitly political changes.

In fact, of the recent shifts in World Bank and IDB activities, one of the most marked is that of private sector development. Both IFIs have started serving as facilitators for private investment in projects, as opposed to providing funding themselves. This constitutes part of a broader trend to create a policy environment conducive to market forces. A concerted effort to coordinate private sector development activities of the World Bank, IFC, and MIGA (Multilateral Investment Guarantee Agency) is currently under way. Together, the operations of this group include evaluating the condition of the private sector in major borrowing countries, acting as a "credit rater" for the private sector, providing technical assistance to host governments in order to enhance their ability to attract foreign direct investment, and guaranteeing private investment against the risks of expropriation, breach of contract, civil disturbance, and the like in host countries. The Business Partnership Center (BPC) at the Bank serves as a central contact point for business inquiries about Bank services for the private sector. The Bank's Business Partners for Development program is designed to bring together business, societal organizations, government ministries, and the World Bank Group, with the aim of establishing programs that meet the mutual interests of these actors.[50] The Private Sector Development (PSD) Department conducts formal training programs, whose topics include "Private Participation in Infrastructure," "Enterprise Restructuring and Privatization," "Business Environment," "Microfinance and Small and Medium Enterprise Development."[51] In short, private sector development enjoys a prominent place at the World Bank. Testimony to its importance is the hiring of new personnel with private sector expertise in an era of downsizing in general. Why the shift to private sector development?

While the United States had long advocated more direct Bank involvement with the private sector, it was the ideological orientation of the Reagan and Bush governments, coupled with the debt crisis (seen as the product of excessive state interventionism) that set the stage for this trend. A more proximate motivation lay in the request by the IFC for more funds in 1990.[52] As the major contributor to the IFC, the United States conceded capital increases conditional upon a reform of the World Bank's approach to the private sector. The diminution of official funds available for development assistance in recent years, discussed by Pamela Starr in this volume, no doubt enhances the justification for such an approach. In short, ideology, backed by economic need and consequent leverage, has raised private sector development to a new level.

Of the Bank's various new agendas, private sector development is arguably the highest priority. And as Michelle Miller-Adams contends, "PSD is the one that accords most readily with the values and beliefs of Bank staff. Designed to support market-oriented economic reform, PSD has been conceived of as a predominantly technical exercise. While PSD impinges on many political issues, these remain implicit."[53] Compared to private sector development, social sector and governance reforms that fall into the category of "capacity building" are often unwieldy from a political standpoint. Even more sensitive politically are governance issues having to do with the media, corruption, and military expenditures, which may well go beyond what the Bank can reasonably hope to influence. And, although the Bank has tried to enhance societal participation via NGOs, participation is not a central goal in and of itself. While these non-PSD initiatives present certain difficulties for a bank staffed largely by economists and intent on retaining an apolitical image, it is important to ask what makes IFIs better than private banks for the development process. Certainly, multilateral banks intent on breaking through some of the most serious obstacles to development must enlist the private sector in ways that go beyond their private counterparts.

Conclusions and Future Considerations

My intent in this chapter has been to present trends and identify forces—ideas, global economic events, and their interaction—that have influenced shifts in IFI policy initiatives since the 1960s. My efforts have undoubtedly raised more questions than provided conclusive answers. The previous description and analysis suggest that IFI policies toward Latin America and other parts of the developing world have been marked by change as well as continuity. The World Bank and IDB have certainly branched out over time in the kinds of projects and programs they have pursued and the kinds of personnel they have hired. Both have become more sensitive to social and environmental issues while pursuing policies that enhance the operation of market forces. Although the research and rhetoric in which they engage reflect many of the changes that have taken place and that are currently underway, an examination of bureaucratic organization, relations with borrowing member nations, and lending patterns (although to a lesser extent) suggest important elements of continuity.

The World Bank and IDB have been both consumers as well as producers and exporters of ideas. The intellectual inspiration for their policies comes from academic circles, other international organizations (such as ECLA, in the case of the IDB) as well as from within their own ranks. Recognition of the importance of human capital for economic productivity and social welfare constitutes a noteworthy example of multilaterals drawing on academic research and the ideas spawned by it. IFI policies have also been driven by global economic events, such as the oil shocks of the 1970s and debt crises of the 1980s. These events are nonideological factors that have had a tremendous impact on development thinking.

As a comparison between private sector development and governance reforms reveals, which ideas IFIs adhere to and elevate to prominence hinges on a number of factors, such as how comfortably associated policy prescriptions fit into their organizational culture, and relations with other actors, including borrowing member countries and NGOs. As exemplified by Robert NcNamara and Barber Conable of the World Bank and Enrique Iglesias of the IDB, leadership seems to be important in "selling" new policy orientations to high-ranking experts and bureaucrats within multilaterals themselves, as well as to bureaucratic and political leaders in borrowing member countries.

The close of the twentieth century provides an opportune moment to ponder the possibilities and problems that lie ahead for IFIs to exert influence in the Latin American region. With no overarching development paradigm defining the present period, IFIs can strike out in new innovative directions. While IFIs have taken on a new set of goals ("postmaterial" concerns, governance, etc.) there is a sense in which they are grasping for new ways to justify their organizations and to earn public approval with the aim of receiving replenishments, rather than acting in the best interest of development and concerning themselves with serious indicators of performance.

Complicating the task of IFIs is the decline in funds available to them in the post-cold-war era, as Pamela Starr points out in this volume. In Latin America and the Caribbean, the bulk of lending has been in the form of market-rate loans from the IBRD. Most of the region has graduated from eligibility for "soft" loans from the IDA. The region as a whole is considered a middle-level borrower able to pay higher rates. And within the region, most of the money goes to the bigger economies. Against this context, it is relevant to wonder what the future influence of IFIs will be. Certainly both the World Bank and IDB have offered their clients ideas and information as well as money. While ideas undoubtedly carry weight, historical example suggests that money does matter. When alternative sources of funding have arisen—for instance, with the petrodollars of the 1970s—the World Bank's leverage did appear to decline, especially among oil producers like Mexico, Nigeria, and Indonesia.[54]

Certainly the potential contribution of IFIs exceeds the capital they can provide. But if the provision of financial resources is in fact the overwhelming source of their influence (and playing the role of "credit rater" for the private sector and related activities a critical way in which IFIs will operate in an era of scarce development funds), IFIs will probably find themselves asking anew what constitutes their distinctive role in development. While "second-wave" institutional reforms and especially governance issues may exceed the competence and legitimate reach of IFIs, making a serious contribution to development in the full sense of the term requires that IFIs be more than banks managing the private sector.

Notes

1. "I.M.F. Lets its Rule on Full Repayment Slip," *New York Times*, Aug. 26, 1998, A-10.
2. "As Economies Fail, the I.M.F. is Rife with Recriminations," *New York Times*, Oct. 2, 1998, A-10.
3. "Dissension Erupts at Talks on World Financial Crisis," *New York Times*, Oct. 7, 1998, A-6.
4. Personal interview with Guiomar Namo de Mello, IDB official, Washington, D.C., May 31, 1996.
5. A host of other factors, however, influences whether and to what extent a given policy is effectively implemented.
6. Robert A. Packenham, *Liberal America and the Third World: Political Development Ideas in Foreign Aid and Social Science* (Princeton: Princeton University Press, 1973), 123–29; and Samuel P. Huntington, "Political Change in the Third World," in *Understanding Political Development*, ed. Myron Weiner and Samuel P. Huntington (Boston: Little, Brown, 1987), 6–11.
7. Devesh Kapur, John P. Lewis, and Richard Webb, *The World Bank: Its First Half Century*, vol. 1: History (Washington, D.C.: The Brookings Institution, 1997), 2.
8. The short period in the early 1960s in which ideas associated with the Alliance for Progress held sway constitutes a partial exception to the claim that IFIs in this decade confined their policy initiatives to economic growth, narrowly defined. The short duration of this conception corroborates the general predominance of the economic focus that modernization theory helped to legitimate.
9. Kapur, Lewis, and Webb, *The World Bank*, 6.

10. R. Peter Dewitt, "Policy Directions in International Lending, 1961–1984: The Case of the Inter-American Development Bank," *The Journal of Developing Areas* 21 (Apr. 1987): 277–84.

11. Michelle Miller-Adams, "The World Bank in the 1990s: Understanding Institutional Change" (prepared for delivery at the Annual Meeting of the American Political Science Association, San Francisco, Aug. 29–Sept. 1, 1996), 1–2.

12. Thomas E. Skidmore, "The Politics of Economic Stabilization in Postwar Latin America," in *Authoritarianism and Corporatism in Latin America*, ed. James M. Malloy (Pittsburgh, Pa.: University of Pittsburgh Press, 1977), 169.

13. Peruvian President Alan García (1985–1990) constitutes a marked exception to this pattern. The cornerstone of heterodoxy under García was the bold decision to limit Peru's debt service to no more than 10 percent of export earnings. Domestic measures, such as an incomes policy tilted toward increasing workers' wages at the expense of profits and running fiscal deficits in order to increase domestic demand, drew less international attention but were also critical aspects of his program. By late 1988, Peru found itself isolated internationally. Unilateral debt restrictions had angered international bankers, who cut Peru off from new external funds. Growth had slowed and inflation had soared. See John Crabtree, *Peru Under Garcia: An Opportunity Lost* (Pittsburgh, Pa.: University of Pittsburgh Press, 1992), 30–31, 40–41; and Manuel Pastor, Jr. *Inflation, Stabilization, and Debt: Macroeconomic Experiments in Peru and Bolivia* (Boulder: Westview Press, 1992), 136–38.

14. Huntington, "Political Change in the Third World."

15. Samuel P. Huntington and Joan M. Nelson, *No Easy Choice: Political Participation in Developing Countries* (Cambridge: Harvard University Press, 1976).

16. Robert L. Ayres, *Banking on the Poor: The World Bank and World Poverty* (Cambridge: MIT Press, 1983); and Martha Finnemore, *National Interests in International Society* (Ithaca, N.Y. and London: Cornell University Press, 1996), chap. 4.

17. Finnemore, *National Interests*, 92.

18. Ibid., 99.

19. Kapur, Lewis, and Webb, *The World Bank*, 6.

20. Diana Tussie, *The Inter-American Development Bank* (Boulder: Lynne Rienner Publishers, 1995), 50.

21. Sebastian Edwards, *Crisis and Reform in Latin America: From Despair to Hope* (New York: Oxford University Press, 1995), 55–58.

22. See Barbara Stallings, "International Influence on Economic Policy," in *The Politics of Economic Adjustment*, ed. Stephan Haggard and Robert Kaufman (Princeton: Princeton University Press, 1992), 41–88.

23. For a viewpoint that downplays the role of IFIs in this regard, see Edwards, *Crisis and Reform*, 56.

24. The World Bank's strong advocacy of human resource development in the form of programs to improve basic health and education constitutes a partial exception to this statement. See World Bank, *Human Resources in Latin America and the Caribbean: Priorities and Action* (Washington, D.C.: The World Bank, 1993); and *The East Asian Miracle: Economic Growth and Public Policy* (Washington, D.C.: The World Bank, 1993).

25. Jonathan A. Fox and L. David Brown, eds., *The Struggle for Accountability: The World Bank, NGOs, and Grassroots Movements* (Cambridge: MIT Press, 1998).

26. Adjustment operations at the IDB have been applied only to sectors and have excluded the broader structural adjustment loans offered at the World Bank. See Tussie, *The Inter-American Development Bank*, 37.

27. Fox and Brown, *The Struggle for Accountability*, 5.

28. For important changes specifically in the IDB under Iglesias's leadership, see Tussie, *The Inter-American Development Bank*, 53–55.

29. Miles Kahler, "External Actors and Adjustment: The Role of the IMF," in *Money Doctors, Foreign Debts, and Economic Reforms in Latin America from the 1890s to the Present*, ed. Paul Drake (Wilmington, Del.: Scholarly Resources, 1994).

30. For a discussion of social investment funds in Latin America, see Philip J. Glaessner, "Poverty Alleviation and Social Investment Funds: The Latin American Experience," World Bank Discussion Paper No. 261 (Washington, D.C.: World Bank, 1994). See also Gabriel

Siri, "Social Investment Funds in Latin America," *Cepal Review* 59 (Aug. 1996), 73–82; and Margaret E. Grosh, *Administering Targeted Social Programs in Latin America: From Platitudes to Practice* (Brookfield, Vt.: Ashgate Publishing Company, 1996).

31. See Shahid Javed Burki and Guillermo E. Perry, *The Long March: A Reform Agenda for Latin America and the Caribbean in the Next Decade* (Washington, D.C.: The World Bank, 1997), 104–6.

32. Kapur, Lewis, Webb, *The World Bank*, 369.

33. Michelle Miller-Adams, "The Challenge of World Bank–NGO Collaboration: Pursuing People-Oriented Development in a Technocratic Culture" (prepared for delivery at the 1997 Annual Meeting of the American Political Science Association, Washington, D.C., Aug. 28–31, 1997), 4.

34. Jane G. Covey, "Is Critical Cooperation Possible? Influencing the World Bank through Operational Collaboration and Policy Dialogue," in Fox and Brown, ed., *The Struggle for Accountability*, 81–119.

35. Kapur, Lewis, Webb, *The World Bank*, 45–47, 375.

36. Moisés Naím, "Latin America: The Second Stage of Reform," in *Economic Reform and Democracy*, ed. Larry Diamond and Marc F. Plattner (Baltimore and London: Johns Hopkins University Press, 1995).

37. Peter A. Hall, "Policy Paradigms, Social Learning, and the State: The Case of Economic Policymaking in Britain," *Comparative Politics* 25, no. 3 (1993): 275–96, especially 277.

38. Kurt Weyland, "Risk Taking in Latin American Economic Restructuring: Lessons from Prospect Theory," *International Studies Quarterly* 40, no. 2 (1996): 185–207.

39. Naím, "Latin America"; and Joan M. Nelson, "Promoting Policy Reforms: The Twilight of Conditionality?" *World Development* 29, no. 9 (1996): 1551–59.

40. World Bank, *World Development Report 1997: The State in a Changing World* (New York: Oxford University Press, 1997).

41. World Bank, *World Development Report*, 41–43.

42. Miller-Adams, "The Challenge of World Bank–NGO Collaboration," 17.

43. Robert L. Ayres, "Crime and Violence as Development Issues in Latin America and the Caribbean," World Bank Latin American and the Caribbean Studies Viewpoints (Washington, D.C.: The World Bank, 1998).

44. World Bank, *World Development Report*, 116.

45. "Call to Arms: A Free Media Can do Battle with Graft," *New York Times*, Oct. 11, 1998, 11.

46. *Social capital* refers to "features of social organization, such as trust, norms, and networks that can improve the efficiency of society by facilitating coordinated actions." See Robert D. Putnam, *Making Democracy Work: Civic Traditions in Modern Italy* (Princeton: Princeton University Press, 1993), 167.

47. Juan Felipe Yriart, "Hacia una Estrategia del Banco Interamericano de Desarrollo para el Fortalecimiento de la Sociedad Civil" (unpublished manuscript prepared for presentation at the Conferencia sobre el Fortalecimiento de la Sociedad Civil, Inter-American Development Bank, Washington, D.C., Sept. 12–14, 1994); and Nelson Stratta, "Estrategia sugerida para el BID para el desarollo de un Programa de Fortalecimiento de la Sociedad Civil en Uruguay" (unpublished manuscript, 1996).

48. Kapur, Lewis, Webb, *The World Bank*, 375. Tussie, writing about the IDB, also notes that the institution's tendency to place economists in charge of overseeing projects has led to a lamentable neglect of the institutional aspects of bank projects. See Tussie, *The Inter-American Development Bank*, 91.

49. Miller-Adams, *The World Bank in the 1990s*, 17–19.

50. "Resource Guide for Business," brochure (Washington, D.C.: The World Bank Group, Sept. 1998).

51. "Private Sector Development Training Program," brochure (Washington, D.C.: The World Bank in collaboration with EDI/LLC, Knowledge Management Team, n.d.).

52. Miller-Adams, *The World Bank in the 1990s*, 10.

53. Ibid., 21.

54. Kapur, Lewis, Webb, *The World Bank*, 321–22.

7

International Financial Institutions in Latin America: Adjusting to the Internationalization of Financial Markets

PAMELA K. STARR

Throughout the post–World War II period, international financial institutions (IFIs) have been active participants in Latin America's economic development.[1] They have left a clear mark in the region from the first World Bank loans and International Monetary Fund stabilization agreements in the early 1950s and the establishment of the Inter-American Development Bank in 1958, to the World Bank's increased emphasis on poverty alleviation a decade later, the temporarily reduced role of IFIs during the 1970s, and their reemergence as the vanguard of economic reform in the wake of the debt crisis. Whether the impact of IFI operations in Latin America has been positive or negative for regional development has been the subject of continuing and often-heated debate for nearly a half century. For good or bad, however, it is generally agreed that IFIs have exerted significant influence over economic decisions and the broader development trajectory of the region. Yet as the twentieth century draws to a close, the central role of IFIs in Latin American development is being challenged by dramatic changes in the international and regional contexts within which these institutions operate. No longer do IFIs operate in a world characterized by significant bilateral aid flows and exclusively national capital markets, and by a region composed of closed economies managed by interventionist, authoritarian states. Declining bilateral flows, the internationalization of financial markets, and the regional process of economic reform and democratization have markedly restructured the environment within which IFIs operate. To preserve its policy efficacy in this new regional order, each institution must modify the way it does business in Latin America. Although this process of institutional adaptation is already well under way, it is far from complete. The relative capacity of the IMF to promote economic stability in Latin America and of the World Bank and the Inter-American Development Bank to promote regional development into the twenty-first century thus depends on how effective this process of adaptation proves to be.

A New Operational Environment

It is not news to note that the internationalization of world markets, and especially world financial markets, have significantly altered the international context of development. Associated with this rise in world market forces, however, are two developments whose impact on the operational context of IFIs has been particularly notable—a marked drop in official flows of development capital during the past twenty-five years (and most particularly of bilateral and concessional flows) coupled with an explosion of private capital flows during the last decade. The combination of these two forces has produced a sharp decline in the relative importance of public funds in international capital markets and the rise of private flows noted for their geographic concentration and in some cases their potential for volatility.

The decline in concessional flows of international capital to developing countries has been under way since the 1970s. Underlying this trend is a growing disillusionment in the industrial countries with the viability of the development project and of the capacity of aid funds to promote it as well as fiscal constraints at home. In the last decade, the impact of "aid fatigue" on aid flows was reinforced by the evaporation of the security-based incentive for development assistance. With the end of the cold war, Russia was no longer economically able to provide assistance to its former allies while Western governments no longer needed to spend money to win the allegiance of strategically located Third World countries in the global struggle against communism. As the industrial countries thereby lost interest in the development project, bilateral aid fell from an average of nearly 1 percent of developing country GNP during the 1970s to only half that sum during most of the 1990s. Further, although nominal flows of official capital (bilateral and multilateral flows) to developing countries remained largely constant throughout the late 1980s and early 1990s, when measured in real terms, official aid flows are now at their lowest point in more than a generation (while demand for these flows has increased with the return of Russia and the former Eastern Bloc countries to the capitalist world economy).[2]

As developing country access to official sources of development capital declined, however, the internationalization of private capital markets has more than filled the void in the aggregate. The 1990s has witnessed an explosion of private capital flows to developing countries. This phenomenon, new to the post–WWII world economy, has been driven by falling barriers to international capital movements (created by competitive pressures in the G-7 countries and by economic reforms in developing countries and in the former Eastern Bloc), advances in information technology, increasingly sophisticated financial instruments, and an eight-year-long expansion in the U.S. economy. In the developing world, these flows have been concentrated in the more advanced economies— the so-called "emerging markets"—and include both loans (bond issues and direct borrowings from private banks) and equity investments (purchases of stocks and direct investment in plant and equipment). From a total only $46 billion in 1990, these private flows to emerging market economies increased to more than $235 billion by 1996. Private flows of this magnitude did not merely supplement official flows, they dwarfed them.

Beyond their size, private capital flows have also reshaped the international context of development as a consequence of their concentration and their expanded potential for volatility. The tendency for private flows to focus on just a few developing countries is striking, even when one considers the significant concentration evident in official capital flows. While the top ten recipients of multilateral and bilateral flows during the 1990–1993 period received 47 percent and 45 percent respectively of these capital flows, the ten top recipients of gross private capital flows during this same four-year period absorbed 70 percent of all private flows to developing countries.[3] This concentration in the provision of private capital is not surprising since investors rationally tend to put their money where they can achieve a high profit while limiting their risk. But this tendency combined with the expanding role of private markets in the provision of development capital suggests that most developing countries will find it more and more difficult to access the funds they require to finance development.

Private flows during the 1990s have also been characterized by the increased role of their most volatile component: portfolio investment. The initial surge of private capital into the developing world during the 1970s was dominated by bank loans and effectively devoid of portfolio flows. The renewed surge during the 1990s, however, has been characterized by large increases in both bank loans and foreign direct investment but combined with a dramatic rise in portfolio investment. Portfolio flows rose from less than half the total for foreign direct investment during the 1980s to a level now rivaling foreign direct investment. Portfolio flows have provided more than one-third of total private development capital to developing countries during the 1990s and accounted for the largest portion of these flows between 1992 and 1994.[4] Although portfolio investment fell off dramatically in the wake of the Asian and Russian financial crises of 1997–1998, its newly expanded role in international capital markets will persist well into the twenty-first century.

This rise in portfolio investment has brought with it a sharp increase in the volatility of private capital flows to developing markets. To a much greater extent than foreign direct investment or bank loans, and very much unlike loans from multilateral development banks, portfolio investment is by its nature highly mobile. A portfolio investor can take money out of any market as soon as a buyer can be found for the stocks and bonds in the investor's portfolio or as soon as the bonds mature (bond maturities in developing markets tend to be relatively short-term in order to minimize investor risk). This mobility generates clear benefits for developing countries. Mobility reduces the risk associated with investing in potentially unstable markets. As risk declines, the willingness of investors to seek out the higher rates of return in developing countries increases. The door to this large pool of investment capital is thereby opened to countries that very much need it.

Mobile capital, however, also can have very negative consequences for developing economies. A sudden, large inflow of capital can weaken a government's efforts to control inflation, appreciate its currency along with asset prices, and produce a large current account deficit that can be sustained only in the presence of continued capital inflows.[5] Should investors lose confidence in such a market, mobility can also generate an even more sudden and large outflow of capital requiring a rapid and painful adjustment whose consequences for economic development and political stability can be extreme. The experiences of Mexico during 1995–1996, Thailand, Malaysia, Indonesia, Korea, and other Asian economies beginning in mid-1997, and Russia beginning in late 1998 clearly and tangibly demonstrate the extent of the economic and political damage mobility can precipitate. This predicament is magnified further by the fact that cyclical external forces (such as the level of industrial country interest rates and the broader perception of risk in emerging markets) have proven to be the most important determinants of portfolio flows during the 1990s. Although economic fundamentals in the recipient country certainly matter, their impact has been secondary to that of external forces. Developing country governments thus have only a limited capacity to influence the direction and size of portfolio capital flows. Reliance on portfolio flows to finance development thereby carries inherent risks that are both significant and different from the developing countries' past experiences with international capital markets.

The impact of the internationalization of capital markets in Latin America reflects these broader developing country trends. Since 1990 (with the exception of 1995, owing to the Mexican peso crisis) official flows into the region have been insignificant relative to private capital. Official flows into Latin America totaled only $13.3 billion during the 1990–1996 period compared with private capital flows of $310.7 billion. Private capital has also been concentrated in only a few of the region's economies with portfolio flows being the most concentrated of all. While the largest and most developed countries of the region absorb the vast majority of private flows into Latin America, poorer countries are left to rely on a shrinking pool of official development assistance. As of 1995, for example, more than 75 percent of capital flows into Haiti were from official sources and nearly 50 percent in Bolivia and Honduras. The rising role of portfolio investment has also been particularly pronounced in Latin America where it has averaged two-thirds of net private flows to the region throughout the 1990s and surpassed foreign direct invest-

Table 7.1

Capital Flows to Developing Countries
(annual averages measured in billions of U.S. dollars)

	1977–1982	1983–1989	1990–1996
Total Net Private Capital Inflows[a]	30.5	8.8	150.7
Net Foreign Direct Investment	11.2	13.3	59.2
Net Portfolio Investment	-10.5	6.5	58.6
Bank Lending and Other Debt	29.8	-11.0	32.9
Official Flows	47.5	36.6	37.7

Sources: Private Flows; IMF, *International Capital Markets* (1995), 33; and (1997), 28. Official Flows; World Bank, *World Debt Tables* (1982–1993); and *Global Development Finance* (1998).

[a]net foreign direct investment plus net portfolio investment plus bank lending.

Table 7.2

Capital Flows to Latin America and the Caribbean
(annual averages measured in billions of U.S. dollars)

	1977–1982	1983–1989	1990–1996
Total Net Private Capital Inflows[a]	26.3	-16.6	44.4
Net Foreign Direct Investment	5.3	4.4	16.4
Net Portfolio Investment	1.6	-1.2	29.2
Bank Lending and Other Debt	19.4	-19.8	-1.2
Official Flows	19.0	9.2	8.1

Sources: Private Flows; IMF, *International Capital Markets* (1995), 33; and (1997), 28. Official Flows; World Bank, *World Debt Tables* (1982–1993); and *Global Development Finance* (1998).

[a]net foreign direct investment plus net portfolio investment plus bank lending.

ment every year until 1995. And following the Mexican peso crisis, Latin America was also the first developing region to feel the powerful repercussions associated with relying too heavily on portfolio investments.[6]

Beyond these changes in international capital markets, dramatic changes within Latin America have also contributed to the altered regional environment in which IFIs must operate into the next century. As is well known, the last decade and a half has been dominated by a transition to market economies and democratic politics throughout the region. This dual transition has made much of the region a more desirable target for private capital, but it also has injected an increased political calculus into economic policy decisions and has intertwined the fortunes of political and economic reform.[7] This reality raises the risk that economic problems could produce negative repercussions for the sustainability of democratic advances in the region and that this will compel regional governments to follow an policy path which may not be the most efficient economically, but which is deemed essential to the preservation of the democratic setting in which market-based economics have been embedded.

The World Bank, Inter-American Development Bank, and IMF thus face the challenge of adjusting their traditional ways of doing business to the new context in which they must now operate. The development banks must find a way to promote development and the IMF a means to encourage macroeconomic stability despite the declining weight of their financial resources and the new challenge presented by mobile capital. Equally important, they must augment the flexibility of their operations in Latin America to accommodate the needs of regional governments struggling to balance the often conflicting demands of democratic politics and market-based economics.

The Development Banks: Preserving Institutional Relevance

The emergence of market reforms and democratic practices in Latin America, and particularly the rise of mobile capital, have prompted the World Bank and the Inter-American Development Bank (IDB) to alter their approach to promoting regional development to preserve their relevance as development institutions into the twenty-first century.[8] Three changes in particular stand out. Each institution has initiated a shift away from autonomous funding of large-scale infrastructure projects in favor of acting as a facilitator for private investment in such projects; launched efforts to improve the regional climate for private investment through the provision of technical assistance and financing for reforms; and increased attention to the needs of small and medium-sized firms and other actors who often are unable to access funds in private capital markets.

The traditional role of the IDB and the World Bank in Latin America had been as the dominant providers of foreign funds for large-scale development projects. If sanitation projects are included, then this effort accounted for more than 85 percent of all IDB lending to Latin America until the late 1980s and of all World Bank lending until the beginning of the 1980s (this percentage fell to 72 percent for the World Bank for the 1982–1984 period). The dramatic expansion of international capital markets in the last decade, however, has undermined the bank's traditional comparative advantage in the autonomous funding of large infrastructure projects. They have thus begun to restructure their operations to maximize the benefit that can be derived from this new distribution of available development funds. By the early 1990s, funding for infrastructure and sanitation projects fell to about 30 percent of each institution's total lending, while a new category of loans—policy-based lending—rose to dominance. Although the initial increase in policy-based loans during the 1980s reflected the emergence of structural adjustment loans to help Latin America through the debt crisis, in the 1990s this category of loans has expanded to include financing for a much wider array of policy reforms. From virtually nothing as late as the early 1980s, this category absorbed nearly 50 percent of IDB and World Bank lending to Latin America by the early 1990s.[9]

Displaced as the dominate source of financing for large-scale development projects and lacking the resources to meet Latin America's huge demand for investment in infrastructure projects (a demand emanating from the investment backlog accumulated during the "lost decade" of the 1980s), the banks have recently redirected their development efforts toward facilitating private investment in these projects. One means of achieving this aim has been to increase the amount of bank funds devoted to providing loan guarantees to the private sector. The banks also have increased their provision of seed money and cofinancing for projects which, as an implicit bank guarantee for the project, helps to reduce private actors' estimation of risk and thereby increase their willingness to invest. Although the World Bank has offered loan guarantees to the private sector since its inception and has lent directly to the private sector since 1960 (through the International Finance Corporation), only recently has the Bank begun to emphasize these tools and the private funds they mobilize as central to the Bank's development efforts. Further, in early 1998 the Bank initiated its new "Business Partners for Development," a three-year pilot program designed to extend business-Bank cooperation beyond infrastructure and into social sector development projects such as education, water and sanitation, natural resources, and youth development.[10] For the Inter-American Development Bank, the shift into cooperating with the private sector in infrastructure development as well as lending directly to private actors without government guarantees is largely uncharted territory. The IDBs private lending wing, the Inter-American Investment Corporation, did not begin operations until 1989 and was not permitted to make loans without government guarantees until

1994 and then only up to 5 percent of the bank's total capital. Yet in 1998, the Inter-American Investment Corporation's capital was increased dramatically and the ceiling on such loans to the private sector was increased to 10 percent of total IDB lending. With this new strategy, the IDB aims to attract private participation reaching 5–7 percent of the bank's investment.[11]

Recognizing that the capacity of developing countries to access private capital markets is now an extremely important development tool, the World Bank and IDB have also increased their efforts to improve the broader climate for private investment in Latin America through the provision of technical support and policy-based loans to finance reform efforts. As one employee of the World Bank noted, "We are no longer a lending bank but a 'knowledgement' bank" providing the benefit of the bank's research, learning, and experience to its client countries.[12] The intermediate aims of this assistance are threefold—to improve the efficiency of domestic markets, to increase the capacity and efficiency of the state, and to develop human capital. The first objective will benefit from the banks' efforts to encourage private sector investment in infrastructure projects and participation in further privatizations, and from the banks' continuing provision of the financial and technical help needed to complete the structural adjustment tasks that remain unfinished. The development banks have also recently begun to provide assistance for the reform and strengthening of domestic financial systems in order to reduce their vulnerability to, and thereby limit the broader economic costs of, rapid outflows of portfolio capital. To augment the policy capacity and efficiency of the Latin American states, the banks have expanded greatly their assistance in designing and implementing regulatory, administrative, and judicial reforms, and for the first time in their history have begun to address openly the development costs of what World Bank President James Wolfensohn has called a "crisis of corruption." Finally, the banks have reemphasized their traditional antipoverty focus under a new rubric. To attract more and higher-valued added private investment, the banks are helping Latin American countries development their human capital resources by expanding the quality of and access to basic education and health care services.

The third major change in the activity of the development banks in Latin America during the 1990s has been an effort to increase assistance to economic activities the market is unlikely to fund. The Inter-American Development Bank in particular has increased its efforts to encourage the establishment, expansion, and modernization of micro-, small-, and medium-scale enterprises and of firms owned by women and other minority groups who have difficulty accessing private capital markets. Both banks have also given increased attention to small-scale lending. The IDB launched a particularly innovative three-year small-scale lending scheme in Guatemala in 1997. Known as Decopaz, the program consists of IDB funding for Guatemalan gov-

ernment loans to poor highland villages to finance small development projects, allowing the villagers to decide precisely how the money will be spent. It
is hoped that the flexibility of this program will fund needed projects in communities too poor to be of interest to private markets while also rebuilding
highland confidence in (and thereby the capacity of) the Guatemalan state in
the aftermath of an extended civil war.[13]

This new development focus of the World Bank and IDB seems to be a
reasonable adjustment to the internationalization of international capital
markets, but it also sets the development banks on a policy path strewn with
obstacles. Some of the rocks in the road toward promoting future development in Latin America are of an enduring institutional sort while others
emerge from the new policies themselves. On the institutional side, many
development bank loans to Latin American countries in the past have not
measured up to their initial objectives. In part this has been due to the banks'
traditional emphasis on ensuring large-scale capital transfers to their member
countries. This focus on simply moving money often resulted in insufficient
attention to project quality leading to some disappointing outcomes and a
backlog of undisbursed commitments. Although the banks have recently
rededicated themselves to emphasizing quality over quantity in their lending,
it will be difficult to change a long-standing institutional culture that measures
success by volume. A continuing bias toward inefficiency will also emerge
from the inevitably differing views about project viability and design among
decision makers within the banks as well as between bank employees and policymakers in the target country. Given the banks' recent efforts to increase
member participation in project design in order to tailor aid to the precise
development needs of member countries, this problem is likely to increase. It
will also be reinforced by the banks' new focus on the "second generation" of
market reforms in Latin America (judicial reform, reform of the state, and so
on), reforms for which there is no clear consensus on how they can best be
achieved. The institutional challenge of development, always daunting, is
therefore unlikely to decline in the near future.[14]

The decision of the World Bank and the IDB to rely more heavily on private sector cooperation in the promotion of development presents additional
challenges. Although efforts to entice foreign capital to invest in Latin America
is likely to bear fruit in the most developed regions and could even meet with
some success in the semideveloped regions of the hemisphere, this strategy
seems much less likely to have a positive development impact on Latin
America's poorest regions. For countries such as Bolivia, Guyana, Haiti, and
Nicaragua, and for regions such as the Brazilian Northeast, the Peruvian Andes,
and southern Mexico, the obstacles to development are more fundamental than
those of their richer neighbors. These regions lack the basic physical and

human infrastructure essential for productive private investment. Until the time-consuming and difficult process of building this infrastructure is complete, the private sector will be a minor source of development finance at best. It was precisely for this purpose—to assist countries and regions unable to contract development capital in private markets—that the development banks were originally created. For Latin America's poorest regions, therefore, there will be no substitute in the foreseeable future to their continuing reliance on the World Bank and the IDB to finance their development needs.

The Latin American regions in greatest need, however, will also find their access to development loans provided on consessional terms more restricted than in the past. Due in large measure to "aid fatigue," the World Bank has found it increasingly difficult to convince donor countries to fund its concessional loan facility. The IDBs concessional loan facility, by contrast, has secured funding well into the future, yet the nominal value of the loans available through this facility has declined by half from its 1979–1981 high and is now virtually the same as it was twenty-five years ago. Measured as a percentage of total IDB resources, the drop off is even more stark: from half of all IDB lending during the 1960s, concessional lending declined to 25 percent in the 1970s and to only 1 percent by the late 1980s.[15]

Even in the more-developed regions of the hemisphere, the expanded importance of the volatile portfolio component of private capital flows means that the development banks' decision to encourage increased use of private development capital carries significant risks. In the wake of the Mexican peso crisis, Latin America's emerging markets dramatically reduced their reliance on portfolio investment and increased their absorption of longer-term capital flows. Despite this success, however, inflows of portfolio investment remain vital to the region's economic health, a fact made abundantly clear following the late 1998 Russian default.[16] As investors' taste for risk imploded, capital surged out of the region threatening both short-term financial stability and medium-term regional development. Faced with this threat, the World Bank and the IDB overcame their initial hesitance to cooperate in any emergency assistance measures believing that this was beyond the banks' already extensive mandate to promote development and fight poverty. Each contributed to a rescue package assembled by the International Monetary Fund to help the region, and specifically Brazil, weather this most recent financial market storm. The International Monetary Fund, meanwhile, has proposed a set of measures to reduce the negative impact of volatile capital flows on developing country growth and economic stability. Success in this endeavor, however, appears unlikely, suggesting that the development banks will continue to feel compelled to divert long-term development resources to preserve short-term economic stability in the coming decades.

The International Monetary Fund: Struggling to Preserve Economic Stability

Not unlike the development banks, the International Monetary Fund has been forced to adapt its operations in Latin America to the demands of a new environment. The IMF has been forced to rethink how to promote exchange rate stability, preserve monetary confidence and cooperation, and ease the duration and burden of payments imbalances in a policy setting dramatically different from the one for which it was created and in which it traditionally operated. Designed to operate in a world of fixed exchange rates and extensive capital controls, the fund successfully adapted to the emergence of flexible exchange rates during the 1970s and is now attempting to adjust to a world dominated by mobile capital.

The sheer size of the capital flows in private markets has undermined the capacity of the IMF to respond to its members' needs for temporary financing in the wake of balance of payments crises, and the mobility of these flows has tended to increase the frequency of such crises. Not unlike the rapid rise in bank lending to developing countries during the 1970s, the surge in portfolio investment during the 1990s has outstripped the resources of the IMF and thereby made it impossible for the fund to do its job autonomously. Instead, the IMF has been forced to rely on an ad hoc syndication of lenders (including multilateral development banks and sovereign lenders) to meet its members' emergency funding needs. Although IMF syndication of loans is not new, it has become much more difficult to accomplish in the current international financial environment. The huge size of the packages the IMF must now organize— for Mexico during 1995, and for Thailand, Korea, Indonesia, Russia, and Brazil during 1997 and 1998—demands the participation of an ever-increasing number of actors. (As is well known, as the size of any group increases the probability that it will remain sufficiently unified to achieve its aim declines.) Further, U.S. participation in future IMF-led loan syndicates has been brought into question by the growing reticence with which the U.S. public and Congress view U.S. contributions to such rescue efforts.[17] Continuing IMF reliance on syndication thus entails significant risks, a situation the fund fully recognizes. In the words of Stanley Fischer, the IMF's first deputy managing director, "The Korean crisis has established that it takes a global coalition to deal with a major financial crisis, where ever it happens. That realization...should have a sobering effect on everyone."[18]

The events of 1997 and 1998 have also raised questions about the capacity of even successful syndication to enable the IMF to do its job. Following multibillion dollar loans to Indonesia, Thailand, Korea, Russia, and Brazil and with billions in loans still outstanding, the fund's resources fell to extremely low levels raising doubts about its ability to provide the seed-money essential to future syndicated rescue efforts. The fund successfully dodged this bullet in late 1998 when the U.S. Congress approved its contribution to the largest replenishment of the fund's working capital in history. The torturous route by which congressional approval was attained (and the real fears that the Congress would refuse the funding increase), however, and the likelihood that private capital flows will continue to grow into the future suggest that resource shortages will be a recurrent problem for the IMF in the coming decades.

In this context, it is not surprising that the IMF has begun to alter its strategy for dealing with balance-of-payments crises. Rather than react to such crises after they emerge, the institution is trying to build the capacity to prevent them from ever developing. This new strategy is designed to improve the effectiveness and utility of the fund's traditional task of surveying developments and problems in member economies, and it has been structured around two core activities: "enhanced surveillance" of the macroeconomic situation in member countries, and "expanded oversight" of their domestic financial markets. Enhanced surveillance aims to take advantage of the growth in global financial markets by enlisting them in the effort to compel emerging market economies to comply with established norms of macroeconomic policy behavior. The most effective means of encouraging countries to adhere to stabilizing macroeconomic policies is to condition their access to needed international capital on the implementation of such policies. As a lender of last resort, however, the IMF possesses the power to condition access to capital only after the withdrawal of private capital has generated a crisis. During the upswing of the investment cycle, the private financial players determine which borrowers will have access to their funds and under what conditions; the IMF hopes to harness this precrisis market power over the flow of international capital.

Informed investors have an incentive to reduce their exposure when the macroeconomic environment in a given market begins to deteriorate. Once made aware of such an increase in investment risk, investors should withdraw their capital at a rate commensurate with the increased risk. Falling capital inflows would increase the pressure on the target country to adjust its economic policy before errors could accumulate and create a crisis. Market forces would thereby nip a potential crisis in the bud. The operational trick to this strategy, however, is providing private actors with the information they needed to estimate risk correctly. This is the task assigned to the IMF's enhanced surveillance—to increase the quality and quantity of data available to private capital markets by encouraging member countries to improve transparency in economic management and expand the disclosure of economic data (its frequency, quality, and completeness) and by disseminating this information on the fund's web page and in its annual reports on member economies.

Enhanced surveillance is to be coupled with expanded oversight of domestic financial markets, especially in emerging economies highly integrated into international capital markets. Weak financial systems are capable of both transforming a balance of payments crisis into a broader economic crisis and helping to transmit a crisis from market to market. In the presence of volatile flows of private capital, therefore, healthy domestic financial systems are an essential bulwark against the ever-present threat of contagion. Expanded oversight would strengthen domestic financial systems by subjecting them to international standards for financial sector regulation. The idea is based on the Basle Accord, a 1988 agreement among the G-10 countries to harmonize financial sector regulations and most particularly capital adequacy requirements. Emerging economies would be encouraged to accept Basle-like standards for transparency, disclosure, and capital adequacy—standards that tend to be stricter than those in force in most emerging markets. The ultimate outcome should be the construction of a firewall against both domestic and international contagion in the form of strong domestic financial systems.

Although both enhanced surveillance and expanded oversight are logical responses to the new challenges posed by the growth of global financial markets and the expanding presence of mobile capital in these markets, neither solution is fully workable. Enlisting private markets to police the macroeconomic policies of national economies is an unrealistic goal. In part this is because the IMF lacks the capacity to provide the information the markets need. From its inception, the IMF has been charged with respecting the economic autonomy of its member countries even as it attempted to integrate them into a global monetary system. This mandate to respect its members' sovereignty means that the IMF is forbidden to disseminate data about any member's economy without the explicit approval of the country involved. And although there have been suggestions that the IMF end this tradition of confidentiality, doing so would only hinder the capacity of the fund to gather data by encouraging members with economic difficulties to provide poor-quality information. The economic information made available to private investors through the IMF will thus continue to be only as timely and comprehensive as member countries wish it to be. And countries that face deteriorating economic conditions—just the moment in which a market-driven economic police force most needs full information to do its job—are precisely the ones who will have the greatest incentive to keep this information from market players.[19]

Relying on market players to discipline economic policy also seems unworkable because the nature of private capital markets suggests that they will not use fuller information in the way the IMF envisions. First, the dissemination of unanticipated bad news about a particular economy could create the very crisis it was designed to prevent. Instead of producing a measured withdrawal of capital, it could spook the markets into overreacting by generating the suspicion that the available information is merely a harbinger of more problems to come. Second, although better information may improve investor decision making, it can never guarantee that their decisions will be right. Markets are composed of individuals susceptible to misperception and subject to error. Financial markets are also prone to herding behavior as investors try to protect their profits or cover their losses in contracting markets. Further, an increasing number of economists have come to the conclusion that capital markets, by their very nature, are more prone to error than their commercial counterparts. Bubbles and crashes are the norm, rather than the exception. Relying on imperfect markets to encourage smooth macroeconomic adjustments in developing countries will thus inevitably be an ineffective strategy.[20]

Like enhanced surveillance, expanded oversight will also be difficult for the IMF to implement successfully. The institutional blueprint for this effort, the Basle Accord, functions in large part because international enforcement is not required. Signatory countries implement the accord willingly because each is satisfied that it meets national needs. Expanding this regulatory strategy to include developing countries, however, will be problematic. Many developing countries have perceptions of how a domestic financial system should operate, which differ from those inscribed in the Basle Accord. Yet without consensus, any attempt to extend this regulatory framework to emerging markets would encounter resistance and therefore inefficient long-term implementation.[21] Equally problematic for any effort either to create a "World Finance Organization" or to expand the purview of the IMF to include regulating and tracking the health of its members' domestic financial markets is the recent decline in the effectiveness of the Basle Accord. Basle has found it difficult to adapt to the creative accounting methods devised by international banks to skirt the accord's capital adequacy requirements and the increasing prominence of nonbank institutions, which operate free of Basle constraints, in the international financial system. If the G-10 precursor of expanded oversight is struggling to maintain its relevance in a world of rapidly changing global financial markets, then its chances of operating effectively in the developing world seem somewhat remote.

What else might the IMF do? In the wake of the Asian and Russian crises of 1997 and 1998 criticisms of the IMF and proposals for reform seemed to be everywhere. Economists, policymakers, and pundits criticized the IMF for either helping to cause the crisis, failing to respond to it with sufficient rapidity, or responding with an incorrect mix of policy solutions. Such criticisms produced a panoply of recommended reforms ranging from limited reforms such as increasing the institution's transparency or demanding that it force the private sector to share the burden of adjustment, to radical reforms such as eliminating the IMF altogether or alternately dramatically expanding its mandate to include explicit oversight of global financial markets. Despite the numerous and vocal critiques of the fund and the clear recognition that the fund did make some mistakes in Asia, there is precious little consensus on what the IMF should do. Without consensus, however, significant institutional change is unlikely. Finally, even if enhanced surveillance and expanded oversight were to be successful in spotting and containing crises such as those which buffeted developing countries during 1997 and 1998, it is unlikely that they will be able to perform the same task for the next generation of financial crises. The constant mutations in the operation of international financial markets suggest that the next crisis is likely to be based on some factor that is not now evident and against which enhanced surveillance and expanded oversight will be ineffective. It appears unlikely, therefore, that the IMF will be able to reduce significantly the turbulence inherent in modern international capital markets

The role of the IMF in Latin America is thus apt to change very little in the coming decade. Unable to control the turbulence in international financial markets, the IMF's ability to promote macroeconomic stability will remain very limited when private capital inflows are strong, and its capacity to preserve stability as private flows exit the region will continue to be threatened by the size of these global capital movements. And the IMF will continue to be surprised from time to time by the sudden appearance of financial crises emerging from previously unseen and hence unpredictable developments.

Protecting Democracy and Markets

Beyond adjusting their operations to the growth of private capital flows and particularly of mobile capital, the development banks and the IMF also must adapt their operations to changing conditions in the Latin American region. Long characterized by authoritarian governance and closed, state-directed economies, Latin America is now dominated by democracies and open, market-based economies. This dual transition will both ease and complicate the challenge facing international financial institutions in the coming century. Economic liberalization will simplify the IFI's tasks by making the region more attuned with the market-based remedies preferred by all three institutions. Political liberalization, meanwhile, will tend to complicate the efforts of the World Bank and the IDB to promote development and of the IMF to promote economic stability. But even as Latin America's dual transition coupled with the global expansion of private capital markets forces international financial institutions to modify their operations in the region, their influence in Latin America will surely remain strong well into the twenty-first century.

Latin America's move toward market-based economic practices has eased the often-tense relationship between regional governments and IFIs. Throughout the postwar period, Latin America's reliance on a development model based on protectionism and heavy state involvement in the economy (import substitution industrialization) conflicted sharply with the mandate of the World Bank and the IMF to promote a more open world economy. The World Bank clashed so strongly with Brazil over its economic policies during the early 1950s, for example, that the bank actually ceased all lending to Brazil between 1954 and 1965, and the policy battles between the IMF and Latin American governments are legion.[22] The recent adoption of market-based reforms throughout Latin America, however, reflects an ideological shift that should improve the relationship between regional governments and the Bretton Woods institutions. These governments no longer view free markets as impediments to growth and development but instead as the most appropriate mechanism to advance these economic objectives. In this context, the development banks' decision to rely more heavily on private capital to promote development in Latin America corresponds neatly with the region's preferred economic practices. Equally, the efforts of the IMF to preserve monetary stability through increased surveillance and oversight dovetails with the stated desire of regional governments to strengthen their domestic financial systems and protect macroeconomic stability. Differences over implementation of these objectives will inevitably create friction from time to time, especially in the case of the IMF. But Latin America's adoption of a development perspective similar to the view long held by the IMF and World Bank will assuredly augment the policy influence of these institutions in the region while also making it easier for them to do their job.

Even as Latin America's economic reform has simplified the hemispheric challenge facing the development banks and the IMF, the region's move toward democratic politics has complicated their operations. Under authoritarian regimes, IFIs could generally count on Latin American governments to push through reforms that, although necessary to improve economic efficiency, were often costly and hence highly unpopular for large segments of the population. Although democratic governments are able at times to employ authoritarian tactics to implement unpopular policies, such a strategy cannot be relied on permanently. The very nature of democracy ensures that citizens have the power to express their opinion about a government and its policies, at a minimum, at election time. A democratic government that systematically ignores the demands of its constituents does so at its own peril.

The democratic constraint on economic policy making, however, extends even further in Latin America. The dubious stability of several of Latin America's democratic regimes means that the implementation of economic reforms, which undermine the well-being of the citizenry even in the short-term, can undermine the foundations of democracy. The presence of mobile capital in such a setting, and especially the periodic short-term crises it can create, can thus be particularly problematic. And even where democracy is fairly well entrenched, a persistent public perception that living conditions have either deteriorated or not improved as promised under Latin America's new liberal order can undermine public support for both market-based economic policies and for the democratic regime supporting them. Throughout the region evidence of this sort of public fatigue with economic programs and governments that do not deliver the goods is growing, as is the emergence of neopopulist politicians willing to ride this wave of dissatisfaction to power. Lastly, the dual nature of Latin America's liberalization means that the future of political and economic reform in the region is tightly intertwined. Success or failure in the economic realm inevitably spills over into the political realm, and vice versa. Promoting a market-based development strategy in Latin America, therefore, is often inseparable from promoting the long-term survival of democracy.

To adapt their operations to such a Latin American setting, IFIs must imbue their institutional mandate to eliminate political considerations from their decision-making process with a measure of flexibility. Their activities must instead seek to preserve and expand both market-based development strategies and the democratic political practices with which regional economic success is frequently integrated tightly. To this end, the development banks must attempt to construct programs that enjoy the support (or at least not the active opposition) of the populations they will effect while all three IFIs must pursue their regional objectives based on a strategy which consciously incorporates flexibility in program design and implementation.

For the World Bank and the IDB, flexibility in part entails tailoring their poverty-fighting and development programs to the precise needs of each Latin American country. One means to this end is an expanded partnership with the target country in both the design and the implementation of development bank projects to ensure that the final project is balanced both politically and economically and that it responds the needs of the Latin American country, rather than those of the development bank. Increased flexibility also implies that the banks will need to broaden their definition of what is an appropriate economic or social policy in order to create the policy space required to respond to the specific political-economic needs of each Latin American country. Such an approach to development assistance will inevitably raise complaints from within the banks (and potentially among donor countries) about sacrificing economic efficiency to meet amorphous and potentially exaggerated political needs, and there will be instances in which such complaints will be highly justified. Yet the alternative seems even more problematic—a program which may be economically efficient but which cannot be supported in the court of public opinion and thereby threatens to undermine, rather than advance, long-term liberalization in Latin America.

The concept of tailoring development assistance to the precise political-economic needs of each Latin American nation would also benefit from an increased partnership between the World Bank and the IDB. Although each institution is similar in the sort of development work they do and the amount of capital they provide annually to Latin America (the IDB provides $7 billion and the World Bank $5 billion), their institutional mandates and their capacity to work closely with each Latin American country is substantially different. For the World Bank, Latin America is just one of the developing regions where the Bank is active, while the focus of the IDB is exclusively on Latin America. This difference has led the IBD to develop a comprehensive network of regional offices situated in every Latin American country and to develop a high degree of familiarity with the local environment. The IDB is therefore well equipped to identify needed projects, potential private sector partners, and the unique needs of a particular community. The history and institutional structure of the IDB also has enabled it to build a large store of confidence among its Latin American members. Latin American countries have always felt that they had significant influence in an institution created solely for their benefit and over which they have always had significant influence.[23] Also, with the exception of the 1980s, the IDB consistently placed responsibility for devising development plans, policies, and priorities in the hands of the member countries, and unlike the World Bank, the IDB's institutional mandate has never included the promotion of a development strategy at odds with Latin American preferences. The IDB thus enjoys a proximity to Latin America's development challenges and a foundation of trust with its member countries essential for the expansion of a viable bank-member partnership in the design and implementation of development projects. Given that the World Bank can never hope to match these advantages of the regional development bank, advancing its aims in Latin America would benefit from a closer working relationship with its regional cousin.

Like the development banks, the IMF also must increase the flexibility with which is operates in Latin America. In particular, Latin American governments need more leeway in designing policy responses to the political-economic risks associated with a heavy reliance on mobile capital. The IMF's mandate calls upon the institution to promote both stability and liberalization in international and domestic capital markets. In the pursuit of these objectives, the fund has long favored reduced regulation and, in particular, the elimination of capital controls. The financial market turbulence of 1997 and 1998, however, has made it abundantly clear that stability and liberalization may not always be complimentary short-term goals in the presence of large flows of mobile capital. This experience has convinced the fund to revise its policy recommendations somewhat. It now argues that member countries with weak domestic financial markets should not open their economies to portfolio capital flows and they may need to make temporary use of limited capital controls. The fund needs to go farther.

Given the improbability that the IMF will soon be able to curb the volatility of capital flows in a region dependent on mobile capital, and the negative impact capital surges can have on the survivability of market-based reforms and the democratic governments which implement them, the fund needs to give Latin American governments more room for maneuver in the management of these flows. Possible measures could include a nonremunerated reserve requirement or an outright tax on inflows of portfolio capital, increased reserve requirements on banks with an excessive amount of short-term funding, and taxation of foreign loans to local banks and businesses. The Chilean, Colombian, and Brazilian governments have used such limited measures to mitigate the upward pressure on the real exchange rate produced by sudden surges of capital inflows, to reduce the economy's vulnerability to capital outflows and devaluation, and to encourage inflows of less mobile forms of capital. Much of the rest of Latin America, however, has shied away from such policies partly because of IMF opposition.

To argue that the fund should respond more sympathetically to Latin American efforts to limit the negative impact of mobile capital is not to suggest that capital controls and domestic regulations are either cost-free or a miracle cure for controlling mobile capital. To the contrary, any effort to limit the free flow of capital across borders will increase the investment risk in the affected market and thereby reduce flows into it. As the supply of capital in the domestic market declines, interest rates will rise and economic activity fall. Further, regulations on capital flows inevitably lose their effectiveness over time as the market discovers ways to circumvent them, and such regulations will only make matters worse if they are used to avoid needed long-term adjustments in macroeconomic policy. In addition, there are more "market-friendly" policy alternatives such as Argentina's successful construction of a privately financed dollar contingency fund (the right to borrow dollars under established circumstances) to protect its currency and its domestic financial system from sudden capital outflows. Nevertheless, given the great potential damage capital surges can inflict on Latin America's dual transition and the impotence of the IMF in the face of capital market turbulence, Latin American governments need more options than the effective counsel of the IMF to "don't do anything, just stand there."

Conclusion

The international financial institutions operating in Latin America thus have a new and difficult task before them: they must find a way to continue promoting development and economic stability in Latin America despite significant changes in the international and regional contexts in which they operate. Each of the three institutions considered in this chapter—the World Bank, the Inter-American Development Bank, and the International Monetary Fund—are fully aware of the challenge before them and have begun the process of adjusting the way they do business in the region in the hope of preserving their policy effectiveness into the new century. The reform process in each institution, however, is insufficient.

The decision of the development banks to rely more heavily on private capital to promote development is a rational response to the evident expansion of international capital markets in the past three decades, but it also raises questions about the capacity of these institutions to harness private flows to meet their public aims. In impoverished regions of the hemisphere where private capital flows are unlikely to venture, the development banks' announced decision to redouble their poverty-fighting efforts is also uncertain to achieve its objectives due to continuing constraints within the banks, a limited supply of concessional funds, and important questions about the way the banks continue to fight poverty. The determination of the IMF to mitigate turbulence in international capital markets is a laudable goal, but one which is quite unlikely to bear fruit.

Yet the struggle to push forward Latin America's dual liberalization process in the decades to come requires that these three institutions meet with some success in their efforts to promote stable growth and development. Latin American countries will continue to need help from the development banks to finance the second generation of market reforms, to fund projects which private markets shy away from, and to help fight poverty. And until the region is able to wean itself off its dependence on mobile capital, Latin American countries will also continue to need monetary assistance from all three institutions to help them cope with the repercussions of occasional capital outflows.

Latin America thus needs IFI operations in the Western Hemisphere to meet with success, and one of the keys to improved effectiveness for all three institutions in their new operational context is increased flexibility. Flexibility does not mean that the IFIs should lose sight of economic efficiency or that they should cease encouraging Latin American countries to sustain policies we know can promote development and stability such as stable fiscal and monetary policies and strengthened domestic financial systems. Flexibility instead means recognizing that economic efficiency and the promotion of democratic practices can conflict in the short-term, and that in a region where both market-based economics and democracy remain in their formative stage, the need for the policy space to mitigate these conflicts when they arise is essential. The absence of such a flexible policy approach could both impair the influence and effectiveness of IFIs in Latin America and undermine the region's dual liberalization process. The successful application of policy flexibility holds the promise of better enabling the development banks and the IMF to complete their institutional missions in Latin America. It also promises to bolster economic reform by embedding it both in the imagination and the pocketbooks of Latin American voters and to strengthen democracy by enabling it to deliver well-being to its citizens.

Notes

1. Although many different institutions may fall within the rubric of international financial institutions, this paper limits its definition of IFIs to the three most prominent multilateral institutions operating in the region: the International Monetary Fund; the World Bank; and the Inter-American Development Bank.
2. The World Bank, *Global Development Finance, Country Tables* (Washington, D.C.: The World Bank, Mar. 1998), 14–15; Dani Rodrik, "Why Is There Multilateral Lending?" *NBER Working Paper* No. 5160, Cambridge, Mass., June 1995, 35; *Economist* (Oct. 5, 1996): 70.
3. Rodrik, "Why Is There Multilateral Lending?" 39.
4. IMF, *International Capital Markets* (Washington, D.C.: The International Monetary Fund, 1997), 28; The World Bank, *Global Development Finance*, 14–15.
5. On the problems associated with capital inflows, see Guillermo A. Calvo, Leonardo Leiderman, and Carmen M. Reinhart, "The Capital Inflows Problem: Concepts and Issues," *Contemporary Economic Policy* 12 (July 1994): 54–66.
6. Statistics on official flows in World Bank, *World Development Report, 1997* (Washington, D.C.: The World Bank, 1997), 246–47. Private capital flow statistics in IMF, *International Capital Markets*, 28; and The World Bank, *Global Development Finance*, 26–27.
7. The interplay between political and economic reform in Latin America is clearly more complex and ambiguous than these two statements imply and obviously varies from country to country. Nevertheless, it seems safe to argue that in the aggregate, these threats to political and economic reform deriving from instability in international markets is valid. On the ambiguous nature of the relationship between political and economic reform in Latin America, see *Markets and Democracy in Latin America: Conflict or Convergence?* ed. Philip Oxhorn and Pamela K. Starr (Boulder: Lynne Reinner, 1999).
8. There are undoubtedly important differences between the operations of the World Bank and those of the IDB in Latin America. The IDB has traditionally been much more active than in the energy and transport sectors; it has a longer tradition of emphasizing antipoverty programs; it is better-suited institutionally for making small and medium-sized loans; and it initiated structural adjustment lending much later than the World Bank. The reforms each has instituted to cope with their changing operational environment, however, have been very similar.
9. Loan distribution figures in Diana Tussie, *The Inter-American Development Bank* (Boulder: Lynne Rienner, 1995), 48.
10. The World Bank, *The World Bank Annual Report, 1998* (Washington, D.C.: The World Bank, 1998), 82–83.
11. On the history of IDB-private sector cooperation, see Tussie, *The Inter-American Development Bank*. Recent changes in lending objectives reported in Stephen Fidler, "Shift towards Private Sector," *The Financial Times of London*, Mar. 17, 1998, 4.
12. Robert Ayres, Conference on the Future of Inter-American Relations (The Brookings Institution, Washington, D.C., Mar. 19, 1998).

13. The structure of the Decopaz program is very much like that of the National Solidarity Program initiated by the government of Carlos Salinas in Mexico.

14. On the history of development bank lending, including the institutional obstacles to effective aid programs, see Roy Culpeper, *Titans or Behemoths?* (Boulder: Lynne Rienner, 1997).

15. Tussie, *The Inter-American Development Bank*, 43; and L. Ronald Scheman, "Banking on Growth: The Role of the Inter-American Development Bank," *Journal of Interamerican Studies and World Affairs* 39, no. 1 (spring 1997): 96. Some economists also have questioned the effectiveness of the development banks' poverty alleviation strategy that focuses exclusively on economic growth and the development of human capital. Although essential to poverty alleviation, these factors might not be sufficient. Recent research undertaken by Nancy Birdsall and Juan Luis Londoño suggests that the relative distribution of assets, such as landholding and access to credit, is fundamental to an effective antipoverty strategy. The current antipoverty strategy of the IBD and the World Bank thus seems destined to under perform even in the best of circumstances. See Birdsall and Londoño, "Asset Inequality Matters: An Assessment of the World Bank's Approach to Poverty Reduction," *American Economics Association, Papers and Proceedings* (May 1997): 32–37.

16. Portfolio flows declined from more than 60 percent of total private flows in 1994 to less than 30 percent in 1996. The dollar value of foreign direct investment more than doubled between 1993 and 1996 increasing from 13.4 percent of total flows to nearly 30 percent. Sebastian Edwards, "Capital Inflows into Latin America: A Stop-Go Story," NBER Working Paper No. 6441, Cambridge, Mass., March 1998, 13; IMF, *International Capital Markets*, 28.

17. Congressional concerns included a Democratic desire to not "bail out dictators," a Republican worry that repeated IMF bailouts would reduce the perception of risk among private investors and thereby increase the frequency and severity of crises in the international financial system, and a bipartisan recognition of the general unpopularity of foreign assistance.

18. Quoted in an interview published in *International Economy* (Jan./Feb. 1998): 59.

19. For example, sections the IMF's 1996 annual report highlighting serious problems in the Thai economy were never made public owing to the refusal of the Thai government to permit their dissemination.

20. On the endemic weakness of capital markets see Dani Rodrik, "Who Needs Capital Account Convertibility?" in *Should the IMF Pursue Capital Account Convertibility? Essays in International Finance*, no. 207, Princeton University, 1998; and Jagdish Bhagwati, "The Capital Myth," *Foreign Affairs* 77, no. 3 (May–June 1998): 7–12. Mitigating the herding effect in modern financial markets is particularly difficult given the nature of most investors in emerging markets. Investors tend to enter these markets with a small proportion of their portfolio with the objective of diversifying their assets. Such investors (quite unlike the big banks which lent to Latin America during the 1970s) have a very small stake in these markets. Their small stake gives them little incentive to protect their investment by focusing on the long-term health of an emerging economy; meanwhile there are limited costs associated with cutting their losses and abandoning the market. They are, therefore, prone to move into or out of a market rapidly and with the herd.

21. On the Basle Accord, see Ethan Kapstein, *Supervising International Banks: Orgins and Implications of the Basle Accord* (Princeton: Princeton University Press, 1991). On the difficulties associated with any effort to extend its application into emerging markets, see IMF, *International Capital Markets* (Sept. 1996): 29–33.

22. Culpeper, *Titans or Behemoths?* 80.

23. Latin America held a voting majority in the IDB until 1994 and now controls half of the votes, although the United States has always had veto power over capital increases and modifications to the Bank's articles of agreement. On the different institutional structures of the IDB and the World Bank, see Culpeper, *Titans or Behemoths?* 23–46; and Tussie, *The Inter-American Development Bank*, 17–34.

8

Some Economic and Strategic Issues in the Face of the Emerging FTAA

ROBERT DEVLIN, ANTONI ESTEVADEORDAL,
AND LUIS JORGE GARAY

The Free Trade Area of the Americas (FTAA) process was launched during the Miami Summit of Heads of State in December 1994,[1] the centerpiece of a broader hemispheric initiative of political and socioeconomic cooperation among thirty-four countries of the Americas. The stated objective is to negotiate, as a single undertaking, a comprehensive and balanced hemispheric free-trade agreement by the year 2005. The preparatory phase, which began in January 1995, was quite successful; indeed, with more advances than the Uruguay Round achieved at a similar stage of development. On the basis of this preparatory work it was possible to launch formal negotiations in April 1998 and hold a first round of negotiations in September 1998 and a second round in the first quarter of 1999. The creation of an FTAA would clearly be the most important chapter in the history of regional cooperation in the Western Hemisphere and mark a fitting culmination to a fast-maturing trade policy framework in Latin America and the Caribbean.

The FTAA process did not emerge out of a vacuum. Rather it is an outgrowth of progressive globalization of the world economy and a profound transformation in the region which finds its expression in: (1) broad-based structural economic reforms in almost all the countries directed at stimulating market activity and a better articulation with the world economy; (2) the emergence, or strengthening, of democratic regimes almost everywhere, and (3) political commitments to once and for all foster peace and cooperation among neighbors with a history of rivalry and conflict. Achieving these simultaneous goals has been difficult, often traumatic, and certainly is still precarious in some of its dimensions.

It is often overlooked that regional integration has been a fundamental complementary tool for achieving these ambitious national objectives, which

permeate the entire region. Latin America and the Caribbean have a long tradition of interest in regional integration. An intense amount of activity in this
area emerged out of the postwar period. However, the initiatives in the first
three decades following the war inserted themselves in the prevailing state-led
import substitution strategy of the time, itself to a large extent a product of
"market skepticism" derived from the Great Depression. In the 1990s, however,
a "new" regionalism emerged in Latin America and the Caribbean that con-
formed to the new national strategies for economic and political transformation and preparation for globalization.

Trade liberalization has been a centerpiece in the structural reform
process, opening Latin American and Caribbean markets to unprecedented
competition from the rest of the world, providing access to new and better
consumer goods and cheaper inputs and technology for production, investment, and enhanced international competitiveness. The extent of the liberalization efforts in the last decade has varied from country to country, but
overall trade in the region is more open today than it has been since the period before the 1930s. Although the credit for trade liberalization should go primarily to the unilateral policies of countries, which became widespread in the
late 1980s and early 1990s, the GATT Uruguay Round negotiations and a wave
of regional trade agreements have continued to play a crucial role. As will be
argued later, regional integration has allowed countries to push forward in
terms of trade liberalization further than they perhaps could achieve in either
the unilateral or multilateral mode and thereby maintain the momentum of
trade reform. But since the objectives and practice of the new integration tend
to go beyond the traditional limited focus on liberalized (often very partial)
goods trade, to include an array of new market-based trade and trade-related
disciplines, the regional agreements often constitute a positive political economy externality, which serves to anchor even more the broader overall national reform process. In addition, there are the political externalities: countries
have used regional integration mutually to cement their new democratic systems and create interdependencies that reduce interest in pursuing historical
rivalries and promote regional cooperation in areas other than trade.

In effect, the FTAA effort is a good example of the new regionalism. Based
on its ambitious formal agenda the FTAA initiative seems to fit well into the
particular stylized facts of a type of regional integration which Ethier has
recently argued is welfare enhancing:[2]

- the integration agreement typically involves small countries linking up
  with large countries;
- the smaller countries have made, or are making, significant unilateral
  reforms;
- the degree of liberalization in the agreement is typically modest;

- the liberalization is primarily achieved by the smaller countries;
- the agreements often involve "deep," or comprehensive, objectives; and
- the agreements are regional in a geographical sense.

While not circumscribing ourselves to Ethier's framework, we share his basic point that it is a mistake to evaluate the prospects of the new regionalism—in this case the FTAA—on narrow Vinerian criterion because much more is at play.

For awhile many doubted the seriousness of the FTAA initiative. But the launching of negotiations in April 1998, coupled with clear signs of gathering momentum, the FTAA now is a regional process closer to becoming a reality. Thus it is worthwhile to review, if only in a limited way, some economic policy and strategic issues that will condition the effects of the FTAA on its member countries.

Our chapter will begin with an overview of the context for the emerging new regionalism and the FTAA, followed by a generic checklist of some of the potential benefits and costs that might be anticipated from an FTAA as well as another checklist of collective and national policy issues that could help to maximize the potential for favorable effects and minimize the costs. The last section will preliminarily develop one particular aspect of the FTAA, which will be an important determining factor of the balance of costs and benefits: the way in which the FTAA articulates with existing regional arrangements in the hemisphere. We close with some brief conclusions.

For the purpose of analysis, the chapter assumes that countries have assessed their alternatives and consequently are actively participating in the FTAA because they effectively share the objective of the Miami Summit, which the hemisphere's trade ministers have reconfirmed in Denver, Cartagena, Belo Horizonte, and San José. It also assumes that the FTAA will effectively emerge on or around 2005. Meanwhile, the chapter's scope does not permit an analysis of the world financial crisis, even though it is quite obvious that the FTAA, world trade, and indeed any meaningful economic initiative is threatened by systemic instability in international financial markets.[3]

The FTAA and the New Regionalism in the Americas

To effectively evaluate its roots, dynamics, and long-run implications, one must understand the context in which the FTAA process was initiated. Since the late 1980s, there has been a growing interest in regional approaches to trade liberalization. One of the earliest manifestations appeared in the southern cone with new sectoral and regional cooperation agreements that marked the incipient development of what we know today as MERCOSUR.[4] It also manifested itself among some developed countries, in particular, the United States's move to bilateral trade negotiations and the deepening of the

European internal market. During the same period most of the developing world was moving toward substantial market-oriented economic reforms, including unilateral trade initiatives. In addition, all of this was happening in the context of multilateral efforts in Geneva to liberalize trade in goods and services around the world, which culminated in the Uruguay Round Agreements in 1994 and the creation of the World Trade Organization in 1995.

By mid-1990s, the regional approaches to trade liberalization had spread throughout the world: in Europe, Asia, and the Americas. The rest of this section is a detailed chronology of these events in Latin America and the Caribbean. It will illustrate how the new regionalism has made its mark in the way trade relations are conducted in the region. If one had to select a single benchmark period in recent times that best captures the features of this "new" regionalism in Latin America and the Caribbean, then it would be around the time of launching of the FTAA at the Miami Summit.

The mid-1990s marks the tenth anniversary of the beginning of the wave of substantive unilateral trade reforms undertaken by the countries of the region.[5] The depth of these reforms is evident when evaluating a number of basic criteria. On average, tariffs in the region fell from 40 to 11 percent, and for most countries those tariff cuts were of the order of 50 percent and were implemented over relatively short periods of time (i.e., two to three years). Average maximum tariffs in the region fell from more than 80 percent to 40 percent with only two countries presently applying maximum tariffs of up to 100 percent on a small number of products. Tariff dispersion, on average, has declined from 30 percent in the mid-1980s to 9 percent today. Both the highest average rate and the highest dispersion rate, as measured by the standard deviation, are currently under 15 percent. There are still, however, some important peak tariffs, particularly in the Caribbean Community. On average, approximately 22 percent of tariff lines are subject to rates above 20 percent. Moreover, there are still some countries with maximum tariffs above 70 percent (see Table 8.1).

In April 1994, the Uruguay Round Final Act was signed at Marrakesh, ending almost a decade of multilateral trade negotiations. The agreements, which made up the final package, entered into force on January 1995, including the agreement establishing the World Trade Organization, responsible for administering the most sophisticated and comprehensive world trade agreement ever signed. In the area of tariff liberalization, this latest round of GATT negotiations achieved an average tariff reduction of 38 percent in industrialized countries and, from the standpoint of the Latin American and the Caribbean countries, implied substantial commitments to dismantle import barriers. The central obligation with respect to tariffs requires countries to limit their levels to a specified maximum, or so-called GATT tariff commitment, or "binding." The latest round resulted in a significant increase in the

Table 8.1

Tariffs in Latin America 1985–1997

		1985	1988	1991	1994	1997
Average Tariff Rates	Argentina	39.3	30.8	14.2	15.4	14.1
(Unweighted Averages)	Bolivia	22.7	16.6	9.2	9.7	9.6
	Brazil	55.1	41.5	20.4	9.7	14.9
	Chile	20.2	15.1	10.8	10.9	10.8
	Colombia	46.5	46.3	16.4	11.3	11.4
	Ecuador	58.7	44.5	16.6	11.0	9.9
	Mexico	33.6	10.2	12.6	12.4	13.7
	Paraguay	18.7	18.6	13.6	7.3	10.0
	Peru	64.4	70.5	16.2	15.6	13.1
	Uruguay	35.9	26.9	21.3	13.6	10.1
	Venezuela	31.6	42.2	15.1	11.3	11.5
Tariff Dispersion	Argentina	9.4	10.3	6.0	8.8	6.4
(Standard Deviation)	Bolivia	4.6	1.3	2.5	1.1	1.4
	Brazil	28.0	19.5	16.8	6.9	7.1
	Chile	1.6	.9	1.5	.9	1.2
	Colombia	16.9	17.4	8.0	5.8	5.8
	Ecuador	56.0	35.0	10.4	6.0	8.3
	Mexico	20.3	6.6	5.2	5.5	14.2
	Paraguay	13.8	13.7	11.8	6.8	6.3
	Peru	24.6	24.4	5.8	3.8	3.6
	Uruguay	14.9	11.3	6.5	5.9	6.4
	Venezuela	25.2	36.3	11.0	6.1	5.8
Tariff Peaks	Argentina	51.5	57.6	25.0	30.0	27.2
(Average tariff rates	Bolivia	32.3	17.0	10.0	10.0	10.0
top 1 percent products	Brazil	108.0	85.0	70.0	20.0	35.0
with highest tariffs)	Chile	27.4	20.0	11.0	11.0	11.0
	Colombia	85.0	88.0	51.4	20.0	20.0
	Ecuador	245.0	125.0	37.0	20.0	24.5
	Mexico	105.5	20.0	20.0	20.0	56.2
	Paraguay	50.0	50.0	52.0	32.0	23.7
	Peru	104.0	109.0	25.0	25.0	25.0
	Uruguay	60.0	45.0	30.0	20.0	22.0
	Venezuela	100.0	139.9	40.0	20.0	20.0

Source: A. Estevadeordal, *Negotiating Trade Agreements in the Americas* (forthcoming).

number of bound tariff lines. In the case of developed countries, the increase went from 22 to 72 percent; and in the case of countries in transition, it went from 78 to 98 percent. Latin America as a whole agreed to bind practically all tariff lines. This is especially significant when compared to the tariff bindings existing before the Uruguay Round began. In Latin America as a whole, only 38 percent of tariff lines for industrial products were bound, equivalent to 57 percent of imports. For agricultural products, the percentages were 36 and 74 percent, respectively.

The same year the multilateral talks ended (1994), there were dramatic advances in the new regionalism, with the Western Hemisphere being a major staging ground. Months before the signature of the Final Act of the Uruguay Round, the North American Free Trade Agreement (NAFTA) was implemented. In addition, important advances were made in the southern cone in preparation for the launching of MERCOSUR in January 1995. Moreover, during the same time period two countries in the hemisphere were in the process of consolidating their positions as strategic trade hubs in the region. Mexico was able to secure in 1994 three important agreements—based on the NAFTA model—with Costa Rica in April, with Colombia and Venezuela (known as the G-3 Agreement) in June, and with Bolivia in September. All three agreements were implemented at the beginning of 1995. For Chile, 1994 marked an acceleration in a series of bilateral agreements in the hemisphere (Mexico in 1991; Venezuela 1993; Colombia 1993; and Ecuador 1994). During the same year, Chile initiated free-trade talks with MERCOSUR countries and Canada and began a second round of negotiations to deepen its agreement with Mexico. These strategic agreements would be signed in subsequent years (1996, 1997, and 1998, respectively). In addition, around the same time, important institutional and policy reforms were carried out in existing agreements such as the Andean Pact (to become Andean Community in 1997), CARICOM, and the Central American Common Market (Table 8.2).

This dynamism was also present at the extraregional level, in particular, in the context of the APEC initiative. Mexico joined APEC as a full member in November 1993, and Chile entered one year later. Moreover, during the II Presidential Meeting of APEC in November 1994 in Indonesia, the leaders agreed to achieve the goal of free trade and investment in the region no later than 2010 for the industrialized economies and 2020 for developing countries. This brief history of the integration efforts in the mid-1990s would be incomplete without reference to the European Union. The EU involvement with Latin America was also renewed in December 1995 with the signature of a trade and economic cooperation agreement with MERCOSUR. This was followed by a Framework Cooperation Agreement with Chile in June 1996 and talks with Mexico toward a new trade and economic agreement in the years to come.

Table 8.2

Regional Trade Agreements in the Americas in the 1990s

Agreement	Date of Signature	Entry into Force
Caribbean Community (CARICOM)[1]	1989	1990
Chile-Mexico[2]	1991	1992
Central American Common Market (CACM)[3]	1990	1993
Chile-Venezuela	1993	1993
North American Free Trade Agreement (NAFTA)	1992	1994
Bolivia-Chile[4]	1993	1993
Colombia-Chile[5]	1993	1994
Southern Cone Common Market (MERCOSUR)	1991	1995
Costa Rica-Mexico	1994	1995
Group of Three (G-3)	1994	1995
CARICOM-Colombia	1994	1995
Bolivia-Mexico	1994	1995
Chile-Ecuador	1994	1995
Andean Community[6]	1988	1996
Chile-MERCOSUR	1996	1996
Canada-Chile	1996	1997
Bolivia-MERCOSUR	1996	1997
Mexico-Nicaragua	1997	1998
Chile-Peru	1998	1998
CACM-Dominican Republic[7]	1998	1999
CARICOM-Dominican Republic	1998	1999

Selected Agreements under Discussion

Regional—Free Trade Area of the Americas (FTAA); Andean Community-MERCO-SUR; Andean Community-Panama; CACM-Chile; CACM-Panama; Chile-Panama; Costa Rica-Trinidad & Tobago; Mexico-Belize; Mexico-Ecuador; Mexico-Northern Triangle (El Salvador, Guatemala, Honduras); Mexico-Panama; Mexico-Peru; Mexico-Trinidad & Tobago; Costa Rica-Trinidad & Tobago.

Extraregional—MERCOSUR-European Union; Mexico-European Union; Chile-European Union; CARICOM-European Union (Lomé Convention renewal); Canada-EFTA; Chile-South Korea; APEC.

Source: IDB, Integration, Trade and Hemispheric Issues Division.

Notes:
1. CARICOM began its reform process in 1989 (Declaration of Grand Anse) and agreed to launch a harmonized CET in 1990.
2. The two countries substantially revised and upgraded this accord in an agreement which was signed and entered into force in 1998.
3. The presidents agreed to re-activate the CACM in 1990 (Montelimar Summit) and opted to definitively pursue a customs union in 1993 (Protocol of Guatemala).
4. Negotiations are currently underway to revise and upgrade the agreement.
5. Negotiations are currently underway to revise and upgrade the agreement.
6. In 1988, the presidents agreed (in the Protocol of Quito) to amend the founding Charter of the Andean Group and alter the existing tariff reduction program. In 1996, the leaders officially agreed to change the group's name to the Andean Community and reform certain existing institutional structures (Declaration of Trujillo).
7. The agreement has not entered into force in some countries as a result of Hurricane Mitch.

The summary account is relevant not only for chronological purposes but also for stressing some of the specific facts that have characterized most of the new regionalism in Latin America, as well as the synergies and complementarities that exist among the different approaches to trade liberalization. First, a key factor in explaining the commitments undertaken by the Latin American and Caribbean countries during the Uruguay Round negotiations was the successful policy reforms—in which unilateral trade liberalization is central—carried out at the national level. In turn, the countries' agreements at the multilateral level acted as a signal to investors of their commitment to external opening and contributed as a lock-in mechanism for the domestic reforms. At the same time, the Uruguay Round agreements set the stage for the pursuit of regional agreements under a common umbrella of global trade rules as well as imposed a clearer set of disciplines under which preferential agreements can be negotiated.[6]

Second, while the reciprocal nature of the multilateral round provides a national political underpinning to further liberalization, and the economic advantages of free trade achieved at the multilateral level are well understood, it is sometimes difficult to evaluate negotiating opportunities in the context of the traditional framework of request/offers that take place in a forum of more than one hundred countries with very different strategic interests.[7] This can delimit the depth of new commitments. Moreover, Latin American and Caribbean countries' control over the initiation, agenda, and pace of a multilateral round is limited.

Regional and bilateral agreements offer certain advantages in this respect. These agreements also offer reciprocity. However, they usually involve a smaller group of geographically defined countries with a very clear profile of shared interests in commercial trade, geo-politics, and regional cooperation. This can provide a better environment for reaching consensus on the complex range of issues in modern trade agendas, for measuring the potential gains from committing scarce resources to a protracted negotiation involving reciprocity, and for private sector understanding and support of the liberalization process. Ethier finds that the incentives for exploiting the advantages of regional negotiations are higher the more successful are multilateral rounds.[8]

In effect, the wave of new regional trade agreements, the deepening of those already in existence, and the launching of FTAA negotiations at a hemispheric level should be seen, first, as a complement to the unilateral reforms and multilateral negotiations. Second, and most importantly, they are laboratories for the development of new paradigms for the design and implementation of trade policy around the world.

From an analytical point of view, traditional economic analysis has distinguished between different stages of economic integration. In this literature, liberalization under a free-trade agreement, as proposed under the FTAA initiative, would constitute a relatively less-advanced stage of integration than a common-market scheme, because it involves preferential trade liberalization among partners, but not the adoption of common protection policies toward third countries and free movement of factors of production. This type of analysis had some validity in a world of relatively closed economies where trade policy is mostly concerned with the management of border measures (i.e., tariffs and nontariffs measures). However, in an increasingly globalized world economy, trade flows are affected not only by border-type measures but also by domestic policies as well. This shift to the so-called "deeper" integration emerged first at the national level where unilateral trade reforms have been accompanied by substantial macroeconomic, financial, and regulatory reforms. The shift has also been very clear in recent multilateral negotiations where a new set of issues has emerged on the trade agenda. These include trade in services, intellectual property, trade-related investment measures and dispute settlement mechanisms. A contentious agenda lies ahead in other areas of possible harmonization efforts, such as competition policy and environmental standards. This increased coverage of areas for the harmonization and reconciliation of domestic policies is also increasingly present in the new regional integration agreements.

Based on these criteria, within the region, a distinction should be made between two existing types of free-trade agreements. First, there are traditional, or "first generation," agreements mostly negotiated in the framework of the Latin American Integration Association (LAIA, or ALADI in Spanish). These primarily focus on traditional market access issues under very simple normative frameworks. They are rightly called preferential agreements and can be subject to a traditional "Vinerian" analysis. These agreements in turn can be divided between "selective and partial" and "universal and automatic" preferential agreements according to the product coverage and the mechanisms used for implementing the preferential treatment for market access purposes. Second, there are the "new generation" of agreements characterized by their coverage of issues in the new global trade agenda, such as services, investment, government procurement, and competition policy. Moreover, in these agreements traditional market access liberalization is characterized by its broad coverage and implemented through automatic phase-out programs. Indeed, the regional integration agreements in Latin America have involved automatic schedules of elimination of tariffs on substantially all trade, with the bulk of liberalization taking place in ten years and exceptions rarely exceeding 6 percent of all tariff lines.[9]

While one must await the outcome of negotiations, the terms of reference for discussions now underway in the FTAA are suggestive of an agreement containing at least most of the elements of the new regionalism.

Preparing for the FTAA: Some Longer-Term Issues

Regional integration is an initiative with a long-run horizon. Many of the most important effects of successful regional integration schemes involve complex interrelationships that develop in a general equilibrium framework over a long period of time.[10] Typically at the beginning, and each time the agreement formally deepens its commitments, there are significant costs to be assumed up front with benefits playing out over a much more extended timeline.

Many economists focus their primary attention on whether regional integration induces what Viner first termed trade creation or trade diversion.[11] From a standard static Vinerian economic model of integration, it is well known that to increase the chances of trade creation there should be an important overlap among potential members in sectors protected by high tariffs as well as wide differences between member countries in the costs of producing the goods in the protected industries. To minimize the potential for trade diversion, there should be, first, a large number of potential members, so that there are few countries whose trade could be diverted; second, initially a low level of trade relative to production; and third, a significant proportion of preagreement trade conducted with future partners. In short, the agreement is going to be less likely trade diverting if formed among countries whose economies are currently competitive, but potentially complementary. Yet these "static" Vinerian effects of a regional integration agreement are only a small part of a successful story.

Dynamic effects are potentially much more important since they are associated with an increase in competitive pressures following the removal of trade barriers. Regional integration is about the "dynamic" economic transformations brought about by intensified competition; reduction of economic rents; exploitation of economies of scale, scope, and agglomeration; marketing and export experience; managerial efficiency, and so on. Today's integration also aims at so-called nontraditional gains such signaling commitments to investors, lock-in of policy reform, strengthening institutions and rules-based procedures, political economy synergies among partners, and geo-political objectives.[12] These effects could raise risk-adjusted rates of return and induce investment (local and foreign), technological change and growth. Indeed, even what may first appear as a cost through trade diversion could in the right circumstances be a platform for an economic transformation with benefits for the subregion and the world economy as a whole. Unfortunately, economists have found the analysis of these latter dynamic effects of regional integration difficult to model and test empirically.[13] Indeed, strong conclusions about regional integration initiatives are all too often drawn exclusively on static analysis, which, aside from providing a very incomplete story, also has its own methodological shortcomings. (The analysis of Yeats concerning MERCOSUR is a good example.)[14]

When national economies integrate there is an important reallocation of resources within and between those economies. When the integrating economies are relatively homogeneous, involved in significant trade with each other and converging in terms of income levels and technological development, the forces of integration could be heavily represented by growing intraindustry trade. In this context, adjustments can be expected to be relatively fast and with moderate economic disruptions.[15] When integration is among very heterogeneous countries in terms of income and technological development, trading relationships are still underdeveloped, and they share an overlapping product mix, the process of regional integration initially may be more heavily represented by development of interindustry trade with more significant lags and displacements during the adjustment process.

The FTAA is clearly an integration scheme involving a heterogeneous mix of countries ranging from the world's richest and most competitive countries to some of the poorest and more economically backward. The heterogeneous nature of the FTAA means that, all being equal, both the costs and benefits of integration could be relatively magnified and their distribution uneven among and within countries. Outlined below are some collective and national policy initiatives that could help Latin America and the Caribbean maximize the benefits of an FTAA and help dampen its costs. But first a generic checklist is presented on some of the longer-term potential benefits and costs, based on the prevailing situation in the hemisphere, which Latin America and the Caribbean could possibly anticipate from a new generation FTAA agreement.

Some Potential Positives

FREE ACCESS TO A HEMISPHERIC MARKET During the 1990s growth of exports to partners within subregional integration schemes has generally outperformed other markets (see Table 8.3). One of the major potential benefits of an FTAA is a more secure and preferential access to that part of the hemispheric market that is outside of the respective formal subregional integration schemes. This "extra subregional hemispheric market" is important for almost all the countries of the region (see Tables 8.4 and 8.5) and some models suggest there would be conditions for considerable creation of trade if an FTAA were to emerge.[16]

Within this hemispheric market, the U.S. is preponderant. Moreover, for countries in the Caribbean Basin the U.S. market weighs heavily, not only in the hemisphere but also in total world trade (see Table 8.6). South of the Caribbean Basin exports to the United States are generally significant, but their share in total trade is a more modest one-third or less. The U.S. market is significant in another important way for many countries: its share as a market for more knowledge-intensive manufactured exports is second only to most country's subregional market. Hence the U.S. market, along with subregional integration,

Table 8.3

Western Hemisphere: Total and Intraregional Exports (millions U.S. dollars and percentages)

		1990	1991	1992
Western Hemisphere[1]	Global Exports	658,234	684,995	727,241
	% growth	7.9	4.1	6.2
	Extrahemispheric Exports	341,515	357,391	364,017
	% growth	5.4	4.6	1.9
	Intrahemispheric Exports	316,719	327,605	363,224
	% growth	10.7	3.4	10.9
	Intra/Total	48.1	47.8	49.9
Latin America[2]	Global Exports	137,781	136,242	145,504
	% growth	10.5	-1.1	6.8
	Extra-LA Exports	121,412	116,249	120,662
	% growth	10.9	-4.3	3.8
	Intra-LA Exports	16,369	19,993	24,943
	% growth	7.3	22.1	24.3
	Intra/Total	11.9	14.7	11.1
Andean Community	Global Exports	31,605	28,630	28,390
	% growth	26.1	-9.4	-0.9
	Extra-Andean Exports	30,310	26,912	26,224
	% growth	26.2	-11.2	-2.6
	Intra-Andean Exports	1,295	1,719	2,156
	% growth	23.5	32.7	25.4
	Intra/Total	4.1	6	7.6
Caricom	Global Exports	4,762	4,771	4,875
	% growth	6.3	0.2	2.2
	Extra-Caricom Exports	4,224	4,308	4,408
	% growth	4.9	2	2.3
	Intra-Caricom Exports	555	463	467
	% growth	23.3	-13.9	0.8
	Intra/Total	11.7	9.7	9.6

1993	1994	1995	1996	1997	1998(e)	Average 1990–1998
765,511	859,185	996,045	1,065,343	1,157,573	1,144,532	
5.3	12.2	15.9	7	8.7	-1.1	7.2
365,905	394,303	472,187	490,588	514,397	476,479	
0.5	7.8	19.8	3.9	4.9	-7.4	4.3
399,606	464,881	523,858	574,755	643,176	668,054	
10	16.3	12.7	9.7	11.9	3.9	9.8
52.2	34.1	52.6	53.9	55.6	58.4	
155,644	181,573	218,989	240,879	268,548	266,068	
7	16.7	20.6	10	11.5	-0.9	8.6
126,011	146,574	177,194	197,204	215,457	211,949	
4.4	16.3	20.9	11.3	9.3	-1.6	7.2
29,633	34,998	41,793	43,675	53,090	54,119	
19.3	18.1	19.4	4.5	21.6	1.9	16.1
19	19.3	19.1	18.1	19.8	20.3	
29,654	34,256	38,843	45,480	47,656	38,787	
4.5	13.5	13.4	17.1	4.8	-18.6	2.6
26,858	30,952	34,268	40,817	42,029	33,233	
2.4	14.9	11.1	19.1	3.0	-20.9	1.2
2,796	3,404	4,575	4,663	5,627	5,554	
29.7	21.7	34.4	1.9	20.7	-1.3	20.0
9.4	9.9	11.8	10.3	11.8	14.3	
4,837	5,933	6,211	-	-	-	
-0.8	22.7	4.7	-	-	-	
4,286	5,346	5,407	-	-	-	
-2.8	24.7	1.1	-	-	-	
551	587	815	-	-	-	
19.1	6.5	38.9	-	-	-	
11.4	9.9	13.1	-	-	-	

continued on the next page

Table 8.3 continued from the previous page

		1990	1991	1992
CACM	Global Exports	4,058	4,138	4,697
	% growth	12.7	2	13.5
	Extra-CACM Exports	3,402	3,356	3,697
	% growth	12.4	-1.3	10.1
	Intra-CACM Exports	656	782	1,000
	% growth	14.6	19.1	27.9
	Intra/Total	16.2	18.9	21.3
MERCOSUR	Global Exports	46,425	45,911	50,561
	% growth	-0.3	-1.1	10.1
	Extra-MERCOSUR Exports	42,302	40,808	43,341
	% growth	-1.2	-3.5	6.2
	Intra-MERCOSUR Exports	4,123	5,102	7,220
	% growth	10.8	23.8	41.5
	Intra/Total	8.9	11.1	14.3
Group of Three	Global Exports	65,162	65,117	67,451
	% growth	22.2	0.9	36.1
	Extra-G-3 Exports	64,127	63,937	65,675
	% growth	15.5	-0.3	2.7
	Intra-G-3 Exports	1,035	1,180	1,776
	% growth	47	14	50.4
	Intra/Total	1.6	1.8	2.6
NAFTA	Global Exports	561,164	591,440	627,933
	% growth	7.8	5.4	6.2
	Extra-NAFTA Exports	320,667	341,997	354,468
	% growth	5.2	6.7	3.6
	Intra-NAFTA Exports	240,497	249,443	273,465
	% growth	11.5	3.7	9.6
	Intra/Total	42.9	42.2	43.6

Source: IDB, Statistics and Quantitative Analysis Unit of the Integration and Regional Programs Department, based on DATAINTAL.

(1) Western Hemisphere includes Latin America (see following definition), the United States, and Canada.

1993	1994	1995	1996	1997	1998(e)	Average 1990-1998
5,065	5,509	6,864	9,018	9,597	10,573	
7.9	9.9	24.6	31.4	6.4	10.2	12.7
3,961	4,290	5,408	7,442	7,730	8,500	
7.1	8.1	26.4	37.6	3.9	10.0	12.1
1,105	1,229	1,456	1,576	1,866	2,073	
10.4	11.3	18.4	8.2	18.4	11.1	15.5
21.8	22.3	21.2	17.5	19.4	19.6	
54,162	62,112	70,401	74,997	83,210	82,931	
7.1	14.7	13.3	6.5	11.0	-0.3	7.5
44,132	50,157	56,018	57,959	62,560	61,537	
1.9	13.7	11.7	3.5	7.9	-1.6	4.8
10,031	11,955	14,394	17,038	20,650	21,394	
38.9	19.2	20.3	18.4	21.2	3.6	22.9
18.5	19.2	20.4	22.7	24.8	25.8	
74,367	86,020	107,625	128,914	144,807	146,333	
10.3	17.1	23.8	19.8	12.3	1.1	10.6
72,023	83,456	104,319	125,749	140,786	142,102	
9.7	15.9	25	20.5	12.0	0.9	10.5
2,344	2,565	3,306	3,165	4,021	4,231	
32	9.4	29.9	-4.3	27.0	5.2	19.2
3.2	3	3.1	2.5	2.8	2.9	
661,752	738,494	856,598	919,918	999,456	996,926	
5.4	11.6	16	7.4	8.6	-0.3	7.4
360,444	396,434	461,079	482,396	514,955	486,147	
1.7	7.2	19.3	4.6	6.7	-5.6	5.3
301,308	352,060	395,520	437,522	484,501	510,779	
10.2	16.9	12.3	10.6	10.7	5.4	9.9
45.5	47.7	46.2	47.6	48.5	51.2	

(2) Latin America here is Argentina, Bolivia, Brazil, Chile, Colombia, Costa Rica, Ecuador, El Salvador, Guatemala, Honduras, Mexico, Nicaragua, Panama, Paraguay, Peru, Uruguay, and Venezuela.

e = Annual estimates are based on date through November 15, 1998.

Table 8.4

Exports of Latin America by Countries and Subregions, 1996 (Percent of Total)

	Intrasubregional	Extrasubregional	Total Hemispheric	Rest of the World
Argentina	33.3	23.4	56.7	43.3
Brazil	15.3	29.8	45.1	54.9
Paraguay	63.3	11.1	74.4	25.6
Uruguay	48.0	14.1	62.1	37.9
MERCOSUR	**22.7**	**27.0**	**49.7**	**50.3**
Bolivia	20.3	46.5	66.8	33.2
Colombia	17.4	52.7	70.1	29.9
Ecuador	8.8	55.8	64.6	35.4
Peru	7.2	32.5	39.7	60.3
Venezuela	7.5	81.0	88.5	11.5
Andean Community	**10.3**	**64.5**	**74.8**	**25.2**
Costa Rica	12.2	53.9	66.1	33.9
El Salvador	43.8	25.8	69.6	30.4
Guatemala	28.5	51.2	79.6	20.4
Honduras	4.1	63.5	67.6	32.4
Nicaragua	15.3	50.5	65.9	34.1
CACM	**20.4**	**49.9**	**70.3**	**29.7**
Mexico	0.9	91.9	92.8	7.2
Colombia	8.2	61.8	70.1	29.9
Venezuela	6.0	82.5	88.5	11.5
G-3	**2.4**	**87.7**	**90.1**	**9.9**
Chile	0.0	36.2	36.2	63.8
Panama	0.0	72.9	72.9	27.1

Source: IDB, Division of Integration, Trade and Hemispheric Issues, based on DATAINTAL.

Table 8.5

Imports of Latin America by Countries and Subregions, 1996 (Percent of Total)

	Intrasubregional	Extrasubregional	Total Hemispheric	Rest of the World
Argentina	24.5	27.9	52.3	47.7
Brazil	15.5	31.2	46.7	53.3
Paraguay	54.3	14.8	69.2	30.8
Uruguay	44.0	19.9	63.9	36.1
MERCOSUR	**20.5**	**29.2**	**49.8**	**50.2**
Bolivia	8.6	58.9	67.5	32.5
Colombia	13.0	50.6	63.5	36.5
Ecuador	16.0	51.7	67.7	32.3
Peru	18.4	45.8	64.2	35.8
Venezuela	8.9	64.4	73.3	26.7
Andean Community	**13.2**	**53.6**	**66.8**	**33.2**
Costa Rica	7.2	71.5	78.6	21.4
El Salvador	19.1	61.7	80.8	19.2
Guatemala	7.7	73.1	80.8	19.2
Honduras	15.4	66.3	81.7	18.3
Nicaragua	24.2	52.9	77.0	23.0
CACM	**12.7**	**67.3**	**80.0**	**20.0**
Mexico	0.4	79.6	79.9	20.1
Colombia	12.9	50.6	63.5	36.5
Venezuela	11.5	61.8	73.3	26.7
G-3	**2.9**	**74.4**	**77.3**	**22.7**
Chile	0.0	55.5	55.5	44.5
Panama	0.0	80.1	80.1	19.9

Source: IDB, Division of Integration, Trade and Hemispheric Issues, based on DATAINTAL.

Table 8.6

Percentage of Latin America's Trade with the USA by Countries, 1996

	% of Exports to USA	% of Imports from USA
Argentina	8.2	19.9
Brazil	19.2	21.9
Paraguay	3.5	10.8
Uruguay	6.7	12.0
MERCOSUR	**15.1**	**20.6**
Bolivia	25.3	27.7
Colombia	38.7	36.0
Ecuador	34.9	31.4
Peru	19.8	26.0
Venezuela	58.8	45.0
Andean Community	**45.6**	**35.3**
Costa Rica	41.0	44.8
El Salvador	18.1	39.3
Guatemala	36.6	43.9
Honduras	58.1	50.3
Nicaragua	44.1	33.6
CACM	**38.7**	**43.2**
Mexico	84.2	75.5
G-3	**76.0**	**67.9**
Chile	15.4	24.4
Panama	51.8	37.3

Source: IDB, Division of Integration, Trade and Hemispheric Issues, based on DATAINTAL.

has been contributing to Latin America and Caribbean's long-sought-after goal of diversifying away from commodity exports to manufactured goods.[17]

In terms of market access, for Latin America and the Caribbean the U.S. market, and North America more generally, is clearly a strategic target of the FTAA negotiations. However, trade with the United States and Canada is already relatively free because of the low average tariffs in those countries and the fact that the majority of Latin American and Caribbean countries already enjoy duty-free access for an extensive range of products on account of an array of nonreciprocal preferential arrangements. Thus the market access benefits of an FTAA will likely focus on three issues. First, negotiating free access for specific products and sectors in North America that face relatively onerous tariffs or nontariff measures (e.g., agriculture, food products, textiles, and so forth). Second, disciplining, beyond what is available under WTO rules, the use in North America of trade-distorting measures and trade remedies (particularly antidumping).[18] And third, more generally establishing a predictable rules-based framework through a hemispheric dispute settlement mechanism to ensure enforcement of a stable free access to this market. Without a major advance in these areas the incentive for Latin America and the Caribbean to make concessions on tariff reduction for North American goods as well as in other areas of the negotiation of special interest to North America (e.g., intellectual property rights, services, government procurement, and so on) could be low. The prospects for a successful FTAA could suffer as a consequence.

Another advantage of an FTAA organized around strict and effectively binding disciplines for openness is that it could provide an escape valve for export to a large market should problems in the world economy begin to undermine open markets elsewhere. However, to afford this opportunity one must emphasize the paramount importance of commitments to openness; only in this way could the experience of Latin America and the Caribbean during the crisis of the 1980s, in which regional markets suffered disproportionately, be ameliorated.

PREPARATION FOR WORLD-CLASS COMPETITION AND GLOBALIZATION Through unilateral, multilateral, and subregional liberalization Latin American and Caribbean governments have been using increasing import competition as a tool for inducing economic transformation.[19] The FTAA promises to open markets much further and induce more head-to-head competition from world-class firms in North America. Indeed, opening to North America, given its size and competitive strength, has effects that parallel in some ways a market opening to the world economy. Preparation for this competition, and the gradual intensification thereof, during a FTAA phase-in period will be a challenge for many national firms in Latin America and the Caribbean. But it also should serve as a major catalyst for microeconomic modernization of the economies. The difference between an opening through an FTAA and one that is unilateral with the rest of the world is that the FTAA offers the benefits of reciprocal liberalization in a legal framework of mutually agreed trade and trade-related rights and obligations. Moreover, the resulting source of high-grade competition is more geographically focused (on identifiable North American firms), which conceivably could provide advantages in the formulation of effective strategic responses by nationals.[20] There is some evidence that NAFTA has served as a catalyst of microeconomic modernization and enhanced competitiveness in Mexico.[21]

ATTRACTION OF FOREIGN DIRECT INVESTMENT Foreign direct investment (FDI) can be a source of technological transfer, modern corporate practice, and access to international export markets.[22] The presence of FDI also can serve to lock-in policy reform.[23] There is great competition among developing countries for this type of investment. The inflows of FDI to Latin America have grown substantially in the 1990s from US$8 billion in 1990 to US$46 billion in 1997. Indeed, prior to the Asian crisis Latin America captured more than one-third of the fast-growing total FDI flows to developing countries.[24]

As Ethier points out, developing country competition for FDI is sufficiently intense that significant distinguishing features in a country or subregion can be decisive in attracting investors, which tend to cluster or locate together.[25] The economic literature recognizes that integration schemes can create an impact that attracts FDI. According to Blomstrom and Kokko the bigger the change in economic environment associated with the agreement and the greater the locational advantages of the country, sector, or subregion, the more likely the initiative will stimulate foreign investment from countries in the agreement and from third parties.[26] An FTAA could be a magnet for foreign direct investment: it would create a preferential market of nearly 800 million people and 10 trillion dollars of GDP. This, coupled with possible lower-risk premia due to the Latin America and Caribbean's locking into (see below) a rules-based agreement anchored by a subregion (North America), which investors traditionally consider highly credible, could be a basis for attracting considerable foreign direct investment. The pattern, however, is not unidirectional. Foreign direct investment that originates in the Western Hemisphere and is motivated primarily by the existence of margins of preference may be withdrawn and be substituted by direct exports from the home country.[27] On the other hand, foreign direct investment that is motivated primarily by locational advantages could expand in the hemispheric market. The FTAA could be a strong magnet for foreign direct investment from outside the hemisphere as well because of preferences of a large market and access, which is secured by a rules-based system. However, some existing extrahemispheric foreign investment could also relocate to exploit the redefined locational advantages of the bigger FTAA market.

As far as intrasubregional investment is concerned, it is difficult to know exactly what is happening due to severe data constraints. However, there are indications that this phenomenon is gradually becoming significant in an environment of open regionalism.[28] In an FTAA this budding intraregional experience could be useful in the formation of alliances and investments that exploit geographical advantages for competing in the hemispheric and world markets.

WIDENING AND DEEPENING OF REGIONAL INTEGRATION The FTAA will probably eliminate some regional agreements and contribute to others deepening and widening. The exact outcome will depend on objectives and the political commitment of the member countries to their respective agreements. As we will see later, this is probably one of the more complex issues surrounding an FTAA. While not all developments in this area will be welcomed by all participants, there are scenarios that would be largely positive for subregional integration, for the hemisphere, and the world economy more generally.

An FTAA promises to enhance transparency and reduce transaction costs of hemispheric trade. Since the 1990s there has been a proliferation of new free-trade areas in Latin America and the Caribbean. These new agreements have served to strengthen political ties, push the trade liberalization process forward, and contributed to growth of trade and investment and diversification of exports. However, the new agreements have created a complex web of tariff preferences, rules of origin, and other disciplines that have reduced transparency in trade, altered investment flows, and introduced their own transactions costs. An FTAA would probably supersede at least the simpler free-trade areas, and—assuming it fulfills its promise of improving on the existing state of the art regarding the normative architecture of free-trade areas—could thereby raise transparency and lower transaction costs in the hemisphere. However, as will be discussed in the following section, the dynamics of this convergence process is complicated and will be aided or abetted by the direction of subregional and regional integration policy between now and 2005.

Since trade ministers in the hemisphere have agreed that only integration schemes with commitments deeper than the FTAA will continue to exist after 2005, there is every incentive for countries with political and economic objectives of deep subregional integration to fortify their community commitments as soon as it is politically feasible. Aside from the short-term benefits of allowing the subregions to better coordinate and project joint positions in the FTAA negotiations, the longer-term advantages of strenghtened commitments are structural change, enhanced investment and competitiveness in the hemispheric and world markets, as well as a more effective vehicle to promote a subregional agenda, which has a logic and legitimacy of all its own. Finally, since the FTAA will most likely be a strictly enforced rules-based system, in the longer term it could have positive demonstration effects on Latin America and the Caribbean regional integration, which still must rely to a significant degree on diplomatic "informality."

On the down side, the negotiations and prospects of a hemispheric agreement could also have the effect in some case of distracting attention from subregional integration and stimulating conflictive opportunistic behavior among subregional partners attempting to negotiate collectively the FTAA. This would be highly unfortunate. We now know that successful subregional integration is never lineal. Hence the collective FTAA process must not aggravate problems in viable subregional agreements and must find ways to flexibly accommodate conjunctural swings in the evolution of deep subregional integration schemes. However, in those cases where fissures reflect inherently weak political commitment and systematic unfulfilled promises of subregional integration, the chances of deepening would not be good anyway and absorption by an FTAA may be in everyone's interest.

STRENGTHENING THE MULTILATERAL SYSTEM   For Latin America and the Caribbean, a healthy and developing multilateral system is strategically essential; after all, as was seen earlier, the extrahemispheric market is still primary, or very important, for all but a few countries. However, some trade specialists argue that regional integration is a threat for the multilateral system. The FTAA is especially alarming from their perspective because of its overall size and the participation of North America.[29]

One cannot dismiss risks in this area. Large regional integration schemes can improve the terms of trade of member countries at the expense of nonmember countries and give rise to incentives for maintaining or increasing preferences and protection. An FTAA can also create defensive reactions on the part of third parties. This would be benevolent if it emerged in the form of a push for a consensus on a new ambitious multilateral round that would in effect erode FTAA preferences. But another possibility is that a defensive reaction emerges in the form of others seeking to widen and deepen their own bloc at the expense of the multilateral system. In any event, it can be argued that in the current policy environment the risks are overstated. Indeed, in today's context of open regionalism, regional integration can serve as a catalyst for development of the multilateral system.

The FTAA process already has had some positive benefits for the multilateral system, e.g., the FTAA preparatory work has greatly increased transparency regarding the rules and norms of trade in the countries and subregions of the hemisphere.[30] Meanwhile, since the WTO is the agreed-upon baseline for the FTAA, the same process is intensively exposing countries to the rights, obligations, and procedures of the WTO and the Uruguay Round. The

FTAA process has even exposed the WTO to better ways to facilitate country notification to that body.[31]

Will a serious FTAA negotiation facilitate or impede another multilateral agreement? This is a highly speculative question full of political uncertainties. The current FTAA negotiations parallel a more narrowly defined WTO built-in agenda (agriculture, services, IPR, and so on),[32] which could very well be expanded into a new multilateral round if there were a broad enough consensus to do so. In the meantime the FTAA has helped countries prepare and exchange ideas and information that could be helpful in their WTO agenda.[33] In any event, since the Uruguay Round is still being digested and the political parameters for launching a new round are complex in the best of circumstances, it was not clear until recently that a new comprehensive round might emerge. Also, without the FTAA the United States might have returned to its original strategy of bilaterally pursuing a trade agenda, which would ultimately aggravate the distortion of the hemisphere's hub-and-spoke matrix. The fact is that for Latin America and the Caribbean the FTAA has been up to now the only available "big market" trade negotiation that could accommodate the trade-offs needed to advance in a broad spectrum of trade issues. Moreover, the voice of the region's countries and subregions in the FTAA negotiation is larger than it would be in a much bigger WTO forum.[34]

It is not implausible that there will be synergies between the WTO built-in agenda and the FTAA negotiations and that FTAA negotiations will serve one way or another as the handmaiden of a new multilateral agreement. Since the FTAA is a single undertaking and interests among the different negotiating topics are far from symmetric between North America and Latin America and the Caribbean, realization of any agreement will likely be better than the WTO in nature.[35] That is to say, in addition to the traditional tariff liberalization on "substantially all trade," to realize itself the FTAA may have to effectively address North American-Latin American and Caribbean trade-offs on the broader spectrum of their respective priority/sensitive issues agenda, leading to agreements in some areas that make the FTAA better, and more balanced, than what is available in the WTO. The specter of a better agreement, on or around 2005, could in turn help induce a world consensus for a multilateral agreement the evolution of which would be influenced by the innovations generated in the FTAA itself. Indeed, some past multilateral rounds have had their origin in the impact of developments in regional integration as outsiders see a round as a vehicle for reducing the preferences they face, or will face, and insiders see it as an opportunity to politically restate their commitment to multilateralism, and perhaps promote their new trade agenda reciprocally at the world level.[36] On the other hand, if a critical mass of sensitive/priority issues are not effectively put on the FTAA table, because countries prefer to negotiate them in multilateral fora, the

FTAA could falter; hence, furthering hemispheric interests in trade liberalization would be dependent on individual unilateral policy and on subregional integration until a world consensus emerged on yet another new WTO round.

LOCK-IN OF POLICY REFORM While economic policy change in Latin America and the Caribbean has been substantial, a successful and balanced FTAA could serve to make reversals more difficult. The importance of this policy instrument would vary greatly among the countries of the region. In any event, lock-in effects were a factor in Spain and Eastern Europe's linkup with the EU and Mexico's participation in NAFTA.

Some Potential Negatives

While there are a number of potential benefits from an FTAA, there are potential costs too. Again, although these will be country specific, a generic checklist—not necessarily exhaustive—can be developed from what is known in the literature and practice of new regionalism.

ADJUSTMENTS Liberalization of trade in the hemisphere is expected to create trade and generate efficiency gains. However, in the process of arriving at the full potential benefits of an FTAA, there are firm, sectoral, and social adjustments on account of the reallocation of resources induced by liberalized trade flows. The more heterogeneous the membership of a new FTA, and the more important trade is as a percentage of GDP, the greater the potential gains from creation of a regional market—but also the more pronounced the adjustment process will likely be. Hence, in an FTAA with heterogeneous countries and many open economies, important adjustments of considerable economic and social magnitude are likely. The costs of these adjustments will depend on many factors such as initial country conditions, the stance of domestic economic policy, and progress in structural reforms, exceptions (if any) and phase-in periods for liberalization, the availability of adjustment assistance, and so forth. Some of these issues will be discussed below.

ASYMMETRIC DISTRIBUTION OF GAINS The FTAA membership will combine heterogeneous countries in terms of their levels of development. Economic theory suggests that, in principle, liberalization of trade can promote convergence among richer and poorer economies. Moreover, there is some empirical evidence that this occurs.[37] However, the process has been observed to be extremely slow and uneven, even in relatively ideal conditions like the U.S. economy where free trade among states combines with the free movement of all factors of production and a degree of uniformity in regulatory frameworks and political institutions.[38] Thus, all being equal, in an FTAA there is the risk of skewed benefits, with some countries and regions gaining much more than others in the short to medium term.[39] There are ways and means to effectively counteract this problem if the member countries so wish to do so. However, if it becomes exaggerated, an uneven distribution of benefits can lead to political tension and stagnation of a trade agreement.[40]

A specific phenomenon identified in the debate over the FTAA is that the asymmetric structure of tariffs in the hemisphere can lead to serious redistributive effects between the North and South.[41] As mentioned earlier, on average, tariffs in Latin America and the Caribbean (Table 8.1) are considerably higher than in North America. (In 1997, the average tariff in the United States was 5 percent and in Canada was 7.5 percent.) Consequently, in the process of preferential tariff liberalization, revenue from duties on imports from North America prior to the FTAA is effectively transferred to producers there as they capture margins of preference. This cost must be weighed against the benefits of entering an agreement.

TRADE AND INVESTMENT DIVERSION   Creation of preferences goes beyond technical issues and obviously has a political component. In principle this is not necessarily bad: a free-trade area represents a compromise among parties with different interests and by definition is part of a second-best world. To the extent preferences emerge endogenously as part of a collective process of trade-offs, they can be the sign of a sustainable free-trade agreement. An agreement among countries that exhibit significantly high tariffs on third parties, coupled with restrictive rules of origin, inevitably has some effect of diverting trade away from possibly more efficient firms that are located in nonmember countries.[42] This has real costs and is part of the price of an agreement which presumably has its compensations for members; and if the agreement promotes sustainable growth, for the world economy as well. But awareness of the problem is important in order to minimize these effects. Meanwhile, to the extent that exploitation of FTAA preferences (including incentives provided by rules of origin)—rather than the transparency and comprehensiveness of disciplines of a large regional market—are the primary motive for foreign investment decisions, there are the risks that some direct investment activity will be diverted from more efficient third markets.[43] Even if diversion of trade and investment flows is more than compensated later by the dynamic effects of integration, there are immediate up-front costs for consumers and producers.

MACROECONOMIC VULNERABILITIES   The FTAA disciplines will emerge in countries at very different stages of structural reform. Hence there is always the risk that in some instances the introduction of a new trade discipline(s) may involve less-than-optimal sequencing vis-à-vis the progress of other reforms. An example might be where the liberalization of financial services precedes strengthening of domestic financial regulatory structures or where that liberalization and creation of the hemispheric market stimulates surges of capital inflows, which in turn generate pressures for a premature appreciation of the exchange rate and weakened trade and balance of payments performance in the new FTAA.[44]

MORE INTERDEPENDENCE While integration schemes provide benefits for participating countries, they also create new interdependencies that may erode autonomy to some degree. With an FTAA new interdependencies will be created; some will be appreciated, and others may not. Since the North American market will naturally be an anchor for an FTAA agreement, one can expect that Latin America and the Caribbean will to a greater extent be under the commercial influence of their northern neighbors. The interdependency could provide benefits—e.g., policy lock-in and investment effects, more formal capacity to influence North American trade policy, capacity to organize balance of payments assistance, and so on—but also be accompanied by more North American commercial vigilance and perhaps indirectly intensifying pressures of particular unilateral noncommercial policies emerging out of this geographic area in subjects such as drugs, labor, and the environment.

Policy Issues

While the above checklist of the potential cost and benefits of an FTAA is a priori, generic and far from exhaustive, it highlights some of the strong economic and political trade-offs that countries could confront as they enter an FTAA. These and other costs and benefits would play out over an extended period of time with the costs weighing in heavily at the initiation of the process. To the extent that the FTAA is successful, these costs should be more than compensated by benefits in the longer term that generate growth and realize other objectives.

How costs and benefits play out in practice will depend on, inter alia, the negotiated architecture of the FTAA disciplines and institutions and the time path of their implementation; the interface between national and subregional economic policy and the FTAA as well as the play of exogenous factors in the world economy. This subsection highlights a generic checklist of collective hemispheric and national policies, which in principle could tend to maximize benefits and minimize costs of an FTAA. Again the relevance of the checklist and its components will vary for each country according to its individual circumstances and the final outcome of an FTAA agreement.

COLLECTIVE NETWORK While avoiding cumbersome bureaucracy and costly infrastructure, it is nevertheless imperative that the FTAA develops a coherent and functionally comprehensive collective institutional network that allows all countries to exploit fully their rights and opportunities as well as monitor and enforce (in a constructive way) the obligations of the FTAA. Not knowing the precise scope and normative architecture of the FTAA inhibits precise comments about this issue. However, among the direct and indirect mechanisms, which should emerge in or around the FTAA are: (1) a fully transparent and participatory dispute settlement mechanism, which builds on innovations found in the WTO; (2) collection and dissemination of information, which facilitates the countries monitoring of their rights and obligations; (3) monitoring of the distribution of benefits of the FTAA, with special attention to the poorer economies; (4) interchange of information and perhaps degrees of coordination concerning certain aspects of national economic policies (e.g., macroeconomics, financial regulation, vigilance of capital flows), which have externalities vis-à-vis countries' performance in the FTAA and affect the ability to deal with systemic problems in an evermore interdependent hemisphere; (5) adjustment and balance of payments assistance;[45] (6) technical assistance; and (7) public outreach to enhance civil society's understanding of the FTAA processes and trade issues more generally.

NATIONAL MACROECONOMIC POLICY   A sustainable macroeconomic environment is fundamental in order for a country to compete and capture the full potential benefits of any economic reform or a trade initiative such as the FTAA. Latin America and the Caribbean have made much progress in reforming macroeconomic policy.[46] However, in Latin America and the Caribbean the sustainability of macroeconomic balances has been adversely affected by international capital flows, which are increasingly volatile, unpredictable, and prone to contagion. The volatility is indeed impressive (see Figure 8.1). In this environment a strong influx of capital cannot be necessarily interpreted as a signal of the market's commitment to a given macroeconomic policy stance or can an outflow be necessarily be interpreted as confirmation of poor fundamentals.[47] Since capital flows affect the level of aggregate expenditure, trade balances, and the real exchange rate, the volatility that is being observed in international capital markets is of fundamental concern for the stability of an FTAA and the ability of countries to maximize their commercial opportunities. More specifically, the volatility of capital flows greatly aggravates macroeconomic management and is conducive to cycles of excess expenditure, crisis, and overadjustment, which in turn is unhealthy for growth, stability, free trade, and integration.

While there is increasing public awareness of the problem of volatile capital flows, international initiatives are usually slow in coming. In the meantime, a defensive national macroeconomic stance that avoids leveraging an economy on volatile short-term external capital may be the best defense to

Figure 8.1

Net Portfolio Investment and Other Short-Term Inflows to Latin America (in billions of U.S. dollars)

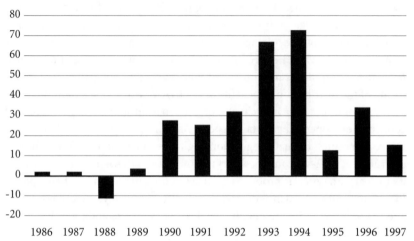

| | 1986 | 1987 | 1988 | 1989 | 1990 | 1991 | 1992 | 1993 | 1994 | 1995 | 1996 | 1997 |

Source: International Monetary Fund.

ward off the destabilizing effects of unpredictable reversals in the psychology of capital markets. Such an approach would aim at establishing a cautious macroeconomic policy stance that, coupled with international reserves, would allow a country to make nontraumatic adjustments should capital flows abruptly slow down or dramatically reverse themselves. This would involve a policy mix of strong fiscal and monetary discipline; cautious external debt management, intervention in the foreign-exchange market (reserve accumulation/sterilization and, when necessary, mechanisms to directly control, or better regulate, the flows of short-term speculative capital), and disciplined financial market regulation.[48] Such an approach could reduce the risk of abrupt macroeconomic adjustments and could contribute to moderating appreciation of the real exchange rate, which protects incentives for domestic production of exports and import substitutes. Indeed, as countries enter into the FTAA, attention to the issue of competitive exchange rates (and even possible overshooting) will be important for facilitating adjustments and effective participation in the hemispheric market.

DEEPENING AND WIDENING REFORMS   Latin America and the Caribbean have made much progress in advancing in its structural reforms, but effective participation in the FTAA will demand deepening and widening of this effort.

Trade liberalization   In recent years Latin America has made marked progress in opening up its economies. Yet MFN tariffs are still relatively high, especially vis-à-vis North America (Table 8.1). A program of further gradual reduction of third-party tariffs would grant exporters cheaper inputs to compete head to head with the North. It also reduces risks of trade diversion and minimizes the redistribution of tariff revenue as FTAA preferences enter into force. Competitive pressures within the FTAA should contribute anyway to lower and converging tariff structures in the hemisphere. The effects of the Asian crisis, however, will probably demand more caution in pursuing MFN tariff liberalization. Indeed in the short term the real challenge may be to avoid or minimize reversals in the market opening up process in the region.[49]

Effective incentives for industrial reconversion and export The FTAA will raise pressures for firms to reconvert in order to face intensified competition from their hemispheric partners. Macroeconomic stability will contribute to this process, but there will also be a need for programs to ensure access to credit and technology (especially for small and medium-sized enterprises), labor retraining and placement, competitive bench-marking studies, identification of market opportunities, export promotion, and so on.[50]

Infrastructure Competing within the FTAA will require more coordinated policy and focus on developing modern infrastructure, not only at the national level but also between and among FTAA partner countries. Improving links among subregional partners is especially important since geography may award opportunities for combining factors of production and creating synergies that enhance competitiveness in the hemispheric market.

Social reform Latin America is the most inequitable developing region in the world.[51] There is a growing consensus that severe inequality can be an obstacle to improvements in international competitiveness and growth. Progress in this area is essential to ensure development of the human capital needed to compete and ensure an equitable distribution of benefits from the FTAA within society. There also is a need for development of transparent and effective regulatory and judicial systems that create a national counterpart to a rules-based hemispheric trading system.

Modernization and coordination of trade-related ministries The ministerial architecture for trade issues in many countries still reflects the function of another era when Latin American economies were more closed, trade was less dynamic, and multilateral and regional trading rules were less complex. Strengthening is now required in many areas including: implementing trade legislation; training to develop professional depth in the nation's corps of negotiators, trade technicians, and lawyers; developing more capacity to analyze and evaluate options for trade liberalization and negotiation, understanding and implementing complex obligations, and exploiting the full rights granted under trade agreements,[52] reinforcing inter- and intraministerial coordination; improving data collection and distribution; enhancing coordination with the private sector and civil society more generally and promoting new exports, investment, and market opportunities.

Deepen and widen subregional integration agreements   Realization of objectives for deep integration in subregional schemes can, among other things, exploit geographic niches for hemispheric investment and export; enhance member countries competitiveness in the hemispheric market; and provide learning experience and negotiating leverage now and in the future evolution of the FTAA. Given substantial interdependencies in some subregional schemes, and the importance of macroeconomic stability for trade performance, some systematic form of interchanging macroeconomic information, with an eye to eventual degrees of coordination, as well as strenghtening rules and procedures for managing destabilizing trade imbalances is desirable for schemes with deep objectives. It also is helpful to pursue extraregional "new" integration agreements, because, apart from their inherent commercial and political merits, they may enhance bargaining power in the FTAA process and may contribute to developing a new multilateral round.

Participation in the multilateral system   A successful FTAA depends on its members complying with WTO obligations and pursuing deeping of the multilateral system. Of particular interest would be promoting another multilateral round and further defining and operationalizing Article XXIV rules guiding the relationship between the multilateral system and regional agreements. This latter consensual framework may help to minimize arbitrary evaluations of regional integration agreements and promote more homogeneous normative structures among them.

International solutions are urgently needed to tackle the destabilizing effects of volatile capital flows. Clearly Latin American and Caribbean countries must individually and together promote a dialogue with the G-7 to reform the international monetary system so that there is a better framework for a stable world economy in which countries and their integration partners can grow and prosper. There are already some interesting proposals on the table. However, it is important for trade ministers to effectively participate in this dialogue directly, or through their finance ministers, because solutions in the area of finance are vital for open markets and trade.

Architecture of the FTAA: Transition, Negotiation, and Implementation

One of the policy areas for minimizing costs and maximizing benefits of an FTAA is its effective articulation of the FTAA with current and future regional agreements. This section will elaborate more on the topic, since it will be one of the central issues for a successful FTAA.

Some Initial Considerations

Given the multiplicity of trade agreements in the hemisphere and the bold decision of the heads of state in the Summit of the Americas to create an FTAA, it is essential that countries carefully design their negotiating strategies so as to take into account both subregional and hemispheric dynamics. In addition, special attention should be given to those countries or subregions with greater political and economic influence in the hemispheric integration process. Unfortunately, the design of any integration strategy raises both theoretical and empirical problems that cannot be solved easily in practice. This is especially true given the coexistence of several basic strategies in the contemporary world trading system; namely, unilateralism, regionalism, and multilateralism.

During the period leading up to the Summit of the Americas, several alternative approaches for hemispheric integration were under serious discussion.[53] The first of these was to look for a convergence path among existing agreements already implemented or under negotiation. The second approach was the accession of all countries to a major subregional agreement. At the time, NAFTA was often promoted as a candidate for this type of expansion.[54] The third option was the initiation of formal negotiations among the various countries or subregions in the hemisphere.

Although the last alternative was the option adopted at the time of launching the FTAA process, the other alternatives have played an important role in shaping the nature of the debate throughout the process. First, the concept of an FTAA, which will be constructed from existing agreements, has been part of the official ministerial language throughout the process (the "building bloc" approach). Moreover, efforts to widen and deepen existing bilateral or subregional agreements have run parallel to FTAA talks and, as such, have been explicitly acknowledged in the FTAA ministerial declarations as evidence of progress toward liberalization in the region. In the meantime, the option of NAFTA expansion has lost credibility on account of the failure of accession negotiations with Chile and failed fast-track initiatives in the U.S. Congress. In contrast, as mentioned earlier, MERCOSUR has secured two important associate members by signing agreements with Chile and Bolivia and is moving to negotiate a free-trade pact with the Andean Community. Moreover, Mexico and Chile are consolidating their hub positions in the hemisphere with continuous efforts to secure new bilateral agreements.

All strategic options have to be evaluated in light of the long-term net social costs and benefits that the particular agreement brings to the member countries compared to those derived from other available alternatives. The net impact of any integration agreement will depend on the type and structure of the trade agreement: namely, the coverage, speed, depth, and timing of liberalization; the selectivity and nature of rules and provisions; the treatment of "sensitive" topics; the application of mechanisms for the distribution of benefits among member countries, and so forth.[55] All of these issues are typical problems encountered when designing a "second-best" policy.

The design of any integration strategy raises a "second-best optimization" problem. Moreover, in subregional strategies reaching for hemispheric scope—which is increasingly the case today in the Americas—there are several alternative paths. If there is no "credible" multilateral cooperative mechanism among all the players, uncertainty will be further magnified and create a more difficult environment for an intertemporal valuation of alternative scenarios. As a result, it is even more difficult to make an "educated choice" among strategic options.

The fact that this situation resembles a "prisoners' dilemma" for the FTAA participants and is conducive to a series of collective decision-making problems may also lead countries to "overvalue" certainty and the benefits from a short-term perspective in decision making. Intimately linked to the foregoing is the fact that any empirical assessment of the relative benefits and sacrifices of each strategic option becomes much less certain.[56] Several factors can contribute to reduce this uncertain environment.

DEFINITION OF A CLEAR ROAD MAP FOR THE FTAA NEGOTIATIONS One of the major achievements of the FTAA initiative to date has been the collective efforts to design a framework and the road map for the process. This has been done by generating clear mandates from the highest national political levels (heads of state and trade ministers); developing a clear definition of the institutional structure (intergovernmental, with technical support of the OAS/IDB/ECLAC Tripartite Committee); consensual principles of negotiation; comprehensive coverage of disciplines as part of a single undertaking, a precise set of terms of reference, preprogrammed performance benchmarks and time frames for different stages of the preparatory/negotiating processes; substantial built-in mechanisms for coordination, and the implementation and consultation with other economic participants.[57] As progress is made in developing these basic points of reference the climate of uncertainty is reduced, which will greatly facilitate the process of preparing countries and subregions for negotiations and development of strategies in anticipation of the FTAA.

CONSISTENCY AMONG BILATERAL AND SUBREGIONAL INITIATIVES Given the complexity of preferential agreements currently in place in the hemisphere, a high priority should be given to progressively encouraging the greatest degree of consistency and coherence among them via ex-post refinements. The same holds for new agreements. Otherwise, there is a risk of reproducing conditions conducive to less transparency in the liberalization process, higher distortions in competition among member countries, and the insufficient use of the advantages of specialization. If this happened, then it would constitute a move away from the observance of the basic principle of "open regionalism," which has characterized regional developments in the hemisphere.

The current situation has seen an increase in the number, variety, and types of agreements, as described earlier. The evolution toward a de facto hub and spoke system—all things being equal—implies:[58]

- the intensification of the search for rents by economic agents in member countries—for example, national or multinational enterprises that plan to consolidate a mono- or oligopolistic position in the regional market, restricting the entry of new competitors;
- the progressive loss of resources because of efforts involved in negotiating, administering, and verifying compliance in each and every agreement, especially where there are overlapping provisions contained in agreements;
- more onerous conditions for liberalization thanks to the relatively higher leverage of a "large hub country" in a bilateral context as opposed to one that is strictly plurilateral; that is, to negotiate with each "spoke country" individually, rather than with all the countries together, which can also lead to granting greater protection relative to the predominant interests of the "hub country"; and
- the restriction of the potential investment in all countries together, at least in comparison to an "ideal" situation of multilateral free trade, and as a result regional income, savings, and growth, because trade barriers remain among some countries—namely, the "spoke countries" of the hub-and-spoke system—without being able to determine a priori its distribution among countries.

In this respect, as we mentioned earlier, the establishment of a free-trade area in the Americas with "subsidiarity" for shallower FTAs agreements, and including a range of some disciplines which go beyond trade in goods, could contribute to the "rationalization" of all the FTAs and integration arrangements in force in the region and also to some degree of adaptation among those with which the FTAA will coexist.

FURTHER CONSOLIDATION OF EXISTING INITIATIVES   Finally, the relative weight that each existing or future subregional agreement will have in the final design of the FTAA and the "rationalization" of the set of integration arrangements in the hemisphere will depend on several determining factors. These include:

- the degree of development of each subregional market, as well as the widening and deepening of the disciplines in the integration process

that goes beyond trade in goods and reflect the spirit of the new regionalism which the FTAA represents;
- the consolidation of the integration process and its projection as a geopolitical and economic arrangement with a sense of identity and with
  the decision-making capacity to engage in broad agendas of economic
  and political cooperation at hemispheric and international level;
- the conclusion, in the next few years, of new generation FTAs among
  groups or countries in the hemisphere that anticipate as best possible
  expected characteristics of the future hemispheric agreement; and
- the strengthening of bilateral relations with decisive hub countries or
  subregions in the areas of trade, investment, financing, and technological cooperation.

On the basis of such considerations, the next paragraphs outline some scenarios for the transition strategies that are available in moving toward the construction of the FTAA.

The Transition Stage in the Negotiation of the FTAA
It is important to start with a brief description of the existing pattern of the
evolution of the hemispheric architecture regarding regional integration
agreements, which, *if it continues unaltered*, would be the stage on which the
FTAA enters into force.[59] With this assumption, the picture that emerges just
before the year 2005, may be the following:

- Consolidation of the most advanced "new-generation" FTA (NAFTA) in
  the Americas. This FTA would cover a broad range of disciplines such as
  trade in goods and services, investment, government procurement, intellectual property, subsidies, antidumping, and countervailing duties,
  comparable to or better than those of the WTO. In addition, it would
  contain partial preferential regimes in favor of the Caribbean countries
  and GSP clauses applicable to the rest of the Americas. However, this
  agreement would not have been expanded because of domestic politics
  in the United States and because of the strategic preparations for the
  negotiations of the FTAA.
- One of the two "hub groups in the hemisphere" (MERCOSUR) would
  have achieved trade liberalization with the rest of South America under
  "first-generation" type agreements, focused basically on trade in goods
  and with rules in market access similar to their own (for example, rules
  of origin similar to those in the MERCOSUR-Chile agreement). That
  would constitute a sort of South American FTA, although less deep than
  the prevailing subregional arrangements in the area (the Andean
  Community and MERCOSUR are customs unions in the process of

consolidation and deepening, but so far with disciplines narrower than the ones contained in the "new-generation" FTAs). In this context, at least in principle, MERCOSUR as a hub subregion, would be expected to strengthen its bargaining power in the design and structure of the FTAA.

- At the same time in both North and South America some "subordinate" hub countries or groups, because of their status as spoke countries or groups in the hemispheric context, would have consolidated their position within their existing integration processes with other Latin American countries. Such will be the case of:

1. Mexico with its "new-generation" type FTA system with Central America, Chile, and some Andean countries;
2. Chile with Canada, Mexico, and Central America under "new-generation" FTAs, and with several Andean FTAs similar to "first-generation" schemes;
3. The Andean Community with FTAs with Chile and several Central American countries by means of "first-generation" type FTAs, as well as with MERCOSUR, although with significant differences in certain rules and disciplines (such as rules of origin), and with CARICOM in "asymmetrical" agreements; and
4. The CACM with "new-generation" agreements with Mexico, Chile, the Dominican Republic, and Panama and a "first-generation" agreement with CARICOM.

In the area of traditional market access, the status of trade liberalization for a select number of FTAs is illustrated in Table 8.7. Under this hypothetical situation it is useful to specify some basic guiding principles for the process of transition and coordination among the countries and "blocs" for the formation of the FTAA.

First, after heated debate in Belo Horizonte trade ministerial, it was agreed that the FTAA would coexist with deeper subregional agreements. As a result, shallow FTAs could be superseded by the basic regulations of the FTAA. In this respect, a decision must be taken on how shallow agreements will be phased out. The decision must take into account the burden of additional administrative costs (e.g., firms and customs authorities will be under two overlapping rules of origin regimes).

Second, in those cases where subregional integration is more profound—in terms of objectives, scope, and coverage—than the FTAA, the problem arises as to the definition of those requirements that will ensure compatibility and coherence in conditions of competition among different regional arrangements and between them and the FTAA (for example, between the levels of preference among the subregional regimes and between them and those of the FTAA).

Table 8.7

Selected Trade Liberalization Programs in the Americas

Agreement		Bilateral Trade	Bilateral Trade Liberalization		
		% bilateral imports of total imports	% items liberalized		% bilateral imports liberalized
		1995	1996	2006	1995
Chile-Mexico	Chile-Mexico	14.9	95.5	98.4	98.8
(1992)	Mexico-Chile	28.3	95.0	98.2	97.8
Chile-Venezuela	Chile-Venezuela	5.6	0.7	96.6	41.4
(1993)	Venezuela-Chile	5.2	0.7	95.7	99.5
Chile-Colombia	Chile-Colombia	3.7	4.1	91.3	88.6
(1994)	Colombia-Chile	6.1	5.3	91.3	93.0
Chile-Ecuador	Chile-Ecuador	5.2	3.9	96.4	35.0
(1995)	Ecuador-Chile	8.9	5.1	96.1	98.4
G-3	Mexico-Colombia	5.5	7.6	90.9	95.5
(1995)	Colombia-Mexico	15.4	4.1	90.8	98.5
	Mexico-Venezuela	12.2	2.4	76.4	99.4
	Venezuela-Mexico	15.3	0.4	76.8	98.6
Mexico-Costa Rica	Mexico-Costa Rica	0.0	86.4	99.3	100.0
(1995)	Costa Rica-Mexico	4.0	73.2	97.8	98.8
Mexico-Bolivia	Mexico-Bolivia	0.3	61.8	96.5	99.9
(1995)	Bolivia-Mexico	3.6	59.2	96.4	98.9
MERCOSUR	Argentina-MERCOSUR	10.3	96.6	99.9	91.2
(1995)	Brasil-Argentina	21.5	99.4	99.9	99.7
	Paraguay-MERCOSUR	91.4	92.8	99.9	
	Uruguay-MERCOSUR	89.9	86.3	99.9	73.6

continued on the next page

Table 8.7 continued from the previous page

MERCOSUR-Chile	Argentina-Chile	8.8	4.4	94.7	63.5
(1996)	Chile-Argentina	34.3	4.4	95.0	32.3
	Brasil-MERCOSUR	11.2	4.4	94.7	58.1
	Chile-Brasil	29.6	4.4	97.6	32.5
	Uruguay-Chile	3.4	4.4	94.8	16.3
	Chile-Uruguay	1.0	4.4	95.4	47.6
	Paraguay-Chile	6.3	4.4	95.0	10.7
	Chile-Paraguay	1.4	4.4	93.5	82.3
MERCOSUR-Bolivia	Argentina-Bolivia	2.3	5.4	97.1	93.9
(1997)	Bolivia-Argentina	23.0	7.3	92.2	72.6
	Brasil-Bolivia	0.2	5.6	97.1	46.9
	Bolivia-Brasil	31.8	7.3	92.2	66.7
	Uruguay-Bolivia	0.1	4.8	97.1	79.0
	Bolivia-Uruguay	0.9	7.3	92.2	20.8
	Paraguay-Bolivia	0.2	5.0	97.1	
	Bolivia-Paraguay	0.2	8.7	92.3	26.7

Source: Estevadeordal (forthcoming).

Otherwise, distortions and inequities would be created in the conditions of competition in the hemispheric market unless the decision was made to opt for the formal harmonization of competition, promotion, and development policies among the member countries of the FTAA.

One of the problems rests in the difficulties of empirical evaluation of those effects; in particular, distortions due to measures and regulations such as rules of origin as well as their distributive and resource allocation impact among countries.[60] Therefore, following a "second-best" policy type recommendation, it would be useful to undertake some adaptation of the regimes and conditions governing competition among countries and prevailing regional integration arrangements in the Americas.

Given the uncertainty associated with the transitional process, the differences among existing regimes and the diversity of participants in this process, the issue of timing with respect to the adaptation of remaining regimes in the hemisphere becomes central. This is even more important if one takes into account the negative effects resulting from inadequate investment decisions or reallocation of production and the loss of efficiency from not anticipating locational and scale economies in the new hemispheric integration matrix. In principle, it is expected that the longer this situation of uncertainty lasts, the greater will be the probability of not seizing the full advantages of future integration in the hemisphere and subregion.

Finally, certain powerful "regional groups" may seize the opportunity to consolidate their integration processes taking into account the disciplines negotiated under WTO agreements or some of the most advanced FTAs in the region, or the scope of the FTAA initiative defined throughout the ministerial declarations. Those groups will then be better positioned to face the critical stage of negotiations of the FTAA with greater bargaining power and also to improve the situation for the transition to the new conditions of competition.[61]

Furthermore, regional groups or "first-generation" FTAs based mostly on the liberalization of trade in goods or that do not deal with a large number of the disciplines included in "new-generation" agreements, could widen and deepen their FTAs with other countries or regional groups. MERCOSUR, the Andean Community, and the CACM are cases that illustrate this type of situation.

As a consequence, through a process of adaptation and coordination of regimes among groups of countries as they effectively move forward with the "rationalization" of their respective FTAs or customs unions prior to the definition of the FTAA, not only can they reduce inefficiencies and administrative costs but also they can create more favorable conditions so that such countries will exert greater influence on the negotiations of the FTAA. Moreover, such rationalization will facilitate the environment for the adaptation and harmonization of different integration arrangements in force while the negotiations of the FTAA are held and can create the conditions for a more efficient negotiating process, where special attention will be focused on the definition of the FTAA in central fields as, for instance, market access.

Under this scenario two factors must be taken into account: first, which regimes will be adopted as the reference benchmark for this process of adaptation; second, how compatible will be the chosen regimes with the ones being negotiated in the FTAA. However, the FTAA regimes under negotiation will be, in turn, greatly affected as a critical mass of countries and groups move forward into this adaptation process.

One of the difficulties for convergence is the choice of reference regimes that contain clear criteria for comparing and selecting alternatives and are also sufficiently precise, transparent, and predictable that their application will not obstruct the process of liberalization.

The existing WTO trading regimes must necessarily serve as one of the key reference points for the analysis of the FTAA architecture. Obviously, this does not imply that the FTAA will deepen those obligations subscribed to under the WTO in each and every one of the disciplines considered. This will probably happen in some cases, but not in others. The final outcome will depend on the negotiations and the degree of progress and harmonization achieved by the most advanced "regional groups" in the hemisphere.

The problem in selecting the reference regime may be illustrated with the rules of origin. In the Americas, at least four basic origin regimes are being applied: (1) that of NAFTA and the "new-generation" FTAs concluded by Mexico and Canada with other countries in the hemisphere; (2) that of ALADI—as the "first-generation" reference regime—for all the partial scope agreements between the signatory countries of the Treaty of Montevideo, for the Andean Community, and the FTAs of Chile with Colombia and Venezuela; (3) that of MERCOSUR for the FTAs with Chile and Bolivia, and eventually the FTA to be concluded with the Andean Community; and (4) that of the CACM as the intermediate regime between "first- and new-generation" regimes. Moreover, the nonpreferential regime being negotiated in the framework of the WTO seems to be tending toward an intermediate framework, based largely on the criterion of change of tariff classification, but with a different degree of stringency between types of goods and using other criteria in those cases where it is necessary to specify origin requirements. Given these circumstances, there arises the issue of which would be the most suitable reference regime to be used in the adaptation process prior to the design of the FTAA. In this particular example, a necessary, though not a sufficient, condition in order to achieve the greatest efficiency and the lowest transition costs is the adoption of some basic principles such as: transparency and predictability; low administrative costs in the application of origin; small number of criteria for classifying origin; a definition of the degree of stringency that will not be higher than that/those in effect among the countries previous to the FTAA's formation; and the nonapplication of rules of origin in those cases where national tariffs to third countries are sufficiently low (for instance, say, below 3 to 5 percent), or where they are similar.[62]

Conclusions

The FTAA has been fathered by a convergence of interests in the hemisphere; on the one hand, North America's acceptance of regional integration as a policy tool complementary to the multilateral system; on the other, Latin America and the Caribbean's combining their long-held interest in regional integration with a new market-based open economic strategy that has fostered a new regionalism and has been an important contributor to a stronger multilateral system. The new regionalism has been a positive influence on Latin America and the Caribbean in the 1990s, helping to promote consolidation of economic reforms, creation of new markets and trade, preparation for globalization, strengthening of democratic regimes, and fostering of regional cooperation.

The FTAA process is a complex venture that undoubtedly bears costs. However, an FTAA could also establish an important new framework of opportunities for regional integration, hemispheric cooperation, and growth. Among other things, it could offer the possibilities of (1) more secure hemispheric market access; (2) a challenging incentive for productive transformation and preparation for globalization; (3) a potential magnet for new FDI; (4) a rationalization of existing strategies of regional integration; (5) synergies that contribute to a stronger multilateral system; and (6) externalities that help to lock-in policy reform.

However, there is a whole spectrum of policy and strategic issues "around" and "outside" of the FTAA process as such that will condition the outcome and effects of the agreement, the ability of participants to maximize potential opportunities and minimize costs, and ensure a reasonable balance in the distribution of benefits among partner countries. In this regard this chapter has presented a short, and far form all-inclusive, checklist of some longer-term collective hemispheric and multilateral issues as well as macro-, micro-, and mesoeconomic national ones that might merit special parallel attention as the formal FTAA negotiations progress.

The national issues are many and diverse. Macroeconomic stability is a sine qua non for effective participation in the FTAA. The volatility of short-term capital flows has, however, become a major threat to macroeconomic stability in the developing world. In view of the fact that international solutions may be slow in forthcoming, countries may have no other choice but to establish an especially defensive policy stance—pragmatically deploying direct policy instruments when necessary—in the face of surges of short-term capital flows. The goal would be to ensure sustainable macroeconomic balances that can support participation in the FTAA's opportunities and accomodate, without trauma, the changes in the psychology of capital markets. However, sustainable macroeconomic balances are not enough; one must address sectoral issues, such as the future strategy of trade policy vis-à-vis the rest of the world and areas involving micro and mesoeconomics—at the level of financing, domestic and foreign investment, human capital development, science, technology and productive resources, physical and institutional infrastructure, public and private coordination, and so on. The future direction of subregional integration is another strategic policy tool for exploiting the opportunities of an FTAA. Only with the creation and exploitation of dynamic competitive advantages, using the possibilities of complementarity and specialization (including opportunities for deep subregional integration) with innovation and technical progress, and with the improvement of competition, can the potential of an integration process such as the FTAA be fully realized.

Also on the checklist are collective issues such as development of a functional, pragmatic hemispheric institutional "network" that directly or indirectly supports an FTAA; there also is a need for national promotion of strategic agenda in multilateral fora: the WTO and any international dialogue that may emerge with the G-7 over the years on solutions to the problems of greater volatility of international financial flows. In the absence of national and international approaches to effectively deal with turbulent international financial markets, ambitious trade initiatives, whether at the national, the subregional, hemispheric, or multilateral level, could be in jeopardy.

In the chapter, particular emphasis was placed on the fact that the successful creation of a transparent and more effective hemispheric market will depend on the progress achieved in the adaptation and "rationalization" of the existing integration arrangements in force in the Americas, as well as the final outcome of an FTAA agreement characterized by a set of rules and disciplines broadly consistent with "regional groups," member countries of the groups, and the remaining countries in the Americas and extrahemispheric arrangements. This would permit, inter alia, more efficient adaptation between a new FTAA and prevailing integration arrangements, deepening of "open regionalism" in the hemisphere, and generate more favorable conditions for facing future progress in the liberalization of competition at the multilateral level.

Notes

1. The opinions expressed here are the authors' and do not necessarily reflect those of the Inter-American Development Bank. We thank Eric Miller, Francois Dionne, and Maria de la Paz Covarrubias for their assistance in data and editing.
2. W. Ethier, "The New Regionalism," *The Economic Journal* (July 1998): 1149–61.
3. The Brazilian crisis and devaluation occurred at the time of finalizing the paper for editorial submission. Hence its repercussions are not dealt with here. However, once the Brazilian and MERCOSUR situation stabilizes the end result should be positive for the FTAA: Brazil's greater price competitiveness will signal many new market opportunities in the hemisphere. For a preliminary analysis of the effects of the Brazilian crisis on Latin American integration and the effects of the Asian crisis on the region's international trade prospects, see Inter-American Development Bank, Integration and Trade in the Americas, "Special Report: The International Financial Crisis: Implications for Latin American and Caribbean Trade and Integration," *Periodic Note* (Washington, D.C.: Integration, Trade and Hemispheric Issues Division and Statistics and Quantitative Analysis Unit, Department of Integration and Regional Programs, 1999).
4. For more details see INTAL, *MERCOSUR Report*, no. 1 (Buenos Aires: July–December 1996).
5. Inter-American Development Bank, "Trade Liberalization," extract from *Economic and Social Progress in Latin America* (Washington, D.C.: Integration, Trade and Hemispheric Issues Division, 1996).
6. This is manifest in the new Understanding on the Interpretation of Article XXIV of the GATT 1994.
7. A. Estevadeordal and C. Robert (eds.), *Market Access in the Americas: Negotiating and Strategic Issues* (INTAL-IDB, forthcoming).
8. Ethier, "The New Regionalism."

9. A. Estevadeordal, *Negotiating Trade Agreements in the Americas* (Washington, D.C.: Integration, Trade and Hemispheric Issues Division, Inter-American Development Bank, forthcoming).

10. R. Devlin and R. Ffrench Davis, "Towards an Evaluation of Regional Integration in Latin America in the 1990s," *World Economy,* March 1999, pp. 26–90.

11. J. Viner, *The Customs Union Issue* (New York: Carnegie Endowment for International Peace, 1950).

12. R. Fernandez, "Returns to Regionalism: An Evaluation of Non-Traditional Gains from RTAs" (Washington, D.C.: New York University and World Bank, 1997, mimeograph).

13. R. Baldwin and A. J. Venables, "Regional Economic Integration," *Handbook of International Economics,* vol. III, ed. G. Grossman and K. Rogoff (The Hague: Elsevier Science B. V., 1995); A. Winters, "Assessing Regional Integration Arrangements" (Washington, D.C.: World Bank, 1997).

14. A. Yeats, "Does MERCOSUR's Trade Performance Raise Concerns about the Effects of Regional Trade Arrangements?" *The World Bank Economic Review* 12, no. 1 (1998): 1–28. For a concise critique of Yeats, "Does MERCOSUR's Trade Performance Raise Concerns about the Effects of Regional Trade Arrangements?" which first appeared in 1996, see R. Devlin, "In Defense of MERCOSUR," *Gaceta Mercantil* (São Paulo, November 19, 1996).

15. The original membership of the European Union approximated these conditions.

16. R. Hinojosa, S. Robinson, and J. Lewis, "Convergence and Divergence Between NAFTA, Chile and MERCOSUR: Overcoming Dilemmas of North and South American Economic Integration," *Working Paper* 219 (Washington, D.C.: Integration and Regional Programs Department, Inter-American Development Bank, May, 1997). Note that the models do not account for the effect of rules of origin, which if very restrictive, would seriously dampen potential trade creation. L. J. Garay and A. Estevadeordal, "Protection, Preferential Tariff Elimination and Rules of Origin in the Americas" (Washington, D.C.: Integration, Trade and Hemispheric Issues Division, Inter-American Development Bank, 1995).

17. For an analysis of the region's export performance, including diversification and potential effects of the Asian crisis, see Integration, Trade and Hemispheric Issues Division and Statistics and Quantitative Analysis Unit, Department of Integration and Regional Programs, "Integration and Trade in the Americas," *Periodic Note* (Washington, D.C.: Inter-American Development Bank, 1998).

18. Chile and Canada are suppressing antidumping measures in their new FTA.

19. Inter-American Development Bank, "Trade Liberalization."

20. Puga and Venables demonstrate that due to geography and externalities from agglomeration, liberalization in a preferential arrangement can provide greater gains in terms of industrialization than a unilateral liberalization. D. Puga and A. J. Venables, "Trading Arrangements and Industrial Development" (Washington, D.C.: World Bank, 1996).

21. See M. Sutler, "Material Gains," *Business Mexico* (September 1997). The FTAA process and initiation of negotiations in 1998 is already raising awareness in Latin America of shortcomings in public and private preparedness regarding international trade.

22. However, as Winters in "Assessing Regional Integration Arrangements," and Garay and Bailliu point out, not all FDI carries net benefits. See L. J. Garay and J. Bailliu, "A Background Note on Foreign Direct Investment in Latin America and the Caribbean" (Washington, D.C.: Integration, Trade and Hemispheric Issues Division, Inter-American Development Bank, 1996).

23. Ethier, "The New Regionalism."

24. A. Calderon, "La inversión extranjera en América Latina y el Caribe: un panorama," in *Inversión extranjera directa en América Latina,* ed. Inter-American Development Bank and Instituto de Relaciones Europeo-Latinoamericanas (Madrid: IRELA, 1998).

25. Ethier, "The New Regionalism."

26. M. Blomstrom and A. Kokko, "Regional Integration and Foreign Direct Investment" (Washington, D.C.: World Bank, 1997).

27. L. J. Garay, "Breve resumen de algunas consideraciones no tradicionales sobre los impactos de la integración regional" (Washington, D.C.: Integration, Trade and Hemispheric Issues Division, Inter-American Development Bank, mimeograph, 1997).

28. L. J. Garay and A. Vera, "Naturaleza y evolución reciente de la inversión intraregional," in *Inversión extranjera directa en América Latina,* ed. Inter-American Development Bank and Instituto de Relaciones Europeo-Latinoamericanas (Madrid: IRELA, 1998).

29. J. Bhagwati and A. Panagariya, "Preferential Trading Areas and Multilateralism: Strangers, Friends or Foes?" (Washington, D.C.: World Bank mimeograph, 1996).

30. By the development and publication of systematic inventories and data bases on trade and trade-related issues that heretofore were unavailable or difficult to secure. The FTAA process has also inspired new research in areas where knowledge is very limited.

31. The Inter-American Development Bank, in its FTAA technical support role, provided the FTAA Market Access Preparatory Group with a simplified system and software for notifying trade and tariff information. The relative success of this exercise contributed to the WTO overhauling its complex and unsuccessful Integrated Data Base, borrowing on some of the innovations that the IDB developed for the FTAA process.

32. See IDB, 1998.

33. S. Otteman, "The FTAA: Its Dilemmas Today and its Prospects in the Future" (Washington, D.C.: Inter-American Dialogue, 1998).

34. It is interesting that in the FTAA negotiations a number of smaller countries can be quite influential in the direction of discussions.

35. Even a simple free-trade area is by definition WTO "plus" since tariffs are eliminated on substantially all trade.

36. K. Bagwell and R. Staiger, *The Economic Journal* (July 1998): 1162–82; World Trade Organization, *Regionalism and the World Trading System* (Geneva: WTO, 1995).

37. D. Ben-David, "Trade and Convergence Among Countries," *Journal of International Economics* 40 (1996): 279–98.

38. R. Barro and X. Sala-I-Martin, "Convergence across States and Regions," *Brookings Papers on Economic Activity* 1 (1991): 107–79.

39. The more extensive the rules and their enforcement in an FTAA the more likely investment will spread and be based on a criterion that goes beyond the home country's local market size.

40. Salgado attributes this problem to the stagnation of regional integration in Latin America in the late 1970s. See G. Salgado, "El Mercado Regional Latinoamericano: el proyecto y la realidad," *Revista de la CEPAL* 7 (April 1979).

41. A. Panagariya, "The Free Trade Area of the Americas: Good for Latin America?" *The World Economy* 19, no. 5 (September 1996).

42. Bhagwati and Panagariya, "Preferential Trading Areas and Multilateralism: Strangers, Friends or Foes?"

43. Winters, "Assessing Regional Integration Arrangements."

44. R. Devlin, R. Ffrench Davis, and S. Griffith-Jones, "Surges in Capital Flows and Development: An Overview of Policy Issues," in *Coping with Capital Surges: The Return of Finance to Latin America,* ed. R. Ffrench Davis and S. Griffith-Jones (Boulder: Lynne Reinner Publishers, 1995).

45. This function perhaps could be carried out by regional organizations.

46. Inter-American Development Bank, E*conomic and Social Progress in Latin America, 1996* (Washington, D.C: Inter-American Development Bank, 1997).

47. R. Devlin, *Debt and Crisis in Latin America: The Supply Side of the Story* (Princeton: Princeton University Press, 1989); United Nations, Economic Commission for Latin America and the Caribbean (ECLAC), *Policies to Improve Linkages with the Global Economy* (Santiago, Chile: United Nations, 1995); and Devlin, Ffrench Davis, and Griffith-Jones, "Surges in Capital Flows and Development."

48. Gavin and Hausmann argue that financial regulation should be even more disciplined than the Basle Accord. See M. Gavin and R. Hausmann, "The Roots of Banking Crises: The Macroeconomic Context," *OCE Working Paper Series* 318 (Washington, D.C.: Office of the Chief Economist, Inter-American Development Bank, 1996).

49. Yet some countries like Chile have scheduled a second stage of MFN tariff reduction, from 11 to 6 percent over five years.

50. Colombia has recently initiated an ambitious study program in this regard. See L. J. Garay et al., *Colombia: Estructura Industrial e Internacionalización* (Bogotá: DNP-Colciencias, 1998).

51. Inter-American Development Bank, "América Latina frente a la desigualdad," *Progreso económico y social en América Latina: Informe 1998–1999* (Washington, D.C.: Inter-American Development Bank, 1998).

52. One of the major areas of adjustment in Canada when it entered into an agreement with the United States was to mobilize a critical mass of trade lawyers accustomed to the aggressive, document-driven litigation techniques of U.S. lawyers in dispute settlement. R. Dearden, "Conflictos comerciales y mecanismos de resolución de controversias bajo el Acuerdo de Libre Comercio entre Estados Unidos y Canadá," in *NAFTA y MERCOSUR,* ed. R. Lipsey and P. Meller (Santiago, Chile: CIEPLAN, 1996); R. Devlin, "Comment on Dearden Paper" in *ibid.*

53. OAS/IDB/ECLAC Tripartite Committee, "Towards Free Trade in the Western Hemisphere" (Washington, D.C., September, 1994).

54. P. Morici, *Free Trade in the Americas* (New York: Twentieth Century Fund, 1994).

55. R. Devlin and L. J. Garay, "From Miami to Cartagena: Nine Lessons and Nine Challenges of the FTAA," *Working Paper* 211 (Washington, D.C.: Integration and Regional Programs Department, Inter-American Development Bank, July 1996).

56. This situation has been illustrated by various authors, such as Hinojosa, Robinson, and Lewis, by means of a computable general equilibrium model. In this case, different scenarios in the process of forming an FTAA were analyzed, in the wake of alternative agreements among "regional blocs"—in particular, NAFTA, MERCOSUR, and the Andean Community. See Hinojosa, Robinson, and Lewis, "Convergence and Divergence Between NAFTA, Chile and MERCOSUR."

57. Devlin and Garay, "From Miami to Cartagena: Nine Lessons and Nine Challenges of the FTAA."

58. For more detail on the analytical framework of hub and spokes, see R. J. Wonnacott and P. Wonnacott, "El TLCAN y los acuerdos comerciales en las Américas," in *Las Américas: Integración económica en perspectiva* (Bogotá: National Planning Department of Colombia and Inter-American Development Bank, 1996).

59. This scenario does not take into account extrahemispheric dynamics, which can potentially be very important and make the picture more complex.

60. L. J. Garay and A. Estevadeordal, "Protection, Preferential Tariff Elimination and Rules of Origin in the Americas" (Washington, D.C.: Integration, Trade and Hemispheric Issues Division, Inter-American Development Bank, 1995).

61. One of the characteristics of a hub-and-spoke network is the advantage awarded to the hub vis-à-vis the spokes and third parties in regard to preferences and conditions of competition. These advantages increase for the hub with the widening and deepening of its network. Likewise, there is a corresponding increase in the influence of its model of integration with third parties and presumably the collective FTAA process. In this regard it is interesting to point out the role Mexico is acquiring as a member of NAFTA, which is rapidly constructing a hub-and-spoke network of new-generation FTAs with Central and South American countries, while at the same time actively participating in an FTAA process, which has a "new-generation" agenda.

62. L. J. Garay and R. Cornejo, "Reglas de origen en acuerdos de libre comercio en las Américas" (Washington, D.C.: Integration, Trade and Hemispheric Issues Division and Statistics and Quantitative Analysis Unit, Inter-American Development Bank, 1998); L. J. Garay and L. F. Quintero, "Caracterización, estructura o racionalidad de las normas de origen del G-3 y ALADI" (Washington, D.C.: Integration, Trade and Hemispheric Issues Division, Inter-American Development Bank, 1997); and L. J. Garay and A. Estevadeordal, "Protection, Preferential Tariff Elimination and Rules of Origin in the Americas."

9

Trade and Investment Issues in the Americas:
A Look Ahead

ROBERTO BOUZAS

The 1990s was a period of major transformations in hemispheric trade and investment relations. While coping with the effects of the external debt crisis had dominated policy debates during the 1980s, trade and investment matters stood at the forefront during the 1990s. The recovery in the rate of growth of trade and investment flows, trade and investment policy change, and a broader agenda of negotiations are the major factors explaining this new emphasis.

In effect, after the stagnation experienced in the 1980s, hemispheric trade and investment flows recovered rapidly in the 1990s. The Latin American and Caribbean (LAC) countries, which under the burden of the debt crisis lost share as outlets for U.S. exports, turned into one of fastest growing markets for U.S. sales during the 1990s. Not only U.S.-LAC trade flows expanded rapidly but also intra-LAC flows recovered after the sharp contraction experienced during the early years of the "lost decade." Investment flows (both direct—FDI—and portfolio) surged as well, responding to the stimulus offered by changing conditions in international financial markets and domestic policy reform.

Similarly, trade and investment policies changed throughout the hemisphere. LAC countries abandoned import-substitution industrialization, replacing it with more outward-oriented trade regimes. But trade policy change was not confined to LAC. In effect, pressures toward trade protection mounted and discrimination gained a more prominent role in U.S. trade policy. The idea of comprehensive and reciprocal trade liberalization arrangements between the United States and LAC countries, which would have seemed odd in the 1980s, unexpectedly took shape in the North American Free Trade Agreement (NAFTA). Shortly afterward, the Enterprise for the Americas Initiative and the launching of negotiations to create a Free Trade Area of the Americas (FTAA) raised the expectation that the shift may be more encompassing. Investment policies also evolved, particularly in Latin America, as new investment regimes, capital account liberalization, and far-reaching privatization programs eased the inflow of foreign capital.

The third feature of the period was the "broadening" of the agenda of trade negotiations. The most remarkable extension came from the inclusion of "new issues" (such as intellectual property rights' protection, trade in services and investment regulations) in trade negotiations. The precedent was laid by the Canada-U.S. Free Trade Agreement (CUSFTA) and NAFTA, both of which included commitments on those issues even before an agreement had been reached at a multilateral level. Mounting domestic pressures also brought to the fore the linkage between trade and the enforcement of labor and environmental standards. This broader agenda raised the specter of protectionism in new clothes, this time not in LAC but in the United States and other developed countries.

These far-reaching changes look pale when compared to the challenges ahead. Over the next decade the nations of the hemisphere will have not only to meet the "prosaic" objectives of maintaining high growth rates of trade and open trade regimes but also to negotiate successfully and implement an FTAA. Certainly, the maintenance of outward-oriented trade regimes cannot be taken for granted in an international financial environment unlikely to be as forthcoming as that of the 1990s, when abundant capital inflows made trade liberalization easier to sustain. Moreover, negotiation and implementation of an FTAA will demand that participants deal with complex issues both of substance and method.

This chapter is organized in five sections. The first assesses the policy significance of changes experienced by hemispheric trade and investment flows and policies, as well as of the gradual broadening of the agenda of negotiations. The second section provides an overview of the challenges that hemispheric trade and investment will have to cope with in the next decade. The third section identifies the main issues likely to be raised by the negotiation and implementation of an FTAA. The fourth section offers an interpretation of the evolving stance of MERCOSUR (e.g., the southern common market, formed by Argentina, Brazil, Paraguay, and Uruguay) in the process. A concluding section summarizes the main points raised here.

Trade and Investment: Flows, Policies, and a Broadening Negotiating Agenda

Trade and Investment Flows

The external debt crisis of the 1980s had a contractionary effect upon hemispheric trade flows. In effect, since most LAC countries were rationed in international capital markets they had few options but to save foreign exchange through import cuts. U.S. exports to LAC performed poorly as a result, increasing from $42.1 billion in 1981 to only $49.1 billion in 1989.[1] Consequently, the share of LAC in total U.S. exports fell from 17.7 percent in 1981 to 13.5 percent in 1989. Intra-LAC trade flows performed even worse, contracting in absolute terms from $16.8 billion in 1981 to $14.7 billion in 1989.

The 1990s brought about a radical change, as abundant liquidity in international capital markets lifted LAC foreign-exchange constraints. Accompanied by more liberal trade regimes, LAC imports recovered fast rates of growth. As a result, U.S. exports to the region increased at an average annual rate 50 percent above that of U.S. exports to the world (12.1 percent as compared to 8.2 percent), a performance which by 1995 had taken the LAC countries' share in U.S. total exports to nearly precrisis levels (16.4 percent). U.S. exports to selected LAC countries expanded at even faster rates, as in the case of MERCOSUR, where they recorded a remarkable 20.5 percent average annual growth rate. LAC countries' thirst for imports also contributed to widening U.S. trade surpluses in the region. One consequence was that U.S. exporters and policymakers turned their attention over to LAC markets once again.

Between 1991 and 1996 intrahemispheric trade (measured by goods' exports) increased at a 13.3 percent average annual rate (Table 9.1). This compared favorably with both the rate of growth of hemispheric exports to the rest of the world (6.4 percent) and of total world trade (7.9 percent). Intra-LAC trade flows increased at an even faster rate (19 percent per year), more than twice the rate of growth of total world trade. Intraregional trade in groups such as MERCOSUR recorded even faster average annual growth rates (27.3 percent per year), more than tripling the rate of expansion of total world trade.

Foreign direct investment flows recovered rapidly as well. While FDI inflows into LAC reached an annual average value of $7.7 billion in 1984–1989, they nearly tripled to an average $20.6 billion per year in 1990–1996. The recovery in foreign investment flows was accompanied by new, rapidly growing intra-LAC flows. In effect, during the 1995–1997 period LAC annual average FDI outflows more than tripled the 1986–1991 average. Since the largest share of LAC FDI outflows is channeled to other countries in the region, intraregional investment ties increased notably. Chilean investments in Argentina and Argentina-Brazil/Colombia-Venezuela bilateral flows stand out among the most significant.

Trade and Investment Policies

During the 1990s trade policies, both in LAC and the United States, underwent a major transformation as well. As far as the LAC countries were concerned, after the external debt crisis of the early 1980s most of them abandoned import-substitution, adopting instead more outward-oriented trade and investment regimes. The roads taken toward trade and investment liberalization were diverse, but mutually reinforcing. Either by joining the General Agreement on Trade and Tariffs (GATT) or, and frequently simultaneously with, the imple-

Table 9.1

The Americas: Export Growth according to Market of Destination (average annual growth rate, percentage: 1986–1991, 1991–1996)

	NAFTA	MERCOSUR	Andean C.	Chile	CACM	CARICOM	FTAA	World
Period: 1986/91								
NAFTA	11.5	10.1	7.5	18.1	12.9	6.9	11.2	12.2
MERCOSUR	3.4	14.5	7.2	25.0	8.9	-4.6	7.4	9.4
Andean C.	24.3	7.3	21.1	13.3	12.0	51.2	21.9	10.9
Chile	8.4	11.1	15.6	na	13.0	5.7	10.2	15.7
CACM	0.8	-20.2	13.4	20.8	13.6	5.0	3.9	1.3
CARICOM	-10.9	32.8	50.0	65.7	-2.8	10.4	-8.4	-1.4
FTAA	11.0	11.2	9.1	19.4	12.8	9.5	11.0	11.6
Period: 1991/96								
NAFTA	13.3	16.3	8.5	19.3	14.2	5.2	13.3	9.8
MERCOSUR	6.9	27.3	10.5	18.5	8.6	7.9	15.4	10.3
Andean C.	12.5	11.2	21.8	9.5	14.6	-2.4	12.9	9.7
Chile	12.4	17.3	19.0	na	10.5	80.6	15.0	11.8
CACM	12.8	33.0	28.8	53.7	15.2	7.2	14.0	13.5
CARICOM	2.3	-8.1	1.5	19.7	24.4	16.3	4.2	3.0
FTAA	13.0	20.1	11.6	18.0	14.1	4.9	13.3	9.8

na = not applicable

Source: Data INTAL.

mentation of ambitious unilateral and preferential trade liberalization programs, most countries in the region revamped their trade and investment regimes away from the protection of domestic markets. Multilateral financial institutions' conditionality made a decisive contribution to the policy shift, in turn eased by readily available foreign finance. By the mid-1990s most LAC countries had significantly cut down average tariff levels, reduced tariff dispersion, and removed quantitative restrictions (Table 9.2). More outward-oriented trade regimes thus became prevalent throughout the region. Unilateral trade liberalization in LAC advanced pari passu with a revival of preexisting preferential trade agreements and enforcement of new ones. Multilateral organizations did not endorse preferential trade arrangements as enthusiastically as they did with unilateral liberalization. But there were strong incentives for the LAC countries to go along, remarkably the U.S. engagement in preferential initiatives (such as

Table 9.2

Latin America and the Caribbean: Trade Liberalization in the Early 1990s

Country	Program Launched in:	Maximum Tariff Rate		Average Tariff Rate		Non-Tariff Barriers
		Initial	*1994*	*Initial*	*1994*	
Argentina	1989	65	30	39	15.8	Between 1989 and 1991 most NTBs and specific import duties phased out.
Bolivia	1985	150	10	12	9.8	Most import prohibitions and licenses phased out.
Brazil	1988	105	35	51	10.7	Most import prohibitions and licenses phased out.
Colombia	1990	100	40	44	11.6	Most import licenses eliminated in 1990.
Costa Rica	1986	100	100	27	11.7	Gradual elimination of import authorizations and other restrictions in 1990/93.
Chile	1973/1985	35	11	35	11	Quantitative restrictions eliminated during the first reform (1973), but price bands and antidumping procedures reintroduced.
Mexico	1985	100	25	24	11.6	Import permits were reduced and official import prices eliminated.
Peru	1990	108	25	66	16.3	Import licenses, quotas, and prohibitions eliminated in 1990.
Venezuela	1989	135	25	35	13.4	Specific duties were eliminated and the number of products with restrictions greatly reduced.

Source: Based on CEPAL, *Políticas para mejorar la inserción en la economía mundial,* Santiago de Chile, 1995; and L. J. Garay and A. Estevadeordal, "Protección, desgravación preferencial y normas de origen en las Américas," in *Integración y Comercio* (Jan.–Apr. 1996).

NAFTA) and the launching of the Enterprise of the Americas Initiative in 1991. The revival of preferential trade agreements in LAC was widespread, but the strategies adopted and the success achieved differed widely.[2]

One of the most successful preferential trade arrangements in LAC was MERCOSUR, the customs union created by Argentina, Brazil, Paraguay, and Uruguay in 1991. Trade among MERCOSUR partners expanded rapidly, taking the share of intraregional exports to total exports from 8.5 percent in 1986 (when Argentina and Brazil launched the bilateral economic cooperation program which laid the basis of MERCOSUR) to 22.7 percent ten years later (see Table 9.3). Not only trade but also investment flows brought the countries of the region closer to each other, a trend which extended into neighboring Chile and Bolivia (with which MERCOSUR signed comprehensive free-trade agreements in 1996). Although MERCOSUR has been criticized for trade diversion, there is scant evidence that the latter (as opposed to trade creation) was the dominant force (except for petroleum). Indeed, since preferential liberalization in the subregion went pari passu with the unilateral dismantlement of trade barriers (and real exchange rate appreciation), total imports (from both within the region and the rest of the world) increased at a rapid pace.[3]

LAC countries' investment policies also shifted away from discrimination and market reserves and toward the creation of a more competitive and forthcoming environment for foreign capital. Most LAC signed bilateral investment treaties with the United States, enforcing many of the demands traditionally posed by U.S. investors and officials (such as new dispute resolution mechanisms). Moreover, far-reaching privatization programs opened new avenues to the participation of foreign capital. The result was a return of foreign investors to the region not only through direct investment inflows but also through more volatile portfolio capital.[4]

In contrast to LAC, where policy change was relatively abrupt, U.S. trade policies evolved along a more gradual pattern. One indicator was congressional activism in the design and implementation of U.S. trade policy, particularly after the passing of the 1974 Trade Act. The more restrictive stance of the legislature was influenced by prevailing public opinion, where pressures for trade protection were on the rise. These, which had been on an upward trend since the early 1970s, translated into a rising number of antidumping (AD) and countervailing duty (CVD) cases brought before U.S. authorities and a more restrictive implementation of U.S. trade-remedy laws.

To counteract the growing influence of protectionist lobbies upon Congress, U.S. trade policy stance shifted toward so-called "aggressive unilateralism," its main purpose being to improve access to third countries' markets for new U.S. export sectors. "Aggressive unilateralism" was instrumental to "broaden" the trade policy agenda, including "new issues" (such as trade in

Table 9.3

The Americas: Regional Composition of Exports
(percentage of total exports: 1986, 1991, 1996)

	NAFTA	MERCOSUR	Andean C.	Chile	CACM	CARICOM	FTAA	World
Year 1986								
NAFTA	42.0	1.9	2.1	0.3	0.6	0.6	48.2	100.0
MERCOSUR	25.6	8.5	4.4	1.3	0.3	0.5	41.0	100.0
Andean C.	23.8	4.0	3.9	1.5	1.3	0.5	36.8	100.0
Chile	23.2	11.1	4.8	na	0.4	0.0	39.9	100.0
CACM	44.6	0.3	0.5	0.0	10.7	0.8	59.2	100.0
CARICOM	76.5	0.3	0.3	0.0	0.2	3.1	80.8	100.0
FTAA	40.3	2.5	2.3	0.4	0.7	0.6	47.7	100.0
Year 1991								
NAFTA	40.7	1.7	1.7	0.4	0.7	0.5	46.2	100.0
MERCOSUR	20.1	11.1	4.2	2.7	0.4	0.3	39.0	100.0
Andean C.	42.1	3.3	6.1	1.7	1.4	2.3	58.9	100.0
Chile	16.8	9.0	4.8	na	0.4	0.0	31.3	100.0
CACM	43.4	0.1	0.9	0.1	18.9	0.9	67.1	100.0
CARICOM	46.0	1.4	2.1	0.2	0.2	5.5	56.0	100.0
FTAA	39.1	2.5	2.1	0.6	0.8	0.6	46.3	100.0
Year 1996								
NAFTA	47.6	2.3	1.6	0.5	0.8	0.4	53.8	100.0
MERCOSUR	17.2	22.7	4.2	3.9	0.3	0.2	48.9	100.0
Andean C.	47.8	3.6	10.3	2.7	1.7	1.3	68.1	100.0
Chile	17.3	11.5	6.6	na	0.3	0.1	36.0	100.0
CACM	42.1	0.2	1.7	0.4	20.4	0.7	68.6	100.0
CARICOM	44.4	0.8	2.0	0.3	0.4	10.0	59.2	100.0
FTAA	45.0	3.9	2.2	0.8	0.9	0.5	54.1	100.0

na = not applicable

Source: Data INTAL.

services, intellectual property rights' protection and investment regulations), which were expected to garner the support of U.S. influential domestic actors (i.e., service suppliers such as the banking and insurance industries; research and development–intensive industries such as pharmaceuticals, software, and entertainment; and foreign investors). Although U.S. trade policy did not bend to domestic groups demanding to link trade policy (and market access) to labor and environmental standards, their rising influence was illustrated by the inclusion of side-agreements into NAFTA (once the pact had been signed) and by President Clinton's failure to obtain congressional support to his request for fast-track authority to negotiate new trade agreements.[5]

These policy changes were accompanied by a reassessment of the role which preferential arrangements and discrimination may play in the advancement of U.S. trade interests. During most of the postwar period nondiscrimination and the most favored nation clause (MFN) were the pillars of U.S. trade policy. In practice, trade discrimination was relegated to the subsidiary role of punishing or rewarding selected partners, usually on security or foreign-policy grounds. However, in the 1980s economic and commercial considerations gained a greater weight in the design of U.S. discriminatory trade policy. Neither CUSFTA nor NAFTA can be adequately understood solely on strategic or foreign-policy grounds. As public and congressional dissatisfaction with the functioning of the GATT system increased, preferential trade arrangements came to be regarded as complements to more effectively advance U.S. trade interests. Although multilateralism remained as the cornerstone of U.S. trade policy, regional trade arrangements gained a more prominent role as complements to nondiscrimination.

For the LAC economies NAFTA was a watershed. For those countries for which the United States was a major partner, NAFTA-induced trade and investment diversion was seen as a real threat. For most of the region, in turn, new NAFTA-like agreements were viewed as lock-in mechanisms or "seals of policy approval" that may contribute to reduce uncertainty and country-risk, in turn stimulating higher direct and portfolio investment inflows. In the context of a structural foreign-exchange constraint, LAC officials were reluctant to pay the price of additional discrimination in the financial markets. The implications of NAFTA were amplified by President Bush's announcement of the Enterprise for the Americas Initiative in 1991 and by the presidential summit held in Miami in December 1994, where thirty-four heads of state undertook the commitment to create a hemispheric free-trade area by year 2005.

A Broader Negotiating Agenda

The results of the Uruguay Round of multilateral trade negotiations (MTNs) confirmed that the international trade agenda was no longer confined to the realm of border barriers and trade in goods. The Uruguay Round sailed in previously uncharted waters, promoting agreements in areas such as the protection of intellectual property rights, trade in services, and trade-related investment measures. Moreover, issues such as competition policies, government procurement, and the link between labor and environmental standards and trade were brought onto the table. The "broadening" of the trade agenda had far-reaching implications. One was that measures traditionally deemed to belong to the realm of domestic policies came under closer international scrutiny and negotiation.

The "broader" trade agenda goes well beyond the "shallow integration" process that characterized the GATT system during most of the postwar period, entering into areas of what has been called "deep integration."[6] One implication of this broader agenda is its heightened potential for conflict. Frequently, new issues touch on sensitive "domestic" practices, a fact which widens the area of potential disagreement. The issue is further complicated by the fact that in many of these new areas there is no established consensus on normative recommendations.

The extension and depth of this novel agenda is still to be agreed upon. However, the U.S. government has been one of its most active advocates, both in multilateral fora and regional and bilateral negotiations. Indeed, as the examples of CUSFTA and NAFTA demonstrate, preferential arrangements have turned into effective vehicles to advance this new agenda. The preparatory negotiations for an FTAA and the mandate agreed in Santiago, Chile, in April 1998 confirm that the new issues will loom high in U.S. priorities for trade negotiations in the Americas.

Hemispheric Trade and Investment: Challenges Ahead

Hemispheric trade and investment relations will face at least two challenges in the short- to medium term. The first one will be to maintain rapid rates of growth of foreign trade and investment flows. This would provide LAC countries with much-needed foreign exchange. Moreover, it would nurture U.S. business and official incentives to engage into constructive negotiations with the countries of the region. The second and related challenge will be to prevent a backlash in trade liberalization in LAC and to keep protectionist pressures at bay in the U.S. market. Both domestic and international factors will shape the environment in which these challenges will be confronted.

Maintaining High Rates of Growth of Trade and Investment

Maintaining high rates of growth of trade and investment flows will matter both for LAC and the United States. During the 1990s the LAC economies took advantage of abundant international liquidity to grow at faster rates than in the previous decade. Rapid import growth widened the current account deficit, but foreign capital easily financed the imbalance, even leading to an increase in international reserves from the depressed levels of the late 1980s. Rapid import growth turned the region into one of the fastest growing markets for developed country exports, raising exporters' interest and drawing trade officials' attention. In the context of more outward-oriented trade regimes, the achievement of high rates of output growth in the future will require the maintenance of a rapid pace of import expansion.

The high liquidity that characterized international financial markets during most of the 1990s is unlikely to prevail indefinitely. The Mexican crisis of December 1994 brought the first signs of alarm about the risks involved in a growth strategy that relied heavily on foreign savings. But its effects were transitory: capital flow toward LAC recovered in 1996 and early 1997, only to plummet again after the 1997 East Asian crisis (later on aggravated by the Russian default). In the late 1990s, the change in the mood of international financial markets may persist longer than during the Mexican episode. Thus the maintenance of rapid rates of export growth will become a key factor to secure badly needed foreign exchange and to prevent a severe growth slowdown. Export expansion may enable LAC to reduce their dependence on volatile portfolio capital flows and to maintain imports growing at rates compatible with sustained economic growth.

The maintenance of high rates of economic growth in LAC will contribute to the nurturing of U.S. private and official interest in the region. This may help to forge a mutually satisfactory trade deal and to maintain U.S. markets open. If LAC continues to be regarded as a region offering attractive opportunities for U.S. business, then U.S. protectionist lobbies may face more effective domestic checks. The odds will thus be in favor of a more constructive approach toward hemispheric trade negotiations.

But in order to sustain high rates of trade and economic growth in LAC, international financial markets will have to avoid major turmoil. The waves of euphoria and panic that have plagued them since the mid-1990s will negatively affect LAC long-term growth prospects. Although private-sector-driven international capital markets have reduced the scope for successful official interventions, the potential contribution of official agencies (such as the U.S. Treasury or the IMF) at times of market turmoil cannot be overestimated, as demonstrated by the role played by the United States during the Mexican crisis of December 1994.[7]

To a large extent, however, maintaining rapid trade growth will depend on the domestic economic and policy environment. Although the outward-orientation of LAC trade regimes is unlikely to be reversed, pressures toward "forced" protection may rise if external conditions deteriorate. By the same token, although a U.S. protectionist backlash is unlikely, the influence of some domestic actors over U.S. trade policy may bring about an increase in protection. To these issues I now turn.

Keeping Protection at Bay and Maintaining Outward Orientation
The change in the trade policy paradigm, which pervaded LAC in the 1980s, was not a transitory event. Import substitution industrialization was full-heartedly abandoned in most of the region by voters, business elites, and public sector officials. But a transitory reversal to protection cannot be discarded out of hand. If the external (foreign-exchange) constraint makes economic growth falter again, then pressures to restrict trade can be expected to mount.[8]

Pressures in favor of trade protection in LAC threaten not only to adversely affect U.S. exporters but also the significant progress made by intraregional preferential trade liberalization. As the fallouts of the external debt crisis of the 1980s clearly showed, intraregional trade flows suffered the most during times of economic contraction. Although the strengthening of outward-oriented business sectors and growing interdependence within the region will constrain policy reversals, a forthcoming international environment will be a key influence over the future course of trade policies.

Similarly, keeping at bay U.S. domestic protectionist pressures will pose challenges both to U.S. officials and export-oriented businesses. Apart from the traditional issues of tariff escalation, agricultural subsidies, and restrictive implementation of trade-remedy laws, U.S. trade policy has suffered mounting domestic pressures on behalf of the protection of environmental and labor standards. If successful, then these may turn into new forms of disguised protectionism.

More intense global interactions have raised the issue of the effects of divergent national practices and policy asymmetries on nations' and groups' welfare to center stage in the trade policy debate. But there is more than a genuine interest to agree on a set of rules to favor mutually beneficial exchange. Indeed, there is a high risk that protectionist interests may capture these issues, using labor and environmental standards to restrict trade. How this imbroglio will be dealt with by the United States (and other developed countries) in their domestic politics will be decisive for the future of the international trading system and LAC countries' market access conditions.

Preserving outward-oriented trade regimes will also require that old and new preferential agreements in the Western Hemisphere be consistent with multilateral rules and the World Trade Organization (WTO). Due to market size and its traditional leadership in world affairs, this imperative will be most compelling for agreements that name the United States as one of its parties.

The FTAA: Coping with Divergent Interests and Agendas
In the Summit of the Americas held in Miami in December 1994 the presidents and chiefs of state of thirty-four countries of the Western Hemisphere agreed to negotiate a regionwide free-trade area by year 2005. The decision

was followed by an intense preparatory activity, which included four trade ministerial meetings in Denver, Cartagena, Belo Horizonte, and San Jose, Costa Rica, and the establishment of twelve working groups in charge of specific issues. Between 1994 and 1998 the process served to collect a significant amount of comparable quantitative and qualitative information on trade flows and trade and investment regimes in the hemisphere and to launch a useful exchange among trade officials. In April 1998, the second presidential summit held in Santiago served to formally launch negotiations.

The preparatory phase has confirmed that trade interests and agendas are not completely coincident throughout the hemisphere. Divergent views prevail about how preferential trade liberalization should proceed, how far should commitments be carried beyond those already undertaken in the WTO (in areas other than market access) or what kind of special treatment, if any, should be granted to the smaller economies. Some of these divergences were not bridged by the presidential declaration that followed the Santiago summit, and they will constitute the core of future negotiations. To a certain extent, these divergences reflect differences in size, trade patterns, levels of protection, and stages of development. But they are also a result of divergent political economies and policy preferences. This diversity will make the negotiation and implementation of an FTAA a daunting challenge.

At least four broad issues will merit special consideration as negotiations develop following the Santiago summit: (1) the scope of the FTAA; (2) its implementation; (3) the distribution of costs and benefits of economic integration; and (4) the interphase of the FTAA and macroeconomic stability. Each of these is briefly discussed below.

The Scope of the FTAA

The record of more than three years of preparatory talks suggests that the scope and nature of the commitments to be undertaken in the FTAA will be at the core of the negotiations. Although protection at the border is still comparatively high in most of LAC, the attractiveness of preferential agreements for U.S. negotiators rests not so much on lowering border barriers to trade in goods, but in WTO-plus commitments (particularly as regards domestic regulations and nonborder issues such as trade in services, protection of intellectual property rights, treatment of foreign direct investment, competition policy, government procurement, and labor and environmental standards). In effect, probably the main U.S. incentive to enter into FTAs with Canada and Mexico was to reach "deeper understandings" on issues still uncovered or inadequately covered—as far as U.S. interests were concerned—by multilateral rules. Many of these WTO-plus issues are sensitive ones for LAC.

Moreover, some of the issues at the top of LAC's priority list, such as agricultural subsidies and enforcement of U.S. trade remedy laws, are unlikely to be adequately dealt with either at the hemispheric or bilateral level (as already demonstrated by CUSFTA and NAFTA).[9] These divergences do not necessarily pose insurmountable obstacles to a successful completion of the negotiations, which will be precisely aimed at bridging them. Yet they do point out areas that will demand considerable energy on the part of the negotiators.

Implementation of the FTAA

The Miami declaration established year 2005 as the limit to conclude the negotiations and to implement the FTAA. Although the agreement should be implemented as a "single undertaking," at least two interpretations of this principle have been offered. According to one, "single undertaking" means that all commitments will be implemented simultaneously and in a single package—that is, nothing will be agreed until all is agreed upon. This formula purports to ensure a deal as balanced as possible in an environment structurally characterized by large asymmetries of size and power. The alternative interpretation takes "single undertaking" as meaning that commitments should be adopted as a whole (no partial enforcement), but that implementation does not need to be simultaneous.

The "single undertaking" commitment has been complemented by that of an "early harvest." The early-harvest principle makes reference to interim agreements that may be enforced in areas in which the participants have been able to strike a deal before all negotiations are concluded. These dual principles may generate tensions if differences emerge regarding the extension and opportunity of such early harvest.

Once again, nothing precludes implementation of certain commitments before year 2005 if all parties find it mutually beneficial. Yet in the context of an unbalanced bargaining process, the way in which agreement on an early harvest is eventually reached will be a key issue.

Distribution of Costs and Benefits

The historical experience with economic integration suggests that there are at least two approaches to deal with the asymmetric distribution of costs and benefits likely to stem from economic integration among widely different partners. Each approach depends on the degree of trust in the market's ability to produce convergence as opposed to polarization among regions with sizable differences in per capita incomes.

Traditionally, the European Union (EU) has given an explicit role to the compensation of asymmetries to prevent the consolidation of vicious circles of stagnation and decay in disadvantaged regions. This is the role played by structural funds and other widely used redistributive mechanisms. In NAFTA, in contrast, these issues have received little attention. Instead, member countries have emphasized the role of domestic policies to compensate for the centrifugal forces that may be unveiled by economic adjustment.

The economies of the Western Hemisphere are characterized by large disparities of size, structure, and levels of development. This will turn the issue of a balanced distribution of costs and benefits into a major one. But promoting a balanced distribution of costs and benefits is likely to go beyond the issue of technical support for the smaller economies, which has been the dominant approach so far.

Macroeconomics and the FTAA

Although trade policy deals mainly with resource allocation, the macroeconomic implications and the issue of the sustainability of trade liberalization can hardly be neglected. The macroeconomic interphase of the FTAA is made more evident by the fact that the WTO-plus agenda fostered by U.S. negotiators goes well beyond border barriers and trade in goods, to include other issues such as capital account liberalization.

In the last decade, the LAC countries have made remarkable progress toward macroeconomic stability and more outward-oriented trade and investment regimes. Yet considerable uncertainty remains about their sustainability and degree of vulnerability to changes in the external financial environment. The economies of the region are still heavily dependent on foreign savings, which makes them vulnerable to volatile capital flows. Moreover, in many countries the nominal exchange rate has played a key role to anchor inflation, raising the question of whether exchange rate regimes may be sustainable in a less-forthcoming international financial environment.

In this context, differences are likely to arise on whether far-reaching trade liberalization (and indeed the broader trade agenda) can be advanced independently of issues such as capital account liberalization, choice of exchange-rate regime, or the establishment of contingent credit facilities to deal with unexpected liquidity crises. As the case of Mexico has demonstrated, growing trade and investment linkages with the United States may raise the issue of whether a monetary union (or a currency board) may be a more efficient policy regime than a flexible exchange rate. The issue of monetary union was also raised (probably prematurely) in MERCOSUR, where Argentine officials would like to see its currency board and peg to the U.S. dollar adopted by the other partners (and particularly Brazil). These issues may not have to be tackled from the start, but they are likely to surface repeatedly throughout negotiations.

MERCOSUR and the FTAA

All MERCOSUR member countries participated in the Summit of the Americas held in Miami in December 1994 and shared the commitment to negotiate and start implementation of a hemispheric free-trade zone by year 2005. However from the start enthusiasm varied widely.[10] While Argentina expressed open interest, Paraguay and Uruguay were largely indifferent, and the Brazilian government mostly reluctant. The reasons are not difficult to understand.

Originally, Argentine authorities seemed most enthusiastic with the FTAA process. The bases for such enthusiasm were lower anticipated transition costs, "expectational" considerations ("lock-in" effects and lower country-risk premia), and the positive influence which the hemispheric agenda was expected to have on MERCOSUR's own intraregional negotiations. For the smaller economies (Paraguay and Uruguay), in turn, economic integration in the subregion was already demanding the bulk of public and private actors' attention. The hemispheric process was thus perceived as relatively distant from the daily demands posed by regional negotiations.

Brazilian reluctance, in turn, rested on several grounds. On the one hand, although the largest MERCOSUR partner stood to gain the most from free and more stable access to the U.S. market, its diversified economic structure also meant that transition costs derived from trade liberalization vis-à-vis the United States would be sizable. Domestic opposition was aggravated by the strains posed by a macroeconomic stabilization program anchored in foreign trade and financial liberalization (in the context of an appreciated real exchange rate).[11] Moreover, since Brazil displays a diversified regional trade pattern and relatively high protection, a hemispheric preferential agreement would involve a high potential for trade diversion. Finally, due to the nature of domestic regulations and the stage of the process of economic reform, Brazilian authorities were reluctant to make reform commitments beyond those already undertaken in the context of the WTO, especially in new nonborder areas. The official argument underlined the need to adapt to the effects of the three-tiered set of liberalization initiatives undertaken in the 1990s: the unilateral program launched in the late 1980s; the adoption of multilateral commitments agreed in the Uruguay Round of multilateral trade negotiations; and the implementation of MERCOSUR agreements.

However, after the Miami summit national positions in MERCOSUR have tended to converge, influenced by several factors. First, the rapid growth of intraregional trade led the smaller partners (particularly Argentina) to appreciate the (mercantilist) benefits of having preferential access to the large Brazilian market.[12] Second, as the FTAA negotiating agenda became more evident, a more balanced assessment of costs and benefits could be made not only by public sector officials but also by the private sector. Finally, as preparatory talks gained momentum and the chances of the U.S. administration obtaining fast-track negotiating authority from Congress diminished, the costs of a recalcitrant and obstructionist position on the part of MERCOSUR increased, while its benefits were hard to see.

MERCOSUR's stance vis-à-vis the FTAA process has suffered the strains posed by not fully convergent perceived national interests. However, these strains were successfully arbitraged and, at the end of the day, member countries succeeded in putting forward a coherent negotiating stance. Certainly, Brazilian views were dominant. Yet they were not immune to other members' perceived interests (such as Argentina's). This accommodation was facilitated by the fact that the phase underway was one of preparations, with no substantial negotiations taking place.

During preparatory negotiations MERCOSUR refused to undertake commitments on issues such as the agreement's WTO-plus scope, early implementation, and inclusion of environmental and labor issues in the negotiations. Overall, MERCOSUR member countries were inclined to emphasize the agreement's WTO-compatibility, rather than WTO-plus scope, except on market access issues. This was revealed by the group's stance in areas such as intellectual property rights protection, government procurement, and services trade. MERCOSUR member countries did not undertake any commitment on early implementation either, except for "business facilitation" measures. The rationale was that a "single undertaking" would be the best way to ensure a balanced result. Opposition to include labor and environmental issues in the negotiations mirrors MERCOSUR's reluctance to go beyond multilateral commitments in areas other than market access.

As preparatory negotiations went along, MERCOSUR successfully put forward the notions that: (1) negotiations should be gradual and achieve a balanced result; (2) the treatment of agriculture, textiles, and apparel should be a priority; and (3) the FTAA should go beyond a commitment to transparency and compatibility with WTO standards in areas such as antidumping and countervailing measures, which pose market access impediments to the region's exports.

The inclination toward a gradual approach to negotiations can best be grasped in MERCOSUR's defeated proposal for a three-phased negotiation made at the Belo Horizonte ministerial summit, or in MERCOSUR's recurring insistence on the subordination of substantive progress to the improvement of basic data and information. The emphasis on priority treatment to agriculture, textiles, and apparel rests on the apparent importance of these sectors (particularly agriculture) for MERCOSUR exports. MERCOSUR member countries rightly fear that treatment of agriculture will be relegated, since many of the market access issues involved may not be adequately dealt with in a regional framework. The same fears gave grounds to MERCOSUR's insistence on making effective progress on antidumping and countervailing duties. These examples demonstrate that MERCOSUR countries are inclined to make progress on new negotiating issues conditional to the achievement of tangible results in long-standing market access obstacles faced by regional exports.

MERCOSUR is likely to remain an important actor in hemispheric negotiations. However, in order to fully take advantage of this potential, the trading partners will have to improve considerably the enforcement of common trade policies. In effect, since the end of the "transition period" in December 1994, MERCOSUR member countries have failed to enforce effectively the common external tariff (CET) and other trade policy instruments (such as a customs code and a regional antidumping and countervailing regime) required to shape a common negotiating stance. Moreover, the "deepening" agenda has been slow to advance.

Conclusions

I have argued that trade relations in the hemisphere have undergone a dramatic transformation in the last decade. This change contributes to the explanation that considerable political energies and taxpayer's money has been invested in the preparatory negotiation of an FTAA.

But this change pales when compared to the challenges that lay ahead. LAC needs to maintain rapid rates of export and import growth. Some of the policy decisions to favor that outcome belong to the domestic realm. But many will depend on international factors and market access conditions. The most daunting challenge, however, will be the negotiation of an FTAA.

Preparatory exchanges have shown that there are significant divergences among the parties. These were expected, taking into account the wide disparities prevailing among the countries of the hemisphere. I have emphasized four issues that will have to be addressed in the course of the negotiations and that are likely to pose the most significant challenges to progress: (1) the scope of the agreement; (2) the method of implementation; (3) the distribution of costs and benefit; and (4) the link between the trade agreement and macroeconomic issues.

Although all participating countries will have a significant role in the negotiations, the United States and MERCOSUR will be two decisive players. If the United States does not push ahead, then the process is unlikely to advance quickly (for which a fast-track authority at some point in the future will prove necessary). As far as MERCOSUR is concerned, as the preparatory negotiations revealed, the regional group has the potential to turn the process into an effective negotiation, rather than a replication of already existing agreements, such as NAFTA. In order to do so, however, MERCOSUR will have to strengthen its common trade policy instruments as well as advance more decisively into the "deepening" agenda.

Notes

1. In the 1981–1989 period the rate of growth of U.S. exports to LAC was one-third of the rate of growth of total U.S. exports. Data on trade flows taken from the IMF (*Direction of Trade Statistics*) and DataIntal.
2. For a discussion on how the U.S. policy stance influenced trade policy design in LAC, see R. Bouzas and J. Ros, "The North-South Variety of Economic Integration: Issues and Prospects for Latin America," in *Economic Integration in the Western Hemisphere*, ed. R.

Bouzas and J. Ros (Notre Dame, Ind.: University of Notre Dame Press, 1994). On alternative strategies about preferential negotiations, see R. Bouzas, "Preferential Trade Liberalization in the Western Hemisphere: NAFTA and Beyond," in *Regionalism and the Global Economy: The Case of Latin America and the Caribbean,* ed. J. J. Teunissen (The Hague: FONDAD, 1995).

3. The sizable difference between the rate of growth of intraregional and total exports (in addition to the fact that trade grew most rapidly in goods in which MERCOSUR countries showed no revealed comparative advantage) was given as an indicator of trade diversion. Indeed, this trend was simply the counterpart of the fact that imports (from all origins) increased at a much faster rate than exports due to trade liberalization, rapid domestic demand growth, and real exchange rate appreciation. In effect, the difference between the rate of growth of intraregional and total imports (26.6 percent compared to 21.7 percent between 1991 and 1996) was not as large as that between intraregional and total exports (27.1 percent compared to 10.3 percent during the same period). Even in the automobile sector (transitorily excluded from MERCOSUR and subject to special bilateral agreement between Argentina and Brazil), imports from the rest of the world increased at a very rapid pace. The original claim was made in A. Yeats, "Does Mercosur's Trade Performance Justify Concerns about the Effects of Regional Trade Arrangements? Yes" (Washington, D.C.: The World Bank, 1996, mimeograph). For a discussion, see R. Bouzas, "El Mercosur: una evaluación sobre su situación y desafíos actuales," in *Regionalización e integración económica. Instituciones y procesos comparados,* ed. R. Bouzas (Buenos Aires: Ed. Nuevohacer, 1997).

4. The total value of new bonds issued by LAC increased from $7.2 billion in 1991 to an estimated $53.5 billion in 1997. Total (disbursed) external debt rose 42 percent between 1991 and 1997.

5. Much of the debate about the 1997 fast-track authority centered on the mandate to be given to U.S. negotiators regarding trade and the environment, and trade and labor standards.

6. For a broader discussion, see R. Lawrence, A. Bressand, and T. Ito, *A Vision for the World Economy: Openness, Diversity and Cohesion* (Washington, D.C.: The Brookings Institution, 1995).

7. During the financial turmoil following the Russian default, the U.S. administration emphasized its interest in preventing a "contagion effect" from spreading to LAC. The U.S. attitude took shape in the official support granted to the organization of an external financial package for Brazil. However, how far any U.S. administration may be prepared—and able—to go is uncertain. Congress may block the executive's policy initiatives, and other governments and international financial institutions may be reluctant to participate.

8. Since the Russian default pressures in favor of trade protection have increased regionwide. Although no government has supported an across-the-board increase in protection, many have engaged in more active implementation of trade remedy laws (such as Argentina, Mexico, and Chile) and procedural protectionism (such as an extension of sanitary requirements in Brazil).

9. NAFTA did not make significant progress in areas such as agriculture (where member countries maintained their own domestic subsidy programs and restrictive rules of origin inhibit market integration—such as in the dairy sector) and the enforcement of U.S. trade remedy laws (where the creation of binational panels to review disputes came short of the Canadian and Mexican aspiration to limit discretion in the implementation of the U.S. antidumping code).

10. For a discussion of the structure of incentives in MERCOSUR, see R. Bouzas, "Mercosur's External Trade Negotiations: Dealing with a Congested Agenda," in *Mercosur: Regional Integration, World Markets,* ed. R. Roett (Boulder: Lynne Rienner Publishers, 1999); and Pedro da Motta Veiga, "El Mercosur y el Proceso de Construcción del ALCA," *Integración y Comercio* 3 (Sept.–Dec. 1997).

11. Motta Veiga, "El Mercosur."

12. The share of MERCOSUR (largely Brazil) in Argentina's total exports increased more than twofold from 16.5 percent in 1991 to 36.2 percent in 1997. For Paraguay and Uruguay regional markets have been traditionally important, but concentration of trade has increased considerably in recent years.

PART THREE

International Civil Society

10

The Future of Migration as an Issue in Inter-American Relations

CHRISTOPHER MITCHELL

Migration, once considered to have little political importance and relegated by governments to the care of consuls and clerks, has arrived as an openly acknowledged theme in the international relations of the Western Hemisphere. Inter-American population movements are now freighted with political, social, and economic consequences, including overall U.S. labor costs, public safety in San Salvador and Guatemala City, and the nature of political regimes in Cuba, Haiti, and elsewhere. Hemispheric governments, including that of the United States, have begun to recognize that their policies must address the significant benefits and penalties that are inextricably linked with migration.

The emergence of migration as a high-priority issue in inter-American diplomacy stems in part from the notable growth of northward migrant flows within the hemisphere during the past twenty years. Table 10.1 displays U.S. Census estimates of migrants from Latin American and Caribbean nations— whether authorized or not—who were living in the United States in 1996. The total (not counting children born in the United States following migration) exceeds 12 million persons, more than 4.5 percent of the U.S. population. Nearly two-thirds of these migrants had arrived since 1980, and in 1997 3.8 million were estimated to lack legal authorization.[1]

Population movement shares an important political similarity with other trends in the hemispheric political economy: in migration, as in commerce and capital movements, individual and transnational decisions maintain an uneasy tension with the goals and efforts of states. Although governments often influence migration trends, individual or group choices frequently bypass or jump over the policies or jurisdictions of states. As political leaders try to enhance their control over the migration process, they must cope with several complex and stubborn facts:

Table 10.1

Persons Born in Latin America and the Caribbean
Residing in the United States in 1996

Nation/Region of Origin	Total	% Who Entered U.S. 1980–1996
Mexico	6,679,000	65%
Caribbean Region		
Cuba	772,000	40%
Dominican Republic	515,000	70%
Jamaica	506,000	63%
Other Caribbean	706,000	63%
Central America		
El Salvador	701,000	75%
Other Central America	1,000,000	73%
South America		
All Countries	1,295,000	64%
Total	**12,174,000**	**64%**

Source: Calculated from U.S. Department of Commerce, Bureau of the Census, *Current Population Survey: The Foreign-Born Population*, 1996, Detailed Tables (PPL-59), Table 6. Internet site:<http://www.census/gov/population/www/socdemo/foreign96.html>.

- Transnational networks of migrants, employers, communities, and supporters have matured in a "virtual geography" that links a dozen important Latin American and Caribbean migrant-sending societies with the United States. These channels of migration and communication, although shaped by borders, states, and laws, are experienced in resisting and minimizing the impact of new governmental initiatives;
- The international and domestic aspects of migration are interrelated, and public policies in each sphere often influence the other. However, Western Hemisphere governments often have limited administrative capacity in both policy spheres and relatively little experience in integrating them; and
- Only limited inter-American diplomatic efforts have been made to craft agreements that would influence, limit, or deflect transnational population flows. For bilateral or multilateral immigration bargains to flourish, experience, expertise, and mutual confidence must all be built up among migrant-sending and migrant-receiving states in the Western Hemisphere.

With this analytic framework and a background in the abundant recent experience of Western Hemisphere migration politics, this chapter will look to the future. I will try to advance insights into how the issue of inter-American population movement will present itself five and ten years into the twenty-first century. I begin with a case study of diplomatic and political interaction between the United States and sending nations in 1996–1998, triggered by changes in U.S. immigration and welfare laws. That case study vividly illustrates migration's emergence as a subject for state-to-state bargaining—negotiations in which transnational actors play major roles and sending nations may cooperate effectively with one another.

My discussion then explores the factors that have turned migration into a highly politicized inter-American issue. I will dive into the rich "soup" of interactions among migration, economic dealings, social change, and state projects in the Western Hemisphere. Focusing special attention on the role of states, I will analyze the sometimes uncertain, ill-coordinated, and even counterproductive policies that have been hatched by governments to influence hemispheric migration flows. Finally, I will speculate on future manifestations of the migration issue. What aspects of migration are likely to matter most to Western Hemisphere governments in 2005 or 2010? What combinations of conflict and cooperation among states may emerge? And what surprises should be expected in this field?

Pioneering in Migration Diplomacy: Sending Nations React to U.S. Legal Changes, 1996–1998

In 1996 and 1997, four changes in U.S. law or administration affecting migration galvanized eight nations of Latin America and the Caribbean into vigorous and concerted protest. Their concerns, their tactics, and the U.S. response made clear how complex and politically charged inter-American migration networks have become.

First, in 1996 President Clinton signed a lengthy bill, entitled the Illegal Immigration Reform and Immigrant Responsibility Act (IIRIRA). This complex law sought to restrict migration, by tightening the U.S. government's handling of asylum claims and by increasing the penalties faced by unauthorized migrants. In addition to being deported, under IIRIRA people who are found to have been "unlawfully present" in the United States for between six and twelve months are barred from reentering the United States for three years; those who have stayed for more than twelve months face a ten-year bar to reentry. The 1996 immigration law also made it more difficult for an "out-of-status" migrant to avoid deportation, even if he or she had developed strong social and family ties in the United States.

At least in theory, IIRIRA heralded a U.S. crackdown on fully 3.8 million unauthorized migrants from Western Hemisphere nations. In practice, it stimulated anxiety and protest by regional governments on behalf of smaller groups of migrants from Central America. Between 240,000 and 280,000 people, though they had fled civil wars in Nicaragua, El Salvador, and Guatemala as early as the 1980s, were threatened with losing all chance to remain in the United States. The governments of those nations feared the loss of funds regularly sent home by these emigrants, remittances that amounted to hundreds of millions of dollars; they also opposed having to reintegrate scores of thousands who had not lived "at home" for decades and who would require jobs, housing, and a voice in local politics.

Second, a larger and more diverse group of migrants was affected by Congress's action in permitting a U.S. law to lapse in 1997: Section 245(i) of the Immigration and Nationality Act. That provision had implicitly recognized the presence in the United States of about one million unauthorized migrants from Latin America and the Caribbean. These persons, slated to receive U.S. visas under various "preference" categories, did not wait in Latin America or the Caribbean until their turn arrived (often a period of several years). Instead, they simply entered the United States by any means available, usually to join other family members. Section 245(i) allowed these entrants to pick up their visas in the United States by paying a fine of $1,000, instead of returning to their nations of origin. As plans were laid by immigration restrictionists in the U.S. House of Representatives to allow the law to "sunset" in 1997, at least several hundred thousand migrants faced a difficult choice structured by IIRIRA: they could return to their native countries to await a visa— but after lengthy residence in the United States, they might not find family support or economic stability in "home" nations. Alternatively, they might remain in the United States, but risked multiyear bars to reentry if they were arrested.

Third, Washington was deporting increasing numbers of foreign citizens who had been convicted of crimes in the United States at the ends of their prison sentences. In Fiscal Year 1997, the INS deported more than 50,000 criminal aliens, a 35 percent increase over the previous year. More than 90 percent of these deportees were sent to Latin America and the Caribbean.[2]

Fourth, the Welfare Reform Act of 1996 appeared to herald increasing hostility in the United States even toward *legal* immigrants, who were made ineligible for Supplemental Security Income (SSI), Medicaid, and food stamp assistance. Although these provisions at first attracted relatively little attention from sending-nation governments, they produced a dramatic increase in applications for U.S. citizenship from resident aliens. By July 1998, the backlog of naturalization applications was between 1.8 million and 2.6 million; applicants were likely to have to wait between eighteen months and five years for their petitions to be processed.[3]

Sending governments and migrants themselves responded vigorously to these new U.S. immigration measures, launching varied efforts to influence U.S. policy making. This process of protest and response had three notable features, which may characterize the politics of inter-American migration in the future:

- *Sending-nation governments gave priority to immigration issues and used diverse tactics to pursue their goals.* Joint diplomatic protests were organized by cooperating governments, and they were transmitted personally to high-level U.S. officials. The foreign ministers of El Salvador, Honduras, Guatemala, Nicaragua, and Costa Rica journeyed to Washington for a breakfast meeting on April 1, 1997, with Secretary of State Madeleine Albright, to urge that she prevent the massive deportation of Central Americans. Immigration issues were pressed vigorously by the presidents and prime ministers of regional nations during President Clinton's trip to Mexico, Costa Rica, and Barbados in early May of the same year. A close adviser of the president reported that this lobbying by Western Hemisphere leaders made a real impact on Clinton, noting, "That's all they wanted to talk about." The presidents of El Salvador and Nicaragua both visited Washington to lobby U.S. officials and legislators during the summer, and a special Salvadoran national commission on immigration made three forays to the U.S. capital for the same purpose.
- *Migrants themselves, and political allies whom they and sending governments mustered in the United States, were active participants in the lobbying effort.* The League of United Latin American Citizens lobbied both for Central American asylum seekers, who appeared menaced by IIRIRA, and for the preservation of Section 245(i).[4] The National Council of La Raza (NCLR), representing organizations including more than two million members, campaigned to restore SSI and other benefits to elderly and disabled legal immigrants, citing suicides among Hispanics who were slated to lose public aid.[5] The Salvadoran and Guatemalan embassies jointly organized and funded a series of legal workshops in eight major U.S. cities, and lawyers and lobbyists hired by sending governments enlisted the aid of the Congressional Hispanic Caucus, the American Civil Liberties Union, the U.S. Catholic Conference, labor unions including UNITE, and elected local officials in Miami, Los Angeles, and other major cities.
- *U.S. policymakers responded with some policy modifications, motivated both by international and domestic-centered political concerns.* The

Clinton administration quickly offered mollifying statements and followed up with specific administrative actions. In San José, the president stated, "these Central American countries are in a rather special category.... In these nations where democracy has prevailed and we want to work with them to succeed, it seems to me we ought to be sensitive to the disruptions that were caused during those tough years that we were involved in as a nation."[6]

After extensive legislative bargaining in response to a proposal from the attorney general, the Nicaraguan Adjustment and Central American Relief Act was passed in November 1997. It granted immediate permanent residency to Nicaraguans who had lived in the United States for two years and permitted Salvadorans and Guatemalans who were already "in proceedings" to pursue their asylum claims unhindered. (Haitian migrants and their allies protested that they should have benefited as well, and nearly 50,000 Haitians were given access to permanent resident status in the United States by a separate law in 1998.) Section 245(i) was allowed to expire, but migrants who had applied for its benefits were "grandfathered," and only future visa applicants stand to be discommoded. In 1997 and 1998 Congress restored SSI and Medicaid benefits to current legal residents who are or might become disabled in the future, and the following year food stamp benefits were reinstated for about 30 percent of legal immigrants: children, the elderly, and the disabled. Criminal deportations continued, but the INS and Washington embassies of concerned states established channels to provide better advance warning of impending expulsions.

In pressing for these limited policy changes, the Clinton administration was concerned to strike a positive stance with Central American nations threatened by social insecurity and highly dependent on remittances. Democratic lawmakers also responded to lobbying by migrants and their allies—and after the 1996 elections many Republicans were inclined to do so as well. They believed their party had forfeited many Hispanic votes by acquiring an anti-immigrant image (e.g., in losing Florida to President Clinton).

A New Environment for Migration Policy: Diverse and Novel Transnational Linkages

Even in the foregoing brief summary of an episode in inter-American migration diplomacy, there is a constant note of perplexity and improvisation on the part of policymakers. Legislators, ambassadors, and politicians were adapting to relatively novel political pressures and social conditions, in an issue-area that is changing rapidly. In this section I examine the unfamiliar new social interactions being created by Western Hemisphere migration—a complex "weather pattern" through which decision makers in nations large and small, rich and poor must try to navigate.

Contemporary Latin American and Caribbean migration to the United States is distinct in some important ways from earlier waves of international population movement to North America. Migrants tend to be more mobile than in past decades and sometimes return regularly to their nations of origin. They tend to remain more involved than earlier immigrants in the societies, economies, and sometimes in the politics of countries outside the United States. Although strong motivations persist for migrants to learn English and to adjust to U.S. culture, they may also move within a social network that links sending and receiving societies, and that transcends both. They may also develop a distinct group consciousness to match their diverse contacts and social exchanges. This pattern, labeled *transnationalism*, is defined by one set of thoughtful scholars as "a process by which migrants, through their daily life activities and social, economic, and political relations, create social fields that cross national boundaries."[7] Analysts have explored transnational linkages between the United States and Mexico, Haiti, the Dominican Republic, and other Western Hemisphere nations.[8]

Within transnational "fields," migrants exhibit a continued mobility that confounds older models of migration as a discrete process followed by settlement and a high level of assimilation. Legal migrants often shuttle back and forth between Latin America and the Caribbean and the United States, for family events or emergencies, seasonally for holidays, or in secular patterns for education or other life phases. Airports in major Caribbean countries are busy year-round with migrants' coming and going, and they strain to bursting during the Christmas holidays and summer vacations.[9] Labor migration—whether authorized or clandestine—often takes place as an ebb and flow across frontiers that is governed by the time of year or the condition of national economies. A major Mexico/U.S. Binational Study on Migration discussed "migrant types" in 1997: "In estimating numbers, or discussing characteristics and impacts, it is not possible to talk of a 'homogenous' Mexican-born population in the United States. It is highly diverse, varying in terms of permanence of residence, legal status, and education and skills. It is made up of persons who stay from only a few hours to a few days to a few years, to those who reside permanently."[10] The San Diego Dialogue, a binational civic group, "estimates that 40,000 people commute from the Tijuana area every day to work on the US side of the border and that 'thousands' of US residents commute daily [to Mexico] to jobs as managers of *maquiladoras* [assembly plants]."[11]

Return migration, either for long periods or permanently, is also a well-established phenomenon. Mexican data indicates that "2.6 million persons living in Mexico as of 1992 had migrated to the United States sometime in the past,"[12] while return migration to the Dominican Republic has spawned the new term *Dominican Yorks* to describe returnees from the U.S. metropolis.

Economic resources also move freely within transnational fields. The best known of these flows are remittances from migrants in the United States to relatives and friends at home. Since large proportions of some migrant groups remit regularly from their U.S. earnings, the financial flows often represent a major source of currency for hard-pressed economies. In 1996, Mexicans in the United States remitted $4.2 billion, while Cuban emigrants sent $800 million to Cuba the same year, placing remittances just behind tourism ($1.4 billion) and sugar ($1 billion) as a source of foreign exchange. El Salvador is estimated to receive $1.1 billion each year, while as much as $400 million is transmitted to Guatemala. Dominicans currently dispatch between $800 million and $1.1 billion annually to their homeland; those living in New York can choose from among fifteen money-transfer companies.[13]

Less obvious forms of economic linkage include the interchange of capital, skills, and trade goods. As Alejandro Portes has written:

> Once abroad, immigrants often find that the types of jobs and wages available to them are...quite poor. This is the case for Caribbean migrants arriving today in New York City....To escape such situations, many immigrants again mobilize their social capital, this time to obtain the necessary resources to set themselves up as small entrepreneurs. Not surprisingly, many of these enterprises are based on connections with the home country, leading to a pattern of back and forth migration and trade.[14]

In addition to the movement of people and resources, transnational social circuits have also fostered the rise of new political resources, statuses, and rights, spanning traditional political frontiers. Many migrants to the United States retain an interest in home-nation politics. Some branches of Latin American and Caribbean political parties thrive in migrant enclaves in U.S. cities, and emigrants are courted by home-nation politicians as political contributors and because their views may influence voters "at home." Mexico, Costa Rica, Italy, and the Dominican Republic have officially sanctioned dual nationality for their emigrants, which the U.S. government does not encourage but tolerates. Colombian citizens can vote in Colombian elections without leaving the United States, and Dominicans will be able to do so in the presidential balloting of 2000. In 1998, a city councilman in Hackensack, New Jersey, of Colombian background, ran for a Senate seat in Colombia's election and would have considered (if elected) holding office simultaneously in both nations![15]

States' Uncertain Search for Control and Advantage in the Migration Field

These new practices, assets, and ideas involving migrants have several important implications for government policies. First, although migrants often carry the multiple burdens of poverty, heavy work obligations, and questionable legal status, they also enjoy more autonomy than in the past. They make choices involving a wider range of resources, over a much longer span of time, than would be true if they made a single decision to migrate definitively. Second, because of transnational linkages, migration exerts a continuing influence in both sending and receiving societies, involving funds, politics, culture, and development. This means that governments can't avoid being interested in migration and in migrants' concerns, in order to carry out the states' own domestic functions. Third, the governments of migrant-sending and migrant-receiving countries also find they must focus on internal events *in the other.* Conditions in sending states (including economic cycles, political conditions, and policy changes) may trigger extensive new population flows to receiving states. Conversely, domestic alterations in the United States may undercut (for sending nations) advantages that they and their citizens have gained from migration.

It would simplify many research problems and policy dilemmas to agree with Robin Cohen's suggestion that the role of states in migration affairs will tend to disappear, since "it will ultimately be impossible to separate the free flow of people from the free flow of capital, goods and ideas."[16] But governments actually exert major influence in all the spheres of international political economy that Professor Cohen mentions—as several of the other studies in this book amply demonstrate—and they will probably continue to do so. In fact, policymakers' active involvement in the field of Western Hemisphere migration has grown during the past twenty years, both in receiving and sending nations. Their efforts have sometimes pointed the way toward better-informed and more-coordinated policies, but at many other times they have been haphazard and ill-considered. I will concisely review the lines of action followed by the United States since 1980, before considering how Latin American and Caribbean nations have sought to influence migration trends. I then note the first tentative moves toward consciously chosen "international policies," devised through negotiation or the separate actions of governments.

U.S. Policies

The most visible strand in U.S. policy toward Western Hemisphere immigration has sought to control and minimize unauthorized migration.[17] Five major policy tools have been utilized to try to achieve this goal since 1980. *Embargoes at sea* have been used to detain and deter migrants from Cuba and Haiti; the

U.S. Coast Guard "interdicted" vessels and flotillas in the Caribbean, sometimes returning emigrants directly to the nation they had fled, and sometimes interning them at U.S. offshore facilities including the U.S. Navy base at Guantánamo Bay, Cuba. *Strengthened border surveillance* has been emphasized in the 1990s, including intensive deployment of border guards, occasional use of military patrols, and elaborate new fences and sensing devices. *Employer sanctions* were stressed in the Immigration Reform and Control Act of 1986 (IRCA). These provisions threatened to punish companies and individuals that hired unauthorized migrants, requiring employers to review documents that might demonstrate U.S. citizenship, legal residency, or work authorization. IRCA also included an *amnesty* for some undocumented migrants, under which more than two million persons received legal permission to remain in the United States. In 1996, as I have shown, *domestic administrative restrictions* were tightened by IIRIRA, the Section 245(i) sunset, and the Welfare Reform Act, to encourage undocumented workers to leave the United States and to discourage potential future entrants.

The U.S. government was offered a significant lesson by the diplomacy and politics of migration during the 1980s and 1990s: it is politically costly to provide immigration access based on ideology or favoritism among nations. In 1980, the twenty-year-old U.S. policy of welcoming and assisting fugitives from Cuba arrived at a turning point. More than 125,000 Cubans were brought to the United States in small boats, when the Cuban government allowed emigrants (along with some criminals and mental patients) to depart from the Port of Mariel. U.S. public opinion rebuked the Carter administration for appearing to lose control of the nation's borders during this episode, even though U.S. officials sought to discourage the boat lift itself, delayed granting favorable legal status to the "entrants," and detained some of the new arrivals for years. In 1990, after the United States had for more than ten years favored Nicaraguan political migrants over those fleeing El Salvador and Guatemala, the U.S. courts ruled in the "ABC case" that such foreign-policy criteria were unacceptable. (To be sure, partiality among sending nations reappeared in the Nicaraguan Adjustment and Central American Relief Act of 1997, which favored Nicaraguans over other Central Americans. A year later, Haitians received benefits similar to those given to Nicaraguans.)

The most obvious shortcomings of U.S. policies toward inter-American migration were: (1) Extensive unauthorized migration continued. As I have noted, in 1997 the INS estimated that 3,800,000 undocumented migrants from twelve Western Hemisphere nations were living in the United States. This continued inflow was deplored by steady majorities in U.S. public opinion surveys. The passage of IRCA was followed by a temporary dip in border arrests, but this effect was probably due to the fact that newly amnestied migrants were no longer being arrested. Vivid if fragmentary reports of persisting unauthorized migration often appear in the U.S. media—e.g., the 1997 case of dozens of deaf Mexicans who had been brought to the United States and kept in virtual slavery by unscrupulous entrepreneurs, who forced them to sell trinkets in New York and other cities. (2) The policies sometimes produced friction with the governments of source countries and with domestic interest groups. Mexico believed that the United States was unduly persecuting honest migrants who wanted only to work—and who were usually hired by U.S. employers; Haitian President Jean-Bertrand Aristide, in his years of exile between 1991 and 1994, criticized U.S. "interception" policies against seaborne migrants from that nation; Mexican foreign minister José Angel Gurría in 1997 termed IIRIRA "grounds for anguish and anxiety."[18] Influential Cuban-American groups bitingly criticized Washington for returning Cuban "rafters" to their nation of origin beginning in 1995, and diverse domestic allies of Haitian migrants trenchantly attacked the U.S. policy of repatriating "boat people." The *Miami Herald,* for example, dubbed President Bush's policy toward Haitians "Operation Racist Shield."[19]

Policies of Sending Nations in Latin America and the Caribbean

Two periods should be distinguished under this heading: before and after the passage of IRCA in 1986. In the *first period,* many source nations were only vaguely aware of emigration as a policy issue and, when they focused upon it, tended to conceive it as a benefit that did not require a policy investment. Overseas jobs, remittances, and thus some limited relief from the social costs of high unemployment and low national incomes resulted from migrants' individual initiatives—and states needed to do little as a supplement. Only Cuba (to be discussed below) and Mexico had well-honed policies toward emigration before the mid-1980s.

Mexico's subtle migration policy was to deal directly with emigrants in the United States and very little with the U.S. government. After the formal bilateral Bracero Program was ended by the United States in 1964, Mexican seasonal workers continued to tread the migration pathway that had been opened by the program during World War II. Mexico established numerous consular offices (forty-two by 1997) in the United States to assist and serve as advocates for unauthorized Mexican migrants. But Mexican authorities repeatedly declined to consult with Washington about contemplated changes in U.S. immigration law. Mexico, they believed, benefited from the status quo, and negotiations might endanger other Mexican interests as well as compromise Mexico's general position that states should not interfere in one another's domestic affairs.[20]

In the *second period,* since IRCA took effect in 1987, countries from which migrants come have tended to be more proactive in recognizing migration as a process that can help or hurt their interests; more imaginative in collaborating with migrant compatriots already in the United States; and more cooperative in linking the endeavors of individual nations into a combined effort at diplomacy and lobbying in the Unites States. While the Mexican government is still somewhat cautious, it "has shifted from a position of deliberate non-engagement on migration matters...to a stance of increasing dialogue with U.S. counterparts to better address migration issues."[21]

While the revised policies that have developed during the past ten years have improved on earlier laissez-faire approaches, they have still displayed a major drawback—one that is all too familiar in inter-American relations. Washington has almost always enjoyed asymmetric power in migration diplomacy. The United States tended to initiate policy controversies and thus could choose the terms of debate. Source countries, by contrast, had few bargaining chips other than their pressing needs for social peace and economic advancement and the human costs that repatriation would involve. U.S. authorities could always claim that their hands were tied by legislation that only Congress could modify.

Negotiation and the Advent of "International" Migration Policies

As the United States and source nations in the Western Hemisphere have come to recognize—albeit fitfully—some shared interests in the migration field, three methods have been used to develop joint policies toward population movement. *Formal written agreements* have been drawn up with Haiti (1981) and with Cuba (1984 and 1994), under which each of those states agreed to restrain unauthorized migration in return for certain U.S. actions. In the case of Haiti, Washington promised economic assistance; in its deal with Cuba, the United States agreed to stop treating seaborne emigrants automatically as refugees, depoliticizing that migrant flow by treating Cubans like any other would-be immigrants. Migration negotiations with Haiti were triggered by the venality and weakness of the Duvalier regime in that country, and they were notably one-sided. The United States made it clear that it would intercept Haitian migrants at sea with or without a formal agreement. The Cuban state, on the other hand, had for long taken the initiative in migration dealings with the United States. Regulating the outflow of emigrants—with significant migration "waves" released in 1965, 1980, and 1994—was a traditional and effective way for Havana to engage Washington's diplomatic attention.[22] The U.S. and Cuban governments negotiated about migration on a more even footing, and they continue to hold regular consultations to monitor implementation of the 1994 accords.

Decentralized informal bargaining was utilized following the passage, in 1986 and 1996, of major U.S. laws affecting immigration. In these communications, states in Central America and the Caribbean opposed U.S. steps that might dictate or encourage a major increase in return migration, or impose new disadvantages on their migrant compatriots within U.S. society. Such U.S. policies included discrimination in granting asylum, enforcement of employer sanctions, reluctance to legalize the status of long-term U.S. residents, and cuts in welfare benefits to legal immigrants.

Migrant-sending nations received largely rhetorical assurances from U.S. authorities in 1987, but procured more concrete administrative and legislative concessions ten years later. This increased effectiveness in lobbying is partly attributable to the quick assimilation of lessons learned about how to influence U.S. immigration actions. The United States government is, to say the least, not usually well organized to bargain over international migration. Negotiating with U.S. diplomats is likely to provide limited benefits, since they cannot repeal restrictive laws or modify the domestic welfare system. However, members of Congress can and do revise laws once they are passed, and their offices are organized precisely to respond to well-aimed persuasion. The relatively independent U.S. court system, in addition, provides points of access where migrants and their domestic allies can win some modifications in U.S. immigration policy. (Prominent examples included Central American migrants' 1990 success in the ABC case, and the U.S. government's retreat after 1986 from prosecuting U.S. citizens who had aided and protected Central American fugitives through the "Sanctuary Movement.")

Latin American and Caribbean nations concerned with migration have also notably increased the political, administrative, and diplomatic resources they devote to dealing with the United States on migration issues. Even small nations—once they see the relevance of migration to their high-priority interests—have coordinated impressive efforts under the guidance of talented envoys and administrators. The embassy of El Salvador proved an effective advocate for Salvadorans in the United States in 1996–1997 and coordinated efforts by other regional governments. Since 1996 the Dominican Republic has marshaled dynamic representation in the United States led by President Leonel Fernández, who spent much of his youth in New York City, and Ambassador Bernardo Vega, an accomplished economist, historian, and political analyst.

Third, a very tentative framework for *multilateral negotiations on migration* has been established in the form of a Regional Conference on Migration (RCM), which has held three annual vice-ministerial meetings since 1996. Members are Mexico, the seven Central American nations, the United States, and Canada; Colombia, the Dominican Republic, Ecuador, Jamaica, and Peru, plus several IGOs and NGOs, recently attended as observers. Fomented especially by Mexico, the RCM has developed a Plan of Action stressing such relatively noncontroversial goals as studying existing migration policies, examining migration's connection with development, combating migrant-smuggling rings, and returning unauthorized migrants from beyond the region (e.g., shipborne emigrants from Asia).[23] However, RCM may add new members (the Dominican Republic has formally applied) and might develop into a forum for multilateral Western Hemisphere bargaining over shared migration policies.

RCM discussions already focus in part on the varied migration issues that exist among Latin American and Caribbean nations. Significant streams of labor migration send workers from Colombia to Venezuela, from Haiti to the Dominican Republic, from Central America to Mexico, from Bolivia and Peru to Argentina, and to Brazil from its neighboring countries. Bilateral agreements on issues arising from these migrant flows have already been negotiated by some of the governments involved, and both MERCOSUR and the Andean Pact have made progress in crafting subregional migration regimes.

The United States may encounter an unexpected benefit if and as migration bargaining becomes more multilateral in the Western Hemisphere. States such as Mexico and the Dominican Republic—which receive migrants from their immediate neighbors, and sometimes deport them as well—may moderate their critique of United States immigration policies to avoid setting precedents that might undercut their local interests.

Looking to the Future

As we look ahead, we can now roughly assess the politics of inter-American migration during the twenty-first century's first decade. The growth of transnational migration links is likely to point the way to significant change in this field. Friction between governments on migration issues will doubtless continue. But limited bilateral and multilateral agreements may be reached to secure common values, as both source and receiving states recognize the persistent shortcomings of their traditional policies. The weaker these agreements are, the more likely it is that hemispheric migration will be affected by economic, political, and perceptual shocks, as well as by natural disasters. Finally, the next ten years will no doubt bring a share of surprises in this field. These unanticipated events and trends will stem partly from the autonomous actions of migrants and other transnational actors, and partly from the unlooked-for consequences of migration policies themselves.

Conflict and Cooperation

For reasons I have already sketched, muted discord will probably continue in Western Hemisphere international dealings over migration. Source countries' interest in continued migration access will probably clash with restrictionist leaders and groups in the United States. U.S. legislators and policymakers will continue to be influenced by the general U.S. public's opposition to unauthorized migration and by the concerns of cultural conservatives, plus some labor unions and environmental groups. In addition, the strong U.S. tradition of legalism in migration affairs stands as a barrier to policy innovation.

On the other hand, the United States and source nations may expand the areas of formal or tacit agreement in the migration field, impressed by the growing overlaps among their interests. Five specific areas for potential negotiation suggest themselves, listed according to their increasing degrees of political and diplomatic difficulty.

COMBATING THOSE WHO SMUGGLE AND TRAFFIC IN MIGRANTS This is an area of near consensus, in which the United States is already collaborating with Mexico and with the Dominican Republic. Advances in this area would also help with narcotics enforcement and might build confidence for other international migration agreements.

REGULATING DUAL CITIZENSHIP A host of potentially complex issues are raised by double nationality: tax treatment, property rights, travel documents, pension payments, voting rights, and others. For source nations, international conventions in these areas could help cement ties to compatriots abroad, and encourage remittances of money, skills, and entrepreneurship. For the United States, such agreements could simplify legal tangles and perhaps head off a backlash from restrictionist political groups. Thus far, the recognition of dual citizenship by source nations in the Western Hemisphere has not raised much political controversy in the United States. But it has the potential to serve as a rallying point for nationalistic U.S. critics of legal migration.

AGREEMENTS ON CRIMINAL DEPORTATIONS In private, some U.S. officials believe it would be more cost-effective to retain migrants, who have been convicted of crimes, in U.S. jails to the ends of their sentences. At present, many are deported before serving their full prison terms, only to return quickly and illegally to the United States. The problem for negotiation might be to devise a program to repatriate and reintegrate convicts in a more orderly way, following a full term of incarceration. Such an agreed program might enable Mexico, Central American, and Caribbean countries to safeguard their societies better against the negative effects of returning offenders.

LIMITING THE LIKELIHOOD AND IMPACT OF MIGRATION EMERGENCIES
Administrators in both source and receiving nations have often had to make far-reaching policy decisions under the pressures of a sudden and massive migratory crisis. In addition to the repeated exigencies involving boats and rafts from Haiti and Cuba, critical periods at the land border with Mexico have resulted from civil strife in Nicaragua and El Salvador, the advent of IRCA in 1987, the Mexican economic crisis of early 1995, and other events. It is often recommended that U.S. government agencies present "migration impact statements," to outline how changes in economic, welfare, or immigration policies might affect population movements. Following that suggested model, negotiating frameworks such as RCM might add migration crisis hotlines. Through these communications channels, governments could consult to head off or minimize disorienting emergencies that cause high costs and may encourage inappropriate long-term policies. This sort of pragmatic channel could be especially helpful in the cases of Cuba and Haiti in the coming decade.

AGREEMENTS LINKING MIGRATION, TRADE, AND INVESTMENT   This would be the most complicated and difficult type of negotiation, but potentially the most fruitful for all. Agreements in this field would involve serious efforts by source countries to discourage emigration, in return for commercial or financial assistance to boost domestic development and reduce incentives for exit. All governments involved would find such international bargaining politically risky, but each might also gain. Source nations would not simply be asking the United States for unilateral concessions but also could offer to dicker over the price of dissuading migrants. The United States might gain, from continental nations, the sort of policy collaboration it has had (intermittently) from Cuba and Haiti since the 1980s. Mexico would be by far the most important potential partner for the United States in such broad-based agreements.

Vulnerability to Diverse Shocks
The option of negotiations aims partly to avoid surges and emergencies in inter-American population flows, seeking "governability" in the migration field.[24] If bilateral and multilateral bargaining is slow to begin or modest in achievements, then Western Hemisphere migration will likely be shaped in important ways by economic, political, and perceptual shocks. The most obvious *political* concern involves the potential for rapid and unmanageable change in Cuba as the revolutionary government evolves and perhaps weakens. The United States maintains better communication with Cuban officials over migration than in most other issue areas, but those neglected areas (politics, the economy, and communications, for example) present the greatest

risks for affecting migration. Haitian emigration could easily be reignited, as the new regime's projects for democracy and development move ahead only glacially. Rural violence in southern Mexico might trigger an outflow similar to the flight of refugees from Central America during the 1980s.

Economic disturbances could flow from the persistent vulnerability of nations throughout Meso-America and the Caribbean to rapid capital outflows, trade declines, and ecological emergencies. *Perceptual* change can also be rapid, especially as public opinion in all nations is buffeted by dramatic news reports involving immigration. The televised beatings in early 1997 of migrant Mexican workers in Riverside, California, galvanized and alienated public opinion in Mexico; the stranding of the ship *Golden Venture* in New York in 1993 served to exaggerate an alleged worldwide wave of migrants headed for the United States. Among the burgeoning issues in the hemispheric political economy, migration is the easiest to portray—or misrepresent—with vivid depictions of individuals and groups. Representation is especially likely to shape social and political reality in this field.

National economies in the Caribbean and Central America are especially vulnerable to *natural disasters* since they often rely on agriculture and tourism—both dependent on terrain that can be laid waste by hurricanes, earthquakes, and floods. Calamities of this sort boost the importance of remittances and worsen the impact of criminal deportations from the United States. Washington demonstrated a new sensitivity to these social and policy links when it temporarily suspended all deportations to El Salvador, Guatemala, Honduras, and Nicaragua following the devastation of those nations by Hurricane Mitch in late 1998.

Predictable Surprises?

Both migrants and government policies will probably bring surprising—and by definition rather unpredictable—events in the coming ten years. Transnational fields are created and peopled by conscious, inventive migrants, who react to their environments and to the policy initiatives of nations and localities. In recent years, observers have been surprised by novel modes of migration, by rapid growth in remittances and return migration, by the level of migrant entrepreneurship, and by the widespread effectiveness of false documentation. Migrants will surely continue adapting to policies recently adopted and to changing economic and political conditions.

Finally, partly because of migrants' reactions, planners should recognize the high incidence of unintended policy outcomes in the migration field. In the past thirty-five years, virtually all major U.S. immigration laws have had unlooked-for consequences. The Hart-Cellar Act (1965) led to much more immigration from developing areas, including the Americas, than its drafters envisioned; the Refugee Act of 1980 wrongly assumed that few migrants would apply for asylum; the employer sanctions included in IRCA (1986) did not function well, and many more agricultural workers gained legal U.S. residency than had been intended.[25] In current policy miscues, welfare cutbacks—designed to encourage unauthorized migrants to return home and to deter new arrivals—actually spurred many legal residents to apply for U.S. citizenship, while effectively pressuring their nations of origin to grant dual nationality. As diplomats and legislators of all nations design new agreements and policies, they would do well to integrate their planning with the best studies available of how their shorthand images relate to—or misconstrue—the real world of inter-American migration.

Notes

1. This estimate is from the U.S. Immigration and Naturalization Service, displayed on the Internet at: <http://www.ins.usdoj.gov/stats/illegalalien/index.html#Table1>. Some Latin American and Caribbean nations, as well, receive sizable numbers of migrants, whether they primarily seek jobs (as in Argentina, Brazil, Venezuela, and the Dominican Republic) or refuge from violence (as in Central America and Mexico during the 1980s).
2. See Margaret H. Taylor and T. Alexander Aleinikoff, "Deportation of Criminal Aliens: A Geopolitical Perspective," Working Paper, Inter-American Dialogue, Washington, D.C., June 1998.
3. National Immigration Forum (Washington, D.C.), fax memorandum, July 8, 1998, 2; also see Mirta Ojito, "A Record Backlog to Get Citizenship Stymies 2 Million," New York Times, Apr. 20, 1998, A1, A16.
4. See statements published on the Internet: <http://www.lulac.org/issues/Immigran/AmnestTP.html>; and <http://www.lulac.org/issues/Immigran/245i.html>.
5. NCLR, "Statement of Raúl Yzaguirre on the 100-Day Campaign," Internet: <http://www.nclr.org/press/1997/suicide-pr.html>. Advocates for immigrants, especially from Latin America, targeted Sen. Alfonse M. D'Amato (R-NY), who faced a difficult (and ultimately unsuccessful) reelection effort. Hundreds of paper plates were sent to the senator bearing handwritten messages such as "Dear Senator D'Amato: How many immigrants work hard to feed you? Restore food stamps for immigrants who need them NOW!!!" James Dao, "Courting D'Amato on a Shoestring: Some Grass-Roots Liberal Groups Apply Election-Year Pressure," New York Times, July 14, 1998, B1, B8.
6. White House Press Release: Press Conference of the President and Central American Leaders, San José, Costa Rica, May 8, 1997.
7. Linda Basch, Nina Glick Schiller, and Cristina Szanton Blanc, Nations Unbound: Transnational Projects, Postcolonial Predicaments, and Deterritorialized Nation-States (Langhorne, Pa.: Gordon and Breach, 1994), 22.
8. See, for example, Robert C. Smith, "Los Ausentes Siempre Presentes: The Imagining, Making and Politics of a Transnational Community between New York City and Ticuani, Puebla" (Ph.D. dissertation, Department of Sociology, Columbia University, 1994); Michel S. Laguerre, "The Role of the Diaspora in Haitian Politics," in Haiti Renewed: Political and Economic Prospects, ed. Robert I. Rotberg (Washington, D.C.: Brookings Institution Press, 1997); Eugenia Georges, The Making of a Transnational Community: Migration, Development, and Cultural Change in the Dominican Republic (New York: Columbia University Press, 1990). For a more skeptical view, based on a study of Salvadoran and other Latin American migrants on Long Island in New York, see Sarah J. Mahler, American Dreaming: Immigrant Life on the Margins (Princeton: Princeton University Press, 1995).

9. A vivid statistic illustrating this mobility involves Puerto Rico. Researchers from the University of Puerto Rico recently conducted a survey in the departure lounges of Luís Muñoz Marín Airport in San Juan. They sought to interview Puerto Ricans who had made three or more trips, lasting several months each, to the U.S. mainland during the preceding two years. To assemble a sample of 250 respondents meeting those criteria, the interviewers only had to approach 311 adults. David Hernández, "Puerto Rican Geographic Mobility: The Making of a Deterritorialized Nationality," panel presentation at the Twentieth International Congress of the Latin American Studies Association, Guadalajara, Mexico, Apr. 17–19, 1997. While the Puerto Rican migrant stream to the continental U.S. began before most other Caribbean migration northward, and Puerto Ricans possess U.S. citizenship from birth, in basic respects Puerto Rican migration now resembles legal migration from other Latin American and Caribbean nations except Cuba.

10. *Migration Between Mexico and the United States: Binational Study* (Mexico City and Washington, D.C.: Mexican Ministry of Foreign Affairs and United States Commission on Immigration Reform, 1998), 6.

11. *Migration News* 4, no. 7 (1997).

12. Ibid., 8.

13. Data on Mexico and Cuba from *Migration News* 4, no. 7 (1997); and 5, no. 1 (1998); estimates for El Salvador, Guatemala, and the Dominican Republic from Deborah Waller Meyers, "Migrant Remittances to Latin America: Reviewing the Literature," Working Paper of the Inter-American Dialogue and the Tomás Rivera Policy Institute, May 1998, Internet <http://www.iadialog.org/meyers.html>. The financial flows are, of course, not all in one direction; Mexico's central bank reported in 1997 that Mexicans had deposited $10.3 billion in savings in U.S. banks. See also Deborah Sontag and Celia W. Dugger, "The New Immigrant Tide: A Shuttle Between Worlds," *New York Times*, July 19, 1997, 28. Remittances sent from New York can be delivered in cash in the Dominican Republic within four hours.

14. Portes, "Neoliberalism and the Sociology of Development: Emerging Trends and Unanticipated Facts," *Population and Development Review* 23, no. 2 (1997), 250–51. References in this passage have been omitted.

15. Sontag and Dugger, "The New Immigrant Tide," 1.

16. Robin Cohen, Introduction to Part Fifteen, "Emerging Trends," in *The Cambridge Survey of World Migration*, ed. Robin Cohen (Cambridge: Cambridge University Press, 1995), 507–8. Cohen subsequently moderates this point, noting that "governments, of course, seek to regulate and control [migration], often with increasingly harsh immigration legislation and internal police measures....They have by no means lost the battle, but the sheer scale of movement is slowly beginning to tire the mightiest Leviathan" (508).

17. In the past two decades, we should note, the United States never imposed new restrictions on legal immigration, although many lobbyists and members of Congress support that goal. (Indeed the Immigration Act of 1990 somewhat expanded authorized population movement from Western Hemisphere nations.) In congressional committee votes preceding the passage of IIRIRA, provisions in the original bill that would have reduced legal migration were deleted.

18. *El Occidental* (Guadalajara), Apr. 18, 1997, 4.

19. Editorial, *Miami Herald*, Feb. 1, 1992.

20. See Richard W. Day, "Keynote Address," and Diego C. Asencio, "The Anticipated Effects of IRCA on U.S. Relations with Mexico," in *Immigration and International Relations: Proceedings of a Conference on the International Effects of the 1986 Immigration Reform and Control Act (IRCA)*, ed. Georges Vernez (Santa Monica, Calif.: The RAND Corporation, 1990).

21. *Migration Between Mexico and the United States,* ix.

22. See Alex Stepick, "Unintended Consequences: Rejecting Haitian Boat People and Destabilizing Duvalier," and Jorge I. Domínguez, "Cooperating with the Enemy?: U.S. Immigration Policies Toward Cuba," in *Western Hemisphere Immigration and United States Foreign Policy*, ed. Christopher Mitchell (University Park: Pennsylvania State University Press, 1992); and Robert L. Bach, "The Cuban Exodus: Political and Economic Motivations," in *The Caribbean Exodus*, ed. Barry B. Levine (New York: Praeger, 1987).

23. RCM documents include: Regional Conference on Migration, "Draft Joint Communiqué," Puebla, Mexico, Mar. 14, 1996, available at Internet: <http://www.quicklink.com/mexico/gob96mar/imi14mar/htm>; and Citizenship and Immigration Canada, Press Release on "Conclusion of the III Regional Conference on Migration," Ottawa, Mar. 2, 1998, available at Internet: <http://cicnet.ci.gc.ca/english/press/98/9813-pre.html>.

24. This general goal is outlined in Lelio Mármora's insightful work, *Las políticas de migraciones internacionales* (Madrid and Buenos Aires: Alianza, 1997).

25. See Kitty Calavita, "Mexican Immigration to the USA: The Contradictions of Border Control," and Naomi Flink Zucker and Norman L. Zucker, "US Admission Policies Towards Cuban and Haitian Migrants," in Cohen, ed., *The Cambridge Survey of World Migration.*

11

Migration Issues: Raising the Stakes in U.S.-Latin American Relations

RAFAEL FERNÁNDEZ DE CASTRO AND CARLOS A. ROSALES

During the period of 1994–1996 the U.S. government enacted restrictive immigration policies, which have had profound consequences for Latin America, the major source of recent migration to the United States (see Table 11.1). In 1994, Californians approved Proposition 187, denying medical services, except in emergencies, and schooling for undocumented children. Nineteen ninety-six alone was an active year for legislation concerning or effecting immigrants. Congress approved three laws: the Illegal Immigration Reform and Immigrant Responsibility Act (IIRIRA); the Antiterrorism Act and Effective Death Penalty Act of 1996; and the Personal Responsibility and Work Opportunity Reconciliation Act of 1996 (i.e., the Welfare Act).

Migration issues have now shifted to the center of U.S.-Latin American relations. Both the ability of U.S. officials to restrict illegal migration and the well-being of the Latin American migrant communities in the United States are emerging as major determining factors in inter-American relations. Many Latin American countries have grown increasingly concerned with immigration because it acts as a safety valve for the region's governments to relieve the pressures of unemployment and economic hardships. It also constitutes an enormous source of foreign currency through the monies migrants send to their home countries in the form of remittances. For example, remittances to El Salvador and the Dominican Republic from immigrant communities in the United States now surpass these countries' exports as a source of foreign currency (see Tables 11.2 and 11.3). Established migrant communities in the United States are also becoming the focus of electoral pressures from the migrant-sending countries. When a migrant community prospers in the United States, it tends to become politically powerful back home, either by influencing preferences in the home country, or by becoming a political force of its own. The Dominican Republic is a case in point: the Dominican community in the United States is an important source of domestic political party

Table 11.1

Total Migration to the United States, 1996 and 1997
(in thousands)

	Foreign-Born Population in the United States	Estimated Illegal Population[c]	Total	Total Population in the Country[d]	% Total Population Living in the United States
Nicaragua	241[a]	70	311	4,349	7
El Salvador	607[b]	335	942	5,924	16
Mexico	7,017[b]	2,700	9,717	94,275	11
Dominican Republic	632[b]	75	707	8,097	9
Honduras	191[a]	90	281	5,981	5

Source:
a. Foreign-Born Population Honduras and Nicaragua, *Census CPS 1996.*
b. Foreign-Born Population Mexico, Dominican Republic, and El Salvador, *Census CPS 1997.*
c. Estimated Illegal Population, INS.
d. Total Population in the Country, Inter-American Development Bank, U.S. Census, *Current Population Survey* (CPS), *1996.*

fund-raising. Of similar relevance, the growing number of criminal aliens deported from the United States to their home countries in Latin America and the Caribbean is reportedly exacerbating the already high incidence of criminal violence and drug offenses (see Tables 11.4 and 11.5).[1]

This paper argues that Latin American and Caribbean countries where migration originates are adopting an increasingly active role in the United States.[2] The governments of these countries are becoming important advocates in the Washington migration policy debate. These governments are engaging in a variety of lobbying activities: from hiring professional lobbyists to helping organize grassroots movements within the migrant communities. In fact, Latin American diplomacy toward migration has begun to resemble the region's trade diplomacy, where Latin American officials are ready and able to play the Washington lobbying game with not only their American counterparts but also other important players including Congress, nongovernmental organizations, and the media.

An Anti-Immigration Sentiment Sweeps the United States

The U.S. debate on immigration waxes and wanes with the economic cycle. When the U.S. economy falters, restrictionist sentiments grow more intense. This sentiment does not translate immediately into policy action and, it usu-

Table 11.2

Total Remittances, 1995

	Nicaragua[a]	El Salvador	Mexico	Dominican Republic	Honduras
Estimated Remittances 1995	$300 million	$1.1 billion	$3.7 billion	$795 million	N/A

a. Data provided by the Nicaraguan Consulate in Washington, D.C.

Source: *Estimated Remittances 1995,* World Bank, *World Development Report, 1997* (Washington, D.C.: 1997).

Table 11.3

Remittances in Comparison to Key Economic Indicators, 1995[a]

	Nicaragua	El Salvador	Mexico	Dominican Republic	Honduras
Estimated Remittances 1995	$300 million[a]	$1.1 billion	$3.7 billion	$795 million	N/A
Gross Domestic Product 1995	$1.9 billion	$9.5 billion	$250 billion	$11.3 billion	—
Exports of Merchandise 1995	$520 million	$998 million	$79.5 billion	$765 million	—
Exports of goods, services, and income	$648 million	$2.1 billion	$93.5 billion	$5.1 billion	—

a. Data provided by the Nicaraguan Consulate in Washington, D.C.

Source: World Bank, *World Development Report, 1997* (Washington, D.C.: 1997).

Table 11.4
Deportation by Country, Fiscal Year 1996

	Total Deportations	Criminal Deportees	Noncriminal Deportees	% Criminal Deportees
Nicaragua	N/A	—	—	—
El Salvador	2,452	1,034	1,418	42
Mexico	50,573	28,143	22,430	55
Dominican Republic	1,934	1,468	466	76
Honduras	2,739	584	2,155	21

Source: Margaret H. Taylor and T. Alexander Aleinikoff, "Deportation of Criminal Aliens:
A Geopolitical Perspective," *Working Paper,* June 1998. Inter-American Dialogue:
Washington, D.C.

Table 11.5
Deportation by Country, Fiscal Year 1997

	Total Deportations	Criminal Deportees	Noncriminal Deportees	% Criminal Deportees
Nicaragua	N/A	—	—	—
El Salvador	3,743	1,491	2,552	40
Mexico	84,899	38,475	46,424	45
Dominican Republic	2,603	1,925	678	74
Honduras	3,732	1,078	2,654	29

Source: Margaret H. Taylor and T. Alexander Aleinikoff, "Deportation of Criminal Aliens:
A Geopolitical Perspective," *Working Paper,* June 1998. Inter-American Dialogue:
Washington, D.C.

ally takes several years to enact immigration legislation. The making of U.S. immigration policy reflects the complexity of the phenomenon. For example, the economic recession of the late 1970s, translated into fear and anxiety for what was perceived as out-of-control immigration coming from Latin America and the Caribbean. President Jimmy Carter appointed a select commission on migration, which in the early 1980s recommended legislation on migration. The Immigration and Reform Control Act (IRCA) was only passed and signed into law in 1986.[3] Similarly, the economic slowdown of the early 1990s can be seen as the triggering event of the 1996 immigration legislation.

Budgetary concerns, at both the national and state levels, have been a considerable stimulant of recent U.S. responses to perceived immigration pressures. Proposition 187 was preceded by studies showing the high cost of providing public services to illegal aliens in California. Similarly, the 1996 immigration legislation was substantially influenced by budgetary considerations. In addition, the provisions of the welfare-reform legislation of 1996 restricting benefits to legal immigrants were prompted largely by federal budgetary considerations.

Although its enforcement is still suspended, the approval of Proposition 187 had spillover effects in the national immigration debate. It led to the promotion of anti-immigrant bills in other states and Congress. Initiatives with contents similar to Proposition 187 were presented in Florida and Arizona. The climate generated by the passage of Proposition 187 in California, coupled with the advent of the Republican majority in Congress in November 1994 and the 1996 presidential campaign, created the fertile ground for legally denying immigrants federal services and to promoting more radical forms of immigration control.

To the dismay of many Democrats, President Clinton signed the welfare-reform bill into law in August 1996. The law denies legal immigrants access to certain free federal services. The measure mainly affects the elderly, by eliminating their access to social assistance and health services. It also affects lower-income groups, mainly seasonal agricultural workers, who depend on food stamps when unemployed. When more benevolent budget winds blew in 1997, President Clinton negotiated with the Republican congressional caucus for the restoration of almost half of the free federal services for legal immigrants that had been cut when the welfare-reform bill was signed into law.[4]

IIRIRA is a complex legislation. It resembles a governmental regulation in its minute detail and numerous clauses with far-reaching effects. It is tougher on undocumented immigrants than IRCA of 1986. One of the main sections of the law is dedicated to strengthening the U.S. Border Patrol. It authorizes an annual increase of one thousand agents for five years, effectively doubling its personnel on the southern U.S. border to ten thousand agents by the year

2001. It also provides for an annual increase of three hundred workers of the Border Patrol support staff for five years, plus more police officers to investigate employers who hire undocumented workers and immigrants with forged papers. IIRIRA also contains various measures to improve control of employment of citizens and authorized foreigners, thereby preventing the employment of undocumented workers.

The law also abolished deportation and expulsion hearings, eliminating many of the rights of undocumented immigrants slated for deportation. This new procedure, called *removal* or *expeditious removal,* allows for anyone who applies at a port of entry without documents or with forged documents to be removed without the right to a hearing. It eliminates the courts' authority to legally review any removal order.

Case Studies

The threat of deportation of thousands of Latin American and Caribbean migrants prompted a reaction from the affected Latin American governments. The sending nations were forced to undertake an unprecedented active role in migration issues. This section analyzes the responses of five Latin American nations to the restrictive U.S. immigration policies implemented between 1994 and 1996. The five countries are Nicaragua, El Salvador, Mexico, Dominican Republic, and Honduras. Nicaragua implemented a lobbying strategy in Washington, which achieved an amnesty for thousands of Nicaraguans living in the United States. El Salvador achieved moderate success in its efforts to get an amnesty. Mexico abandoned its traditional position of deliberate nonengagement and developed and pursued dialogue with Washington. Honduras missed the opportunity to benefit from the legislation passed by the U.S. Congress that benefited Nicaraguans, Salvadorans, and Guatemalans. The Dominican Republic has initiated a series of diplomatic activities aimed at establishing a dialogue with U.S. officials. The Dominican embassy in Washington has encouraged the migrant community to organize and exert political pressure on U.S. policymakers.

Nicaragua[5]

On April 1, 1997, the day the IIRIRA was enacted, the Central American foreign ministers met in Washington with Secretary of State Madeleine Albright to urge her to prevent the massive deportation of Central American migrants. Also, at the ministers' urging, migration was at the top of the San José, Costa Rica, summit agenda scheduled for May 1997. In this meeting between President Clinton and his counterparts from Central America and the Dominican Republic, the presidents of Nicaragua and El Salvador pressed vigorously for changes in U.S. immigration laws.

President Clinton responded by pledging that there would be no mass deportations and that the law would be enforced in a manner "which avoids destabilizing the nations and the economies of Central America, or creating enormous hardships for children and families."[6] He pledged a commitment to work "with Congress to implement the new law so that it does not produce these unintended results."[7] Clinton delighted his hosts by stressing that the thousands of Central American migrants who would be subject to deportation under the new law deserved special consideration because of the U.S. role in the civil conflicts that forced them from their countries during the 1980s and suggested that the U.S. Congress might recognize them as "a rather special category."[8]

The implementation of IIRIRA in April 1997 caused widespread panic among the estimated 70,000 undocumented Nicaraguans in the United States. The struggle to obtain a "green card" became the priority for thousands of Nicaraguans, and immigration became the single most important bilateral issue for Nicaragua. "We are very worried," admitted then-Foreign Minister Emilio Alvarez Montalván.[9] With close to 50 percent unemployment and annual income per capita income of $425—the hemisphere's second lowest—Alemán's government was concerned that a "human tidalwave" would only worsen the already precarious economic and social situation of the country. "We need to make arrangements in order to slow the deportation process," otherwise the return of thousands of Nicaraguans will "increase unemployment and violence," asserted Alvarez.[10]

Until 1997, Nicaragua did not have a strategy on migration vis-à-vis the United States. Nicaraguans who had migrated to the United States after fleeing their country's civil war during the 1980s had been allowed to stay and work in the country under temporary amnesty programs set up by the Reagan and Bush administrations. The implementation of IIRIRA forced the government to put in place a strategy to deal with the looming threat of the return of thousands of Nicaraguans. The Nicaraguan strategy ended up blending active diplomacy and a lobbying effort to press for corrective legislation.

NICARAGUAN DIPLOMACY AND LOBBYING   Shortly before taking office, President-elect Alemán ruled out the possibility of hiring a professional lobbyist in Washington to influence immigration policy, blaming lack of resources. Alemán stated that it would be up to his embassy in Washington to get the job done. Aided by a small embassy staff, Francisco Aguirre-Sacasa, Alemán's ambassador to the United States, designed a lobbying strategy to press for changes in the U.S. immigration policy. Aguirre-Sacasa himself served as the "quarterback" of the effort.[11] Instead of a "shot-gun approach" of flooding the U.S. Congress and administration officials, the ambassador's strategy involved targeting the principal obstacle for a more flexible application of U.S. immigration laws: conservative Republicans in the U.S. Congress. The Nicaraguan lobbying effort emphasized two basic messages: anti-immigrant rhetoric and policies antagonize Hispanic voters; and there was a need to follow through on the Reagan legacy and take care of the "unfinished business of the cold war."

The first message used to lobby congressional Republicans was simple but effective. It was based on the demographics of U.S. electoral politics. It argued that given the current demographic trends, the Republican Party needed to improve its standing with the country's fastest growing minority, U.S. Latinos.[12] Even though the 1996 immigration law was not strictly a Republican law—since it had received bipartisan support and had been signed by Clinton—the most fierce opposition against softening its impact came from Republicans, particularly Rep. Lamar Smith (R-TX), chairman of the House Immigration Subcommittee. The message inferred that the forced return of hundreds of thousands of Central American migrants would only consolidate the image of Republicans as anti-Hispanic.

The Nicaraguan effort was helped enormously by the fact that its migrant community is largely concentrated in Florida. It also helped that the Aguirre-Sacasa family owns an influential Spanish language daily newspaper in that state. It owed nothing to coincidence that Reps. Lincoln Díaz-Balart and Ileana Ros-Lehtinen, both Cuban-American Republicans from Florida, later spearheaded the Nicaraguan effort in the U.S. Congress.

Equally important in the lobbying campaign was the use of ideological nostalgia to soften the hearts of Republican "cold warriors." Old Nicaraguan heroes of the 1980s were flown in to help in the lobbying effort. Adolfo Calero, former leader of the U.S.-backed counterrevolutionary forces (Contras) and currently a national legislator, visited Washington to lobby his conservative friends in the U.S. Congress.

Through personal relationships, Aguirre-Sacasa was able to enlist the help of key Republicans to send reinforcing messages. Among them was conservative columnist Robert D. Novak, who wrote an eloquent appeal for Republicans to provide respite to Nicaraguan migrants. Novak's *Washington Post* article blended both the demographic argument and the cold-war-inspired plea for special consideration to Nicaragua.[13] A number of Republicans proved to be receptive to the message. The day after the article by Novak was published, Newt Gingrich, who understood the importance of the Hispanic vote, instructed Lincoln Díaz-Balart to meet with Lamar Smith to find a way to stave off the deportation of Central Americans. The result was the Nicaraguan Adjustment and Central American Relief Act (NACARA) signed into law in November 1997.

NACARA provides what amounts to an immigration amnesty to as many as 150,000 Nicaraguans[14] and 5,000 Cubans who entered the United States before December 1, 1995. It also benefits, but to a lesser extent, an estimated 200,000 Salvadorans and 50,000 Guatemalans who entered the country before 1990 and also faced possible deportation. They are allowed to apply for "suspension of deportation" under the more lenient pre-1996 laws and are required to demonstrate "extreme" hardship if returned to their home countries.

NACARA's preferential treatment for Nicaraguans over Salvadorans and Guatemalans created a major rift among Central American refugee communities. Nicaraguan community leaders were quick to echo differences among the countries. "We were allies of the United States in the struggle against communism," said a Nicaraguan community leader who heads a Virginia branch of the Nicaraguan Brotherhood community group. "We are well-disposed to help the Salvadorans, and we admire many of them. But let there be no doubt: We are of the right, and they are of the left."[15] NACARA was also viewed as a Republican move to change their party's image with U.S. Hispanics.[16]

Nicaragua's success in achieving corrective legislation to the 1996 law also owed to the activism by Nicaraguan migrant groups. While the embassy-led effort focused its lobbying mostly in Washington, migrant community advocates worked at the local level, pledging future electoral support. Congressional lawmakers felt the pressure from all angles. Nicaraguan community representatives also came to Washington on several occasions to pressure legislators. Although acting separately, the Nicaraguan embassy and community activists remained in constant communication, providing mutual encouragement.

El Salvador[17]

El Salvador represents the second largest source of illegal immigration to the United States (see Table 11.1). The money migrants send back to their homeland represents the biggest source of income for the national economy: almost $1.4 billion for 1998, or 10–11 percent of GDP[18] (see Table 11.3). As remittances have increased and become a major source of support for families, the government and the economy in general, emigrants have been transformed into national social heroes.[19] The potential implications of IIRIRA threatened the economic stability of the country.

Given the economic importance of remittances, the government of El Salvador has made securing the legal status of Salvadorans in the United States the single most important issue of its bilateral agenda. The Costa Rican summit with President Clinton marked the start of a diplomatic and lobbying effort by the Salvadoran government to press for changes to the new law.

Salvadoran President Armando Calderón Sol asked his American counterpart for an amnesty for all Central American migrants in the United States. He received a political commitment of support from Clinton, who encouraged Central American officials to visit Washington and lobby the U.S. Congress. In 1997, Calderón Sol, as well as other leaders, traveled to Washington, D.C. to press administration and congressional leaders for changes to the new laws. Governmental lobbying was conducted at the highest levels.

Shortly before the Costa Rica summit, the Salvadoran government retained the services of Rick Swartz, an experienced immigration advocate and political organizer. Swartz's mandate was to mobilize the Salvadoran migrant community in the United States. Swartz developed a strategy to form a coalition of U.S.-based grassroots organizations to exert political pressure to press for changes to immigration policies. The coalition would include Salvadoran migrant groups, as well as established nongovernmental organizations advocating migrants' rights.[20] Significant government resources were made available to finance the effort.[21]

Starting in 1992, leaders of the Salvadoran community in the United States have made overtures to the government of President Alfredo Cristiani. A delegation traveled to El Salvador to meet with Cristiani in an unsuccessful attempt to enlist the government's help in dealing with the looming "suspension of deportation" programs. Subsequent meetings with Salvadoran diplomats in Washington also proved ineffective. Groups like the Central American Resource Center (CARECEN) were largely perceived as "subversive" for defending the rights of immigrants, most of whom had fled the country's twelve-year civil war.[22] There was also a clear lack of interest by the conservative government of El Salvador. It did not understand the magnitude of the problem and furthermore found no political use for the issue. However, in 1995, the Salvadoran community found a more receptive embassy in Washington under the government of President Armando Calderón Sol. Ambassador Ana Cristina Sol became aware of the anti-immigration sentiment sweeping the United States. She also understood the political gains to be had at home by helping Salvadorans in the United States.[23]

Influenced by the Mexican experience of supporting Mexican Americans,[24] the Salvadoran foreign ministry developed programs to support migrants. The embassy in Washington created a position "Counselor for the Community." The counselor developed an outreach program to help migrants organize, assisting groups to send money for specific community development projects and teaching migrants their rights in the United States.

The Salvadoran government went one step beyond its Mexican counterpart. Having a clear target in mind—amnesty—the Salvadoran government launched a lobbying effort, which involved the National Immigration Forum and the liberal wing of the Democratic Party, which had been a critic of the Salvadoran government during the country's twelve-year civil war. The lobbying efforts crystallized in the inclusion of El Salvador and Guatemala in the legislation known as NACARA, approved by Congress in November 1997. The benefits of this legislation to Salvadorans and Guatemalans were of a lesser extent than those to Nicaraguans.[25]

It is clear that not many inroads have been made with conservative Republicans in the U.S. Congress, either by the Salvadoran government or Salvadoran migrant groups. President Calderón Sol found that despite ideological like-mindedness, conservative Republicans are likely to support restrictive immigration policies. Moreover, even though many Republicans understand the importance of the Hispanic vote, the perception of many is that Salvadorans in the United States left a country ruled by a democratically elected government. Nicaraguans, on the other hand, fled a country ruled by a communist dictatorship (Sandinista regime). The Nicaraguan success in achieving NACARA owes a great deal to the activism of Cuban American Republicans who fought to benefit their Nicaraguan American constituents.[26]

Mexico

Few U.S. political debates have drawn more attention in Mexico than the one created by California's Proposition 187. This referendum was viewed in Mexico as a watershed moment in U.S. immigration policy. It not only represented the first time that a state attempted to develop its own migration regulation but also it had negative ramifications on the living standards of new immigrants, both legal and undocumented. The passage of IIRIARA two years later was perceived in Mexico as a national version of Proposition 187.

Mexican officials became increasingly convinced that the growing hostility toward migration was creating not only an episodic series of restrictions against Mexican migrants but also demonstrated that the U.S. "half-open door" policy—permanent rhetorical threat of closing the border without acting on it—was coming to a close. This adverse climate jeopardized the two main objectives of Mexico's bilateral migration policy: first, to avoid abrupt changes in U.S. immigration policy and the flow of immigrants, i.e., keeping "the U.S. door open"; and second, to protect the rights of migrants in the United States.

These concerns explain the change in the Mexican government's position on migration: from nonengagement to an active search for a new understanding. As Foreign Minister Angel Gurría said, "Mexico is looking for a new formula where Mexico and the United States could jointly manage this complicated phenomenon."[27] The current Mexican position sharply contrasts from its nonengagement policy on migration from the end of the

Bracero Program in 1964[28] to the early 1990s. For almost three decades Mexico had a "no-policy policy."[29] During this time, Mexico was content with the status quo. It purposely allowed the forces of supply and demand to determine the flow of Mexican immigration into the United States. The Mexican government limited its actions to the protection of the human rights of its nationals within U.S. territory. This position was consistent with the prevailing perceptions about migration. Rooted in the socioeconomic structures, migration was considered a straightforward supply-demand model: as long as demand existed for the migrants in the United States, there was little one could do to curb migration.

Unlike the attempts of Nicaragua and El Salvador to change Section 245(i) of IIRIRA, Mexico's new migration policy is limited to a new engagement: to pursue bilateral consultation on various issues where dialogue was previously nonexistent. Bilateral consultation has taken place on specific migration issues, such as the development of mechanisms to regulate border crossings. The Mexican efforts have been limited to specific areas and to the executive branch. The Zedillo administration has not pursued potential linkages between immigration and foreign policy. It has been argued that foreign-policy considerations can be a moderating factor in U.S. decision making on migration issues.[30]

The new migration policy of the Mexican government consists of four main elements: active diplomacy in Washington and throughout the United States; the emergence of a process of institutionalization of migration affairs; the creation of a Program for the Mexican Communities Living Abroad; and the traditional consular role of protecting the human rights of Mexican legal and undocumented immigrants.

Migration is so prominent in Mexico's domestic and foreign affairs that a public position has been unavoidable. However, for years this position has been limited to political rhetoric. The president, the minister of foreign affairs, and the ambassador to the United States usually made public statements on migration and continue to do so. This rhetoric, nevertheless, is now accompanied by a hands-on approach and an active presence in not only Washington but also in cities and states with a large migrant population.

The Mexican embassy in Washington under the Zedillo administration created two positions to oversee migration matters. The embassy also has hired a consultant on migration issues. This advisor is responsible for assisting in the development of a strategy to counteract the restrictive policies enacted in 1996.

The institutionalization that has taken place in other areas of U.S.-Mexico intergovernmental affairs has spillover effects in the migration realm. Relations between the U.S. and Mexican governments reached a watershed during the 1989–1992 period. The relationship evolved from nonengagement to cooperative problem solving. Formalization of the bilateral dialogue and consultation has been the preferred strategy used by the Zedillo administration to manage U.S.-Mexican affairs. This explains the current disposition of Mexican officials to strengthen existing mechanisms and to create new ones for dealing with complicated immigration issues. Some examples of this trend toward institutionalization include: the strengthening of the Working Group on Migration and Consular Affairs of the Binational Commission; the recent creation of border liaison mechanisms, such as the one on Activities of the INS and Consular Protection; the 1996 Memorandum of Understanding dealing with the protection of the rights of Mexican nationals in the United States; and, most recently, the joint statement on migration signed by Presidents Zedillo and Clinton during Clinton's visit to Mexico in May 1997.

In 1990, the Salinas administration created the Program for the Mexican Communities Living Abroad (PMCLA). This program was a response to frequent demands from Mexican Americans to the Mexican government for more support for their communities living in the United States. The establishment of the PMCLA represents the Mexican government's recognition of the potential of Mexican Americans as a source of political support within the United States, and also the possibility of the community to develop closer economic ties with Mexico.

President Zedillo's administration has continued to make the PMCLA a priority in the bilateral relationship. Moreover, in 1997, the Mexican Congress approved a presidential bill to allow dual citizenship. This legislation seeks to facilitate Mexicans living abroad, particularly in the United States, to adopt U.S. citizenship, without losing any privileges guaranteed by the Mexican nationality. In pursuing this direction of permitting Mexicans living in the United States full privileges, Congress is debating whether there will be absentee voting in the next presidential election in the year 2000.

Protecting the rights of immigrants have traditionally been the essence of governmental action toward migration. While the United States has focused its policy toward Mexico on the protection of property, investments, and goods owned by its citizens, Mexico, by contrast, has focused mostly on the protection of its labor force. Protection activities of the Mexican government have sometimes been confused with political rhetoric. Foreign-policy speeches, especially those regarding relations with the United States, usually include a reference to these protective activities. Since the end of the Bracero Program, and more so since the passage of California's Proposition 187, the Mexican government has emphasized the strengthening of this system of protection. At the turn of the century, Mexico has developed the largest consular network in the world—forty-two consulates in the U.S. territory. There have been efforts to modernize the system by training and updating programs and improving technical infrastructure, such as the development of databases.

It is too early to assess the effectiveness of the new Mexican approach to migration matters. The recent activities of the Mexican government have produced bilateral consultation on a variety of issues where dialogue was previously nonexistent. Thanks to the increase in bilateral mechanisms in the border area, there is better coordination between Mexican and U.S. officials on important issues such as deportations. The growing intergovernmental dialogue has led to greater attention to the human rights of unauthorized Mexicans in the United States. Finally, an important achievement was the conduction of a binational study on migration between Mexico and the United States, which was the first bilateral analysis by academics from both countries. The study was coordinated by the Mexican Ministry of Foreign Affairs and the U.S. Commission on Immigration Reforms.[31]

Dominican Republic[32]

There are an estimated 707,000 Dominicans in the United States (see Table 11.1), making them the third largest immigrant group to the United States from the Western Hemisphere. The implications of this statistic are multifaceted and have come to be an important factor in terms of the bilateral agenda between the Dominican Republic and the United States. With the introduction of IIRIRA, immigration issues have been thrust into the forefront of U.S.-Dominican relations.

Immigration now represents a vital portion of the Dominican economy in the form of remittances, which provide the second-highest source of revenue for the country (see Table 11.3). In addition, immigration has served as a "strategy of income accumulation for middle-class or aspiring middle-class households that cannot solidify their class position within the confines of the Dominican national economy."[33] Dominican politicians now recognize the interests of Dominican-born immigrants to the United States, who account for 9 percent of the total Dominican population, as they are inextricably linked to the economic development of the Dominican Republic.

The increasing hostility toward migrants, which found concrete expression in the IIRIRA, caused the Dominican diplomacy in Washington to become active on migration matters. As stated by the Dominican ambassador to the United States, Bernardo Vega, three interrelated concerns made him and his embassy try to influence U.S. migration policies: the increase in the number of criminal deportations (see Tables 11.4 and 11.5), the more stringent provisions for acquiring legal status and its consequent impact on the level of remittances.

In 1997, the United States deported approximately 1,925 criminal aliens to the Dominican Republic, 74 percent of total U.S. deportations to the country (see Table 11.5). According to the embassy, close to 90 percent of these deported criminals were engaged in narcotics. These criminals return to the Dominican Republic with dangerous skills acquired in the United States, while the Dominican government lacks the means and ability to effectively fight crime. This is demonstrated in the rise of drug-related crime, particularly narco-trafficking, in recent years.[34]

In general terms, IIRIRA has made it more difficult for Dominicans to settle in the United States. The "family sponsor" terms for acquiring an U.S. visa have become much more stringent. Sponsors must provide an affidavit of support and prove they will be making the required minimum income to be eligible as a sponsor. Since 98.7 percent of Dominican immigrants come to the United States through a "family sponsor" agreement, this has become a major concern for the government of the Dominican Republic. The embassy estimates that almost half of the resident aliens in the United States do not have enough income to apply. Moreover, the embassy has found that in 1998, 72 percent of the family reunification claims were rejected, which represents an important increase from the 52 percent that have been traditionally rejected. According to embassy estimates, this growth in rejections represents approximately 16,000 new visas.[35]

Dominican Republic's diplomatic reaction to the increasing hostile climate toward immigration consisted of three main elements. First, it developed a series of studies to assess the significance for the Dominican Republic of the harsher new laws. Second, diplomats attempted to make their positions heard in different policy decision centers of Washington. Finally, embassy officials helped to organize the Dominican American community. The efforts to analyze the impact of the new regulations were developed in three fronts: the ambassador and senior staff devoted a good amount of time to study the issues; the embassy hired a well-known immigration advocate, Rick Swartz; and Ambassador Vega asked a Washington-based think tank, the Inter-American Dialogue, to conduct research on criminal deportations.[36] Meanwhile Ambassador Vega directed his efforts toward two agencies, the Immigration and Naturalization Services and the State Department. He has also approached some members of Congress. He has argued that Congress is not ready act, especially in regard to criminal deportations. While acknowledging that he has been unable to get tangible results, Ambassador Vega sees his role as the articulator of the Dominican position.

The Dominican Embassy in Washington has developed an important effort to raise awareness to Dominicans in the United States in regard to the new immigration challenges. In addition, the embassy is advocating the establishment of a coordinating office in Washington, D.C. to serve the Dominican American community there.[37] It is noteworthy to mention that Dominican political parties traditionally come to the Dominican American communities to raise funds for their campaigns. Recently, absentee voting has been approved, but no decision has been made yet, whether in the year 2000 election, there are going to be voting facilities in United States territory. To Ambassador Vega, this seems unlikely given the financial burden that this will represent.

Honduras[38]

Honduras represents the third largest source of Central American migration to the United States (see Table 11.1). While the Nicaraguan and Salvadoran migrant communities were able to respond to the IIRIRA, Hondurans were slow to understand the implications of the law and unable to organize and mobilize against it.[39]

Despite warnings about the law from his embassy in Washington since 1996, President Carlos Roberto Reina failed to assign any importance to the plight of the estimated 90,000 Hondurans in the United States.[40] Although Reina's bilateral agenda in Washington included migration issues, trade and foreign debt were by far the foreign ministry's greatest priorities. It was not until late 1997 that the Reina government started to react to the potential implications of the U.S. immigrations laws. Only then was the Honduran embassy in Washington instructed to give priority to immigration. Foreign Minister Delmer Urbizo-Panting visited Washington and met with officials at the White House, National Security Council, and the State Department, to express concern on immigration. He also sought advice from Central American community groups and from immigration advocates on possible actions the government might take to prevent the forced return of Hondurans.[41]

As NACARA approached the final stages of approval in the U.S. Congress, Hondurans suddenly realized that they had missed an opportunity to achieve any reprieve on deportations. The Honduran government felt unfairly singled out by NACARA. It argued that their nationals should receive the same treatment as their Central American neighbors. But Honduras, where no wars were fought and no asylum granted, did not have the clout or the arguments to achieve the political recognition in the United States to be taken into account.

Increasing media coverage of the plight of Hondurans in the United States made immigration an important political issue in the Honduran presidential campaign in the fall of 1997. In early 1998, President Reina, President-elect Carlos Flores Facussé, and Salvadoran President Armando Calderón Sol, met in Honduras with a visiting U.S. congressional delegation and expressed concern to them over the application of the restrictive new U.S. laws.[42]

Soon after taking office, President Flores Facussé met with representatives of Honduran migrant community in Miami and pledged to support their cause. Flores made immigration the most important issue in his bilateral agenda with the United States. In April 1998, the Honduran foreign ministry gave its embassy the mandate to make immigration its priority.

In September 1998, President Flores Facussé dispatched his foreign minister, Fernando Martínez Jiménez, to the United States. His mission was twofold: to lobby policymakers, and to meet with representatives of Honduran migrant community. The president of the Honduran Congress, Rafael Pineda Ponce, came with Foreign Minister Martínez. Upon returning from the United States, Pineda Ponce announced his intention to seek the presidency. He also announced that he would make absentee voting for Honduras a key priority in the congressional agenda.

Governmental expressions of concern have not translated into any coherent or effective lobbying effort. Honduran authorities recognize that any measure to provide Hondurans with reprieve from deportation will require lobbying the U.S. Congress. Even though the possibility of hiring a professional lobbyist has been discussed at the highest levels of government, no resources have been made available to follow through.

Conclusions

The case studies show that Nicaragua constitutes the most successful lobbying effort undertaken in the United States on immigration issues. El Salvador represents a moderately successful lobbying strategy; while Mexico, Honduras, and the Dominican Republic are still seeking ways to secure better conditions for their conationals in the United States.[43]

Table 11.6 illustrates the different responses undertaken by selected Latin American and Caribbean countries in reaction to the toughening of U.S. immigration laws. The five countries show differences in their objectives. The three Central American countries concretely sought an amnesty for their migrants in the United States. The key to Nicaragua's success was its effectiveness in reaching out to conservative Republicans in Congress. Two elements explain this receptiveness of Republicans to Nicaragua's concerns: the geographical concentration of Nicaraguans in Florida, and the ideological dimension of their lobbying message. Nicaraguans were able to rekindle the relations that were built during the 1980s between the Contra leadership and the conservative Republicans in the U.S. Congress. Despite the fact that El Salvador was the country that implemented the most comprehensive lobbying effort, its

Table 11.6

Comparison of Diplomatic Activities on Migration in Washington, D.C. of Selected
Latin American Countries

	Main Objective	Embassy Staff Working on Migration Issues	Involvement of Ambassador	Professional Lobbying	Legal and/or Expert Advice	Support of Migrant Communities	Absentee Voting	Results
Nicaragua	Amnesty	0	High	No	No	No	No	High
El Salvador	Amnesty	1	High	Yes	Yes	Yes	No	Moderate
Mexico	To keep the "half open door" policy	2	Moderate	No	Yes	Yes	Approved but not implemented	Moderate
Dominican Republic	Stop criminal deportees	1	High	No	Yes	No	Approved but not implemented	Nil
Honduras	Amnesty	0	Moderate	No	No	No	No	Nil

Source: Interviews with embassy officials.

limited success can be explained by its inability to make significant inroads with conservative Republicans. Honduras's lack of activism represents the case of a country that was not prepared to play the Washington influence-peddling game.

The experience of the Central American countries show that despite shared interests and similar objectives, no effort was made to coordinate their actions. The exceptions were El Salvador and Guatemala, which joined efforts and presented a united front.[44] Central American nations saw each other as a competitor in their search of concessions for their migrants.

As shown in Table 11.6, Mexico and the Dominican Republic did not have concrete or viable objectives. Mexico's goal of keeping the door open for migrants going north, both legally and illegally, is a general one that did not allow for a concrete strategy. The Dominican Republic's objective to minimize the flow of criminal deportees faces a hostile domestic environment in the United States.

The most significant element of the Latin American and Caribbean response to the restrictive U.S. immigration regime is the relation these governments are developing with their migrant communities in the United States. Latin American and Caribbean countries are becoming increasingly aware of the role of the U.S. Hispanic community as a potential political ally. The relationship between the Latin American governments and their migrant communities in the United States will be a defining element in the future of inter-American relations. This will be reinforced by the growing demographic and political importance of the U.S. Hispanic community.[45] As shown in Table 11.6, Mexico and El Salvador have already established formal programs to develop closer ties with their migrant communities in the United States. Nicaragua, Honduras, and the Dominican Republic are following suit.

The Mexican migration experience, which is the longest and the most significant in terms of numbers, shows that migration has been considered as an area of conflict in U.S.-Mexican bilateral affairs. Since migration is becoming such a formidable element in U.S.-Latin American relations, the challenge for policymakers is to transform the terms of the debate to make migration an area of cooperation. To that end, it will be important to recognize that migration issues are as important to both the sending nations and the United States.

Notes

1. Several media reports have linked the deportation of criminal aliens from the United States to increases in violent crime in sending nations. See, for instance, Glen Garvin, "Civil War Over, but Violence Goes On," *Miami Herald*, August 4, 1997, <http://newslibrary. krmediastream.c.../n12_auth? DBLIST=mh97&DOCNUM=48433>; Carlos Castillo, "Salvadorans Fear Expatriates' Return," *Ottawa Citizen*, November 24, 1994, A9; Arsenio Ramírez, "Sanz Jiminián recononce el incremento de la criminalidad en la sociedad dominicana," *La República* (Santo Domingo), May 22, 1997, 14A. "Nuevo Jefe de la PN Promete Acabar Corrupción," *El Caribe* (Santo Domingo), May 22, 1997, 5.
2. Christopher Mitchell has previously examined the implications of U.S. immigration laws in inter-American relations. See his "New U.S. Immigration Policies and Contemporary Inter-American Relations" (paper presented at the Conference on the Impact of New U.S. Immigration Laws on U.S. Foreign Policy in the Americas, organized by the Inter-American Dialogue, the Carnegie Endowment for International Peace, the Tomás Rivera Policy Institute, and the Hispanic Council on International Relations (Washington, D.C., Nov. 21, 1997).
3. For a good analysis of IRCA passage see, Manuel Garcia and Griego and Mónica Verea Campos, *México y Estados Unidos frente a la migración de indocumentados* (Mexico City: UNAM-Miguel Angel Porrúa, 1988).
4. Manuel Garcia y Griego and Mónica Verea Campos, "A Paradox of the 1990s, the New U.S. Immigration Law," in *Voices of Mexico* (spring 1988): 89–90.
5. Unless otherwise indicated, the case study on Nicaragua is based on an interview with Francisco Aguirre-Sacasa, Nicaragua's ambassador to the United States. The interview was conducted in Washington, D.C. on Oct. 14, 1998. We are grateful to him for his candidness and support.
6. Statement issued May 8, 1997. "Clinton-Figueres-Text-2," *Washington Post*, http://.washingtonpost.com/wp-sr/WAPO/19970508/V000183-050897-idx.html.
7. Ibid.
8. See Terence Hunt, "Clinton at Summit in Central America," *Washington Post*, May 8, 1997, Internet: <http://search.washingtonpost.com/wp-srv/WAPO/19970508/V000488-050897-idx.html>; Elizabeth Shogren, "Clinton Seeks to Ease Deportation Concerns," *Los Angeles Times*, May 9, 1997, <http://www.latimes.com/HOME/NEWS/NATION/t000041907.html>.
9. InterPress Service report by Roberto Fonseca, March 27, 1997.

10. Ibid.

11. He was particularly well placed to be in that position. His broad understanding and deep knowledge of the American political system and the U.S. Congress as well as his familiarity with the key players in Washington served him well in his quest for influencing U.S. policy-makers.

12. Based on U.S. Census Bureau projections, the National Academy of Science predicts that by the year 2050 the U.S. population will be 51 percent white, 14 percent black, 26 percent Hispanic, and 8 percent Asian. The argument for Republicans to bolster their position with Hispanics on the strength of their growing electoral importance has been made since 1997 in several articles in the printed press. See, for example, John Harwood, "Parties Mull Agendas in High-Stakes Battle for Hispanic Voters," *Wall Street Journal*, Apr. 22, 1997, A1; and René Sánchez, "Both Parties Courting Latinos Vigorously," *Washington Post*, Oct. 26, 1998, A12.

13. See Robert Novak, "A GOP Strategy that Alienates Hispanic Voters," *Washington Post*, Oct. 9, 1997, A23.

14. Note the discrepancies between the number of Nicaraguans estimated by the INS and the number of beneficiaries of NACARA. According to Ambassador Aguirre-Sacasa, the real number of Nicaraguans in U.S. territory is hard to determine. Many immigrants remain clandestine.

15. Quoted from Pamela Constable, "A Sore Spot among Refugees," *Washington Post*, Oct. 18, 1998, B3.

16. "I suppose the Republican Party is trying to repair its reputation with Hispanic voters they alienated in 1995 and 1996," said Frank Sharry, executive director of the National Immigration Forum. Carol Rosenberg, "Relief Plan for Central Americans," *Miami Herald*, Oct. 10, 1997, A1.

17. The case study on El Salvador is based primarily on personal interviews conducted by the authors with: H. E. René León, El Salvador's ambassador to the United States, Oct. 26 and 31, 1998; Saúl Solórzano, Executive Director of the Central American Resource Center (CARECEN), Oct. 16, 1998; and Rick Swartz, Washington, D.C., Oct. 28 and 31, 1998. We are grateful to them all for their candidness and support.

18. Personal interview by authors with El Salvador's ambassador to the United States, René León, Washington, D.C., Oct. 26 and 31, 1998.

19. "Salvadoran migrants are 'la gallina que pone los huevos de oro' (the goose that lays the golden egg),"said Saul Solorzano, Executive Director of the Central American Resource Center (CARECEN), at the Washington, D.C. conference entitled "Family Ties and Ethnic Lobbies: Latino Relations with Latin America," organized by the Inter-American Dialogue and the Tomás Rivera Policy Institute, June 25, 1998.

20. Working with the U.S. organizations was crucial so the effort would not be accused of meddling in U.S. domestic policies. Personal interview by authors with Rick Swartz, Washington, D.C., Oct. 28 and 31, 1998.

21. According to Swartz, close to half a million dollars were allocated by the Salvadoran government.

22. CARECEN was founded in 1982. It has become the leading advocacy group for the rights of Central American migrants in the United States. CARECEN is based in Washington, D.C. and has chapters in different states. Personal interview by authors with Saul Solorzano, executive director of CARECEN, Oct. 16, 1998.

23. Personal interview by authors with Rick Swartz, Oct. 28 and 31, 1998.

24. Tomás Rivera Policy Institute Policy Brief "Family Ties and Ethnic Lobbies: Latino Relations with Latin Ameirca," Jun. 1998, 4.

25. NACARA provides an immigration amnesty to as many as 150,000 Nicaraguans who entered the United States before December 1, 1995. An estimated 200,000 Salvadorans and 50,000 Guatemalans who entered the country before 1990 are allowed to apply for suspension of deportation under the preexisting laws and are required to demonstrate extreme hardship if returned home.

26. Rep. Ilena Ros-Lhetinen (R-FL) cosponsor of NACARA, argued for special consideration for Nicaraguan refugees because they had direct impact and participation "when we

fought the military battle." See Pamela Constable, "A Sore Point among Refugees," *Washington Post*, Oct. 18, 1998, B3.

27. Angel Gurría was Mexican foreign affairs minister during the first three years of the Zedillo's administration. These remarks were pronounced in a meeting held between Minister Gurría and the Mexican members of the Binational Mexico-U.S. Migration Study, in May 1997.

28. The Bracero Program was a guest-workers program for Mexican workers implemented from 1943 to 1964. See Manuel Garcia y Griego, "The Importation of Mexican Contract Laborers to the United States, 1942–1964: Antecedents, Operation, and Legacy," in *The Border that Joints: Mexican Migrants and U.S. Responsibility*, ed. Peter G. Brown and Henry Shue (Totowa, N.J.: Rowman and Littlefield, 1983).

29. For a more detailed discussion, see Sidney Weintraub, Franciso Alba, Rafael Fernández de Castro, and Manuel Garcia y Griego, "Responses to Migration Issues," in *Migration Between Mexico and the United States*, Binational Study, vol. 1, Thematic Chapters (Mexico City: Mexican Ministry of Foreign Affairs and Washington, D.C.: U.S. Commission on Innigration Reform), 437–510.

30. For example, foreign-policy considerations played a key role in the opening stages of the Bracero Program and counteracted U.S. unilateral actions that would have harmed the program. When U.S. domestic considerations dominated, the Bracero Program was undermined and unilaterally dismantled. See Carlos Rico, "Migration and U.S.-Mexican Relations," in *Western Hemisphere Immigration and U.S. Foreign Policy*, ed. Christopher Mitchell (Pittsburgh: Pennsylvania State University, 1992), 221–84.

31. The Binational Study was published by the Mexican Ministry of Foreign Affairs and the U.S. Commission on Immigration Reform in 1998.

32. This case study was based on a personal interview conducted by the authors with H. E. Bernardo Vega, the Dominican Republic's Ambassador to the United States, Washington, D.C., Jan. 22, 1999. We wish to express our gratitude to Ambassador Vega for his support.

33. Sherri Grasmuck and Patricia Pessar, *Between Two Islands: Dominican International Migration* (Berkeley and Los Angeles: University of California Press, 1991).

34. Arsenio Ramírez, "Sanz Jiminián recononce el incremento de la criminalidad en la sociedad dominicana," *La República*, May 22, 1997, 14A. "Nuevo Jefe de la PN Promete Acabar Corrupción," *El Caribe*, May 22, 1997, 5.

35. Personal interview by authors with Bernardo Vega, Domincan Republic ambassador to the United States, Washington D.C., 1999.

36. The Inter-American Dialogue Working Paper, "Deportation of Criminal Aliens: A Geographical Perspective," is a product of Ambassador Vega's initiative.

37. According to Ambassador Vega, $50,000 were raised in the business community in the Dominican Republic to promote the establishment of a coordinating office in Washington.

38. The case study on Honduras is based primarily on personal interviews conducted by the authors with: H. E. Edgardo Dumas Rodríguez, then–Honduras ambassador to the United States and Minister Counselor, Oct. 15, 1998; Benjamín Zapata, Deputy Chief of Mission of the Honduran Embassy to the United States, Oct. 22, 1998. We are grateful to them for their time and support.

39. Interview by authors with Honduran ambassador to the United States, H. E. Edgardo Dumas Rodríguez, October 15, 1998; Interview, Minister Counselor Benjamín Zapata, Oct. 22, 1998. We are grateful to them both for their time and support. See also James Wilson, "Hondurans Miss Out on Washington's Immigrant Asylum Deal," *Financial Times*, July 29, 1998, 7. Honduran officials readily admit that their government *no estaba despierto* (was not awake) to the situation brought about by IIRIRA.

40. Interview, Benjamín Zapata. According to Zapata, during a trip to Washington in the summer of 1997, President Reina only timidly brought up immigration concerns in meetings with administration and congressional leaders.

41. Interview, Benjamín Zapata.

42. See "Reina, Flores y Calderón Sol abogarán por inmigrantes hondureños y salvadoreños," *La Prensa*, Jan. 7, 1998, <http://www.laprensahn.com/natarc/9801/n07001.htm>.

43. As part of the efforts to assist the countries affected by Hurricane Mitch, the Clinton administration announced in late December 1998 temporary deportation relief for an estimated 90,000 Hondurans and 60,000 Nicaraguans who have resided in the United States as of Dec. 30, 1998. INS statement, "Honduras, Nicaragua Designated for Temporary Protected Status Following Devastation from Hurricane Mitch," Dec. 30, 1998, <http://www.ins.usdoj.gov/public_affairs/news_releases/tpsrel.htm>.

44. Guatemala was not selected to be a case study for its similarities to El Salvador. In addition, it is widely recognized that El Salvador led the effort and that Guatemala jumped on the "vanwagon."

45. Hispanics are the fastest growing population group in the United States. Based in U.S. Census Bureau Projections, the National Academies of Sciences predicts that by the year 2008 Hispanics will surpass the African American community as the most numerous minority group in the United States.

12

International Assistance for Democracy: A Cautionary Tale

ANITA ISAACS

International assistance for democracy has become a booming field of activity and inquiry in recent years.[1] The scope of programs, the diversity of participating players, and the intellectual energy spent tracking and assessing initiatives all attest to the growing interest in stimulating action and understanding of the international contribution.[2]

This chapter builds on existing analysis, taking stock of the trajectory of research and activity on the theme and encouraging a cautious rethinking of the policy frame. The goodwill and many positive contributions of international actors will be acknowledged. But it will also be argued that international democracy assistance continues to fall short of its intended objectives. These shortcomings stem in part from an overambitious rhetoric. But they also reflect mistaken and at times contradictory assumptions about the challenges of democratization in the region. In missing the proverbial boat, international actors risk creating mistaken illusions about potential impact. Equally importantly, they contribute to deterring the course of democratization in the hemisphere.

The chapter is divided into three parts. The first part provides a synopsis of the state of democracy in the region, noting both the gains registered of late and highlighting the remaining challenges. The second section offers an overview of the history of international support for democracy, followed by a presentation of major actors and programs. The third part assesses the international contribution, stressing recent achievements and underscoring the limitations of current efforts to nurture democracy in Latin America.

The State of Democracy in Latin America

Democratic Gains

The demise of military regimes throughout the continent, the waning of dominant-party rule in Mexico and the advent of peace in Central America all offer encouraging signs. They suggest that Latin America has emerged from the shadows of dictatorship in which it lurked for the better part of the twentieth century. A glance around the hemisphere hints at substantial progress in consolidating procedural democracy, as defined by fair, inclusive, and competitive elections, respect for political and civil liberties and associational autonomy.[3]

From Mexico to Argentina, free and fair elections are now well-entrenched mechanisms governing the transfer of political power. The end of the civil wars in Central America, the failure of coup attempts in Guatemala, Paraguay, and Venezuela, and even the 1998 election of former Venezuelan coup leader Hugo Chavez, confirm the legitimacy of the ballot over all other means for gaining political office. Victories of opposition candidates in countries such as Mexico and Venezuela, where traditional ruling parties have long enjoyed hegemonic status highlights the intensification of political competition. In Central America former revolutionary movements have entered the democratic political fray, and historically marginalized groups, including women and indigenous peoples, have gained greater representation in national legislatures.

Civil and political liberties are more respected today. Democratically elected regimes show greater respect for human rights. They also support efforts to strengthen the rule of law, whether through the enactment of judicial reform and human rights legislation, the establishment of ombudsmen offices, or the development of civic education initiatives targeting schools, poor communities, and the region's security forces.

A vibrant civil society and a committed political leadership propel these transformations. Often created to oppose military regimes, civic organizations have struggled since the transition to adjust their agendas to assist democratization. The current era is also marked by the growth of an unprecedented normative commitment to democratic governance among citizens and leaders alike. Survey after survey underscores a strong preference for democracy among Latin Americans, while political leaders pledge their allegiance to democracy in summit declarations and Organization of American States (OAS) resolutions. Their words are backed by deeds, as manifested in their newfound willingness to commit the resources of regional organizations to democratic defense and strengthening.

Outstanding Democratic Challenges

Latin American democracies continue to face serious challenges. However free, fair, and competitive, elections do not always yield regimes truly representative of the popular will. In the current economic era, the region's leaders are often more responsive and accountable to international economic actors than to their own citizens—in desperate need of social services to cushion the blow of years of economic austerity and restructuring.

Violations of human rights persist. Public authorities routinely abuse suspects, the poor continue to find access to the judicial system blocked, and the powerful still enjoy considerable impunity. Politically motivated violence has ebbed, replaced by common crime. Indeed crime rates have soared to the point where Latin America is now considered the most violent region in the world.

Civil society is a reflection of the broader society in which it has emerged. Deeply rooted clientelistic and authoritarian traditions define relationships between the leadership, rank and file, and constituents of many civic organizations, including those formed to undermine dictatorial rule. Civil society also tends to reproduce existing relations of power. Organizations that are representative of elite interests or that benefit from the expertise of a well-educated leadership are likely to enjoy greatest access and influence.

Latin American political parties are similarly clientelistic. Furthermore, they tend to function primarily as electoral vehicles, offering little in the way of ideology or program and with poorly developed links to their constituents and to organized civil society. These characteristics reflect the persistence of traditional, particularistic ways of doing politics. But they are also aggravated by the slowness with which viable alternatives to the neoliberal model have emerged, even among most parties on the left. Democratic governance suffers as a result. Deputies elected as members of these parties transform Congress into a forum for policy obstruction, rather than for the formulation of responsive legislation. The executive often reacts by seizing delegative powers, and popular disillusionment with political parties and politicians sets in—a feeling also captured in opinion polls and contributing to the rise of populist movements and outsider candidates.

The state is ineffective in performing either its coercive or administrative duties. Establishing the rule of law requires judicial reform.[4] It often also means establishing a presence in regions where state absence leads to the emergence of alternative centers of power and typically violent means of exercising authority. The state's developmental capacities have been severely strained by economic crisis and restructuring with attendant economic, social, and political consequences. While elites benefit from privatization, the elimination of social services exacerbates poverty and inequality and heightens the alienation of poor majorities.

International Actors and Democratization: An Overview

Continuity and Change

Observers of the history of hemispheric relations have identified moments during which U.S. policy appeared to favor the encouragement of democratic rule. Similar dilemmas, however, plagued each attempt. Most obviously, the

United States embraced democracy inconsistently, preoccupied with competing security and economic interests. Internal obstacles further constrained
U.S. effectiveness. Powerful sectors whose interests were not served by democracy resisted its imposition. But so too did a variety of other domestic actors,
who may have favored democracy, but denounced its imposition by the United
States as a violation of national sovereignty. Finally, U.S. policymakers tended
to project a paternalistic, limited, and ethnocentric vision, viewing the U.S.
role as one embodied in Woodrow Wilson's stated commitment, "to teach the
South Americans to elect good men."[5]

The implications were both sobering and chastening. As an essay on the
topic, subtitled "Learning from History," noted, "The overall impact of US
policy on Latin America's ability to achieve democratic politics was usually
negligible, often counterproductive and only occasionally positive."[6]
Scholars tracking Latin American transitions to democracy during the 1980s
became more tentative about the U.S. contribution. Domestic political
actors were placed at the forefront of efforts to undermine dictatorship, rel-
egating the international community to the sidelines where it could applaud,
nudge, or reinforce the process. Scholars suggested, moreover, that this was
as it should be. Emerging consensus stressed the connection between sustainability and the indigenous quality and character of the democratic
regime. Informed by new understandings, the international dimension of
democratization thus became of peripheral importance for the first-generation
transitions literature.[7]

The end of the cold war stimulated a reappraisal of the international contribution to democratization. Scholars struggling to make sense of the myriad
ways in which international players have become actively engaged in efforts to
consolidate fragile democracies concede that they underestimated the international role in the process of regime change. A lexicon that includes terms such
as *contagion, control, consent,* and *conditionality* now defines the contours of
international involvement in transition and consolidation.[8]

This reconceptualization highlights patterns of continuity and change. At
one end of the spectrum, contagion captures the benign, almost unintention-
al international impacts. The popular "wave" metaphor is a prime example of
contagion, underscoring the inexorable way in which democracy spreads at
various historical junctures (including this, the third wave) as one country
after another gets swept up in a powerful trend. The term also hints at simu-
lation. In crafting transitions, domestic actors may apply models and emulate
strategies that facilitated democratization elsewhere. At the other end of the
spectrum, coercion and control emphasize ways in which international actors
have sought, on occasion, to impose democracy. If postwar Germany and
Japan offer the most clear cut examples, then the term also captures the

dynamic of U.S. policy in Central America during the 1980s. Coercive methods have also survived the cold war. Often now referred to as conditionality, the term highlights the pressures and sanctions to which international actors resort in defense of threatened democracies.

The term consent portends a changing political landscape in which a diverse cast of international players play friendly parts, spoken with greater self-assurance. As we know, the recent democratic wave reached epidemic proportions. Propelled by the end of the cold war and the demise of the Soviet Union, and accompanied by the rising currency of neoliberalism, the contemporary wave also narrowed the range of democratic alternatives. However grossly exaggerated, the "end of history" reflected the seeming agreement, or growing consent, on the value of liberal, procedural democratic forms and a neoliberal economic course.

Understandably, the appearance of consent had a noticeable impact on the international community. The sobering lessons of attempts to export democracy were only just being absorbed, and debate over democratic definition, content, course, and pace promised to engage a broader set of scholars and policymakers than ever before. Yet with one stroke of the brush, those debates became irrelevant. Liberal democratic values suddenly appeared so attractive and so contagious as to preclude serious consideration of alternative models, regardless of the particular social, cultural, economic, or political circumstances of each emerging democracy. Furthermore, if the complex realities of specific countries could be ignored, then committed political actors could simply will their countries into becoming democracies by following a recipe: spreading values and replicating techniques which seemed to work in the most secure liberal and procedural democracies.

The same could be said of the accompanying economic strategy. Only a few decades ago, Latin American scholars employed dependency analysis to explain the natural affinity between authoritarian rule and capitalist development in the region. But, in another striking historical turn, scholars and policymakers alike now celebrate the harmonious and self-sustaining relationship between democratic governance and capitalism in the same region. Those so committed have a similar recipe at their disposal.

Growing acceptance of a legal right to democratic governance has buttressed these transformations, enhancing the self-confidence with which international actors pursue democray assistance as well as the democratizing leadership's receptivity, or willingness to tolerate international intrusion. When first proposed, the right to democratic governance sounded excessively radical—for some almost off the wall.[9] Yet with consensus achieved on a liberal, procedural destiny for emerging democracies, the notion shed its radical image and entered mainstrean political discourse. Not only did it gain credence because of its circumscribed democratic vision but also it did so because of the astuteness with which its proponents made the case that the right to democracy already existed. The argument that democratic rights are mere extensions of the right to self-determination stuck. So too did the idea that they are already enshrined in the universal declaration of human rights, which stipulates that governmental authority resides in its embrace of the popular will. Would-be democratizers, then, can make both a moral and legal case for pressures and assistance in the name of democracy, while leaders who may violate democratic principles find themselves on shakier ground today, no longer able to denounce international pressure by invoking national sovereignty and obliged to pay homage to democratic principles.

Finally, the post-cold-war support for democracy also rests on a strategic redefinition of interests within democratized and democratizing worlds alike. In the case of the United States, the absence of an adversary, coupled with the rise of new political and economic orthodoxies, enhanced the appeal of democracy promotion and permitted more diverse forms of international engagement. Latin American elites have likewise been converted to the democratic cause. The economic failures and unanticipated brutality of military regimes discredited authoritarianism in elite eyes. Elites also accept that sustained economic prosperity in the current global order will depend significantly on their willingness to abide by democratic procedures. Thus for instance, the Arzu government of Guatemala, an administration representative of business interests, clearly understood the new rules of the game when it embraced peace in the mid-1990s. Given the degree of repression experienced during the authoritarian era and the sudden vacuum of ideological alternatives, Latin America's popular sectors have also endorsed liberal and procedural democracy. Using the same example, representatives of Guatemalan civil society and its guerrilla movement understood the stakes when they joined forces with Arzu in negotiating the 1996 peace accords. Continued popular adherence to democracy depends on the capacity of regimes to guarantee political freedoms and to facilitate enhanced participation. As in the case of elite groups, it also depends on satisfying the economic needs of poorer sectors of society.

Democracy Assistance Programs

ACTORS AND ACTIVITIES: A SURVEY OF THE FIELD The field of democracy assistance has become increasingly cluttered in the past decade.[10] Clearly, governments and government agencies are active participants. In the case of the United States, the U.S. Agency for International Development (USAID) launched a democracy initiative in late 1990, subsequently reaffirmed following the 1992 election of Bill Clinton. Still the United States is by no means the only, or even the most important, state actor in the field. Other nations, including some with a long history of engagement in the field, such as Canada and the Scandinavian countries, as well as relative newcomers, such as Spain and even Japan, target substantial portions of their foreign-assistance budgets to assisting democratic development in Latin America.[11]

Bilateral assistance does not necessarily represent the most significant contribution. To begin with, governments share billing with a diverse cast of nongovernmental organizations (NGOs). These include so-called QUANGOs, or quasi NGOs, who receive government funds but retain independence in deciding how to allocate their support. Dutch and Italian funds, for instance, tend to be funneled through domestic church-based organizations long active in relief and solidarity in the region—Central America in particular. German political assistance, meanwhile, is filtered through the country's political foundations *(stiftungen)*, who first became active in the region as part of an international effort to contain the Cuban Revolution by encouraging the development of an anticommunist political and labor left.[12] Although the Christian Democrat Konrad Adenauer Stiftung has been the most prominent of the German foundations historically, both the Social Democratic Friedrich Ebert Stiftung and the Free Democrat Friedrich Neumann Stiftung steadily increased their commitment to the region during the 1970s and 1980s. By the end of the 1980s, for instance, up to one-third of the Ebert budget was allocated to Latin America, while the Adenauer Stiftung spent more than 50 percent of its funds on the region. In addition to providing technical and political assistance to like-minded parties and unions, the Adenauer foundation provides support for governance-related research and media development.

The success of the German political foundations has spawned several look-alikes in other countries, including Britain, France, Canada, and the United States. Of these, however, it is the U.S. National Endowment for Democracy (NED) that is the most visible in Latin America.[13] Funded by the U.S. Congress and established during the Reagan administration with the explicit aim of promoting democracy abroad, the NED both administers its own discretionary grant-making program (which consumes some 60 percent of its resources) and underwrites the programs of its four core grantees: the American Center for International Labor Solidarity (ACILS, formerly the Free Trade Union Institute); the Center for International Private Enterprise (CIPE); the International Republican Institute (IRI); and the National Democratic Institute for International Affairs (NDI). Because of the perceived progress of democracy in the region, the NED's Latin American program currently commands fewer resources than do its programs in Eastern Europe, Asia, or Africa. Within the region, the NED views its challenge as that of nurturing democratic trends in countries that have yet either to experience or to complete transitions (Cuba and Mexico). It also seeks to protect and advance democracy in places where it appears most threatened (Colombia, Peru, and Venezuela). In pursuit of these objectives, and much like the German *stiftungen* after which it is modeled, the NED and its core institutes tend to collaborate with like-minded Latin American organizations.

A range of other NGOs also boast a vigorous presence in the field. The U.S.-based Washington Office on Latin America (WOLA), Americas Watch, and the Lawyers Committee figure among the better-known advocates for human rights and democracy in the hemisphere. During the 1970s they played a key role in providing timely information to the international community about the human rights abuses of military regimes, forming an integral part of what scholars have come to describe as a transnational activist network.[14] They continue to serve as conduits today, monitoring progress and disseminating information regarding human rights and broader democratization issues. Latin America's turn toward democracy provided an opportunity for several of these organizations to become more active in the field. For example, they have begun to offer training to local civic associations, as these seek ways to access and influence their democratic political process.

The Carter Center and the Council for Freely Elected Heads of State, which operates under the center's auspices, are most intensively involved in election monitoring and mediating. On occasion, the center's mediation efforts have taken it beyond the electoral realm. President Carter's timely and forceful intervention secured the 1994 restoration of President Aristide in Haiti, while a year later the center provided a forum to air grievances surrounding property issues that threatened to stymie democratic progress in Nicaragua.[15]

Perceived democratic gains registered in Latin America have meant a decline in private philanthropic commitment to the hemisphere in favor of regions where democratic advances have been more tentative. All the same, the private foundation community, which includes the Ford and MacArthur Foundations, maintain a significant profile in Latin America, where they continue to assist individuals and organizations engaged in human rights and governance-related work. In a move against the current grain, moreover, the Soros Open Society Institute recently established its first Latin American field office. In choosing Guatemala as its site, it signaled a commitment to support local efforts to build peace and democracy following the signing of the 1996 accords.

Intergovernmental and multilateral financial organizations have been added recently to the list of actors involved in democracy promotion in Latin America. In recent years, European countries have devoted increasing shares of their foreign-assistance budgets to underwriting political-assistance programs supported through the European Union. Closer to home, the OAS which has oscillated historically between the commitment to democracy implicit in its founding charter and a parallel concern with protecting national sovereignty, tilted decisively in favor of guaranteeing democracy during the 1990s. It established a Unit for the Promotion of Democracy, which carries out a broad range of activities from technical assistance and supervision for elections, to the clearance of land mines in Nicaragua, to assistance for the demobilization of warring parties and the resettlement of refugees in postconflict Central America. In adopting Resolution 1080 and ratifying the subsequent Washington Protocol in 1997, its membership outlined a series of measures (a progression of pressures and sanctions) to follow in the event of an attempted overthrow of democracy in the hemisphere.[16] The United Nations has also become active, again most notably in Central America. Its role has evolved from electoral observer, to facilitator of the negotiation and implementation of peace accords in El Salvador and Guatemala. Not only is a UN mission thus monitoring the implementation of the Guatemalan accords but also its development wing, the United Nations Development Programme (UNDP) has developed a program of political assistance designed to facilitate the enactment of pledges contained in specific accords.[17] Finally, by the early 1990s both the World Bank and the InterAmerican Development Bank (IDB) had come to emphasize the connections between popular participation and sustainable development on the one hand, as well as those between democratic governance (the rule of law and government efficiency, accountability, and transparency) and economic investment and growth, on the other. As a result, these organizations too developed programs intended to foster judicial reform, the modernization of the state, and enhanced civic participation.[18]

MAKING SENSE OF PROGRAMS International actors tend to sort the laundry list of activities in which they are engaged into piles organized according to the kind of democratic challenge faced by the recipient country. Allowing for a certain messiness, three sets of piles emerge, corresponding to democratic transition, defense and deepening.

Transition During the transition phase the international community's most widespread and effective form of intervention has been electoral. Representatives of the entire cast of international actors—governmental, intergovernmental, and nongovernmental—converge around elections. At times they almost stumble over each other, as they provide the technical assistance and monitoring deemed essential to conduct and certify the fairness of elections.[19]

The visible international role in fostering peace in Central America also warrants inclusion under the transition rubric, if only because these accords mark a critical first step toward democracy in the war-torn isthmus. In both El Salvador and Guatemala, the United Nations, as well as individual countries, "friendly states" from the region and beyond, provided an environment conducive to negotiation. At key moments they also applied pressure upon recalcitrant parties that prevented the peace process from stalling.

In the case of peacemaking (and also frequently in the case of electoral assistance), apparent agreement (consensus) between the international and domestic political leadership regarding the role and legitimacy of international intervention prevails. Domestic political actors accept the need for negotiated democratic transition. International engagement is favored and solicited in order to facilitate that change. It also serves to certify the freedom and fairness of the process.

International support for democratic transition becomes more complex in cases where the domestic political leadership is less committed and less willing to tolerate international intrusion. It is also more subdued when foreign governments worry that democracy promotion could clash with the pursuit of other, usually economic, interests. Cuba and Mexico offer relevant examples.[20] In both these cases, the domestic political leadership resisted international efforts. Foreign governments also tended to tread lightly. Faced with competing economic concerns, European and Canadian governments in the case of Cuba, and the United States in that of Mexico, tended to emphasize the benefits of constructive engagement as a means to foster democratic progress and to use summit pageantry, official state visits, and private discussions to urge reform. Soft diplomatic persuasion was the instrument of choice, cloaked in a rhetoric loaded with references to the integral relationship between capitalist development and democracy and to the sweep of the third democratic wave, whose contagious effects neither Mexico nor Cuba will ultimately prove able to resist.

The international community as a whole, however, is neither silent nor inactive in either Mexico or Cuba. In both these cases, international NGOs have taken up the slack, actively supporting groups within civil society that aim to push forward a peaceful democratic transition. In the case of Mexico, for instance, during 1997 alone, the NED and its core institutes earmarked some $800,000 to civil society organizations. Those funds underwrote electoral observation and civic education activities surrounding the 1997 election, a landmark contest that signaled the end of single-party rule in Mexico. Cuba is another NED priority. The endowment underwrites the dissemination of information about the human rights situation in Cuba and abroad. It also supports the work of individuals and groups seeking to foster greater openness and inclusiveness in discussions about the current situation in Cuba, as well as about the prospects for peaceful political change on the island.[21]

Democratic Defense Multilateral organizations, including the OAS, the UN, and the IDB, have responded most firmly to threats to democracy in the region. As noted, the interruption of democratic government is now deemed to constitute grounds for collective action by the OAS membership. OAS members, many of which consider themselves still fragile democracies, have a strong self-interest in establishing mechanisms to preserve constitutional rule in the hemisphere. Safeguarding mechanisms encompass an escalating set of pressures, which range from diplomatic exhortations and threats, backed up by the imposition of economic sanctions and culminating in the eventual suspension of the offending country.

The OAS has been called upon to so respond on at least three occasions: in the aftermath of military intervention in Haiti and *autogolpes* (or self-staged coups) in Peru and Guatemala.[22] In all three cases pressures involved threats, followed by a temporary suspension of Peruvian loan disbursements by the IDB and, in the Haitian case, by a UN call for an oil and weapons embargo and a freezing of assets. The effectiveness of international efforts in the three cases was wide-ranging. At the risk of oversimplification, international pressures seemed to work best in Guatemala, where they triggered a swift repudiation of José Serrano's attempted coup. Reacting to the threat of economic sanctions, the Guatemalan business community wasted little time in joining with other sectors of civil society to denounce the *autogolpe*. The country's vacillating military thus received a clear signal that prompted them to withdraw their initial support of the president. The Peruvian situation was more complex. Fearful of international isolation and sanctions, Alberto Fujimori reacted to the withholding of loans by agreeing to an electoral timetable mandated by the international community. Yet popular support for his actions enabled him to retain power (and to continue to govern autocratically) while adhering to that timetable. International efforts were least successful in the Haitian instance. The imposition of sanctions had relatively little effect on the Haitian leadership. Because the country already enjoy pariah status, there was less at stake. Furthermore, the impact of the embargo was diminished as a result of routine violations by members of the international community who stood to gain by turning a blind eye.

Analysis reveals that successful international defense is predicated on at least three factors. First, effectiveness depends on the degree of international resolve and consensus, as manifested in part by the consistency with which sanctions are applied. Second, it reflects the extent to which the offending country is prepared to be shunned by the international community. And third, success is determined by the degree to which international pressures reinforce organized domestic opposition.

To a certain degree, the defense of democracy is a sign of the times. It represents the search for consensus on international action; it involves a diverse set of international players and presents a multilateral face; and it deploys instruments which combine familiar coercive techniques with a newer approach, stressing conditionality. Yet the conditions under which international efforts prove successful suggests that the current climate may have changed less than might be assumed. Competing concerns may still preclude effective international action: to wit the violations of the Haitian embargo. Democratic norms have yet to become deeply entrenched: Latin American political leaders and citizens alike still make instrumental calculations as to the benefits of adhering to democratic principles. Finally, we are reminded of the forgotten premise of the early transitions literature: democratization is ultimately a domestic affair.

Democratic Deepening The process of democratic deepening has elicited the most enthusiastic international response. The entire cast of international actors are in some fashion engaged in activities designed to strengthen democratic governance in Latin America, mainly through the provision of technical assistance.[23] Aid can be organized into five main categories: electoral assistance; support for political institutions; judicial reform; modernization of the state; and aid to civil society.

Considered part of a long-term effort to nurture and sustain fragile democracies in the hemisphere, electoral assistance straddles the transition and deepening phases and also serves to buttress fledgling democracies. It includes the provision of international observers and the training of domestic monitors, support for the local media during campaigns, technical assistance and training for electoral commissions, and voter registration drives. Although by its very nature, this kind of assistance tends to be clustered in countries in the midst of elections, electoral assistance is not always easily distinguished from other forms of democracy assistance. For instance, to the extent that programs designed to strengthen political parties or civil society focus on political campaign reform or the emergence of a more informed electorate they may have a spillover effect on electioneering.

Examples of electoral assistance include the technical support and monitoring teams sent to observe the 1996 Nicaraguan, 1997 Mexican, and 1998 Colombian and Venezuelan elections. The NDI and IRI supported voter education and mobilization drives held in anticipation of the Venezuelan ballot also qualify under the same rubric. So too will much of the current USAID program in Peru. Centered around the projected 2000 elections, some USAID-supported activities are geared toward electoral observation, while others are intended to enhance the role of civil society in the design of a democratic campaign agenda.

Driven by a concern with rendering the political process more representative, accountable, and efficient, political institution building focuses principally on legislative reform at the national and local levels. Bilateral assistance from a variety of countries, including Canada, Spain, Sweden, and the United States have been central to these efforts. Assistance has tended to be highly technical, at times (as in the case of Spain) involving parliamentarian exchanges.[24] A prime example of democratization through contagion, these programs have stressed the sharing of strategies and the replication of structures that inform the legislative process in donor countries. The development of research services and library facilities, the reconfiguration of the legislative process and structures; the exercise of oversight functions and budgeting; the conduct of opinion polls; and the dissemination of information regarding the passage of laws are all supported as part of an endeavor to enhance legislative capacity and responsiveness in Latin America.[25]

Targeted efforts to strengthen political parties are fewer and further between. Where they exist, they are often pursued under the auspices of international political party foundations, historically the German *stiftungen* but increasingly also the NDI and the IRI. Party foundations establish ties with local political counterparts with the long-term aim to nurture the development of a competitive and institutionalized party system, anchored in society and shaping, aggregating, and channeling functions of political intermediaries. As with legislative reform, party assistance is both technical and premised on the notion that Latin American political parties can be strengthened through a process of emulation and replication. Foundation representatives thus lend their expertise in membership recruitment, fund-raising and campaign strategies, and in the building of communication networks linking national and local branches, party leadership, rank-and-file and constituent groups, and parties and civil society organizations.

Reform and modernization of the Latin American state also attracts international attention. The consensus view is that the tremendous expansion of the state during the postwar era failed to ensure development, reduce poverty and inequality, or guarantee law and order. Sustained economic growth and successful integration into the post-cold-war global economy consequently entails a redefinition and restructuring of the state in ways that would enhance its accountability and effectiveness.[26]

Because the successful implementation of economic reforms relies on improved governability, both the IDB and the World Bank have become central participants in state reform. An early IDB document succinctly stated, "Economic reforms do not occur in an institutional vacuum,…inadequate government institutions, and the absence of governability can frustrate their results. The goal, then, is to incorporate economic reform, social reform and reform of the State into a single integrated development agenda."[27] In practice, whether the objective is one of defining the comparative advantage of the state, improving public sector accountability and competitiveness, or facilitating economic decentralization, the familiar technical-contagion model prevails, flavored with a dose of conditionality. International technocrats offer a road map and share know-how. And they offer incentives in the form of grants and loans so as to cajole countries along the chosen path.

The international community converges in its support for the two final clusters of democracy assistance: judicial reform, and the strengthening of civil society. This being said (and although there is some crossover) international actors have tended to approach the field of judicial reform from different directions. In the case of the international NGO community, the entry has been primarily through the avenue of long-standing human rights concerns, reconfigured to keep pace with the course of democratization. Activities pursued under this rubric have been concentrated of late in the Andean region and Central America. They include civic education and human rights training, legal aid and advocacy, alternative forms of dispute resolution, and even the professionalization of the police forces. The common thread linking the varied programs lies in sustained NGO interest in enhancing access to the judicial system and preventing abuses of human rights. Multilateral organizations, meanwhile, approach the rule of law through a concern with protecting property rights, regulating business activity, and curbing corruption, thereby creating a secure economic climate.[28] Without downplaying the need to improve access to justice, the multilaterals have shown a particular interest in helping modernize judicial systems in the region. Considerable focus is placed on lending the technical expertise and providing the financing required to reform the court system: by relieving case backlog; sponsoring revisions to legal codes; and professionalizing judges and judicial personnel. Finally, bilateral donors, whether of Canadian, European, or U.S. origin, enter the arena through both doors. Official rule of law and administration of justice programs are governed by rights, access, and modernization concerns.[29]

Civil society building is the new mantra of international democracy assistance. Bilateral donors, the multilateral banks, and the NGO community all coincide in highlighting the fundamental link between civil society, on the one hand, and democratic governance and sustainable development, on the other.[30] Enhanced popular participation provides a key to gaining political access and influence, to holding the political leadership accountable, and to fostering development by providing beneficiaries with a role in the process and subsequent stake in the outcome. Seen as a means to a variety of desirable ends, the international community's function becomes that of unleashing and harnessing civil society's energies. So conceived, assistance is targeted principally at those organizations most able to contribute to economic development or who most actively seek to influence the political process.

A Tentative Assessment

The Cast of Actors

The expanding universe and the diversity of international actors currently engaged in democracy assistance offer potential benefits. Most obviously, the presence of so many players increases the potential funding available for political development. This becomes particularly significant once organizations such as the World Bank and the IDB, which command substantial resources, decide to accord priority to governance issues.

Beyond sheer numbers, the presence of diverse players allows for more extensive programming. Mandate, comparative advantage, historical self-definition, and interest tend to determine the kinds of initiatives that specific members of the international community are likely to support. Whereas party foundations seek out their political colleagues in Latin America, multilateral financial organizations are drawn toward support for institutional reforms conducive to economic security and growth, and international human rights and democracy NGOs are attracted to issues and groups that bear some connection to a long-standing history of NGO activism on behalf of human rights in the hemisphere.

The comparative advantages and weaknesses of any set of international actors are potentially compensated for by those of others. In some ways the participation of multilateral banks, intergovernmental organizations, and bilateral donors is a dream come true. These organizations often command substantial resources and, either through their membership or their ties to government partners, enjoy direct political access and substantial influence. By contrast, the NGO community is generally less well endowed. Latin American governments for the most part also remain highly suspicious of NGOs, a fact that serves to limit the role of NGOs to that of exercising pressure from the outside. In other respects, however, governmental, multilateral, and intergovernmental actors are all more constrained than NGOs. For example, bilateral donors are reluctant to be overly harsh in their criticism of democracy in Latin America. For better or for worse, Latin American governments are partners with whom foreign governments must cooperate on a broad variety of issues which transcend the democratic quality of any given regime. Intergovernmental organizations and the multilateral banks are similarly stifled in this regard. In the case of these organizations, it is the governmental character of their membership and institutional mandate that tempers the vehemence with which they take government policy to task. On occasion, it also curbs their freedom to work with groups perceived as excessively critical of government initiatives. One World Bank official was succinct in stressing the importance of maintaining positive relationships with governments: "They are our clients."[31] By contrast, international NGOs enjoy the greatest scope for involvement. Not only do they forge natural relationships with civic organizations, but if given half a chance they would also combine forces with most local and many international players.

Collaboration among international players has improved in recent years, owing to emerging consensus over the definition, terms, and legitimacy of democracy assistance, as well as growing appreciation of the perceived rewards of engagement. Formal arrangements, such as donor consultative groups, guide involvement in the Central American peace processes. These more formal processes coexist alongside a variety of ad hoc mechanisms that also serve to ameliorate coordination. Increasingly, international actors share information and seek advice over the phone, at lunch, or by posting grant information on their web pages. At times they even jointly fund initiatives in areas such as civil society, where donor interest coincides. Occasionally, the players surprise themselves by the ease with which they manage to collaborate. Commenting on a successful joint venture intended to strengthen Guatemalan civil society, a representative of a UN agency with several years experience in the region, observed, "We actually loaned money to USAID so that it could get in on the ground and participate with us. Who would have thought this was possible a few years ago?"[32]

Improvements notwithstanding, coordination among the international democracy community has yet to reach the levels needed to prevent duplication of efforts. Though cognizant of the potential benefits, international actors claim to have insufficient time to network routinely with their counterparts. It is not only, however, a question of priority. These days, the international community is reluctant to admit to rivalry, preferring to emphasize multilateral cooperation. Nevertheless, competition prevails. One individual with ties to Spanish democracy assistance disparagingly noted the limited contribution that Canadian, U.S., or Scandinavian aid could make to democratization in Latin America, contrasting it with Spain's potential: "Only Spaniards can truly understand Latin America's needs. After all, Spaniards and Latin Americans are brothers."[33]

Lingering misgivings also preclude effective collaboration. Early attempts by Clinton administration officials to engage NGOs in formulating policy toward Latin America created considerable consternation. In the opinion of some, the advantages of participation would be offset by the costs, measured in terms of diminished NGO autonomy, objectivity, and credibility. Those concerns were magnified by the fact that representatives of the NGO community had been named to key decision-making positions. One human rights advocate mused worriedly at the time, "We are reluctant to criticize now. These people were our colleagues. They are still our friends. Look, we see them socially."[34]

Relationships between multilateral financial institutions and representatives of the international NGO community also remain distant and tense. Both the World Bank and the IDB have made a concerted effort to reach out to NGOs, seeking to integrate them to a greater degree than ever before in policy design and implementation. Yet the banks have developed closer ties with local NGOs, whose participation is deemed crucial to program success, than with international NGOs. The distance between the two is partly of the NGO community's own making—a reflection of the tenacity with which NGOs cling to their autonomy. But persistent conflicts also stem from divergent operating styles and differing interpretations of development and democracy.[35] The prevailing hostility is captured in the observations of a World Bank official: "NGOs are very schizophrenic. Do they want to go mainstream and get coopted, or do they want to stay out and criticize the heck out of us? International NGOs pretend to be (or maybe they are) both international, highly empowered diplomats and people with grassroots connections. They flip flop.... I feel like smacking them and saying that they can have it one way or another. Either tell me about the international community or [about] poor mountain villages."[36]

PROGRAMS AND ACTIVITIES

Positive Trends International actors have assisted democratization in Latin America, bearing some measure of responsibility for the impressive list of democratic accomplishments recorded at the outset of this chapter. The legitimacy of elections, the rise of political competition, the heightened respect for civil and political freedoms and the invigoration of civil society all attest to the fact that Latin American regimes are heeding a procedural democratic course.

How much credit can be claimed by the international community is extremely difficult to ascertain. As always, the difficulty stems in part from the fact that international support is entangled in a web of domestic pressures and processes that work, both independently and in relation to those of the international community, to reinforce democratic tendencies. In part it is also because democratization is an ongoing process, encountering obstacles, registering setbacks, and often painfully slow to bear fruit.

Nevertheless, it is undeniable that qualitative changes in the international environment have provided a climate conducive to foreign engagement in the promotion of democracy in the hemisphere. The end of the cold war has reconfigured the political and ideational landscape, through the embrace of liberal democratic norms and a neoliberal economic agenda, alongside declining adherence to state sovereignty and heightened acceptance of a right to democratic governance. Adding to this packet of transformations, an old constraint on U.S. hegemonic behavior—the absence of an adversary in the region—has been removed, while a new one has been added—diminishing levels of foreign assistance. This is expressed in the opening of spaces that permit a broad spectrum of international players to enter freely into the democratization arena.

These changes enable international actors to march in step. Support for democracy is increasingly multilateral, both in the sense that multilateral institutions, whether financial or intergovernmental, play a central role, and in the sense that greater collaboration (however far still from the ideal) reigns among international players and between international and Latin American protagonists. One of multilateralism's principal virtues lies in the message it conveys. It reminds those who would thwart democracy that they will now contend with a unified community of nations committed to its defense, if need be through the use of traditional coercive instruments. At the same time it suggests that efforts to deepen democracy in the hemisphere are more likely today to be characterized by consent and cooperation.

These transformations also expand the reach and potential impact of assistance. In addition to multiplying the resources available for the task, the diversity of the cast of actors permits a plurality of approaches and emphases. Democracy assistance takes place on a number of fronts—legislative, judicial, state, political party, and civil society. Within each of these domains, moreover, the specific interests and expertise of each international actor lends a special character to the assistance effort. This is true even in the more-cluttered fields, such as judicial reform and civil society. As noted, for example, in the case of judicial reform, human rights NGOs maintain a strong rights and legal access focus, while multilateral banks stress the modernization and professionalization of the legal system. Approaches and emphases are similarly diverse with respect to civil society. Indicative of a new era, U.S.-based advocacy NGOs are increasingly assisting local NGOs develop the means to influence their own governments. With USAID backing for instance, WOLA has developed an advocacy-training program in Guatemala that targets leaders of local civil society organizations.[37] Equipped with its own sets of understandings of the role of civil society in development, the IDB seeks to link civil society strengthening efforts to specific development projects. Instead of pursuing civil society building independently, therefore, it fosters civic participation in the design and implementation of bank projects. International actors thus tend to approach democracy assistance with a particular frame. Were each to exist in isolation, the given frame of any particular actor could limit the reach of international democracy assistance. But the presence of multiple and juxtaposed frames yields a veritable collage of initiatives, together producing a richly textured field of democracy assistance.

Continuing Constraints Enthusiasm among U.S. policymakers engaged in democracy assistance is essential, if only to justify the continued commitment of resources to a public skeptical of foreign assistance and for whom the promotion of human rights and democracy rank low on a scale of foreign-policy priorities. Behind the confident public face, however, lies a puzzled corps of democracy activists, increasingly aware of the difficulties of their task.

The euphoria that marked the onset of the current wave has gradually receded, to be replaced by the somber realization that the battle for democracy is not about to be won. However significant the gains, the democratic record remains mixed. Whether on the state, legislative, party, or civic front, progress has been halting and uneven. Democratic institutions and procedures remain fragile in many countries. Substantive democracy is conspicuous by its absence.

If it is difficult to determine how much credit to award international actors for democratic success, then it is equally hard to decide how much blame to apportion for its failings. Indeed, it is appealing to exculpate the international community, on the grounds that it was all a big mistake. Whereas international actors originally appeared to heed the scholarly consensus that democratization was essentially a domestic affair, they got caught up in the frenzy of the present moment, wrongfully assuming that they could engineer democratic deepening.

Obviously, international engineering alone cannot produce democratic consolidation. Conceding the truism, however, should not let international actors off the hook. Naiveté conceals errors of judgment and failures to consider trade-offs—both of which themselves impede the sustained deepening of democracy in the hemisphere.

This chapter has presented the phases of democracy assistance in much the same vein as international actors perceive them. Three distinct phases exist: democratic transitions, followed by democratic deepening and, on occasion unfortunately, also by democratic defense. Furthermore, success in the transition phase is predicated largely on the commitment of powerful domestic actors. The deepening and defense phases, meanwhile, are deemed more responsive to international assistance and susceptible to international pressure.

The use of the terms *assistance* and *pressure* highlight differences that characterize the international approach to deepening, as contrasted with defense. Deepening elicits a consensual, collaborative approach, symptomatic of the warm, fuzzy feeling that pervades democracy assistance in the post-cold-war era. By contrast, the international community is stern in its defense of democracy, as the cases of Guatemala, Peru, and Haiti underscore. It uses scare tactics and resorts to traditional coercive measures—imposing sanctions and deploying military force to persuade offenders to heed democratic procedures.

Nevertheless, this categorization misses significant connections between phases, as do its techniques and instruments. The distinctions between phases are not as clear cut as they are often portrayed. Rather than discrete, sequential moments of varying duration, they are more accurately viewed as points along a continuum, with each phase blending into the others. By stressing the interrelationships between phases key questions about the dynamics of democratization can be raised. For instance, are not the most fragile democratic regimes those most vulnerable to challenge? If so, does it not follow that the challenges of deepening and defense are reverse sides of the same coin? By the same token, how do transitions sow the seeds of democratic strength or fragility, thereby facilitating deepening, or hastening challenge?

This reformulation and the questions it provokes must inform the thinking of international democracy activists. This is not because it is in their power to determine the trajectory of democratization. Rather, it is because greater sensitivity to the overlap between phases raises anew the notion of preventive diplomacy, and does so with a novel twist. The international defense of democracy need not begin only once that regime is visibly threatened by a coup maker. As fragile regimes are particularly vulnerable to collapse, and as weak institutions as well as extreme poverty and inequality are all symptoms of fragility (and warning signs of eventual collapse), preventive measures to address the symptoms can be taken. In so doing, defense is secured; in the long run, so too may democratic deepening.

The reconceptualization of phases and, ultimately, of the trajectory of democratization challenges conventional wisdom about democracy and democracy promotion. Most immediately, it suggests that coercion, even in its mildest and most persuasive forms, is at best an instrument of last resort. Democratic defense can be assisted more effectively through a proactive use of consensual and collaborative methods. As democratic defense is inseparable from democratic deepening, then the collaborative programs designed to assist the deepening phase should also secure defense.

The catch, however, lies in the quality of the tools. It is not just that the less coercive tools in the international democracy assistance kit may get the job done better. It is also that the job itself becomes harder because some of the tools in the kit obstruct the assembly of the democratic edifice, while other key implements are missing. The neoliberal economic model, imposed by international actors, works to obstruct democratic deepening. Contrary to the new orthodoxy, the relationship between capitalism and democracy is neither automatic nor necessarily harmonious. Privatization in the region has intensified corruption, revealing and exacerbating the limitations of Latin America's judicial systems. Cuts in public expenditures have contributed to producing levels of poverty and inequality that appear increasingly incompatible with democracy. Not even minimalist notions of political equality prevail in much of Latin America, while the challenge of enhancing popular participation in contexts where citizens are struggling merely to survive is particularly daunting. Neoliberalism's toll can also be measured in declining institutional legitimacy and capacities. Governmental accountability is skewed as political leaders become finely tuned to the requirements of the global market and to the demands of international financial institutions, upon whom they depend for investment, trade, and aid. In the process they disregard the demands of their citizens who require basic social services, which are either absent from the neoliberal menu or which hollowed-out states are too weak to provide. Without the tools to build social democracy in Latin America, procedural democracy stands on shaky ground.

Assistance to civil society also warrants critical examination. To begin with, resources are not distributed evenly among civic associations, but rather tend to favor certain organizations disproportionately. Some of these are umbrella organizations, including in the Mexican case, peak human rights and democracy organizations such as the Civic Alliance, the Centro Civico, and the Citizen's Democracy Movement. The advantages seem obvious. These groups are usually headquartered in the capital; thus they are easily accessible to foreign donors and work from a base from which they can directly access the political system. They also tend to be run by committed, well-educated, and cosmopolitan leaders. And they claim a broad reach, purporting to perform the role of spokesperson and to offer training to the local organizations whom they represent.

Assistance has also gravitated toward advocacy organizations and groups that work on a well-defined set of issues—ones that usually coincide with those the international community deems key to democratic success. As one representative of a Guatemalan organization awash in international support, observed, "If you work on human rights, women or indigenous peoples—all the trendy Western issues—then you have no problem getting funds."[38] Again, the rationale is clear: these are groups specifically concerned with central challenges to democracy. Moreover they seek to access, influence, and monitor the political process, hence their contribution to democratization is obvious and relatively immediate.

Finally, donors tend to support the more professional organizations. More adept at proposal writing, skilled at accounting and already well positioned to influence the political system, or to make an impact on development, the capacities of these groups gives them an enormous advantage in applying for international funding. When asked, for instance, how the IDB selects its NGO partners, a Bank representative in Guatemala explained, "We have a competition, we solicit proposals from NGOs and we choose the best proposal. We are now designing a proposal for technical cooperation with rural women. And the executor will be an NGO. Five or six NGOs will compete, submit proposals and we will choose the one that we think is the best.... *This is how we are opening spaces and strengthening civil society*" [emphasis added].[39]

Skills aside, there is a question of comfort. The more professional organizations are those run by the better-educated and usually better-connected leadership, well plugged in to local and international networks. They possess a particular savvy, reflected in their ability to formulate polished proposals, easily justifying an expenditure of funds. But personal rapport may also be part of the equation, facilitating as it does a good working relationship between donor and grantee. One representative of an international NGO that is supporting a rural Latin American indigenous organization emphasized how much more difficult (though ultimately more rewarding) it was to work with this type of organization. By way of illustration, he noted the difficulties of cross-cultural communication, confessing that different body languages alone made for potential misunderstandings.[40]

Given this scenario, the conventional wisdom about the inherent benefits of strengthening civil society elicits challenge. Simply put, dominant approaches to grant making in this area risk doing as much harm as good, reinforcing undemocratic tendencies within civil society and hampering democratization. Support for key umbrella organizations, for instance, carries with it the enormous advantage of economy of scale. Yet by their very nature, these organizations tend to aggravate the prevailing penchant for hierarchical and clientelistic relationships, which are as characteristic of Latin American civic organizations as of other institutions in the region.

Moreover, by supporting the usual suspects the international community contributes to further marginalizing and indefinitely retarding the development of other groups, which may not enjoy the same skills, access, or polish and which appear to be working on more peripheral themes. In a way it also highlights the potentially ephemeral quality of the success of any given civic organization, tied as it appears to be to the continued engagement of key individuals who possess the right combination of skills. This suspicion is confirmed in a recent evaluation of civic education programs in the region. The most successful programs reviewed, such as the Mexican Escuela de Capacitacíon Civica, clearly owed their success to their founders. Commenting on this, the evaluators wrote, "[They] provide the vision and the driving power. Without them, the school is not likely to survive, at least this time." Leadership also explained the decline of another initiative, a Guatemalan institute figured among the least effective of those assessed, and whose "program and credibility suffered after the departure" of its founder in 1993.[41]

Finally, the impact transcends that which it has on any individual civic organization. Patterns of international assistance create a dependent civil society. Like the political leadership in the current global economic era, civic organizations are prone to valuing their relationships with international donors to the detriment of those they need cultivate with local constituents. International agenda setting renders this problem particularly acute. Financial survival dictates that civic organizations tackle problems in ways that reflect donor priorities. At best these are an incomplete reflection of how local communities understand the dynamic of democratization in the region.

Errors of omission also limit the effectiveness of assistance. While international actors trip over themselves in the rush to fund rule of law and civil society initiatives, they pay less-sustained attention to political party reform and even less to reform of either the state bureaucracy or the executive branch. For the most part, political party foundations tend to tinker with like-minded moderate parties; multilateral banks espouse modernization in ways consistent with their vision of a minimalist and transparent state sector and decentralized government; and the executive branch is virtually absent from the grant-making portfolio of the international donor community. These omissions reflect liberal democratic biases, seasoned with a neoliberal economic flavor, in which state and executive powers are to be held in check. Yet if the challenges facing Latin American democracies today are to be met, institutional reform will also need to tackle a reality in which an extremely powerful executive is also frequently unaccountable. A strengthened state, able to advance however modest a vision of the common good must also emerge. In fact, the democratic cause may actually require that the reconfigured state enjoy degree of insulation from a political process, particularly so long as access remains highly inequitable. And political party reform will require wholesale institutional innovation, reinvigoration, and rejuvenation in order to assuage widespread popular misgivings about parties and politicians.

Omitting an emphasis on interactions between the component parts of democratic governance also exacts a potentially steep price. For example, efforts to reform legislatures can only be truly effective if legislatures are composed of renewed political parties, and if they are able to improve their relationship with the executive. Similarly, civil society will have greater political impact, to the extent that its strengthening occurs in tandem with that of political parties and the state. Unless it does so the political access of civic groups will remain circumscribed and popular demands will be frustrated. Instead of deepening democracy, democratic deterioration may ensue, manifested in further alienation from an unresponsive political leadership and in heightened disillusionment with the meager perceived benefits of political participation.

Finally, the strengths and weaknesses of a technical approach to democracy assistance must be weighed.[42] The perceived advantages of technified assistance are several. They reflect the context within which such an emphasis has developed. Indeed, it mirrors the new era, marked by a convergence around liberal strands of democracy and capitalism. Furthermore, as those strands inform the beliefs and define the structures of much of the international democracy community, international actors seem particularly well positioned to lend their expertise to those intent on emulating a Western model but who are in need of technical know-how.

While herein may lie the international community's best contribution, conviction in the total success of such an approach sets up the international community for failure. It is a political and narrow vision, predicated in the belief that a universal democratic recipe exists and that democratic institutions can be exported through training and sharing techniques. As a result, it ignores the broad historical context within which the region is democratizing. That context is reflected, for instance, in the persistence of authoritarian and clientelistic tendencies and in the challenges that these create for efforts to construct accountable and representative institutions. It is equally apparent in the extreme poverty and inequality and in the obstacles that these pose for the construction of a participatory and democratic order.

Concluding a Cautionary Tale

International democracy assistance has taken great strides during the past decade. The reach and range of actors, programs, and activities are broader. The international manner has evolved, becoming more collaborative and consensual. And the technical nature of support emphasizes the comparative advantage of international actors, maximizing impact and minimizing political interventionism. The successes are significant. They lie in the steadfastness with which democracies have survived despite considerable odds. They are also apparent in the gradual strengthening of democratic institutions and procedures throughout the region.

The limitations of international contributions, however, are equally impressive. To begin with, the international community has overestimated change. On the Latin American front, substantial challenges persist, whether the desired end point is a more liberal or social variant of democracy. More generally, the path to democracy is no more linear in Latin America today than it has been elsewhere at other historical moments. Staying the course cannot be guaranteed by exhortations, punishments dished out to democracy usurpers, or through the transfer of democratic technology.

To the extent that mistaken assumptions about the course of democracy in Latin America inform international assistance, the cost is potentially steep. The impact of technical aid, for instance, is inherently limited. Technological know-how can reshape institutions, but behind the institutional facade lurk embedded illiberal practices, an underlying cause of democratic fragility. More obvious damage is incurred in areas where the international community has acted with greatest zeal and conviction. In the rush to underwrite civil society building, for instance, international actors reinforce undemocratic tendencies. They also skew the focus and growth of these organizations, hampering the development and impact of a sector deemed a cornerstone of democracy. As significantly, the until recently unquestioned belief in the appropriateness of liberalism and neoliberalism for Latin America blinded international actors to considering the potential trade-offs. As a result, poverty persists, inequality is exacerbated, and popular disillusionment with the democratic process grows apace.

On the international front, there is as much continuity as change. The coercive imposition of democracy has waned but has yet to cede fully to a collaborative pursuit. Coercion remains the instrument of choice when democracy is threatened, while political conditionality constrains the everyday policy decisions of political leaders. Furthermore, rooted in the rhetoric of liberalism and neoliberalism lies a particular, familiar model of democracy. Whether justified by the right to democratic governance or by a perceived vacuum of ideological alternatives, international actors again engage in the export of a Western-centric democratic model.

In making democracy in its own image, international actors are also prone to neglect certain issues, actors, and arenas. In a 1996 Washington workshop on U.S.-based efforts to promote democracy in Latin America, a panelist suggested that the democratic cause would be served better if development agencies paid greater attention to rebuilding state capacity and if political party assistance expanded to include the Latin American political left. A stunned audience seemed unsure how to respond. Someone in attendance glibly dismissed the observation, noting that it stemmed from "too much time spent away from Washington." This may well have been the case. All the same, too much time spent in Washington, elsewhere on the international circuit, or even among elite organizations in Latin America colors one's democratic understandings and priorities. Furthermore, it exposes a gulf that separates the vision of democracy that many within these communities hold, from that embraced and experienced by substantial sectors of Latin American society. Programs designed in pursuit of this vision, therefore, may prove ineffective. They may also serve to render the democratic goal more elusive than it seemed at the onset of the third democratic wave.

Notes

1. Research for this paper was conducted with the assistance of grants from the Century Fund (formerly the Twentieth-Century Fund), the United States Institute of Peace, and Haverford College. The chapter has benefited from the assistance and insights of a number of individuals inside and outside of government in the United States, Canada, and Europe. I respect their wishes to remain anonymous and am deeply appreciative of their help.
2. Recent scholarly analysis of international democratization issues includes: Thomas Carothers, "Democracy Assistance: The Question of Strategy," *Democratization* 4, no. 3 (1997):109–32; Larry Diamond, "Promoting Democracy in the 1990s: Actors, Instruments and Issues," in *Democracy's Victory and Crisis*, ed. Axel Handenius (New York: Cambridge University Press, 1997), 311–70; Tom Farer, "Collectively Defending Democracy in the Western Hemisphere: Introduction and Overview," ed. Tom Farer, *Beyond Sovereignty: Collectively Defending Democracy in the Americas* (Baltimore: Johns Hopkins University Press, 1996), 1–25; and Laurence Whitehead ed., *The International Dimensions of Democratization* (New York: Oxford University Press, 1996).
3. This discussion draws on Michael Shifter, "Tensions and Tradeoffs in Latin America," *Journal of Democracy* 8, no. 2 (1997): 114–27; and Jorge I. Domínguez, "Latin America's Crisis of Representation," *Foreign Affairs* 76, no. 1 (1997): 100–10.
4. On the state, see Guillermo O'Donnell, "The State, Democratization and Some Conceptual Problems," in *Latin American Political Economy in the Age of Neo-Liberal Reform*," ed. William C. Smith, Carlos H. Acuña, and Eduardo A. Gamarra (New Brunswick, N.J.: Transaction Publishers, 1994), 157–79.
5. See, for instance, Abraham F. Lowenthal ed., *Exporting Democracy: The United States and Latin America* (Baltimore: Johns Hopkins University Press, 1991); Lars Schoultz, *Beneath the United States: A History of U.S. Policy Toward Latin America* (Cambridge: Harvard University Press, 1998); Peter H. Smith, *Talons of the Eagle: Dynamics of U.S.–Latin American Relations* (New York: Oxford University Press, 1996); and Tony Smith, *America's Mission: The United States and the Worldwide Struggle for Democracy in the Twentieth Century* (Princeton: Princeton University Press, 1994).
6. Abraham F. Lowenthal, "The United States and Latin American Democracy: Learning from History," in *Exporting Democracy*, 243.
7. See Guillermo O'Donnell and Philippe C. Schmitter, *Transitions from Authoritarian Rule: Tentative Conclusions about Uncertain Democracies* (Baltimore: Johns Hopkins University Press, 1986).
8. This discussion draws on Philippe C. Schmitter, "International Context and Consolidation," in *The International Dimensions of Democratization: Europe and the Americas*, ed. Laurence Whitehead (New York: Oxford University Press, 1996); and Laurence Whitehead, "Three International Dimensions of Democratization," in *The International Dimensions*, 3–25. On political conditionality, also see Steven H. Hook, "Building Democracy through Foreign Aid: The Limitations of United States Political Conditionalities, 1992–96," *Democratization* 5, no. 3 (1998):156–80; and Joan M. Nelson and Stephanie Eglinton, "The International Donor Community: Conditioned Aid and the Promotion and Defense of Democracy," in *Beyond Sovereignty*, 169–86.
9. For a discussion of the right to democratic governance, read Thomas M. Franck, "The Emerging Right to Democratic Governance," *American Journal of International Law* 86 (1992): 49–52.
10. This discussion draws on Carothers, "Democracy Assistance"; and Diamond, "Promoting Democracy."
11. For information and analysis on USAID programs see *USAID Strategic Plan* (Washington, D.C.: USAID, 1997). For information on Canadian assistance, consult http://www.acdi-cida.gc.ca. On Denmark, see http://www.undp.org/missions/denmark/policy/plan9620.htm. On Sweden, see http://www.si.se/eng/esverige/developm.html. On Japan, see http://www.infojapan.org/policy/oda/guide/index.html; and on Spain, consult "España y América Latina: Relaciones y Cooperación en el Cambio de Siglo," *Síntesis* 27–28 (1987).
12. The German *stiftungen* are discussed in Wolf Grabendorff, "International Support for Democracy in Contemporary Latin America: The Role of the Party Internationals," in

Whitehead, ed., *The International Dimensions*, 201–26; and Michael Pinto-Duschinsky, "International Political Finance: The Konrad Adenauer Foundation and Latin America," in Whitehead, ed., *The International Dimensions*, 227–55.

13. On NED and other QUANGO programs, see http://www.ned.org/cgi-bin/SFgate. Also consult *National Endowment for Democracy [NED]: Annual Report 1997*, Washington, D.C.

14. See Kathryn Sikkink, "Nongovernmental Organizations, Democracy and Human Rights in Latin America," in *Beyond Sovereignty*, 150–68. Also see Margaret E. Keck and Kathryn Sikkink, eds., *Activists Beyond Borders: Advocacy Networks in International Politics* (Ithaca: Cornell University Press, 1998).

15. On the Carter Center, see *The Journey to Democracy 1986–1996: Latin American and Caribbean Program* (Atlanta: The Carter Center, n.d.). Also consult http://www.emory.edu/CARTER_CENTER.

16. For more on the OAS, consult Heraldo Muñoz's article in this volume. Also Viron P. Vaky and Heraldo Muñoz, *The Future of the Organization of American States* (New York: The Twentieth Century Fund Press, 1993).

17. The UN's role is discussed in Thomas G. Weiss, David Forsythe, and Roger A. Coate, eds., *The United Nations and Changing World Politics* (Boulder: Westview Press, 1997); and Thomas G. Weiss and Leon Gordenker, eds., *NGOs, the UN and Global Governance* (Boulder: Lynne Reinner Publishers, 1996). This section also draws on interviews with UNDP officials, Guatemala City, Guatemala, Oct. 1997.

18. On the World Bank, see *Governance and Development* (Washington, D.C.: The World Bank, 1992); David Gillies, "Human Rights, Democracy and Good Governance: Stretching the World Bank's Policy Frontiers," in *The World Bank: Lending on a Global Scale*, ed. Jo Marie Griesgraber and Bernhard G. Gunter (Washington, D.C.: The World Bank, 1994); and Bernard De Vries, "The World Bank's Focus on Poverty," in Griesgraber and Gunter, eds., *The World Bank: Lending*. On The Inter-American Development Bank, see *Modernization of the State* (Washington, D.C.: Inter-American Development Bank, 1994); and *Marco de Referencia para la Acción del Banco en los Programas de Modernización y Fortalecimiento de la Sociedad Civil* (Washington, D.C.: Banco Interamericano de Desarrollo, 1996).

19. There is a vast literature on election monitoring. See Jennifer McCoy, Larry Garber, and Robert Pastor, "Pollwatching and Peacemaking," *Journal of Democracy* 2 (1991): 102–14; Robert A. Pastor, "Mediating Elections," *Journal of Democracy* 9, no. 1 (1998): 154–63; and Michele Wozniak Schimpp and Lisa Peterson, *USAID and Elections Support: A Synthesis of Case Study Experiences* (Washington, D.C.: USAID, 1993).

20. See, for instance, Jorge I. Domínguez, "Cuba in the International Community in the 1990s: Sovereignty, Human Rights and Democracy," in *Beyond Sovereignty*, 297–315; and Denise Dresser, "Treading Lightly and without a Stick: International Actors and the Promotion of Democracy in Mexico," in *Beyond Sovereignty*, 316–42. USAID has become much more active in Mexico of late and now has a full-fledged governance program in that country.

21. See *NED: Annual Report 1997*.

22. See Domingo E. Acevedo and Claudio Grossman, "The Organization of American States and the Protection of Democracy," in *Beyond Sovereignty*, 132–49; Anthony P. Maingot, "Haiti: Sovereign Consent versus State-Centric Sovereignty," in *Beyond Sovereignty*, 189–213; and David Scott Palmer, "Peru: Collectively Defending Democracy in the Western Hemisphere," in *Beyond Sovereignty*, 257–76.

23. Carothers discusses the technical character of assistance in "Democracy Assistance."

24. *Convenio de Cooperación Parlamentaria entre el Congreso de los Diputados de España y el Congreso de la República de Guatemala* (Madrid: Congreso de los Diputados, 1996).

25. See Diamond, "Promoting Democracy"; and Ryan S. McCannell, *Legislative Strengthening: A Synthesis of USAID Experience* (Washington, D.C.: USAID, 1995).

26. See *World Development Report 1997: The State in a Changing World* (New York: Oxford University Press, 1997), 19–40.

27. "Modernization of the State" (Washington, D.C.: Inter-American Development Bank, 1994), 4.

28. See, for instance, Edmundo Jarquín and Fernando Carillo, eds., *Justice Delayed: Judicial Reform in Latin America* (Washington, D.C.: The Inter-American Development Bank, 1988).

29. See Harry Blair and Gary Hansen, *Weighing in on the Scales of Justice: Strategic Approaches*

for Donor-Supported Rule of Law Programs (Washington, D.C.: USAID, 1994); and Carothers, "Democracy Assistance."

30. World Bank, *Governance and Development;* Inter-American Development Bank, *Modernization of the State;* and Harry Blair, John Booth, Ricardo Cordova, and Mitchell Seligson, *Civil Society and Democratic Development in El Salvador: A CDIE Assessment* (Washington, D.C.: USAID, 1995).

31. Anonymous interview by author, Washington, D.C., Sept. 1997.

32. Anonymous interview by author, Guatemala City, Oct. 1997.

33. Anonymous interview by author, Oct. 1997.

34. Anonymous interview by author, Washington, D.C., Mar. 1994.

35. The same is true of NGOs and the UN System. See, for instance, Ann Marie Clark, Elisabeth J. Friedman, and Kathryn Hochstetler, "The Sovereign Limits of Global Civil Society," *World Politics* 51 (1998): 1–35; and Weiss and Gordenker, eds., *NGOs, the UN and Global Governance.* On the World Bank, see Paul J. Nelson, *The World Bank and Non-Governmental Organizations* (New York: St. Martin's Press, 1995).

36. Anonymous interview by author, Washington, D.C., Sept. 1997.

37. Ibid.

38. Anonymous interview by author, Guatemala City, Mar. 1998.

39. Ibid.

40. Anonymous telephone interview by author, Dec. 1998.

41. Sally Yudelman and Lucy Conger, *The Paving Stones: An Evaluation of Latin American Civic Education Programs* (Washington, D.C.: The National Endowment for Democracy, 1997), 36–49.

42. See Carothers, "Democracy Assistance."

13

Toward a Regime for Advancing Democracy in the Americas

HERALDO MUÑOZ

When the Organization of American States (OAS) General Assembly met in Santiago in 1991 and approved the Santiago Commitment to Democracy and Resolution 1080, both landmarks in the development of the "emerging right to democracy" in the Americas—that is, a growing acceptance in the region that democracy can and should be defended through peaceful collective action—all countries participating in that important meeting had democratically elected governments.

That positive environment, which contrasted with the period of dictatorships of the 1970s and 1980s (as late as 1979 elected leaders governed in only two of the South American nations), did not allay a widespread sense that the countries in the region still faced lingering threats of authoritarianism and other even more complex problems that hovered over the newly regained democracies.

During the 1990s, the illegal interruptions of democratic processes in several countries were reversed, stopped, or reduced. At the same time, international public opinion became increasingly sensitive to human rights violations and to dictatorial rule. Hence, what preoccupies most democratic leaderships in Latin America nowadays is not so much the fear of a coup d'état, but the frailty of democratic institutions, the lack of effectiveness of democratic processes, and the low intensity of the prevailing democratic regimes.

In this perspective, this chapter intends to evaluate the complex state of democracy in the region and to propose some ideas in three key areas: the promotion of the consolidation of democratic rule, the prevention of new breakdowns of democracy, and, if necessary, the efficient reaction to attempts to overthrow democratic regimes.

The State of Democracy in the Region

It has been pointed out repeatedly in countless reports on Latin America that today democratic governance is deeply troubled; that democracy is in jeopardy. Of course, it is no minor achievement that most countries in a region formerly plagued by dictatorships with their consequences of jailings, torture, disappearances, exile, and fear continue to enjoy democratic rule and that the presidency has passed from government to opposition, or to the same government through reelection with impressive regularity and peacefulness in the late 1980s and 1990s. As Jorge Domínguez and Abraham Lowenthal wrote, "the recurrence of elections, the resilience of constitutional government and the defeat of coup attempts are all well-deserved causes for celebration."[1]

However, the fragility of present-day democracies can be perceived in coup attempts against elected civilian presidents in the 1980s and 1990s in Argentina, Ecuador, Guatemala, Venezuela, and Paraguay. Moreover, the classic military coup is giving way to new phenomena. In Peru, democratically elected President Alberto Fujimori staged a "self-coup" against Congress and the courts, after which he pressured for constitutional reform to allow for his reelection; while in neighboring Ecuador, the Congress, wielding constitutional arguments, removed democratically elected president, Abdallah Bucaram. While it is true that none of these situations wound up in a complete breakdown of democracy and that most saw constitutional rule restored, these turbulent moments signaled the existence of formidable tensions and weaknesses affecting democratic rule in the region. The positive aspect has been that elected regimes have survived adversities and *cuartelazos* (or attempted coups), whereas in the past they would have most likely fallen into dictatorship. These unsuccessful overthrow attempts are warnings about the deep problems of present-day democracy in Latin America. To name but a few: widespread government corruption; grave economic inequities; ineffective political institutions; and shortsighted political leadership.

Poll after poll in Latin America demonstrates that the electorate is disenchanted with politics and politicians; that citizens increasingly prefer to express themselves "directly" regarding public affairs, circumventing the traditional instruments of political representation, such as political parties or even Congress; that growing numbers of citizens, particularly youths, are apathetic and refuse to participate not only in civic affairs but also in sporadic major elections; that people do not trust their courts, their police, or their parliaments. Disenchantment with politics in Latin America is aggravated by the perception that large economic groups and the mass media wield an exaggerated influence. Television coverage that privileges action—particularly the unusual—as well as simple and direct messages tends to further devalue political debate in general and conventional approaches to politics in particular. Moreover, there is a widespread perception of unkept promises by politicians and pervasive inequality in the distribution of economic progress. In this context, how will democracy in Latin America look within the next five or ten years?

First of all, the survival of democracy cannot be taken for granted, even though today there are legitimate collective instruments to act multilaterally to impede or reverse abrogations of democratic rule. Most countries of Latin America are attempting to consolidate democratic gains and have successfully resisted coup attempts; but the situation in the region is more complex than a simple division between democracies versus dictatorships.

In the future, the challenge may be to curtail "nonliberal democracies," as Fareed Zakaria has called those democratically elected governments that ignore constitutional limitations to their own authority and even act against the basic freedoms and rights of their citizens.[2] "Delegative democracies," in the words of Guillermo O'Donnell, are certainly better than the dictatorial regimes of the past, but they are still "very far from the boring beauty of con-solidated democracies."[3]

Nonliberal or delegative democracies gain legitimacy by the fact that they are "reasonably democratic." Being democratically elected leads some politi-cians to believe they can act as they please, dispensing with the inconveniences of power constraints posed by congress or the judiciary. These so-called democracies are a danger in the near future of Latin America. Another perilous situation is presented by "self-complacent democracies," those too-confident democratic regimes that have experienced longevity and are backed by a strong national traditional of openness and pluralism, but now face stagnation or setbacks in civic commitment and participation, or are not responding ade-quately to the demands for change. The sharp decline in voter participation in the 1998 presidential elections in Costa Rica is a case in point. The troubles faced in the early 1990s by Trinidad and Tobago and other democracies of the English-speaking Caribbean provide other examples.

In sum, fostering democracy in the region must have a three-focused approach. First, keep weak, unconsolidated democracies from relapsing into dictatorships; second, keep democratic governments from developing into "nonliberal democracies"; and third, promote new means to strengthen already consolidated democracies, so that they do not evolve into "self-complacent democracies."

Actors, Instruments, and Measures for Advancing Democracy in the Hemisphere

In recent years, multiple actors have played significant roles in the promotion, defense, or recuperation of democracy in Latin America. Formal intergovern-mental organizations like the OAS, informal groupings of countries, such as the Rio Group, and a vast network of nongovernmental institutions have contributed to the advancement of the cause of democracy in many countries of the region. Often, these actors have behaved on a same case with varying perspectives, sometimes in clear contradiction with one another. But the experience and commitment to democracy of these actors is valuable and should be enhanced and stimulated in an attempt at a greater coordination among them while maximizing their comparative advantages.

It is necessary to work for an integrated and well-coordinated system of democracy promotion and defense in which everyone has a place. In practice, of course, real life may not correspond to theory; in some cases, discrepancies and lack of coordination will continue to exist. But it is desirable to attempt coordination and to identify sets of instruments and measures for fostering and defending democracy to be implemented while also differentiating according to the type of threat and the degree of consolidation in the country concerned. In addition, recommended measures should go beyond the prevalent approach of rescuing democracy once it has collapsed. Hence, I suggest that the coordination of efforts on behalf of democracy focus on three broad categories: (1) promotion of democracy; (2) prevention of breakdowns of democracy; and (3) reaction to a collapse of democracy.

Promotion

Without a doubt, nongovernmental and international organizations have been involved for some time in the promotion of values and practices that favor the consolidation of democracy. However, many of these efforts have been short-lived and have tended to disappear in the postauthoritarian context of the late 1990s. Thus, there should be a continuing effort to work against the causes that erode democratic rule and to use incentives and creative ideas to solidify the basic foundations of democracy in the region. Promotion of democracy and, beyond this, fostering democratic governance may also be the most efficient way to deal with "nonliberal democracies" and to reinvigorate "self-complacent democracies."

Nongovernmental institutions are particularly well suited to engage in democracy enhancement activities, given the experience many of them have acquired and the flexibility and independence inherent in a nongovernmental entity. The Chilean NGO "Ideas" emerged in the 1980s in the context of the struggle to recuperate democracy, but after democracy was reinstalled in 1990, it began to lend its experience to other countries. Thus Ideas implemented electoral assistance and education for democracy projects in Haiti and Paraguay. But at times and in certain countries, NGOs can raise suspicion in the eyes of government officials. This is why promotion of democracy should also be a key activity for formal international organizations and much less so for informal arrangements of countries like the Rio Group.

Programs such as the OAS "Unit for Democracy" should be strengthened
and expanded to continue cooperation with the improvement of democratic
institutions in interested countries. Education for democracy is one of the
areas of concern of the Unit for Democracy. Likewise, the XI Summit of the
Rio Group, held in Asunción, Paraguay, in August 1997 agreed on various
measures to be adopted at the national level by individual member-states and
oriented toward fostering a "democratic culture," such as incorporating democratic guidelines in the contents and objectives of educational projects,
reforming the teaching of history to emphasize knowledge and cooperation
among nations, and appealing to communications media to pay greater attention to the promotion of democratic values and principles.

The courts and congress should be other top objectives of efforts at
democracy promotion. The modernization and depoliticization of the courts
are vital steps to reestablishing the judiciary as a respected, credible institution,
since in many Latin American countries it does not enjoy such necessary trust
and respect. National legislatures could be assisted in nonpartisan ways in the
development of technical research services, staff training programs, and
exchange programs with other parliaments. Nongovernmental agencies could
play a role in this respect, along with specialized international organizations,
such as the Parlamento Latinoamericano, based in São Paulo, Brazil.

Technical assistance to political parties and social organizations is also
desirable, so as to endow the public work of these actors with a more professional outlook that favors negotiation and proposal creation and avoids dem-
agogy and confrontation. The technification of politics and the rejection of
traditional "career politicians" are already evident in the curriculum of the
majority of recent presidents in Latin America. Assistance in modernizing
political parties and social movements should be preferably channeled
through private organizations, political party internationals, and other nongovernmental entities, since any formal governmental participation, be it
national or international, may be impractical and generate objections. The
purpose of assisting political parties and social organizations should also aim
at improving their capacity to better represent the interests of traditionally
underrepresented geographical, social, and ethnic sectors.

The Socialist International played an important role in promoting
democratization in Latin America during the 1980s, but its regional presence
has declined in the 1990s. Other less formal party arrangements have
become active in recent years, such as the São Paulo Forum that congregates
leftist parties throughout the region. Even conservative parties have gathered
regionally with democracy promotion as an objective. In August 1998 the
Unión de Partidos Latinoamericanos (UPLA) met in Colombia to lend support to Colombian democracy and to the new president of that country,

Andrés Pastrana, who presided over the conservative party alliance in the region.

In many countries of Latin America, rising crime, in conjunction with corrupt, brutal police forces, have diminished public confidence, thus becoming a threat to democratic governance. This is clearly an area for democracy promotion through support for measures such as the training or retraining of police agents, with the goal of sensitizing them to the respect for human rights criteria; professional improvement through bilateral and multilateral exchange and assistance programs; more joint community-police activities, augmenting civilian presence in the management of public security policy; promotion of the participation by police officials in international peacekeeping operations; increase in antidrug efforts to curb the violence of narco-traffickers and other organized criminals who corrupt police officers and erode confidence in public authorities, and so forth. Chile maintains programs of cooperation in police training with Guatemala and El Salvador and fellowships to enroll at the police academy of Carabineros de Chile are in high demand in other Latin American countries. When President Jorge Serrano attempted a "self-coup" in Guatemala in May 1993, the Chilean government immediately suspended its police assistance program, only to reinstate it once democracy was fully restored.

Without a doubt, profound socioeconomic inequalities and pervasive poverty in most of the region constitute a major threat to democratic rule. As Jorge Castañeda put it, since Latin America has always been the most unequal of the world's poorer regions and given that Latin America is nowadays more unequal than before, "the fragile democracy whose birth or resurrection it has witnessed in the past decade is likely to be short-lived."[4] Although reducing inequality is obviously a long-term exercise, urgent initiatives should be undertaken to ameliorate such a grave situation.

Here is a key role for international financing agencies, such as the World Bank, the Inter-American Development Bank, and the International Monetary Fund. Fortunately, in recent times these organizations have reoriented their perspectives toward supporting programs that fight poverty and inequity, a trend that should be promoted and heightened. Although not a tendency of these new times, bilateral aid programs to poorer nations should be encouraged to continue or to be instituted where they can exist. Interestingly, Latin American countries now have their own international cooperation programs to assist poorer countries in the region. Chile, for example, has an active cooperation program with Central American and the English-speaking Caribbean nations. Argentina and Brazil instituted similar aid programs for the Caribbean in the framework of the OAS. Although democracy promotion as regards socioeconomic inequality should be mainly an endeavor at the governmental level, nongovernmental organizations also can help with well-focused programs to favor the more vulnerable sectors of Latin American societies. Finally, reducing trade barriers, minimizing protectionist pressures, and increasing market access for Latin American goods to the developed countries of the hemisphere should also be favored.

Prevention

Along with the challenge of orienting the integrated system for the advancement of democracy primarily toward the long-term goal of promoting democratic governance, a closely related permanent key objective is the prevention of abrogations of democratic rule. The following measures seem important in this respect. First of all, in order to avoid the all-too-common dangers of electoral fraud, manipulation, and violence, it is desirable that international organizations and nongovernmental entities provide technical assistance, as well as monitor campaigns and elections in fragile democracies of Latin America. The OAS has been successful in this respect and needs to continue this work. However, given the limitations of intergovernmental organizations, it is recommended that private agencies also be active in this area, to speak out, when necessary, with no restrictions.

Electoral assistance should not be limited to the observation of electoral acts. For example, assistance should be for longer-term initiatives, such as the creation or strengthening of impartial electoral tribunals, free from government control, or for improving the technical aspects of elections. Active electoral assistance either bilateral or by the interamerican community could save many costly efforts to reverse materialized interruptions of democracy. An interesting example in this sense is that the Electoral Service of Chile has contributed its electoral expertise in the cases of Panama and Paraguay and, more recently, has been a recipient of cooperation from Brazil with regard to the possibility of introducing in Chile computerized voting, already common in Brazilian elections.

Informal intergovernmental groups, such the Rio Group, should play a central role in another desirable initiative: to establish an "early-warning mechanism" to avoid democratic ruptures. Here, the Rio Group or subregional blocs such as MERCOSUR should, at the first sign of critical domestic tension in a given country, offer their good offices to promote dialogue, propose fact-finding missions, assist in national reconciliation, and stimulate peaceful political interactions. This type of initiative was exhibited in Argentina and Brazil's actions in March 1998, in defense of the democratic process in Paraguay. While accepting that presidential elections could be postponed if the Paraguayan Congress so decided, Brazilian and Argentinean authorities publicly suggested that the MERCOSUR consider August 15, 1998, to be an inflexible date for the transfer of presidential power in Paraguay, a date that eventually was indeed respected.[5]

Beyond concrete crises, measures should be adopted to offer more permanent forms of assistance to achieve negotiated settlements in countries that face drawn-out guerrilla conflicts, and, once agreements are reached, to demobilize warring parties and consolidate peace. The OAS was quite effective in this latter area in Suriname and Central America through its International Commission for Support and Verification (CIAV).

Any early-warning mechanism should include not only offers of diplomatic mediation—which may imply establishing minimal structures for such initiatives—but also quiet pressure and, in extreme situations, public statements from the international group of nations or formal international organization criticizing actions endangering democracy in the country in question.

Lastly, perhaps one of the best investments in preventing democratic breakdowns would be to stimulate a permanent civil-military dialogue geared toward reinforcing civilian authority. This is a role principally for formal international organizations, but contributions can also be made by nongovernmental institutions. In fact, in some cases where there has been serious distancing between civilian sectors and the armed forces, an academically oriented exercise of discussions among individuals representing both sectors may be a required first step toward a later formal civil-military dialogue. This is exactly what occurred in Chile in the late 1980s when the NGO Centro de Estudios del Desarrollo (CED) gathered a group of leading intellectuals, political leaders, and military officers in a series of private meetings that paved the way to civil-military dialogue.

The Inter-American Defense Board and the Inter-American Defense College—if they are to continue to exist—should undergo a major overhaul to serve the objective of civil-military convergence. Merely having a few more civilian students at the college, for example, will not suffice, since these institutions still operate under a quasi-cold-war mentality and as meeting places for military officers of the region.

Subregional groupings such as MERCOSUR or the Rio Group could play an interesting role in this area, implementing pilot programs to foster regional discussions on military budgets, peacekeeping, integration, and other related topics with a strong civilian presence, so as to increase their weight and technical expertise in national security affairs. In this sense, in August 1998 authorities from the ministries of defense of Argentina and Chile jointly requested that ECLAC (the Economic Commission for Latin America and the Caribbean) develop a methodology to measure military spending in both countries. In any case, the encouragement of civil-military dialogue is a patient and delicate work that should be pursued with a long-term view; but in the end, it could be an excellent antidote against military insubordination and dictatorial temptations.

Both the *promotion* of democracy and the *prevention* of democratic ruptures involve deep-rooted problems that, therefore, require persistent work and attention. However, the inter-American community must also coordinate efforts to *react* in the short run with speed and good sense, to eventual overthrows of democratic governments. Here, formal international organizations and the international civil society have experience and a key role to play.

Reaction

The collective defense of representative democracy through peaceful means has been a salient feature of the inter-American system in recent years. Endowed with the Santiago Commitment to Democracy and Resolution 1080, the OAS in the 1990s has reacted swiftly and with relative success in the face of the illegal interruptions of democracy in the crises registered in Haiti, Peru, and Guatemala.

Moreover, the "right to democracy" is being defended at a subregional level in Latin America. The Rio Group, for example, stressed that democracy was a key component of the constitution of the group, condemned through various declarations attempted coups in member countries, and even suspended from its deliberations two members—Panama and Peru—due to incidents of illegal interruption of democracy.

Likewise, in April 1996, when a coup was attempted in Paraguay by General Lino Oviedo, MERCOSUR, led by Brazil and Argentina, reacted quickly, condemning that attempt and warning about its eventual repercussions for that country in the economic bloc, thus playing a vital role in impeding the overthrow of the democratically elected government of President Juan Carlos Wasmosy. As a consequence of that, MERCOSUR issued the "Presidential Declaration on Democratic Commitment in Mercosur" that allows for various degrees of suspension from the economic bloc of a member-state government that emerges through a coup d'état. This text was turned into a formal treaty protocol at the 1998 MERCOSUR Presidential Summit and must now be adhered to by any future member of the integration scheme.

In the inter-American system a major step beyond the Santiago Commitment and Resolution 1080 was the reform of the OAS Charter—the Protocol of Washington—approved in December 1992 and fully ratified in 1997, which permits the suspension of a member-state from the organization if its democratically elected government is ousted by force. That reform of the OAS Charter was highly praised in the region. One editorial in a major Latin American newspaper stated in this respect that it represented "a major advancement in the political process in the region, arriving as a crowning achievement of a period in which renovating ideas emerged against the authoritarian exercise of power."[6]

In this same vein, the Declaration on the Defense of Democracy of the XI Summit of Heads of State and Government of the Rio Group, held in Asuncion in August 1997, stated in one of its paragraphs that in case of any occurrence of an alteration of the rule of law or a rupture of the constitutional order, the secretariat would immediately convene a meeting of foreign ministers to deal with it.

In sum, it is now conventional wisdom that coups will no longer be tolerated in the region and that democratic solidarity has evolved from a moral prescription to an international legal obligation with strong political underpinnings. Moreover, in the global and interdependent world of the post–cold war, dictatorships can no longer control what their people see or hear. When a government violently represses its people, instant communications make it known worldwide. The new times, therefore, challenge sovereignty as never before and call into question the narrow notion of nonintervention conceived as a bulwark against other fundamental principles, such as the exercise of representative democracy.

In this context, it would be advisable to systematize the concrete measures of reaction that international organizations, groups of countries, and nongovernmental institutions can implement in the face of a rupture of the democratic order in a given country of the hemisphere. Depending on the concrete conditions that may be confronted, we suggest a widening spectrum of options, ranging from declarations to the use of force (only in the most extraordinary of circumstances).

Declarations can be a powerful instrument to react following a democratic breakdown. In some cases, they have been a key deterrent for stopping the successful consolidation of a coup. Various observers stated that, in the attempted upset of the democratic order in Paraguay in 1996, the strong declarations on the part of the OAS and the MERCOSUR countries, especially Brazil, condemning such attempt were fundamental to saving democracy in that country.[7] Declarations can be a robust weapon for nongovernmental entities such as Americas Watch or Amnesty International. Written or verbal denunciations, public reports, and other statements may provoke strong repercussions in the public opinion of the affected country, thus contributing to generating concrete changes in the previous situation. In the 1996 Paraguay crisis mentioned above, a firm condemnation of the attempted coup by the Council of Latin American Entrepreneurs (CEAL), an important regional businessmen's association, added decisive pressure from an influential sector to impede the consummation of the planned overthrow of democracy.[8]

A second broad category of measures is that of *sanctions.* If a coup d'état materializes in a given country, a strongly worded condemnation may not suffice. Hence pressure in the form of sanctions may have to be imposed. The overall criteria for the approval and implementation of any sanction should be pragmatism and negotiation. A sanction is not an end in itself, so that it should never be imposed precipitously. Often, sanctions may be unpopular; they can be manipulated by the dictators to toughen repression; or they may simply not achieve the desired end. Most importantly, negotiation should always be in the background of the course of action. That is, sanctions should be a pressure directed at the "de facto" power holders to encourage them to engage in dialogue with the democratic forces, so as to return the country to constitutional rule. The type of sanctions will depend, obviously, on the legal framework of the concerned organization.

A first level of sanctions should be of a "political-diplomatic" nature. As in the case of the OAS actions against Haiti, they could include the recognition of the deposed authorities as the sole legitimate representatives of the nation-state, the denial of travel visas to coup leaders and key supporters, the withdrawal of diplomatic missions from the country, leading when necessary to the formal exclusion of the member-state from the international organization or group.

A successful case of political-diplomatic isolation of a dictatorial regime occurred after General García Meza staged a coup d'état in Bolivia in 1980. The Andean Pact members developed a joint strategy to pressure for democracy restoration: Ecuador broke relations with La Paz, while Colombia, Venezuela, and Peru did not recognize the new Bolivian authorities. As a reaction, Bolivia stopped attending Andean Pact meetings and announced its intention to withdraw from the integration bloc. European nations and the United States reduced their contacts with the Bolivian military regime. All of this facilitated the collapse of the dictatorship and a return to democratic rule in Bolivia. If the dictatorial government refuses to engage in negotiations to restore democracy, then sanctions applied could pass to a higher stage.

Escalation should be to the level of "military and economic" measures. The threat of economic sanctions is already institutionalized in MERCOSUR through the eventual suspension of preferences for a member-state. The interruption of all military aid and sales is another measure that should be considered. Multilateral financial organizations may suspend aid programs and, except for humanitarian assistance, multilateral and bilateral economic aid could be canceled in a progressive fashion. If needed, then a total trade embargo and a severing of economic and commercial ties could be imposed. Caution is advised when considering this type of measure, due to the eventual hardship imposed on the population and because of power politics considerations (for instance, the reticence of some countries to apply economic and military sanctions on neighboring countries) that could erode international consensus and, thus, reduce the efficacy of said measures. In the case of Cuba, economic sanctions against the Castro regime have not produced a democratic opening, but on the contrary have actually wound up closing political spaces that could have developed as channels for the expression of pluralism.

The last-resort level of sanctions should be the "use of force" in its various forms. This is not a viable alternative in the hemisphere, except in extreme cases. In many instances, it would not be a legal option. However, when there are humanitarian interests involved, a solid international consensus, and the proper legal framework, like in the case of Haiti, measures such as the imposition of a naval blockade or even direct intervention could be considered. In the end, the threat of the use of military force could be more effective in the perspective of forcing a peaceful and negotiated restoration of the abrogated democratic order.

The protagonists of alternative courses involving sanctions will be generally the nation-states, be it individually or, preferably, multilaterally. However, nongovernmental organizations may play a complementary role. Unilateralism should be avoided. Today collective and peaceful approaches to defend democracy are a more efficient and less costly option than unilateral actions.

Some Conclusions

International events and forces have had a great deal to do with the wave of democratization of the 1980s and 1990s and with the present situation of democracy in the Americas. As globalization progresses, this will be even more so the case in future times. Clearly, there are no predetermined formulas to advance democracy, nor is this a task only of nation-states. The whole inter-American community composed of formal international organizations, informal groups of states, subregional governmental institutions, and private organizations (national and international) can and must be part of an integrated system to promote and defend representative democracy in the region. Although in some particular instances they will want to act independently, most actors interested in democracy should seek convergence and coordination to increase the likelihood of success. Although strategies will vary according to the concrete case in question, efforts should stress, first of all, the long-term and patient task of democracy promotion, then that of prevention, and only when it is unavoidable, that of efficient reaction to an abrogation of democratic rule.

There is some reason for optimism despite the serious troubles that democracy faces in the region. The democratic institutions in Latin America are more firmly rooted than in the past. Civil society is stronger, the middle classes are larger, sensitivity for respect for human rights is greater, and means of communication are more prone to investigate and denounce repression. In fact, as Jorge Domínguez has argued, Latin American democracies are now within the international norm; that is, democratic standards in other regions of the world are—unfortunately—not much higher than in this hemisphere.[9] Moreover, the international context is more favorable to democracy now than in recent decades. The end of the polarization that characterized the cold war and the deepening of economic and technological interdependence have generated a growing acceptance of collective action in favor of democracy and more effective ways to achieve such goals.

Although the international community indeed has a transcendent role to play, democracy in any country ultimately rests in the hands of its people and depends on the existence of a civil society that can effectively use the instruments democracy provides. National leaders must be willing to compromise and accept potentially unfavorable electoral outcomes; they must commit firmly to democratic principles and practices. The consolidation of democracy is a long-term process, and it is unlikely to occur by imposition from outside. On the contrary, as Lowenthal points out, "because democracy inherently involves self-determination and autonomy, outside efforts to nurture it must be restrained, respectful, sensitive and patient."[10] Moreover, such a difficult task must include, as suggested in this work, incentives and positive measures to cope with socioeconomic problems, especially extreme poverty, that in developing countries are just as serious a threat to democracy as coups d'état. This challenge is today more likely to bear positive fruits than ever before in the past and, therefore, should remain a high priority in the inter-American agenda.

Notes

1. Jorge I. Domínguez and Abraham Lowenthal, "The Challenges for Democratic Governance in Latin America and the Caribbean: Sounding the Alarm," *Inter-American Dialogue Discussion Paper,* Apr. 1994, 2.
2. Fareed Zakaria, "A Ascensão da Democracia Não-Liberal," *Foreign Affairs* (Brazilian ed.: *Gazeta Mercantil*), no. 15 (Dec. 1997).
3. Guillermo O'Donnell, "¿Hacia Una Democracia Delegativa?" Interview by Jorge Heine, *LASA Forum* XXIII, no. 2 (summer 1992): 7.
4. Jorge Castañeda, "Democracy and Inequality in Latin America: A Tension of the Times" (paper presented to the Inter-American Dialogue, Apr. 1994), 10.
5. See "Argentina e Brasil aceitam eleição adiada," *Folha de São Paulo,* Mar. 14, 1998, 16.
6. Editorial, "Impulso Democrático," *Correio Braziliense,* Sept. 28, 1997, 30.
7. See statement by José Luis Simón in *Jornal do Brasil,* Apr. 28, 1996, 20; Arturo Valenzuela in *La Nación,* June 7, 1998; and "Tudo pela Democracia," *IstoÉ,* June 19, 1996, 102–3.
8. See *Gazeta Mercantil* (Brazil), Apr. 29, 1996.
9. Jorge Domínguez, "El Avance de la Democracia en América Latina," *Carta Internacional,* USP, no. 2(1997): 4.
10. Abraham Lowenthal, "Learning from History," in *Exporting Democracy,* ed. A. Lowenthal (Baltimore: Johns Hopkins University Press, 1991), 262.

Contributors

Roberto Bouzas is a Senior Research Fellow at the Latin American School of Social Sciences (FLACSO) in Buenos Aires. His latest book is *Regionalización e integración económica: Instituciones y procesos comparados* (Nuevohacer, 1997).

Robert Devlin is chief of the Integration, Trade, and Hemispheric Issues Division of the Inter-American Development Bank. He has published four books and numerous articles on international economics and economic development.

Jorge I. Domínguez is the Clarence Dillon Professor of International Affairs and Director of the Weatherhead Center for International Affairs at Harvard University. His most recent books are *Toward Mexico's Democratization: Parties, Campaigns, Elections, and Public Opinion* (Routledge, 1999) and *Democratic Politics in Latin America and the Caribbean* (Johns Hopkins University Press, 1998).

Antoni Estevadeordal is a trade economist with the Integration, Trade, and Hemispheric Issues Division of the Inter-American Development Bank. His most recent working papers include "Negotiating Preferential Market Access: The Case of NAFTA" and "Regionalism in the Americas: The Case of Mercosur," both for the Inter-American Development Bank.

Rafael Fernández de Castro is Chairman of the Department of International Studies and Professor of International Relations at the Instituto Tecnológico Autónomo de México (ITAM). He is coeditor of *The Controversial Pivot: The U.S. Congress and North America* (Brookings Institution, 1998); and *U.S.– Mexico: The New Agenda* (University of Texas Press, forthcoming). He was one of ten scholars from the United States and Mexico who wrote *Binational Study on Migration*, the first such study conducted by the Mexican and U.S. governments (1995–1997).

Luis Jorge Garay is a consultant for the Integration, Trade, and Hemispheric Issues Division of the Inter-American Development Bank. He has published fourteen books and numerous articles on international trade, foreign debt, industrial organization, international competitiveness, and globalization.

Ivelaw Griffith is a Professor of Political Science and Associate Dean of the College of Arts and Sciences at Florida International University. His most recent books are *Drugs and Security in the Caribbean: Sovereignty Under Siege* (Penn State University Press, 1997) and *Democracy and Human Rights in the Caribbean* (Westview Press, 1997).

Wendy Hunter is Associate Professor of Political Science at Vanderbilt University. Her publications include *Eroding Military Influence in Brazil: Politicians against Soldiers* (University of North Carolina Press, 1997) and "World Bank Directives, Domestic Interests, and the Politics of Human Capital Investment" (with David Brown) in *Comparative Politics Studies* (spring 2000).

Anita Isaacs is the Stinnes Professor of Global Studies at Haverford College. She is the author of *The Politics of Military Rule and Transition in Ecuador* (1993) and is currently writing a book about the Guatemalan Peace Process.

David R. Mares is Professor of Political Science and Adjunct Professor of The School of International Relations/Pacific Studies at the University of California at San Diego. Among his most recent publications are *Civil-Military Relations: Building Democracy* and *Regional Security in Latin America, Southern Asia and Central Europe* (Westview, 1998); and "Deterrence in the Ecuador-Peru Enduring Rivalry: Designing Around Weakness," *Security Studies* 6, no. 2 (winter 1996/97).

Christopher Mitchell is Professor of Politics at New York University. He has recently published "The Impact of the U.S. Policy on Migration from Mexico and the Caribbean," in *Migrants, Refugees and Foreign Policy*, ed. Rainer Münz and Myron Weiner (Berghahn Books, 1997); and "Urban Elections in the Dominican Republic, 1962–1994," in *Urban Elections in Democratic Latin America*, ed. Henry A. Dietz and Gil Shidlo (SR Books, 1998).

Heraldo Muñoz, a political scientist, was Chile's Ambassador to the Organization of American States (1990–1994) and to Brazil (1994–1998). His most recent books are *Latin American Nations in World Politics* (Westview, 1996), coedited with J. Tulchin; and *Política nacional de los nuevos tiempos* (Editorial Los Andes, 1997).

Carlos A. Rosales is an Associate and Program Director at the Inter-American Dialogue in Washington, D.C. Prior to joining the Dialogue, he was a project officer at the Ottawa-based Canadian Foundation for the Americas (FOCAL). He was an international elections observer for the International Foundation for Election Systems (IFES) to Panama's 1999 general elections, as well as for the Organization of American States (OAS) in Nicaragua's 1996 general elections. He has published several articles on inter-American issues and Central American affairs in the United States, Canada, Peru, and Central America.

Mónica Serrano is a Professor in the Centro de Estudios Internacionales at El Colegio de México and Research Fellow at Oxford University. She is the editor of *Governing Mexico: Political Parties and Elections* (1998) and was guest editor for the special issue of the journal *Foro Internacional* devoted to Public Order and National security in Latin America (no. 151, 1998).

Pamela K. Starr is a Professor of International Studies at the Instituto Tecnológico Autónomo de México (ITAM). She is the coeditor of *Markets and Democracy in Latin America* (Lynne Rienner, 1999). Her recent articles focus on international capital flows and the politics of economic reform in Latin America.

Boris H. Yopo is Professor at the Instituto de Estudios Internacionales, Universidad de Chile and at the Academia Diplomática "Andrés Bello," Chile's Foreign Ministry. His most recent publications include "Experiencias de integración y concertación política en América Latina," *América Latina Hoy: Derecho y Economía* (Milan, 1996); "Factores externos en la transición a la democracia en Chile," *Síntesis* (Madrid) (1997); and "New Regionalism in the South," in *Looking Sideways: The Specifics of South-South Cooperation* (Johannesburg, 1998).

Index